Valincour

Valincour

The Limits of *honnêteté*

Charles G. S. Williams

The Catholic University of America Press
Washington, D.C.

Publication of this book has been funded in part by a gift
to the Associates of The Catholic University of America
Press by Dr. Mary Ann F. Rizzo.

The paper used in this publication meets the minimum
requirements of American National Standards for Information
Science—Permanence of Paper for Printed Library materials,
ANSI Z39.48-1984.

∞

Library of Congress Cataloging-in-Publication Data
Williams, Charles G. S.
    Valincour : the limits of honnêteté / by Charles G. S. Williams.
      p. cm.
    Includes bibliographical references.
    1. Valincour, Jean Baptiste Henri du Trousset de, 1653–1730.
    2. Authors, French—17th century—Biography. 3. Authors,
    French—18th century—Biography. 4. Naval biography—France.
    5. Social ethics in literature. 6. France—Social life and
    customs—17th–18th centuries. I. Title.
PQ1930.V28Z95   1990
841′.4—dc20   89-25205
ISBN 0-8132-0721-5 (alk. paper)

Contents

Acknowledgments

It is an honor to thank S.A. le comte de Paris, and the Fondation Saint-Louis, for the access I have had to the papers of the Maison de France. I thank also the Trustees of the British Library for permission to reproduce the letters of Valincour to Cardinal Gualterio.

Librarians in "my" libraries have treated me with special kindnesses that have spoiled me: the Ohio State University Library, especially Scott Seaman and the interlibrary loan staff; the Taylorian Institution, Oxford, and Mr. Giles Barber; the Sterling and Beinecke libraries at Yale. I wish to thank, for special attention and copying, the library of the Institut de France and the Bibliothèques municipales of Aix, Besançon, La Rochelle, Lille, Rouen, and Vitry.

Professors Edward Harvey and the late Henri Peyre, for encouragement and reading early drafts of some of my chapters, have my gratitude for this and much more. I am also grateful to Professor Bruno Neveu for kind evaluation and encouragement in his review of an earlier form of Chapter 4. I wish to acknowledge here the generosity of the late René Jasinski, who took time at the Bibliothèque Nationale for discussion of some bibliographical problems. Finally, my friend and colleague John C. Rule has been an invaluable interlocutor and has generously shared references from his researchers on Torcy.

I thank the Department of Romance Languages and the College of Humanities at the Ohio State University for a quarter's leave to complete my manuscript. I wish also to reiterate my gratitude to the American Council of Learned Societies for a grant that made research on the Bouhier papers possible. In preparing the manuscript I have been especially fortunate for the help and care of Dr. Mitchell Imhoff, Eleanor Sapp, and Thelma Singer Williams. My good fortune continued at The Catholic University of America Press with the kindness, concern, and care taken with my manuscript by David McGonagle, Director of the Press, and my editor, Susan Needham.

C. G. S. WILLIAMS
Columbus, August 1988

Portrait of Valincour (1699), Artist unknown. Collection of the Académie française, the Château de Versailles. Reproduction from an engraving, Bibliothèque Municipale, Lille.

Peu après la mort de Racine, Valincour fut choisi pour travailler à l'histoire du Roi, en sa place, avec Despréaux. Je ne sais quelle connoissance il avoit eue auprès de Mme de Montespan: ce fut par elle qu'il fut mis auprès de M. le comte de Toulouse dès sa première jeunesse reconnue, et bientôt après, fut secrétaire général de la marine. C'était un homme d'infiniment d'esprit et qui savoit extraordinairement, d'ailleurs un répertoire d'anecdotes de la cour, où il avoit passé sa vie dans l'intrinsèque et parmi la compagnie la plus illustre et la plus choisie, solidement vertueux et modeste, toujours dans sa place, et jamais gâté par les confiances les plus importantes et les plus flatteuses; d'ailleurs très difficile à se montrer, hors avec ses amis particuliers, et peu à peu, très longtemps, devenu grand homme de bien. C'était un homme doux, gai, salé sans vouloir l'être, et qui répandoit naturellement les grâces dans la conversation, très sûr et extrêmement aimable, qui avoit su conserver la confiance du Roi, être considéré de Mme de Maintenon, et ne lui être point suspect en demeurant publiquement attaché à Mme de Montespan jusqu'à sa mort, et à tous les siens après elle. M. le comte de Toulouse avoit aussi toute confiance en lui.

Saint-Simon, *Mémoires* [1699]. Pléiade [1953 ed.] 1:625

To Edward Harvey, *honnête homme*

Valincour

Introduction

Il faut donc, pour être honnête, joindre à la noblesse de
l'âme les lumières de l'esprit. Quiconque rassemble en
soi ces différens dons de la nature, se conduit toujours
sur la boussole de l'utilité publique.

Helvétius, *De l'Esprit, II, vi*

In his long life, Jean-Baptiste Henri du Trousset de Valincour (1653–
1730) was a poet, a critic of literary texts, an historian who became
"historiographe du roi," member of three academies, an active believer
who engaged himself in polemic on behalf of his church and faith,
and a philosopher. His life was rich in friendships; he especially
acknowledged those of Bossuet, Boileau, and Racine. He moved in
many circles, from Boileau's gatherings at Auteuil to the salon of Mme
de Lambert or the nights at Sceaux, from the library of the Abbey of
Saint-Germain-des-Prés to discussions of poetry and philosophy at
Fresnes with the Daguesseaus or of astronomy with Cassini, whom he
delighted in entertaining at his own retreat at Saint-Cloud. His career,
however, lay elsewhere. For more than four decades he served in the
household of the comte de Toulouse, first as *secrétaire des commandements,* then as *secrétaire général de la marine* when Toulouse actively
assumed his charge of *Amiral de France.* Service to the admiral and to
naval affairs of a most varied nature brought him into other, official
circles, as he skillfully represented them to successive ministers, com-
mittees, and commissions, from the naval administration of Seignelay,
through the regency councils, to the ministry of Fleury.

From this brief overview alone, and the systematic bibliography I
have compiled (Bibliography I), it is clear that Valincour's claims to
distinction exceed the outlines of this active life offered in the two

I

short biographies of him that have appeared.[1] It is also evident that the symbolic crystallization of distinction as "honnête homme" derived from much more than the able "critique mondaine" of Valincour's early *Lettres à Madame la marquise*** sur le sujet de La Princesse de Clèves* (1678).[2] The primary goal of my chapters on Valincour's writings (2–4, 6–8), which are the heart of my book, has accordingly been to trace the textualization, the constitution through writing, of the "honnête homme" as it is shaped by the verse, literary criticism, history, Academic eloquence, and letter writing that succeed one another chronologically but progressively become concurrent parts of his life in writing. In each of these domains, I have discovered unpublished documents, some mentioned but not utilized by earlier biographers, others seemingly unknown to them. Among the latter, the most important is the extensive correspondence with Cardinal Gualterio (discussed in Chapter 7). These letters alone, in themselves and intertextually, suffice to shift the major focus of biographical narrative from the rituals of polite society to Christian humanism. The epistles of Paul and Pascal's thinking, the *De officiis* and *Crito,* are far more significant for the "honnête homme" Valincour sought to be than any manuals of civility. And however formative contacts and affinities with Boileau and Bouhours were, it is those with his friends among learned and high-minded magistrates—like Jean Bouhier and Henri-François Daguesseau—that complete the textual portrait of the "honnête homme" Valincour came to represent.

In Chapters 1, 5, and 8 in part, I have attempted to reconstruct as fully as possible Valincour's career, especially in naval affairs. Generally ignored or summarily judged by literary historians, but acknowledged for its "honorable contributions" by historians of French naval administration from Eugène Sue to Etienne Taillemite,[3] this career is the

1. Albert Cazes, ed., *La Princesse de Clèves* (Paris: Bossard, 1925), 1–87; Paul Demailly, *Notice sur la vie et œuvres de J. B. H. de Valincour* (Ham, 1884). The latter is often inaccurate and now of little use. Foisset's *Biographie universelle* article (1827) remains a frequent source despite numerous errors (corrected long ago by A. Jal, *Dictionnaire critique* (1872), s.v. "Valincour").

2. The studies of Valincour's criticism by J. Ramsay and G. Genette (both in 1968) gave new impetus to "Valincour studies," recently renewed by feminist readers (N. Miller [1981], J. De Jean [1983, 1984]). See Bibliography II.

3. The qualifier "honorable" is recurrent. See E. Sue's high praise in *Histoire de la marine* (Paris: Bonnaire, 1836), 4: 38–40 and similarly G. Lacour-Gayet, *La Marine militaire de la France sous le règne de Louis XV* (Paris: Hachette, 1910), 66; more recently, Baron Armel de Wismes, *Jean Bart et la guerre de course* (Paris: Julliard,

armature of Valincour's life and the fundamental and most far-reaching context of his distinction. Reconstructing it has necessarily led to the need to piece together from documents, for the first time, the household, fortunes, and career of the comte de Toulouse. Although Valincour's fortunes, I have discovered, began with Colbert and remained attached to his clan, it was the unsteady patronage of Toulouse (as R. E. A. Waller has suggestively outlined it)[4] that gave Valincour the position from which he could serve his sovereign and France. In tracing the careers of the two men, and the close and complex relations between them, Valincour the man of action for the first time comes clearly into view, negotiating the politics of power relations with the values of a humanist and the skill of a diplomat. Toulouse demanded much in the way of service and in turn gave as he could—in the event, to Valincour, an enduring seal of *honnêteté*.

In addition to a recovery of the diversity and particularity of Valincour's life, which re-views the "critique, homme du monde" (in the broadest sense of the terms), I have wished by the organization of my biography to explore in his life two linked forms of exemplarity. On the one hand, I have accepted François Bluche's invitation to contribute to prosopographic studies of a group of "new men"[5] (paradoxical as that may at first seem for Valincour), civil servants or *Plume* constituted as a meritocracy by service to Louis XIV. On the other hand, the exemplary *honnêteté* praised after Valincour's death—in more unexpected places than the Academic eulogies offered by his friends Fontenelle and La Motte—suggests that Valincour's career represents the social ideal of the "honnête homme" at a significant moment of transformation and redefinition. In its inclusiveness of multiple vantage points for viewing transitions, Valincour's *honnêteté* offers historically, to its history as to his own, an especially revealing passage through the famous "crise de conscience européenne."[6]

1965), 27, and Etienne Taillemite, *L'Histoire ignorée de la marine française* (Paris: Perrin, 1988), 421–34.

4. R. E. A. Waller, *The Relations between Men of Letters and the Representatives of Authority in France, 1715–1723.* D.Phil. Diss. (Oxford, 1971), 421–34.

5. François Bluche and Jean-François Solnon, *La Véritable hiérarchie sociale de l'ancienne France. Le Tarif de la première Capitation (1695)* (Geneva: Droz, 1983), 74–75, 79–81. See also on this "catégorie professionnelle," R. Mousnier, *La Plume, la faucille, et le marteau* (Paris, PUF, 1970), 7–26 and passim.

6. Paul Hazard cites Valincour's Academic discourse of 1717 in *La Crise de la conscience européenne* (1935; rpt. Paris: Fayard, 1961), 318–19. On his misrepresentation of it, see below chap. 6. n. 50, and text.

Valincour's "civil service," to sovereign and France, was shaped by the demands made by the historical realities of the Nine Years' War (1688–97). Service during these years, if it was to be seen as "meritorious"and to distinguish the "honnête homme," could not be accomplishment simply by an artistically successful performance of sociability.[7] To succeed by the pen first of all meant to work, successfully and gracefully, to be sure, but also to be guided by the proper spirit of civic engagement. And the guidance of proper religious principles could not be dissociated from that spirit.[8] *Honnêteté* during these harsh years of war and its attendant trials (as in the remaining years of the reign of Louis le grand) seems scarcely conceivable without those guiding principles well in evidence, no more than "uprightness" would be for a high Victorian functionary not possessed of them. "To become a perfect 'honnête homme,'" Racine wrote to his son Jean-Baptiste in 1698, then in diplomatic service, "you understand, one must render unto God his due . . . , there is nothing so sweet in this life as a good conscience."[9] A keen sense of social realism blends with conviction in this career counseling, as the two do in the contemporary turnings of Valincour's career, and both suggest that a new primary meaning of "honnête homme" is fully in place.[10]

Shortly after Valincour's death, he was admitted into Titon du

7. The esthetics of "honnêteté" has been beautifully anatomized and documented by Domna Stanton in *The Aristocrat as Art: A Study of the Honnête Homme and the Dandy in Seventeenth- and Nineteenth-Century French Literature* (New York: Columbia University Press, 1980). For its implications in critical theory, see Jean-Pierre Dens, *L'Honnête homme et la critique du goût: esthétique et société au XVIIe siècle* (Lexington: French Forum, 1981). On Valincour, pp. 127–38.

8. J.-P. Dens's valuable rediscovery of the manuals of "honnêteté" by abbé Goussault (pp. 30–36), representative of a current of "conception chrétienne," in fact emerging during the Nine Years War, may with further research on the actual status, functions, audience of the authors of manuals reveal itself to be central rather than eccentric among the *honnêtes gens* of, or allied with, the *robe* and *plume*. On a powerful model from the same years, see J.-J. Demorest, "L'Honnête homme et le croyant selon Pascal," *Modern Philology* 53 (1956), 217–20.

9. "Pour devenir un parfaitement honnête homme, vous concevrez qu'on ne le peut être sans rendre à Dieu ce qu'on lui doit. . . . Il n'y a rien de si doux au monde que le repos de la conscience." Letter of 21 July 1698, Racine, *Œuvres complètes,* ed. R. Picard (Paris: Gallimard, 1966), 2:619–20.

10. According to Dens, by 1695 the earlier definition (primarily esthetic, I would add) is felt to be "dépréciée par un galvaudage langagier." Saint-Simon complains of it and in 74 of 140 portraits observes a "semantic neutrality": for him "'honnête homme' signifiait tout bonnement 'homme honnête,'" Dirk van der Crysse has concluded. See "L'Honnête homme selon le duc de Saint-Simon," *Revue belge de philologie et d'histoire* 48 (1970), 775–83.

Tillet's elaborate plans for a Parnasse François with a long list of qualifications. To a talent for salty verse, expected in the older esthetic ideal of the "honnête homme," are added the less-expected "occupations considérables" of study of physics and mathematics.[11] Shortly thereafter, the *Armorial général* (1738) added more. Beyond its genealogy it is a nobility of service that consecrates *mérite*: "Les grands talents de feu M. de Valincour, & son génie heureux dans tous les genres de la littérature, lui méritaient l'honneur d'être choisi par le feu Roi Louis XIV pour écrire les Annales de son Règne."[12] But the high point comes in Goujet's edition of Moréri's *Dictionnaire* (1759).

Valincour étoit un homme si rempli de grandes qualités, que l'on peut dire qu'il a fait un des principaux ornemens du siècle dernier & du nôtre. Tout le monde a connu son mérite, la justesse de son esprit, ses idées nobles, sa prudence conformée, son expérience dans les grands emplois, & sa capacité particulière pour concilier habilement les intérêts des souverains. Il a reçu dans la république civile & littéraire la plupart des honneurs où l'on peut élever un homme de ce mérite.[13]

Valincour was a man so replete in great qualities that it can be said that he was one of the principal ornaments of the last century and our own. Everyone knew his merit, the justness of his mind, his noble ideas, his consummate prudence, his experience in high positions, and his particular ability to conciliate skillfully the interests of princes. He received in both civil and literary republics the greater part of the honors to which a man of this merit may be raised.

When these specially chosen terms of praise are accepted, rather than dismissed as rhetorical extravagance, and particular attention is given to the inclusive "last century and our own" (as well as the date), Valincour's *honnêteté* so fully and carefully depicted here may well offer an unusual instance of transformation and transition. The honors paid to the sometime student of Bouhours and the man to whom Boileau dedicated his "Satire XI" on honor (1701) have weathered the demythicizing and transformation of the concept of the "honnête homme" by the *philosophes*.[14] Indeed even after recasting history, after

11. Evrard Titon du Tillet, *La Parnasse françois* (Paris: Coignard, 1732), 647. On the grand scheme, see Judith Colton, *The Parnasse françois: Titon du Tillet and the Origins of the Monument to Genius* (New Haven: Yale University Press, 1979).

12. *Armorial général de la France, Premier Registre* (Paris: Collombat, 1738), 2: 574–75.

13. Louis Moréri, *Le Grand Dictionnaire ... augmenté par l'abbé Goujet* (Paris: Libraires associés, 1759), 10:436.

14. On the difficulties of the transition, read from Le Maître de Claville's *Traité*

Le Siècle de Louis XIV, Voltaire continued to find in Valincour's history of Guise "one of the best books I know in regard to history."[15] And both Voltaire in *Le Siècle de Louis XIV* and d'Alembert later,[16] from an Académie française now *tout philosophique,* praise Valincour's Academic ideals and his service through them to the Académie, a fortiori a newly constituted *République des Lettres.*

As my subtitle, in one of the senses of the limits of *honnêteté,* has been meant to suggest, each area of Valincour's writing may then in fact be interpreted as partially open intellectually to the Enlightenment. His position and practices of writing often suggest parallels with Bayle. Beginning with his almost entirely neglected verse and its progressive individualism,[17] there is always a critical spirit at work in Valincour's writing. At different times, but continually, it reshapes genres, examines evidence, re-examines rhetoric, finally begins to rethink the language of metaphysics. From the perspective of the past, however, the limits emphasized in my subtitle suggest a second, different aspect of the qualities and developments of Valincour's writings. By striving, lucidly and personally, for a certain kind of perfection of models of discourse, Valincour always remains within the limits of the time-honored humanism of a *Republica literaria.*[18] His verse remains overwhelmingly Horatian in inspiration; criticism, within an Aristotelian frame. Some formal features of his historical writing are as old as the Italian Renaissance arts of history.[19] And the Cartesian method that

---

du vrai mérite de l'homme (1734), see Corrado Rosso, *Les Tambours de Santerre. Essais sur quelques éclipses des Lumières au XVIIIe siècle* (Pisa: Goliardica, 1986); on the *philosophes'* "occupation" of the Académie, Lucien Brunel, *Les Philosophes et l'Académie française au XVIIIe siècle* (Paris: Hachette, 1884).

15. See below, chap. 4, n. 6.

16. "Eloge de Villars," *Œuvres complètes* (Paris: Belin, 1821), 3:179.

17. The term is used as Robert Finch elaborates it in *The Sixth Sense: Individualism in French Poetry, 1668–1760* (Toronto: University of Toronto Press, 1966). See also debate on experimentation with poetic form, Sylvain Menant, *La Chute d'Icare: la crise de la poésie française, 1700–1750* (Geneva: Droz, 1981), 87–91 and passim.

18. Although not often cited, I have much profited from Marc Fumaroli's analyses of Parlementary ideology and eloquence in *L'Age de l'Eloquence: Rhétorique et 'res literaria' de la Renaissance au seuil de l'époque classique* (Geneva: Droz, 1980) and "Rhétorique d'école et rhétorique adulte: remarques sur la réception européenne du traité 'du sublime' au XVIIe et au XVIIIe siècle," *Revue d'Histoire littéraire de la France* 86 (1986), 33–51.

19. Problems in general with the older form of humanistic historiography are explored by Oreste Ranum (who stops short chronologically of Valincour): *Artisans of Glory: Writers and Historical Thought in Seventeenth-Century France* (Chapel Hill: University of North Carolina Press, 1980). On the "arts of history," see Donald R.

suits him temperamentally can only partially accommodate Lockean revision. But as the role of mediator he so often sought to play and the procedures of dialogue that in some manner mark all his writing promise, Valincour was not a dogmatic Ancien. He attempts to readapt the best of an idealized past to the present, a present also often felt in need of welcome new directions (especially from the sciences). The letters to Bouhier and others during Valincour's last years, as I shall show in Chapter 8, "conclude" the life of thought in this manner and thereby set its final shape within dialectic limits already discernible in his first writings.

Bibliographical Problems

Documents concerning Valincour's career remain sparse and elusive in the earlier periods of his life but are surprisingly abundant for others (especially from 1690). Scattered through various archives in France and elsewhere, in a large assortment of papers of state, legal documents, genealogical papers, ecclesiastical records, and literary remains, there are sufficient documents to show Valincour's career and life in the significant directions that they took. While I cannot claim to have exhaustively sorted out all these resources, and have been unable to consult some collections as freely or long as I should have liked,[20] I believe that enough "traces" have been found to justify the scope of my inquiry as appropriate to the questions they pose.

At least two drastic losses of Valincour's papers have complicated problems for any research (and most probably deterred earlier expansions of the existing biographical sketches). The first was the fire, the night of 13 January 1726, which totally destroyed Valincour's house at Saint-Cloud. According to long-standing anecdote, Valincour offered twenty louis to a retainer to rescue the manuscripts of the history of

Kelly, *Foundations of Modern Historical Scholarship: Language, Law, and History in the French Renaissance* (New York: Columbia University Press, 1970), especially pp. 21–28, and George Huppert, *The Idea of Perfect History* (Urbana: University of Illinois Press, 1970), 15–18 and passim.

20. This is especially true for the Toulouse papers to which access is by special permission for items approved in advance. They are not so disappointing on Valincour as thought to be on Toulouse himself. See Suzanne d'Huart, *Archives de la Maison de France (Branche d'Orléans)* (Paris: Archives Nationales, 1976), 1:14–15. The *fonds* is in extreme disorder. Similarly, account books and other papers of Ancien Régime, Série G[5] have often been withdrawn due to deterioration, making a rigorously quantified study of Toulouse's finances and establishments now impossible.

the reign on which he had worked with Racine and Boileau. In the midst of confusion, his man mistakenly returned with a bundle of *Gazettes*.[21]

The extent of the loss in this fire of official papers, personal letters and writings, finished works of his youth and unfinished outlines of later years can only be surmised. A manuscript note of documents taken from the comte de Toulouse's archives indicates that the loss of personal records, for the comte, was extensive and included original copies of some of his most important letters of charge.[22] Daguesseau spoke of an "infinité de mémoires manuscrits dont la perte serait irréparable,"[23] whereas Fontenelle alluded as inclusively (and as imprecisely) to "des recueils, fruits de toutes ses lectures, des ouvrages ou ébauchés ou finis."[24] During Valincour's last four years, as I shall show in my last chapter, the recovery of some of these manuscripts that had been entrusted to others, the rewriting of others, and the reconstitution of certain dossiers, will tell much about both the values that had guided a lifetime of work and the shape he wished his life to retain—if not for posterity at least for the compilers and readers of his posthumous papers. A committee of friends, headed by Daguesseau and including Torcy along with the cardinals de Polignac and Fleury, in due course had collected two volumes of *Ouvrages posthumes* consisting of 1623 pages.

These manuscripts were in the nineteenth century owned first by A. M. H. Boulard,[25] who lent them to the Oratorian Adry (for use in preparation of his 1807 edition of *La Princesse de Clèves*, which was accompanied by the first modern reprinting of Valincour's *Lettres*), and to Sainte-Beuve. After Boulard's death, they passed into the great library of J. L. N. Monmerqué and were sold with it at public auction on 6 April 1861.[26] Since that date, these papers have in their turn disappeared. Paul Mesnard advertised unsuccessfully for them in 1867,[27] indicating that the auction house of Charavay had no records (or were

---

21. Recounted by Tyrtée Tastet, *Histoire des quarante fauteuils* (Paris: Lacroix-Comon, 1855), 3:39. On the fire, see below, chap. 8.

22. See below, chap. 8. pp. 271–72.

23. *Œuvres*, ed. Pardessus (Paris: Fantin, 1819), 16:331.

24. "Eloge de Valincour," *Eloges* (Paris: Salmon, 1825), 2:255.

25. *Catalogue des livres de la bibliothèque de feu Mr A. M. H. Boulard* (Paris, 1833), 4:146.

26. No. 4185 of *Catalogue des livres imprimés, manuscrits et autographes faisant partie de la bibliothèque de feu M. de Monmerqué* (Paris, 1861), 449.

27. *L'Intermédiaire des chercheurs et curieux*, no. 73 (10 Jan. 1867), 8.

unwilling to divulge them),[28] and what remained of Valincour's family had no knowledge of their new owners or location.[29] Cazes hoped again to find the manuscripts in 1925 but was no more successful. I repeat that hope, however dim it may now seem, that my book may serve to unearth the *Ouvrages posthumes* and in turn be happily served to a second, revised edition. In the meanwhile, all is far from lost. As I have already emphasized, much remains scattered in archives; other writings, as will be seen, have been buried in the collected works of contemporaries. Two partial inventories of the posthumous collection of manuscripts also suggest that, while some losses are of course irreparable, enough has in fact been salvaged from them to allow us yet to see in broad outline the prospectus of Valincour's different writings and to infer that what remains is representative of the particular concerns, scope, and qualities of their writer.

Adry's note, accompanying two prose pieces (one the transcribed dialogue from Auteuil whose authenticity may thus be established from a manuscript) and five poems, is particularly informative:

On trouve dans ce manuscrit plusieurs dialogues sur la littérature et sur les lois, dans le genre de ceux de Platon; des dissertations métaphysiques, géométriques, théologiques même, des mémoires très curieux sur l'état de notre marine, qu'il composa sans doute en qualité de secrétaire de M. le comte de Toulouse, amiral; des lettres critiques sur les voyages de Cyrus, etc.; un fragment d'une traduction de la quatrième Tusculane; des mémoires sur les finances, une critique très bien faite de la célèbre harangue du cardinal du Perron aux Etats généraux en 1614; et enfin un recueil fort étendu, intitulé *Vers et Pièces libres,* ouvrages de société, composés pour l'amusement de M. et Mme la marquise de Torcy, de Mme la marquise de Bouzols, de Mme la marquise de Castries-Vivonne, et de M. de Valincour, où chacun fournissait quelque morceau de sa façon.[30]

Monmerqué published with his edition of the memoirs of the marquis de Villette the "mémoires très curieux sur l'état de notre marine" (1724–25), which end Valincour's long association with naval affairs with a scope and detail that have been highly appreciated by later

28. Neither my requests nor Henri Peyre's on my behalf for access to Charavay's archives were acknowledged. An annotated catalogue has not been located.

29. The marquis d'Héricourt, grandson of Valincour's brother Bénigne, had aided Monmerqué in the edition of the letters of his father to Mme de Simiane. See *Lettres de Mme de Sévigné* (Paris: Hachette), 11 (1862): 57, n. 1.

30. *La Princesse de Clèves* (Paris: Sourds et Muets, 1807), 2:290. On the group, see below, chap. 6. nn. 79–81 and text.

historians.[31] Monmerqué adds Fleury to the valuable list of participants in an audience for Valincour's later verse. He described the group of "dissertations" somewhat differently, adding some precision to the subjects generally identified by Adry that in dialogue form were developed in the last writings Valincour was at work revising at the time of his death: a double series of dialogues treating metaphysics on the one hand and, on the other, esthetic matters with a central focus on theatre (a tantalizing approximation to the outline of Condillac's *Essai sur l'entendement humain*). The group of writings

se compose de dialogues philosophiques sur les matières les plus graves, telles que les vérités éternelles, l'infini, les spectacles, des lettres sur la vérité et sur la justice, etc. Valincour y combat le cartésianisme, qu'il regarde peut-être avec raison, parce que l'homme abuse de tout, comme le germe de cette philosophie hardie, qui soumit tout à la raison, et ne s'arrête pas devant les vérités révélées.[32]

One might have been glad of less moralizing and something more in place of the "etc.," but Monmerqué's moralizing is a precious confirmation of Daguesseau's passing comments on Valincour's last writings. The writings on metaphysics and related topics were to be collectively focused in a manner suggesting that Valincour's "final words" were to be in writing that put all the resources of his mind and craft to an apologetic design. After the presence of Bossuet in his early life, and the testimony to his faith of later years now visible in the letters to Gualterio, Valincour's writing and life indeed seem to have ended—appropriately to his mind—with "humanisme dévot."

The translation of Cicero's *Tusculanarum disputationum* (abbé d'Olivet solicited translations by divers hands and published them finally without Valincour's collaboration)[33] may be regretted, but a translation of the *Crito* remains, as does some of Horace. Reflections on the eloquence of Du Perron may also be missed, done as they probably were for a session of the Académie; but others on a great variety of authors are extant, in his "Avis" (1714) to the Académie, for example (long mistakenly taken as a first draft of Fénelon's *Lettre*). The notes on travel literature, doubtless undertaken for Toulouse's instruction,

31. E.g., Geoffrey Symcox, *The Crisis of French Sea Power 1688–1697: From the "guerre d'escadre" to the "guerre de course"* (The Hague: Nijhoff, 1974), 9 and passim.

32. *Mémoires du marquis de Villette* (Paris: Société de l'Histoire de France, 1854), xlvi.

33. See letter to Bouhier, 24 Oct. 1726, *Revue d'Histoire littéraire de la France* 31 (1924), 385.

would have added to the sense of Valincour's pedagogic methods; but memoirs, largely neglected until now, are still there to give a clear view of the qualities of the "tutor" and the responsibilities they assume. The memoirs on finance, like those on naval affairs, would be only too welcome to historians, even though the most finished of them may have been published. The greatest loss remains, finally, the all but completed last dialogues, scarcely recoverable now in outline and intention from correspondence.

The inventories of Valincour's paper perform one last service. The "honnête homme," whose principal writings were published anonymously, all but ceased on the evidence of the surface record to be a writer after 1701. The verse, eloquence, memoirs, and letters published thereafter were either pirated or left to the editors of collections. The inventories add their confirmation to the evidence left in the archives: the "honnête homme," for all his modesty, surely cannot be said to be defined by the celebrated maxim—"Le vrai honnête homme ne se pique de rien." For Valincour, as his friends knew and others who had known him attest long after his death, the true "honnête homme" prides himself legitimately on matters of high principles, as on the style that befits them. Valincour remained always a writer, anything but indifferent to the esthetics or the ethics of writing.

Note on Translations

For reasons of space and the real needs of readers, I have not systematically translated all quotations into English. In Part III, which may be of more general interest to students of various histories, I have consistently given English translations, especially for the difficult texts of Chapter 7. In the chapters of Part I that involve literary texts of interest mainly to literary historians I have cited only the French. Secondary sources have almost always been translated, except when the form of the language of the original (e.g., contemporary tributes, documents) is significant. All translations are my own. The orthography and punctuation of the original texts have been maintained without modernization or regularization.

Part I

The Making of an *honnête homme*

Chapter 1

Honnêteté in the Making

Family: Du Troussets and Duprés

Jean du Trousset was baptised on 18 March 1653 in his family's parish church of Saint-Louis en l'Ile Notre-Dame.[1] His father, Henri du Trousset, Ecuyer, was at the time *receveur général des décimes* for Berry. He had held that position of agent for church moneys at least since his marriage a year earlier to Marie du Pré, daughter of a *maréchal des logis* of the duc d'Orleans.[2] The dowry had been a quite suitable though not handsome 20,000 livres. Jean du Trousset was the first of five children[3] born before the early death of their father in January of 1661. Only he and his brother Bénigne (later d'Héricourt, b. 14 May 1655; d. 10 October 1733) lived to maturity.[4] Born scarcely a month after the conclusion of the civil war of the Fronde and the

1. Auguste Jal, *Dictionnaire critique* (1872), 1218–19 cites the no-longer-extant parish register.
2. Jacques II Dupré, also sometime *receveur général des rentes du clergé,* may in that position have directed his son-in-law, Henri du Trousset, to his similar charge. Ties to the Orléans family go back to the fifteenth century and were maintained also by Louis I (b. 1629), son of Jacques II, counselor of Mme de Montpensier. See *Grand Armorial de France* (1949 ed.), 3:245; François Bluche, *L'Origine des magistrats du Parlement de Paris au XVIIIe siècle (Mémoires . . . Paris et Ile-de-France,* 5–6 [Paris: Klinckseick, 1956]), 164–65.
3. Jal lists four, additionally Eustache (b. 28 Apr. 1654) and Jacques (b. 2 Oct. 1656). Institution of guardianship (D'Hozier, Dos. Bl. 648, p. 14v) adds Louise-Claude, then fifteen months. Eustache has disappeared in this list (25 Jan. 1661).
4. No genealogical registers include Eustache, Jacques, or Louise-Claude. For genealogy see *Armorial général de France. Registre Premier* (1738), 2:574–75, slightly more detailed than *Grand Armorial de France* (1949 ed.), 6:363. For convenience (accurate and adequately detailed), La Chenaye-Debois, Badier, *Dictionnaire de la Noblesse* (3rd ed., 1876), columns 237–39.

fifteen-year-old Louis XIV's return to Paris, Jean with his family may have known hard times, as many in positions like Henri du Trousset's did.

The family titles nonetheless satisfied the newly exigent legal requirements, of five unbroken generations, set for maintenance of nobility in 1663. The head of the family, Eustache du Trousset, Ecuyer, seigneur de Renoncourt, produced the necessary documents for Caumartin in November 1663, tracing the family to Henri, sieur du Trousset, chevalier, seigneur de Walincourt, de Renoncourt, noble du Cambrésis en 1529.[5] Eustache himself, a soldier since 1639, held the rank of captain in the regiment of Saint-Maur (1651) and had been awarded the Ordre de Saint-Michel. He was the most distinguished of four brothers who had military careers. Only Henri du Trousset, the second of the five sons of Jacques II du Trousset, continued the second family tradition—administrative service to the crown. Jacques II had represented it as *secrétaire du roi* at Saint-Quentin.[6] It was in this second tradition that the eldest son of Henri du Trousset, later known as Valincour, brought new distinction to the family.

The Parisian du Troussets had little contact with their Picard relatives, who continued in military careers and by 1721 became dispersed.[7] But when Marie du Trousset was left a young widow, with five minor children and a sixth to be born after her husband's death, they came to her aid. Philippe du Trousset de Rinville was named subrogate guardian/tutor. He may have become that from gratitude as well as duty, since Henri du Trousset's generosity in matters of inheritance had allowed him to pursue his career as far as the elite Grey Musketeers (after also having been captain with the Saint-Maur).

5. For Eustache's *requête,* see D'Hozier, P.O. 2890, 64,220, pp. 2–5. The complete D'Hozier papers contain elaborate drafts, with the documents 94pp. Nobility was maintained in 1659, in 1670 with extension to Henri's sons ("Valincour" is Jean-Henri), then in 1721, when Bénique-Jérôme d'Héricourt was awarded the Ordre de Saint-Lazare.

6. *Conseiller secrétaire du roi Maison Couronne de France* at the time of his death (13 Nov. 1656), he was earlier *lieutenant de la ville de St Quentin* (and as such figures in the arrest of Théophile. See F. Lachèvre, *Le Libertinage devant le Parlement de Paris* [Paris: Champion, 1909], 1:211–14). For the renunciation of inheritance (17 Dec. 1656) by Eustache and Henri du Trousset in favor of Rinville, see D'Hozier, Dos. Bl. 648, p. 14; P.O. 2890, 64,220, p. 68v.

7. Héricourt alluded to "... héritiers, de jeunes gens présentement écartés à droite et à gauche." Letter to Clairambault, 2 Nov. 1721, D'Hozier, P.O. 2890, 64,220, p. 39.

Of the widow almost nothing is known, beyond a capability that was later praised by Fontenelle.[8] In 1662, she remarried and for her family married well. '

Valincour's stepfather was Jean Hocquart, Ecuyer, seigneur d'Assenlis et de Muscourt.[9] An old friend of the family, who had signed the du Troussets' marriage contract, he lived nearby on the Ile Saint-Louis. The new family resided from 1662 at 8, rue Poulettier, where the du Troussets had lived perhaps for a decade, in one of the blocks of buildings on independent parcels adjacent to the Hôtel de Bretonvilliers (one end of which may be seen in the engraving of the Hôtel by Pérelle).[10]

Rather than Eustache de Renoncourt, it had been Jean Le Ragois, son of the *receveur général des finances,* Claude Le Ragois de Bretonvilliers (who built the Hôtel), that stood as Valincour's godfather; Claude's widow, Marie Accarie (d. 1653), as his godmother. Bénigne Le Ragois in his turn followed as godfather to the du Troussets' third son, named for him in 1655. At the signing of the marriage contract, Bretonvilliers were in fact almost as numerous as members of either spouse's families: in addition to Mme de Bretonvilliers, Jean Le Ragois (*conseiller du roi en ses conseils et maître des requêtes*), Alexandre Le Ragois (*Prêtre*), Bénigne Le Ragois (*conseiller du roi en sa Chambre des comptes*) all signed the document.

Henri du Trousset, with a modest personal fortune, had obviously owed his position to the protection of the wealthy financier and speculator Claude de Bretonvilliers[11] and established bonds of friendship

8. "Il demeura entre les mains d'une mère propre à remplir seule tous les devoirs de l'éducation de ses enfants." *Eloges* (1825 ed.), 2:251. In addition, three "quittances" of 1673, 1676, 1679, D'Hozier, P.O. 2890, 64,220, pp. 8–8v. She does not figure in the contract of Bénigne's marriage (see below, n. 97).

9. Jean III Hocquart. The family was distinguished in *épée* and *robe* as well as finances. He had also been previously married. See F. Bluche, *L'Origine des magistrats,* pp. 214–15; *Les Magistrats du Parlement de Paris au XVIIIe siècle, 1715–1771* (Paris: Les Belles Lettres, 1960), 145, 156; below, n. 30.

10. On the Hôtel and development of the Ile (and Pérelle's drawing), Bernard de Montgolfier, *Ile Saint-Louis* (Paris: Ville de Paris-Carnavalet, 1980), 44–53. One plan (A. N. Cartes et plans, F²¹ 3596, no. 2) labels Hocquart and du Trousset residences (approximately designated in the 1661 guardian institution).

11. Claude was *conseiller d'état* and speculated from 1631. On his financial dealings, Françoise Bayard, *Le Monde des financiers au XVIIe siècle* (Paris: Flammarion, 1988), 160, 182; 271 for place in financial world. For contemporary (negative) views: Tallemant des Réaux, "Mesdames de Bretonvilliers," *Historiettes,* ed. A. Adam (Pléiade,

between the families that lasted surely to the benefit of his sons.[12] Valincour spent a part of his childhood at least with the same view from the sumptuous Hôtel whose prospect, from the southeast corner of the Ile, Tallemant des Réaux declared the most splendid in the world after that from the harem of the Grand Turk. In its Galérie de Phaëton, completed when Valincour was scarcely an adolescent, he may too have had his first introduction to an art whose raison d'être was allegorical celebration of the brilliant beginnings of Louis XIV's personal reign. Beside depictions of the Liberal Arts, figures of Security, Concord, Peace, Constancy, Liberality, and Magnanimity provided an impressive array of the emblems of beneficient monarchy.[13]

The other signers of the du Troussets' contract were also well-to-do or frankly wealthy. They exhibit also, along with some older titles of nobility, a sprinkling of literary "titles" and associations that makes the group something of a microcosm of the foursquare, cultured society of *robe* and *plume* in and through which Valincour later found his way and to which he remained temperamentally attached. In addition to the Le Ragois and Hocquart, François du Trousset and two other kinsmen (Ambroise Maupointet, *receveur des tailles forraines* at Saint-Quentin and Tourdieu, *conseiller du roi, lieutenant criminel* at Loursy), friends of the groom included the well-connected Louis de Bailleul, seigneur de Soissy, *conseiller du roi en ses conseils et dans le Parlement,*[14] and the writer soldier Jacques de Cailly, Ecuyer.[15] The remaining signers are all financiers or fiscal agents: Etienne de la Fonds, Ecuyer, *contrôleur général de la Chambre des comptes* and Etienne Hénault,

1961), 2: 654–55, 1427–28; see Bayard (p. 341) for an attack on Mme de Bretonvillers, Sept. 1648; Daniel Dessert, *Argent, pouvoir et société au Grand Siècle* (Paris: Fayard, 1984), 355 and 777 (quoting from Jean Vallier's *Journal*).

12. Bénigne (1622–1700) also signs Héricourt's marriage contract (see below, n. 97). He was *président de la chambre des comptes* from 1657 to 1671. On his financial dealings, see Bayard, p. 271 and passim. I have found no record of direct financial dealings.

13. On the gallery and paintings, Jacques Wilhelm, "La Galérie de l'Hôtel de Bretonvilliers," *Bulletin de la Société de l'histoire d'art français*, 1956, pp. 137–50; B. de Montgolfier, *L'Ile Saint-Louis,* pp. 49–53.

14. Louis de Bailleul (d. 1701) married Marie Le Ragois, sister of Bénigne (with a dowry of 600,000 livres). See Bayard, p. 442. On the family, ibid., 280; F. Bluche, *L'Origine des magistrats,* 71–72 and *Les Magistrats du Parlement,* pp. 100, 314–15; D. Dessert, pp. 281, 369, 372.

15. 1604–73. *Diverses petites poésies* (1667). See F. Lachèvre, *Bibliographie des recueils collectifs* 3 (1904), 239–45; Georges Mongrédien, "Un épigrammatiste du XVIIe siècle …," *Revue de France* 1 (1931), 300–33.

conseiller du roi, contrôleur général des rentes de l'Hôtel de ville;[16] finally, Jean de La Bruyère, *conseiller du roi, contrôleur des rentes,* the wealthy uncle of the future author of *Les Caractères.*[17]

Separated by eight years, La Bruyère the nephew and Valincour may have known each other very early, almost certainly in the years 1667–74.[18] In advanced age Valincour recalled very familiarly the personal life and career of the *moraliste,* in an often-quoted portrait.[19] Along with their common background, there are a number of parallels in their lives and careers: early loss of their fathers, celibacy, positions in noble households, great admiration for and personal debts to Bossuet, and finally (and perhaps most tellingly) a distancing in writing from the milieu in which they were raised. If in his "bible de l'honnête homme"[20] La Bruyère effects this distance by taking his vengeance on the financiers, the city, and would-be courtiers, Valincour finds his way through them more easily and fortunately, suppresses his *moraliste's* account settling (except with selected friends), and finally makes his own "plume" count in and with a different manner.

Valincour's later reminiscences of his youth are almost exclusively literary. When late in life he discovered that his cousin Nicolas Dupré de Saint-Maur, later a distinguished economic and legal thinker, had just published a translation of *Paradise Lost* (and his brother was promising one of *La Divina Commedia*),[21] Valincour wrote to Bouhier that he was astonished: "je n'avais aucune connoissance de leurs talents, qu'ils m'ont tenu cachés, et j'ai été étonné de voir un tel débordement

16. *Secrétaire du roi* in 1652, Etienne La Fonds was sent to examine the *commis de l'Epargne* in Berry as well as Poitou and served thereafter as *receveur.* See Bayard, p. 71. Etienne Hénault is seemingly related collaterally to François (d. 1710), grandfather of the historian and uncle(?) of the wealthy tax-farmer Jean-Rémy. Not mentioned in printed genealogies of the family.

17. On Jean II de La Bruyère (b. 1617; d. 27 Dec. 1671), see G. Servois, ed., *Œuvres de la Bruyère* (Paris: Hachette, 1912), 1:clxxiii-clxxiv and Tableau généalogique.

18. Years between his father's death and move to Caen, perhaps when the *Caractères* were begun, are for La Bruyère almost totally unknown. There is nonetheless a strong probability. Valincour certainly knew him before the entry into Condé's household (1684–85).

19. Quoted below, chap. 8, at n. 58.

20. André Stegmann, *Les Caractères de La Bruyère* (Paris: Larousse, 1972), especially on "mérite," pp. 30–32 and passim.

21. Nicolas-François Dupré de Saint-Maur (1695–1774), *maître des comptes,* Académie française (1733); *Le Paradis perdu de Milton avec les remarques d'Addison* (1729 and six reprintings to 1775). No translation of Dante by Pierre Dupré de Saint-Maur appeared. On the family, see F. Bluche, *L'Origine des magistrats,* p. 165.

de bel esprit dans ma famille, où je croyais être seul; encore trouvais-je que c'était trop."[22] ["I had no knowledge of their talents, which they have hidden from me, and was astonished to see a flood of literariness in my family, in which I believed I was the only literary type—and at that, I thought, one too many."] For a time when he began to write, despite the verse of Jacques de Cailly that must have been some of the first to point the young du Trousset in one future direction, Valincour may well have thought he was alone in his family. He was alone, if an anecdote by Fontenelle is to be believed, when a special, personal experience of writing crystallized. An indifferent boy at school, Fontenelle reported, he found a love of literature with a copy of Terence only when schooling was behind him.[23] At about the same time, he found another lifelong passion: for Racine. Again to Bouhier, in advanced age, he recalls his excitement in going to the theatre, for what would have been one of the performances of the original run of Racine's *Britannicus*. It seemed to him, he remembered, that all the carriages in the streets were conspiring to block his way.[24] Only one other reminiscence came to mind while writing to Bouhier, in its way also an experience of solitude; alone at Saint-Cloud, the elderly Valincour was visited by the image seen in his youth of the once keen-minded abbé d'Aubignac sunken in senile torpor.[25]

No mention is ever made, nostalgic or other, of the school that Fontenelle also left nameless, or of any masters. It was, according to records seen by Doncieux but now lost, the illustrious Collège de Clermont,[26] where his path could just have crossed that of the marquis de Seignelay (Valincour most likely was an "externe"). Père Bouhours, who played a decisive role in Valincour's life from 1678, would then

22. Letter of 20 Sept. 1729, *RHLF* 31 (1924), 396.

23. *Eloges* (1825 ed.), 2:251: "Il le [Terence] lut d'abord avec assez d'indifférence, et ensuite avec un goût qui lui fit bien sentir ce que c'était que les belles lettres."

24. Letter of 13 Nov. 1726, *RHLF* 31 (1924), 386: "Je me souviens que la première fois qu'on me mena à la Comédie, c'était à *Britannicus,* j'imaginais que tous les carosses qui passaient celui où j'étais allaient prendre ma loge, et je souhaitais que leur chevaux prissent le mors aux dents."

25. Letter of 5 Dec. 1726, *RHLF* 31 (1924), 386: "Je me souviens d'avoir vu dans ma jeunesse l'abbé d'Aubignac dans cet état et cela faisait horreur et pitié en même temps."

26. The registers are no longer extant. Georges Doncieux, *Un Jésuite homme de lettres au XVIIe siècle* (Paris: Hachette, 1886), 25. On Clermont and the *robe,* see R. Chartier, M. Compère, and D. Julia, *L'Education en France du XVIe au XVIIIe siècles* (Paris: SEDES, 1976), 171–75 and F. Bluche, *Magistrats du Parlement,* pp. 263–64. On Bouhours's "tuition" of Valincour, below Chap. 3, nn. 58–59 and text.

have entered it first literally as a schoolmaster. Although Valincour, in his enthusiasm for science and mathematics, does not reflect the *ratio studiorum,* much in his early writing and in permanent features of it does: particularly his way with quotations, the repertory of texts that expands the *florilegia,* and finally an inclination to "explication de textes" combined with a sense of their actuality.[27] A lifetime's ambivalence toward Jesuits may also have begun at Clermont, as it would for Voltaire, with the positive pole of attraction set for Valincour by Père Dominique Bouhours, S.J.

Places and *occupations*

A manuscript note to one of Valincour's earliest extant unpublished poems identifies its author as du Trousset, Parisian, and "not yet twenty-five." The addressee of the openly autobiographical verse, Olimpe, is also identified as "Mme Poncet, wife of the Intendant of Berry."[28] The poet presents himself as a *commis,* and pays court to the lady in his spare time between the drawing up and the delivery of legal papers with which he besieges her husband.[29] Identifying himself fictively with the persona of Boileau's first satire, the *commis*/versifier leaves little doubt that there is "dans la poudre de la greffe, un poète naissant," who would prefer to take flight to Parnassus or, more simply, to remain in the salon. But even the life of a *commis* may have seemed preferable to that of a more demanding and time-consuming career in the laws.

The relations with the Poncets thus seen, and the link with Berry, suggest his father's Berry connection. But for all of being that, it does not appear from the poems, or other indications, that the young du Trousset worked for Poncet. During the years 1675–77, when he paused for some welcome poetic recreation with these perhaps old friends, he appears to have been directly or indirectly in Colbert's employ. Valincour's stepfather, Jean Hocquart (with whom, to all evidence, he always remained on excellent terms), was Colbert's sometime *premier commis.*[30]

27. On the "school for poets," see Sylvain Menant, *La Chute d'Icare* (Geneva: Droz, 1981), 7–45.

28. B.N. MS. fon. fr. 19144, p. 90. On Mme Poncet, née Marie Bétault, see below, chap. 3, n. 57.

29. Mathias Poncet de La Rivière, comte d'Ablis and baron de Presles (1626–93), *président au grand conseil* (1676), among other posts, was intendant at Bourges in 1674. See also below, n. 34.

30. From 1655 to 1664, then again in service to the family, 1696–1703.

In 1710, while negotiating some tricky paperwork between the comte de Toulouse and the crown, around the minister Pontchartrain, Valincour echoes the pride of the young poet who dissociated himself from the business of the courts. He was and remained a simple *gradué*, he maintains with some pride, more than implying that it was nothing to be held against him that he had advanced without purchasing a charge, beginning with that of *maître des requêtes,* which opened the way for the ambitious.[31] It would seem that the simple *gradué* and budding *bel esprit,* who did not wish to enter the laws, was put to work by his stepfather, either for him or in some other capacity for Colbert. Hocquart's own son began a career thus, in naval administration,[32] as did Valincour's younger brother, Bénigne, with whom he always worked closely. In 1691, Bénigne became one of the four new holders of the office of *conseiller du roi, maître ordinaire en la Chambre des comptes* created in 1690. In commendation, he was cited "en considération des services qu'il avait rendus sous les srs Colbert et le Pelletier Contrôleurs généraux des finances et ceux qu'il rend maintenant" (since 1686, as *trésorier du roi* at Metz).[33] Valincour most probably also rendered such services; Poncet as an intendant was in regular administrative correspondence with Colbert.[34]

By the end of the 1670s, Valincour's place in service to Colbert is clarified. Like his stepbrother, he becomes attached to the Marine, assigned to Lambert d'Herbigny in the work of elaborating the landmark naval ordonnance published in August of 1681.[35] This particular

31. Lettre de Mr de Valincour à Mg le chancelier [Louis Pontchartrain], B.N. MS. fon. fr. 16731, pp. 67v–68; "J'aurois pû en acquérir [des charges] comme beaucoup d'autres qui se sont enrichis sans avoir eu ny plus d'occasion que moy pour cela, ny peut estre guère plus de capacité. Je ne repens pas de ne l'avoir pas fait, et je me flatte que vous ne m'en estimerez pas moins." For context, see below, chap. 5, pp. 142–48.

32. Jean Hyacinthe I Hocquart (1650–1723) was from 1691 *intendant de la marine* at Toulon. From beginnings with the Le Pelletier financial administration he became a *fermier général* (1687–91).

33. B.N. D'Hozier, Dos. Bl. 648, p. 13v.

34. Appointed as *intendant d'Alsace* in 1672, then posted at Metz in 1673–74. See *Lettres, instructions, et mémoires de Colbert,* ed. Pierre Clément (Paris: Imprimerie Nationale, 1865–67), 2: ccxxxviii, 319 and passim; 3:493, 4:70–71, 98–99. Also Georges Livet, *L'Intendance d'Alsace sous Louis XIV, 1648–1715* (Paris: Les Belles Lettres, 1956), 363–79, 942.

35. Eugène Sue, *Histoire de la marine* (1836), 4:38; Baron Armel de Wismes, *Jean Bart et la guerre de course* (1965), 22–38. On the commission, Charles de La Roncière, *Histoire de la marine française* (Paris: Plon, 1920), 5:418–20.

apprenticeship had some perhaps unforeseen results. First, Valincour began what would be in the end almost a half a century of work with maritime matters, which gradually absorbed him. From a first conscientious application to matters at hand there developed, possibly surprising him, a real love of the sea, of ships, even of seafaring. "Horace is good at all times and in all places," he wrote to Adrien-Maurice de Noailles; but while beside the sea at Toulon, he changed his mind and wrote that "if I had Horace here, I would make him retract his verse against the sea."[36] Perhaps equally unexpected was the qualification that work on d'Herbigny's commission gave him for a place that became his permanent "occupation" and was his first real charge: appointment to the household of Son Altesse Sérénissime (S.A.S.) le comte de Toulouse. And it is at this point that Bossuet and Mme de Montespan seem to have played their part in Valincour's fortune. They were not its polestars, as has invariably been claimed,[37] but served him more as relays in a system of protection begun with the Bretonvilliers and well in place with the patronage of the Colbert connections. In one respect, however, Mme de Montespan decisively influenced the new man whose position in the world rose with the new responsibilities of the 1680s: she renamed him. Having teased him with the puns on "Trousset," she persuaded him to a change to the more dignified "Valincour."[38] It is on the commission from Toulouse that his name takes its full form: Jean-Baptiste Henri du Trousset de Valincour.

36. Letter of 10 June 1704, *RHLF* 10 (1903), 678: "Si je le tenois icy, je lui ferais faire une ode à l'honneur de la mer, et rétracter ses vers fameux 'illi robur et aes triplex.'"

37. The lead followed by virtually all subsequent studies of Valincour was set by Fontenelle, who states in 1685 (altered seemingly by Foisset's misreading oddly followed by Jal, 1218B). *Eloges* (1825 ed.), 2:253: "L'illustre évêque de Meaux qui ordinairement fournissait aux princes les gens de mérite dans les lettres dont ils avaient besoin, le fit entrer en 1685 chez M. le comte de Toulouse." Bossuet specialists have agreed: Cardinal de Bausset goes further: "Valincour, à qui Bossuet a adressé le dernier ouvrage qu'il ait fait imprimer peu de jours avant sa mort, fut placé de sa main dans la maison du comte de Toulouse" (*Histoire de Bossuet,* Paris: Outhenin-Chalandre, 1841, p. 361). See also A. Adam, *Histoire* 5:98; Thérèse Goyet, *L'Humanisme de Bossuet* (Paris: Klincksieck, 1965), 1:159–62.

38. The anecdote is maintained by Pierre Clarac, *Œuvres complètes de Racine* ("L'Intégrale," 1962), 552, n. 250. Cf. Louis Racine, "Mémoires," *Œuvres de Racine,* ed. P. Mesnard (GELF, 1865), 1:287; Saint-Simon, *Mémoires,* ed. G. Truc (Pléiade, 1953), 1:625. Saint-Simon remarks that "Toulouse l'aimait fort" (1:323).

The years 1683, 1685, and 1688 have all been proposed as the date of Valincour's entry into Toulouse's household, each with a logical probability to recommend it. The year 1685 seems to me most likely: that year, the seven-year-old comte would pass from his first governesses into men's guidance. Toulouse later commended Valincour for services rendered, indeed the "soins qu'il a pris de notre éducation longtemps avant qu'il entrast dans le maniement de nos affaires."[39] As I shall presently show, some of Valincour's memoirs for Toulouse indicate, explicitly and indirectly, that he first served as part-time tutor, perhaps as gentleman (1683?) attached to Toulouse's staff. There he joined the marquis d'O (Toulouse's governor and, like Valincour, attached to him for life)[40] and the somewhat bizarre baron de Longepierre, whose principal tutorial responsibilities until he was dismissed were in the Orléans household.[41] The year 1683 had, of course, been that of Colbert's death (6 September) and, a month later, of Louis's secret marriage to Mme de Maintenon. As though sensing the changing "conjoncture," Valincour had earlier in the year written a letter to Du Cange that announced prospective changes of his own.

The long-known but previously unpublished letter to Du Cange (10 April 1683)[42] announced Valincour's intention to follow up his successful *Vie de François de Lorraine, duc de Guise* (1681) with an ambitious series of similar historical biographies. Along with his compliments to Du Cange, the sometime poet, who now felt himself more attracted to history and erudition, may also have been angling for an historiographical appointment.[43] The *Vie* and these new intentions were a

---

39. On the date and provisions of this commission, see below, n. 87 and text.

40. Gabriel-Claude, marquis de Villiers d'O (d. 1728) and his wife, Marie-Anne de la Vergne de Guilleragues (1657–1737), are harshly described by Saint-Simon as intriguants placed in Toulouse's household by Mme de Maintenon, which is unlikely (1:323–25, 674). A quarrel with Valincour is also mentioned (1:625). His fidelity and Toulouse's attachment to him seem never to have been in question.

41. Hilaire-Bernard de Requeleyne, baron de Longepierre (1659–1731), successful dramatist in the 1690s, was dismissed by the king in 1700 for matchmaking with Toulouse (and Charlotte de Lorraine, Mlle d'Armagnac). See Saint-Simon, *Mémoires*, ed. Truc (Pléiade), 2:8, R. E. A. Waller, *The Relations Between Men of Letters and the Representatives of Authority in France, 1715–1723*, p. 424.

42. For the text, see below chap. 4, n. 4 and text.

43. Du Cange had been charged by Colbert with continuing the corpus of medieval chronicles begun by Duchesne. See Lionel Gossman, *Medievalism and the Ideologies of the Enlightenment: La Curne de Sainte-Palaye* (Baltimore: The Johns Hopkins University Press, 1968), 235. On the project, Institut de France, MS. 1451.

much stronger recommendation to Bossuet than was his criticism of *La Princesse de Clèves*, which (via Bouhours) gained introductions to Racine and Boileau later to be so valued and so valuable to him.[44] The history of his *Vie,* as I shall later show (Chapter 4), was aligned with the positions of Colbert (and Seignelay), who had in the royal council spoken for moderation in the face of the growing threat of violence in the cause of "conversions" of the Religion Prétendue Réformée (R.P.R.).[45] Bossuet's position was also at this date conciliatory. And if he was asked, as he was in the similar case of La Bruyère as a tutor in the Condé household, to vet the credentials of the author of the *Vie,* nothing in it or its author's life would have disqualified him.[46] Made admiral of France, also in 1683, Toulouse could obviously do with the help of a proven historian; and there are other reasons why Valincour, with his tested service to the Colberts (and, of course, incidentally, his wish to pursue historical writing), was a good choice for the future in the position.

In the 1669 reforms of naval administration, which set the stage for the golden age of French sea power to come, the retention of the title of Amiral de France was an anachronism.[47] Named and serving at the king's pleasure, the admiral was responsible only to him and was thus outside the newly established hierarchy that linked the intendants and intendant general to the minister for marine affairs. Although he might command, he was not de jure commander-in-chief of the royal fleets (nor in the event ever de facto their commander).[48] The charge,

44. In his reception Valincour refers to Racine as "près de vingt années son ami de toutes les heures" (p. 6), i.e., since c. 1679–80. That Bouhours introduced the two is revealed by J.-B. Racine, letter of 10 Nov. 1745 to Louis Racine, *Cahiers Raciniens* 1 (1957), 55.

45. See Elizabeth Labrousse, *"Une foi, une loi, un roi?": La Révocation de l'édit de Nantes* (Paris: Payot, 1985), 94, 115.

46. In 1685 Bossuet gave La Bruyère an oral examination on Descartes, which Valincour could have "passed" as well as the ideology of his *Vie* may a doctrinal test. See *Correspondance de Bossuet* (GELF ed., 1909), 4:18, n. 3.

47. In this context, see Etienne Taillemite, "Les Problèmes de la marine de guerre au XVIIe siècle," *XVIIe Siècle* 86–87 (1970), 21–36: "charge purement honorifique" (p. 23). In greater length, E. Taillemite, *Colbert, Secrétaire d'Etat de la marine et les réformes de 1669* (Paris: Académie de Marine, 1970).

48. That the anomalous position of the admiral was a principal factor in the crisis of naval command is shown by E. Taillemite, "Le Haut-Commandement de la marine française de Colbert à la Révolution," *Les Marines de guerre européennes* (Paris: Université de Paris-Sorbonne, 1985); rpt. as "Une crise du commandement," chap. 7

still possessing considerable privileges, had its traditional provisions[49] but was without strictly legal specification by statute, since its authority issued directly from the king's and represented it. Commissions of officers, naval justice, the administration of provincial admiralties and policing of their environs, all within the admiral's domain, were as many potential sources of contestation with the overlapping jurisdictional claims of local parlements or the centralized administration. In wartime, the admiral's *congés* (passports with his seal, required of all vessels leaving French ports) and the adjudication of prizes taken at sea or litoral salvage (from whose liquidation the admiral received a prize tenth) in particular became matters of contention, as combat strategy increasingly depended on the rapid and profitable private licensing of royal ships.

What the admiral's charge really would be, in short, what the admiral would amount to, depended then very much on the man. Since the first two appointments were of boys, the comte de Vermandois having preceded Toulouse,[50] what the admiral would be depended to a great extent on his staff, and on no one more than his *secrétaire général de la marine*. He could, of course, also by various means reduce the potential conflicts of interests and ultimately turn matters in the administration's direction. Since the appointment of Vermandois, that position had been held by Le Fouin, who was totally loyal to Colbert,[51] but by the time of the comte's death, and Colbert's, was showing signs of his age (notably in a lawsuit with the princesse de Conti that embroiled his office).[52] Grooming a successor of proved ability, and loyalty, was

of *L'Histoire ignorée de la marine française* (Paris: Perrin, 1988), 150–76. On the crisis, for Toulouse, after 1704, see below, chap. 5. pp. 137–138.

49. Provisions granted by the king (23 Nov. 1683) with the charge, registered by Parlement on 22 Dec. 1683, are in A.N. MS. API 300: 89. Pp. 1–5 are followed by an account of the ceremony of Toulouse's investiture (23 Dec. 1694), "sur l'avis donné ce jour'huy par M. de Valincourt, secretaire general de la marine" (5v–11v). See also E. Taillemite, *Colbert* (1970), 25–27; "Le Haute commandement . . ." (1985), passim.

50. On the short unhappy life of Louis, comte de Vermandois (1667–83), *fils naturel* of Louis XIV and Mlle de la Vallière, admiral in 1669, see the graphic account of Eve de Castro, *Les Bâtards du soleil* (Paris: Orban, 1987), 152–61, 164–65.

51. Le Fouin (d. 1688) was commissioned by the king on 9 Dec. 1683 to "regir et percevoir pendant la minorité de S.A.S. les droits et attachés a ses dtes charges d'amiral." (A.N. MS. Marine G 140, p. 124v.)

52. Mme de Conti's lawsuit, for recovery of moneys due to her as an heir of Vermandois, brought seizure of some of Le Fouin's papers in June 1688 and caused, then and with his death, several readjustments in Toulouse's staff. See A.N. MS. Marine G 140, pp. 135–36v.

in order. Valincour duly, if not entirely dutifully, assumed the appointment on 21 October 1688, just in time for the new war declared against
the Dutch in the following month. (In one of Toulouse's ledgers, the
next entry for the year's events after Valincour's appointment is that
war.)[53] What Valincour made of the charge, which the usually precise
Jal defined only by its lack of definition,[54] was in the decade following
his official appointment perhaps not entirely what was expected by
Seignelay—or Colbert—and advisers. But as I shall presently show,
the way he defined it in large part set the solid foundation of his
"mérite" as a servant of the crown.

As tutor to Toulouse, unofficially or otherwise, Valincour set about
collecting books—nautical treatises, atlases, collections of voyages.[55]
He read Caesar with the boy and, he admitted in one of his memoirs,
looked forward to reading more with him. That memoir and one
other from Valincour's extensive writings for the prince's instruction[56]
reveal a great deal. As Eugène Sue long ago pointed out, they are both
the work of a talented expositor and, it should be added, pedagogue.
Both the short treatises, on *congés* and on *prises* (composed most probably in 1688–89),[57] leave no doubt that their author had a taste for
erudition. Texts from antiquity and medieval chroniclers are cited with
apparent pleasure. Both are subordinated, however, to information

53. The registration of Valincour's provisions "de la charge de secrétaire de la
marine" is recorded in A.N. MS. G 140, p. 136v (and 300 AP1: 877, p. 195v). It is
followed by the "Ordonnance du Roy portant la declaration de guerre par mers et par
terre contre les Hollandais qui revoque les passe-ports et sauve-gardes, fait defense
d'avoir aucun commerce" (26 Nov. 1688).

54. Auguste Jal, *Glossaire nautique* (Paris: Firmin-Didot, 1848), 1338: "Titre donné
à un fonctionnaire placé près de l'amiral jusqu'en 1792, depuis 1795 près du ministre,
et chargé d'attributions divers, dont la nature et le nombre ont souvent varié." To
supplement, significantly, it is Valincour's confirmation by Pontchartrain that is cited
(for the text, see below text with n. 71). For the most complete treatment of the charge,
see Auguste Dumas, "Le Conseil des prises sous l'ancien régime (XVIIe–XVIIIe
siècles)," *Revue historique du droit français et l'étranger,* 3e Série, 29 (1905), 367–71.

55. Book orders (including Bayle's *Dictionnaire historique et critique*) were placed
during the war through the Rouen merchant Pierre Legendre. See Charles Beaurepaire, "Pierre Legendre, marchand de Rouen," *Normandie* 10 (1895), 193–205.

56. "Des prises" and "De l'origine de l'établissement des congés," Eugène Sue,
Histoire de la marine française (1836), 4:40–52; 53–58. Valincour also promises for the
comte a "Histoire de la navigation."

57. Placement in Sue's internal chronology (1680) is misleading. Use of a 1688
ruling as well as the attitudes toward Holland and England suggest the dates Nov.
1688–May 1689. Consequently, the memoirs are practical for the "teacher" dealing for
the first time actively with both "prises" and "congés" as well as the pupil.

about the origins of the admiral's privileges and the history and nature of his office.

Two other aspects of the memoirs are of particular interest for the future of the admiral and his secretary. First, both are practically oriented. Pains are taken while instructing his noble pupil or, as Valincour put it, "with the honor I have to inform Your Serene Highness of the rights that belong to his charge, without uselessly tiring him with the details he will later learn, as he will acquire a deeper understanding of the difficult and important questions his charges involve." Flattery, minimal but decidedly there ("You have succeeded all the gods," the tutor allows himself to say, after citing some mythological and biblical precedents for the admiral's prize tenth), is like the exquisite tact put to the service of pedagogy. There are in fact many practical details: precise identifications of the kinds of passports (and even what their forms look like), explanations of the ways ships are identified, an accounting of the papers they must carry, and perhaps most significantly a careful exposition of the legality of seizures at sea, supplemented by an account of the practical means by which they are made, assured, then certified and liquidated by judges attached to the admiralties. The writer, in his explanations of legal procedures, stays close to the 1681 naval code that he knew well.

If Toulouse's position was meant to be a privileged sinecure, Valincour does not make the presupposition and goes about his instruction as training for informed and able practical action. By invocation of the "difficult and important questions his charges involve," Toulouse is also being given a sense of responsibility rather than pure privilege. In modulations of his instruction from legalities (and information) to situational ethics and moral principles, Valincour was also doing his pupil a particular service. As the tutor knew, but the boy perhaps did not yet fully understand, an illegitimate son—even legitimized (1681) by a great king—would be obliged to prove himself and to depend on self-reliance in ways that a prince of the blood would not. Toulouse, who continued to receive this kind of advice through very difficult times in his life when his titles would be questioned, had good reason to be grateful for it. And there are a good many indications that from the time of his maturity he in fact was.

As a second focal point of interest, the memoirs plainly show Valincour as a humanist. In his efforts to instill principles, Valincour seeks qualities that had illustrated the lives of noble commanders, like that of François de Guise as Valincour himself had written it. The first maxim of the sea is that it is free to all, he instructs (contrary to English contentions, he also alerts the future commander). God made no boundaries in the seas. Any seizure, he declares, is contrary to the principles of peace and liberty. But wars, like laws themselves, must be accepted as necessities, since laws will not undo the world's evils or make men good. And law must always be obeyed—on ships, which are "like little cities," as elsewhere within the realm. Seamen summoned to prove their identities, the moral tutor adds, sometimes reply shockingly that they have no religion (especially Hollanders, he continues, again strategically). This too, the teacher allows it to be inferred, is against God's order; but to Valincour's credit he refrains from identifying the nonbelievers as "supposedly reformed" (R.P.R.). Unlike instruction later offered to the duc de Bourgogne—thought by aristocratic critics to be overly scrupulous for the needs of a leader—Valincour's for Toulouse never allows the critique of war or religious principles informing it to put into question the nobility of the man of arms legitimately waging war in service to his sovereign. In an equally conscientious Cartesian, indeed Colbertian, spirit, Valincour, to the best of his ability and resources, also did his part to assure that Toulouse would be well informed (even if less grandly than memoirs for the duc de Bourgogne were intended to ensure).

The real testing ground for the *secrétaire général,* in the admiral's interests and with him, opened before him with the 1688 declaration of war that took them both into the field and also kept Valincour long hours with the comte's clerks and councils.

From *charges* to *mérite*

Traditionally, and symptomatically limiting in the formation of an admiral, Toulouse's introduction to combat was in the field. At thirteen, he was taken by the king on the campaigns of 1691. Valincour, accompanying him, was present with the comte at the siege of Mons, and was not entirely pleased by what he saw and heard. He reported hearing a commander say, in all seriousness, that the "boulets" of the English fleet, being lighter than the French, could not do as much damage. "Je me contentai de plaindre le Roi," he commented, "de ce qu'on l'instruisait si mal de ses plus importantes affaires" ["I contained myself from voicing pity that the king was so badly instructed in his most important affairs"]. He was again with Toulouse the following year for the spectacular pageantry and grandiose military deployment that attended the siege of Namur. Racine, who was fatigued by them, wrote to the other royal historiographer, Boileau (who had stayed at home): "Je laisse à M. de Valincour le soin de vous écrire la prise du château neuf."[58] In 1693, Valincour was again in the comte's entourage when he first commanded his own regiment at the siege of Charleroy; business letters were received by Valincour's *commis* Vauerin and others from the field at Harlemont and Dinant.[59] At the war's conclusion, he still accompanied Toulouse, whose education was practically extended by a voyage to witness the beginnings of negotiations for the peace treaty of Ryswyck.[60] The balance sheet of activity at home showed an equal devotion to service and on a much broader scale the same guiding principle of loyalty to the king.

A month before formal declaration of war against the United Provinces, Seignelay established a *conseil des prises* under the presidency of Toulouse, which had to be administered by Valincour. Valincour refers, in a placet of 1711 to Louis XIV to which I shall return, specifically to "twenty-three years" of service in "all that regards prizes."[61] From its institution, the work involved with this council, which put the secretary in constant contact with Seignelay's *commis* and his interests, was extensive and difficult. The council was established to deal with the rapidly burgeoning enterprise of licensing private *armateurs*, in progress while the fleet was being readied. Seignelay himself armed some four frigates, with his own financing and in syndicate with Colbert de Croissy, and his doing so sparked a run among noble investors at court on this kind of high-yield investment.[62] One year after the institution of the council on prizes, almost to the day (20 October 1689), an *arrêt* of the royal council decentralized its adjudication of prizes, on the grounds that its slowness had created a bottleneck dangerous to the

---

58. Letter of 24 June 1692, *Œuvres complètes* (Pléiade, 1966), 519. Valincour had thus his own part in the enthusiasm of Boileau's "Ode sur la prise de Namur." On the spectacle, see F. Bluche, *Louis XIV* (Paris: Fayard, 1986), 630–33. For the anecdote on Mons, told by P. Demailly without citing source and attribution of the speaker as the duc de Beauvillier, see "Notice sur Valincour" (Ham, 1884), 84.

59. 5 and 13 June 1693, *Normandie* 10 (1895), 201.

60. On Toulouse's presence, Saint-Simon, *Mémoires* (Truc, ed., Pléiade), 1:422–24. By this moment, after command of Boufflers's cavalry, he was *lieutenant-général*. This moment would seem to provide the context for Valincour's *conte en vers,* "Le Rossignol" (see below, chap. 2, pp. 66–67).

61. See below, n. 68 and text.

62. Dangeau, *Journal* 2:183. See also J. S. Bromley, "The Loan of French Naval Vessels to Privateering Enterprises, 1688–1713," *Les Marines de guerre européennes* (1985), 65–66 and passim.

war effort. Local admiralty courts were henceforth empowered to judge cases, unless a captured vessel's nationality was in question.[63]

The issuing of passports, which grew apace with the drive of privateering, was similarly streamlined, pressure being exerted from the beginning for swift action on the part of the admiral's staff. As it has been explained for a later moment by Thomas Schaeper, the passport's path through bureaus was indeed circuitous. Once foreign trade policy had been set, the controller-general's office sent forms to his *premier commis,* who supervised their expedition to the minister for the marine for his signature and the admiral's with his seal. It returned thence to the controller's office for initialing, then proceeded to the naval secretary who "dispatched" it to the requester.[64] Having ready-stamped forms at hand would be expeditious for the minister, if the *secrétaire général de la marine* were to agree to it; there is no indication that Valincour was so inclined. Special difficulties arose also over commissions for vessels issued directly by James II, which involved Valincour in repeated correspondence with the minister (Pontchartrain) and others. Officers of the admiralty at Saint-Malo created difficulties, refusing as they did to acknowledge the signatures of either Toulouse or Valincour, since prior to 1695 there continued to be an Admiral of Brittany (the duc de Chaulnes).[65]

Procedures of the *conseil des prises* may have been slow, as Seignelay complained; but as his exchange of letters with Valincour shows, delays were in part the result of careful monitoring of the admiral's interests.[66] These interests were considerable and also slow to be realized, since the council's judgments were subject to appeal and nonpayment of Toulouse's tenths could provide additional investment capital. After Seignelay's death, Toulouse's council was obliged, for example, to take

63. On the first council, see Geoffrey Symcox, *The Crisis of French Sea Power 1688–1697* (The Hague: Nijhoff, 1974), 76–78. Following the articles of 1676 the council was under the admiral's presidency with at least three *conseillers d'état,* three from the *conseil des finances,* three *maîtres des requêtes,* the *secrétaire d'état de la marine,* and the *secrétaire général* (without deliberative voice).

64. Thomas J. Schaeper, *The French Council of Commerce, 1700–1715: A Study in Mercantilism after Colbert* (Columbus: Ohio State University Press, 1983), 141, n. 17. This reconstruction factors in the council of commerce (which fixed trade policy).

65. Dame Lucy Sutherland, "The Jacobite Privateers in the Nine Years War," *Statesmen, Scholars and Merchants,* ed. Anne Whiteman, et al. (Oxford: Clarendon Press, 1973), 31.

66. Letter from Seignelay to Valincour (A.N. MS. Archives de la Marine, $F^2$7 (1689), p. 261) complains of slowness in response to Valincour's insistence that all prize records be submitted to the council. See also A. Dumas, "Le Conseil," p. 370.

measures to collect "considerable sums" from his heirs, adjudged but not yet disbursed to Toulouse's treasurer.[67] In 1711, in his retrospective accounting of his years of administrating "all that regards prizes," the net sum quoted by Valincour is no small temptation to malversation (possible in a number of places). Valincour's declaration of his own scrupulous accountability, being in a placet to his sovereign, amounts to a solemn oath. It also reveals his conscientious attention to staffing, among other ordinary war duties, experience that would again be called upon in the next war (the Spanish Succession).

Il y a vingt-trois ans, Sire, que sous les ordres de M. le Comte de Toulouse, je suis chargé de tout ce qui regarde les prises. Il m'en a passé par les mains pour plus de deux cent millions. Beaucoup de gens y ont gagné des richesses immenses, en faisant de leur industrie ou de leur crédit un usage qui paroissoit légitime, & que je n'ai pas cru devoir suivre, parce qu'il me paroissoit douteux. Aussi oserois-je assurer V.M., que durant un si grand nombre d'années, & parmi une si grande multitude d'affaires où la moindre chose décide de la main-levée ou de la confiscation, jamais il n'est arrivé aucun sujet de plainte de la part des Armateurs, ni des Réclamateurs, & que j'ai toujours été en état de répondre de la fidélité & de la probité de mes Commis comme de la mienne propre.[68]

For twenty-three years, Sire, I have been charged by the orders of M. le comte de Toulouse with everything that concerns prizes. More than two hundred million [*livres*] have passed through my hands. Many persons have, by their use or credit, made immense fortunes, legitimately to their mind in such circumstances, practices I have believed I should not follow because they seemed to me doubtful. Therefore I dare to assure Your Majesty that during such a long period of years, and in such a multitude of affairs that depend on the slightest detail for judgment of restoration or confiscation, there has never been any misunderstanding or any subject for complaint on the part of armorers, or investors, and that I have always been in a position to answer for the loyalty and probity of my staff as for myself.

The years 1690–95 gave ample proofs of Valincour's "industry" and gained him a steadily increasing reputation for probity, *mérite* for a functionary whose "credit" by 1695–96 was widely known beyond Toulouse's councils. It was consecrated by actions of Toulouse himself framing this five-year period that also ended the comte's minority with his installation as admiral, appointment as governor of Brittany, and

67. In September of 1691, Toulouse's council takes measures to regain from Seignelay's heirs "considérables sommes" owed to Toulouse (A.N. MS. G⁵ 215, p. 3).
68. *Mémoires et lettres de Madame de Maintenon* (Maestrich, 1789), 8:178–79. On the context of the placet, see below, chap. 5, n. 69 and text.

acquisition of the duchy-peerage of Penthièvre. Fontenelle, and other eulogists who follow his account of Valincour's life, emphasize the personal sacrifices of writing, study, and time demanded of him by Toulouse's expanded domain in Brittany alone.[69] The Breton admiralty correspondence, including even occasional direct legal representation, was time consuming, the more so as Toulouse's replacement of Chaulnes was unpopular, at court as in Brittany,[70] and demanded tact. But the years before had been equally demanding, beginning with the campaign voyages, Toulouse's continuing education, and more that is specially acknowledged by the comte in 1695.

In 1692, Valincour continued to insist (the word is not too strong) to Pontchartrain that full records on prizes be forwarded to Toulouse's council. The response was a circular letter to the admiralties (17 December 1692): "Messieurs, le sr de Valincour ayant esté nommé secrétaire général de la marine, l'intention du Roy est qu'à l'avenir vous luy addressiez les procédures des prises qui seront amenées dans votre juridiction, dans les temps et suivant les règlements faits par sa Majesté pour l'instruction de ces procédures."[71] He continued also to attend assiduously the small council "du vendredi" that began to meet at M. Billard's to deal with a variety of financial and naval matters concerning Toulouse.

Originally and until 1695 only four in number—Billard, Valincour, Dupré (his kinsman),[72] and Cossin— replaced successively by the long-serving treasurers Chardon and Brossard, the members of this council made decisions on requests, directed correspondence to proper destinations, and deliberated on possible litigations. The full *prise* council was convened when legal matters demanded. Records of litigation and ledgers of prize adjudications were kept separately from its minutes.[73]

69. *Eloges* (1825 ed.), 2:253.
70. See Mme de Sévigné, letters of 25 Mar. and 15 Apr. 1695 (Duchêne ed., Pléiade, 1978), 3:1091–93.
71. Cited by A. Jal, *Glossaire nautique* (1848), 1338. Copy in the Archives du commissariat des classes, Honfleur.
72. Either Louis I Dupré or Louis II (d. 1754), *avocat au Châtelet* (1711) and according to Bluche "chef du ceil du cte de Toulouse et du duc de Penthièvre" (*L'Origine des magistrats,* p. 164). The minutes of the Friday council are in A.N. G⁵ 215-33, 256 (for years 1695–1701).
73. The registers of the "prises" are A.N. G⁵ 263, 265 (for 1694–97). Names and pertinent identifications are entered but sums due to Toulouse are not (seemingly, these are entered in Brossard's treasury ledgers, preserved only from 1705–06, 1720–22, and at present withdrawn from circulation). The legal appeals and related matters are G⁵ 263, 265 for 1694–97.

This "council" or steering committee was also separate from the household council, which was not fully formed until 1695.[74] Estate and notary records then fell to the treasurer (who kept his own records) or to the *avocat* Benoise. But all transactions were monitored and countersigned by the full group in regular weekly meetings (altogether then at least three series of weekly meetings for Valincour from 1695). Earlier on, in the smaller committee, functions were less specified and often shared. Valincour verified and reported in 1691, for example, on renovations of Toulouse's newly acquired *hôtel* in Versailles and his Marly residence.[75] About the same time, Valincour himself changed his residence, from the Ile to the Cloître Notre-Dame, where he became Boileau's neighbor and where he remained through 1715,[76] "as contented and at ease as a canon," Pontchartrain joked in 1694.[77]

If Valincour kept a residence of his own in Paris, his place in Toulouse's household was nonetheless as sure by 1693 as it was in his councils. There is in Toulouse's papers a "Projet d'ordre de la maison de son Altesse Serenissimme ...," a twenty-page notebook dated 1 January 1693, which confirms this place and in itself is of particular interest.[78] Though it does not constitute a full *livre de raison* and includes no information on wages or pensions, the notebook reveals the size of Toulouse's staff, of interest both for the comparison it allows with later records of a more elaborate household establishment and for the record of reality it offers behind the fantasies of those at court (including Madame, duchesse d'Orléans, the Palatine)[79] alarmed by the prospective magnitude of Toulouse's establishment. Toulouse's fortune, literally speaking, was from the beginning and ever after the subject of much gossip, especially after Penthièvre was purchased and paid for in louis d'or down at practically the full sale price of 1,500,000 livres.[80]

The functions of the officers of the household are first listed and

74. These are the ledgers and minutes of A.N. 300 AP1: 856–57 (for 1695 through 15 Dec. 1702).

75. A.N. 300 AP1:89 Liasse on the Hôtel de Versailles and on the Maison de Marly.

76. The *Almanach royal* that begins to appear in 1699, as well as the Académie listings, gives this residence. Cf. also the *Livre commode des addresses de Paris pour 1692* (ed. E. Fournier, 1878).

77. Letter of 15 July [1694]. A.N. Marine B^{2}95, p. 35.

78. A.N. 300 AP1:90.

79. Letter of 16 Mar. 1695, *Lettres de la Princesse Palatine,* ed. Olivier Amiel (Paris: Mercure, 1982), 117: "On fait à ce jeune homme un établissement magnifique. Ce sera le plus grand et le plus riche seigneur de France."

80. See D. Dessert, *Argent, pouvoir, société,* p. 178; Valincour to Pontchartrain, letter of 10 June [1695], B.N. MS. D'Hozier, P.O. 2890, 64,220, p. 26.

briefly described: *intendant, premier escuyer, secrétaire-général des commandements, gentilhomme ordinaire, controlleur-général, aumonier, médecin, chirurgien, apothicaire.* Understaff functions are also carefully described, from *valets de pieds* to kitchen help, with directions spelled out for the latter on the handling of silver and the purchase of wood and candles. Valincour's duties, as described here, sound deceptively simple against the known realities that earned him the rations designated for the regular diners in the household. "Le Secrétaire des commandements est pour expedier tous les livres, dresser toutes les expeditions, les faire signer à S.A.S., les contresigner, les sceller des sceaux de S.A.S. et garder les sceaux."

At "high table," the prince's, there were regularly eight diners, not identified as to function in the notebook and visibly a different group assembled for the comte's dinner conversation. They are listed as M. le Marquis d'O and Madame la marquise, Mons l'abbé Langle,[81] Mons Desplassons, Mons de Valincour, Mons de Longepierre, Mons de Terramey. Each of these diners was served daily a pound and half of bread and one bottle of "vin de bouche" (at 1 livre a bottle). Fifty-eight other regular diners are identified (with lesser, varying portions), at four tables of pages (7), valets de chambre (9), garçons (7), valets de pieds (15), gens d'écurie (12). Others (a Swiss, a porter, a valet for the pages) are designated as receiving "nourriture en argent." Portions are carefully noted, as are daily kitchen provisions itemized from meat and fruit (7 liv.) down to artichokes (1 liv. 10s.) and cress (8s). The total daily expense in this fastidious itemization is 99 liv.1s.6d.

If the comte were shown this book, there was surely a lesson in economy to be learned from it. That kind of economy is highly indicative of the care taken by the conservative household council evident over the years in its ledgers and minutes of accounting for the comte's finances (that in the early years are obviously also thought to be the king's). Toulouse had from his beginnings bad luck—a slight musket wound at Namur, scarlet fever during a later campaign—which menaced his fortune more seriously in later years. He was, however, fortunate in his council of long-serving, devoted overseers; of solid common sense, careful with funds, they were also men of shrewd judgment and not penny proud when it came to good investments. By 1693, something of their capabilities, and even tone, seconded

---

81. Pierre de Langle (b. 1644) served as preceptor (and aumônier?). He has assumed charge of the library by 1696. Letter of 9 Aug. to Legendre, *Normandie* 10 (1895), 204. He was later bishop of Boulogne.

surely by the marquis d'O (despite Saint-Simon's portrayal of him as an opportunist) had served to form the comte. In good fortune, favored by the king, he appeared modest and "sage," enough so even to win over the Palatine.[82] The staff of 1693, and the establishment it represents seemingly for the Versailles hôtel, may appear princely indeed for a fifteen-year-old. But it was not yet on a scale to justify the alarm of gossips and was managed with a conscientiousness that could have disarmed them.

On 23 December 1694, the pageantry changed for Valincour from the battlefield to the Parlement, with the Grand' Chambre and Tournelle assembled to attend the oath of fidelity to the king of Louis-Alexandre de Bourbon as he received his sword and was solemnly installed as admiral. In the procession to the Palais for the installation Valincour had his place, with his own drummer; after Toulouse had been received and then judged a first case of the admiral's justice, the secretary proposed "plusieurs articles" to the premier président. It is typical of the admiral's high sense of his dignity, shared by his secretary, that the specific article mentioned in the minutes of the ceremony[83] is the erecting of a dais. The premier président replied that the Parlement was an ancient house of the kings of France and that in its traditions a dais was constructed only for the king when he came for his *lits de justice*. Blustering tactfully, however, the judge declared himself unable to give immediate judgment and agreed that Pontchartrain should be dispatched forthwith to inquire of the king. No less symbolic than the question of the dais itself for the admiral who took his oath with a full sense of the duty of service is that of the henceforth unavoidable presence of the intermediary, whom the premier président designated to speak with the king. The minister—Pontchartrain especially—was to continue to be a factor in the realization of the admiral's intentions, ambitions, and actions. The problems already outlined of administrative tensions were of greater import than the envy and gossip and courtiers, existing as they did between an admiral (now visibly a

82. Letter of 19 Apr. 1701 (Amiel ed., 200): "Le comte de Toulouse a peu d'intelligence, mais il a un bon caractère et il est très libéral." "Le coucou du nid," Eve de Castro puts it in her portrait (*Les Bâtards du soleil,* pp. 266–67): "Un jugement droit et juste en lui supplée à l'esprit, qu'il a fort court, mais la précision et la clarté mêmes. D'accueil aussi gracieux qu'un froid naturel, mais glacial, le peut permettre; toujours civil, prévenant avec les dames, prêtant volontiers, l'oreille et le bras à qui le vient solliciter, le cœur généreux et tendre, avec pourtant dans ses façons une sécheresse, une distance qui leur ôtent la grâce qu'on leur voudrait trouver."

83. A.N. 300 AP1:89. "Provisions de la Charge d'Amiral," p. 7v.

responsible and capable adult) and a young minister in 1694–95 proving his own administrative capabilities. It is in this context of tensions that the recognition for service that Valincour received from Toulouse in 1695, in the reissuing of his commission, has a special significance.

Despite the fact of the circular letter already cited, Pontchartrain refused in 1695 to accord Valincour the full privileges of his charge, on the grounds that he had not been properly commissioned as *secrétaire général de la marine*. A note and accompanying documents in the D'Hozier papers leave no doubt of the reason for the clarification of Valincour's activities and titles for 1692–94 detailed in the commission. "M. de Valincour n'a esté employé dans l'Estat des principaux officiers de la marine es années 1692, 1693 et 1694, que comme commis par arrest du conseil pour signer avec l'Estampille de l'Amiral quoyque jusques en 1691 on luy eut toujours donné la qualité de secretaire de la marine. L'ayant effectivement suivant les provisions cy-jointes de M. l'Amiral du 2 janvier de la presente année 1695, il demande a estre employé en ladte qualité sur le Petit Estat de cette année."[84] Along with this note there is a group of letters written by Valincour to Pontchartrain that show him continuing to function in his charge over the years 1694–98 and on excellent terms with the minister, who was at the beginning of this correspondence still in the early stages of his administration.

What was most probably an oversight of registration of Valincour's specific charge, during the busy first campaign years, became, with the reissue of his commission of 1695, a reaffirmation of the articles of 1688 (and 1676) that defined the charge and with it the admiral's rights. In Auguste Dumas's analysis and clarification, this reconfirmation by and large fixes both for the rest of the ancien regime. In particular this meant maintenance of the presidency of the *conseil des prises* and the procedures for it defined by the articles and previously observed by Seignelay and Louis Pontchartrain. It remained in fact the commission extraordinaire of the *conseil du roi* it had clearly been in its earlier functioning. But a successful battle had been won—not the last to be fought—for the letter of the admiral's charge, a victory not perhaps just for his "illusion"[85] of service but for his discretionary actions in its spirit.

A day before the reissuing of commission of the *secrétaire général,*

84. B.N. MS. D'Hozier, P.O. 2890, 62,220, p. 29.
85. A. Dumas, "Le Conseil des prises," p. 352.

Toulouse had also reissued that of the *secrétaire des commandements* (both just in time to include their holder in the revision of "Pontchartrain's" capitation tax tables).[86] The provisions of this first commission generally includes those of the *secrétaire général,* and its duties now declared necessary to Toulouse had preceded the administration of marine affairs and first proved their holder's worthiness; more specifically, we may see, recent services had again proved that service. "Estant necessaire pour le bien de nos affaires et de notre service d'avoir pres de nous un secretaire de nos commandements, Maison et finances, pour expedier et signer les lettres de notre volonté," the comte makes known his choice of "le sr Jean Baptiste Henry du Trousset Ecuyer, sr de Valincour dont la capacité et fidélité nous sont particulierement connus par les preuves qu'il nous en a donnés dans l'administration de nos affaires depuis plusieurs années, et voulant en outre reconnaître les soins qu'il a pris de notre education longtemps avant qu'il entrast dans le maniment de nos affaires." There follow then the specifications—"pour en ladite qualité signer toutes lettres, commissions, provisions, brevets des charges des officiers de notre maison et autres, toutes lettres patentes et clauses, tous estats de gages, pensions, expeditions de notre gouvernement de Guyenne et generalement toutes autres qu'il appartiendra."[87]

In the same year and in 1696, Valincour's *mérite* and the credit it bestowed were acknowledged by two quite different petitioners. Racine wrote to his son Jean-Baptiste that when at court he should consult M. de Valincour, who indeed watched over the beginnings of his friend's son's diplomatic career and continued to do so after Racine's death.[88] The following year, Vauban (whom Pontchartrain especially admired) wrote to the admiral's secretary to ask him to use his influence and skill to direct 40,000 livres of Toulouse's tenths on Dunkirk

86. Valincour's position figures in the *Onzième classe* (thirty-seventh within it) taxable at 100 livres. The addition was made 1 Jan. 1696. See F. Bluche and J.-F. Solnon, *La Véritable hiérarchie sociale de l'ancienne France* (Geneva: Droz, 1983), 105.

87. My copy is La Rochelle, B.M., MS. 2725, no. 14; another B.N., MS. Clairambault 557, pièce 5500. The governorship of Guyenne was exchanged for Brittany later in the year.

88. Letter of 3 June 1695 (Pléiade ed.), 2:557. Jean-Baptiste was *gentilhomme ordinaire du roi, à la petite écurie;* for later attentions from Valincour, see J.-B. Racine to abbé Renaudot, letters of 9 Sept. 10 Dec. 1699, 24 Aug. 1700. F. K. Turgeon, "Unpublished Letters of Jean-Baptiste Racine to the abbé Renaudot," *Modern Language Notes* 54 (1939), 174, 179. Louis Racine, too, acknowledged in Valincour "un ami fort vif pour moi et je lui ai eu dans ma jeunesse plusieurs obligations." *Mémoires (Œuvres de Racine,* ed. Mesnard), 1:61.

toward much needed repairs of the port. "Only you," Vauban wrote to Valincour, could effect this delicate negotiation, "entirely in your hands."[89] However worthy Valincour doubtless thought this cause, for its military advantage or simply as a good investment, he characteristically safeguarded Toulouse's funds (frequently solicited for worthy causes) and did not take the matter to his council. The request and the expense were forwarded to Pontchartrain.

Standing on his record during the war years, Valincour stepped out of Toulouse's council on 6 September 1698[90] to allow the treasurer Chardon to present Valincour's memoir asking in effect for a raise. From his charge as *secrétaire général* he regularly had 1,500 livres a year.[91] Other financial benefits went with the charge (a tax on commissions in his granting, among others). A number of these rights, some lost by Le Fouin in his lawsuit, are itemized by Valincour; he asked specifically for the restitution of only some of them (according to the provisions of 1695), significantly and characteristically requested for the "dignity of the charge," not directly and explicitly as personal compensation for services rendered. Toulouse approved the request with his initials, granting that the *secrétaire général* "a droit & peut disposer des commissions d'interpretes, courtiers, chirurgiens, maistres de quay, pilotes & aumoniers, et autres de la mesme qualité dont S.A.S. ne retire point de finance, attendu que ceux qui l'ont précédé dans l'exercice de ladite charge en ont disposé." The *secrétaire des commandements* was also granted a regularized compensation for dispatch costs, "droit de sceau et expéditions . . . des officiers dont les charges dépendent de S.A.S.," according to fixed rates.

The restored benefits may have served in part for the purchase of Valincour's second residence. Sometime at the end of the 1690s he acquired, in the cul-de-sac Louvart at Saint-Cloud,[92] a country house

89. A.N. Marine B^{3}95, pp. 494–99. Vauban's letter is dated 10 June 1696; Valincour forwarded it to Louis Pontchartrain on the 11th. I am grateful to my colleague Ben Trotter for first calling this reference to my attention.

90. A.N. G^{5}215, pp. 122–24.

91. A. Dumas, "Le Conseil des Prises," p. 371. The additional emoluments that seem to Dumas considerable financial supplements, it should be remembered, were not regularly paid. Estimate of Valincour's staff is also questionably small in Dumas's estimation. The one *commis* (Vauerin) was supplemented by several "écrivains." On Valincour's pension, see below, chap. 5. p. 141.

92. The location is given by Charles Urbain, *Correspondance de Bossuet* (GELF ed., 1909), 2:143, n. The first appearance in Valincour's letters of a dating from St. Cloud is on 27 June 1701 to Noailles (*RHLF* 10 (1903), 671).

of venerable age that was his continued delight in advancing age. He created there, all his eulogists recall, a life that included good conversation with a variety of friends, the kind of far from austere "learned solitude" that he enjoyed through the decade as Boileau's frequent guest at Auteuil. "It is far from the lavish hospitality of Villeroy you have been enjoying," the owner of this "hermitage" later wrote in an invitation to Harlay, and added also significantly that it lay handily on the way to Versailles.[93] Meetings of Toulouse's weekly council had ceased meeting at Billard's and from at least 1695 demanded Valincour's regular attendance in his residence at Versailles or Fontainebleau, as the court moved. The house was not a gift; nor were the carriage and horses frequently needed from the 1690s onward by the secretary, who was often on the move between Paris, Versailles, Fontainebleau, and Marly.

The consecration of Valincour's *mérite* by Toulouse's actions in 1695 were foreshadowed by events of 1690–91, in which Pontchartrain's participation also had a special place. On 13 January 1690, the list of signers of the contract of marriage of Bénigne d'Héricourt and Marie Marguerite Bousitat de Courcelles, "fille du deffunt Mr Pierre Bousitat Seigr de Courcelles," was headed by the "tres haut et tres puissant Prince" Louis Alexandre de Bourbon accompanied by the "tres haute et tres puissante Princesse" Marie Françoise de Bourbon, princesse de Blois (the future duchesse d'Orléans, wife of the regent, who always doted on her borther Toulouse)[94] and included their mother, Françoise Athanase [*sic*] de Rochechouart. Pontchartrain also figured among the signers and a year later stood as godfather to Bénigne's first son, Bénigne-Jérôme, whose career, also pursued in naval administration, continued and confirmed the family's new tradition. And according to Mme de Simiane, his later friend and correspondent, the manner in which that tradition was embodied by the family had brought a "lasting esteem for it in Provence."[95] In the meanwhile, the Héricourts

93. Letter of 25 Aug. [1710] to Achille III de Harlay (B.N. MS. fon. fr. 16731, pp. 51v–52).

94. Later support from the regent's son may well also have come through the duchesse; in any case, family ties with the Orléans were enhanced by Valincour's knowledge in Toulouse's entourage of both the duc de Chartres and Mlle de Blois very early in their lives.

95. Letter of 28 July 1735: "Vos parents sont adorés dans ce pays-ci, jusqu'au plus petit cadichon." *Lettres de Mme de Sévigné* (ed. Monmerqué, 1862), 11:220. Bénigne-Jérôme d'Héricourt was *commissaire de la marine* (1716), *intendant des galères* (1729), *conseiller au Parlement de Provence* (1732).

were comfortably established in the parish of Saint-Eustache and the rue Vivienne.

The group of signatories of Héricourt's marriage contract, in contrast with the smaller and relatively more modest group represented in his parents', testifies in dramatic fashion to the heightened standing of the brothers, whose rise the elder had led already at some sacrifice (given the cost of 120,000 livres of Héricourt's 1690 office) in the interest of their consolidated fortune and titles. The accumulation of the latter, based on the merit of acknowledged administrative service, is an impressive index to the real prestige of their standing[96] confirmed also by the distinction of the signatories. Some names, though in a new generation, are familiar: both Dominique and Philippe de Bailleul reappear among them. So does Jean Hocquart, "beau père." Le Peletiers, whom Bénigne served, now far outnumber Bretonvilliers (simply Bénigne Le Ragois). With them and the great names of the realm are some of the most illustrious of the *robe*: The chancellor, Louis Boucherat, M. d'Aligre, Bignon (Jérôme), Arnauld de Pomponne, Harlay (Nicolas), Jean-Pierre Dargouges de Reniers and Joseph de Rosambol (both known from the *conseil des prises*). The entire document deserves quotation,[97] offering as it does, beyond evidence of the broth-

96. According to the formula suggested by Bluche, *La Vraie hiérarchie,* pp. 91–96 ("Usage d'une grille"), Valincour's position (Class XI, place 37) is about the same as his father's (XI, 26). Appointment in Toulouse's household is not factorable, since not taxed. But Bénigne's charges as *trésorier à Metz* (IV, 14) and *Maître des requêtes* (V, 1) lead to a base (IV) of 27 points, which with 1st and 2nd "cumuls" yields 33 as an index (as opposed to Henri du Trousset's 13).

97. B.N. D'Hozier, Dos. Bl., 648, 17,193, pp. 13–16: The contract was signed in the presence of "tres haut et très puissant Prince Monseigneur Louis Alexandre de Bourbon, Comte de Toulouse, Grand Amiral de France et Gouverneur de Guyenne; de très haute et très puissante Princesse Madame Marie Françoise de Bourbon, Princesse de Blois; du très haut et très puist Seignr Mgr Louis Boucherat, Chancelier de France, Seigneur de Comparan et autres lieux et de très haute et très puiste Dame, Dame Anne Francoise Loménie de Brienne, son épouse, de très haute et très puiste Dame, Dame Françoise Athanase de Rochechouart de Mortemart; de haut et pt Seignr Mr Phelypeaux de Pontchartrain, conseiller du roy en tous ses conseils et contrôleur général des finances et de haute pte De Marie de Maupeou, son épouse; de haut et pt Seign Mr Claude Le Pelletier, Conseiller du Roy en tous ses conseils et au Conseil Royal des finances et Ministre d'Etat; de haut et pt Seignr Mr Louis Le Pelletier, Conseiller du Roy en tous ses conseils et Président de son Parlement et de la haute et pte Dame Généreuse Josephe de Rosambo, son épouse; de Mr Charles Maurice Le Pelletier, abbé de St Acekig d'Angers; de Mr Michel Le Pelletier, Conseiller D'Etat ordinaire, Intendant des Finances et de De Marie Maydelene Guevin, son épouse; de haut et pt Seign Mr Dominique de Bailleul, Chlr Seigr de Chateaugoutier, Président au Parlement; de haut et pt Seignr Mr Phillipe de Bailleul, Chlr Seignr de Chateaugou-

ers' social ascension, a picture of the network of working relations that underpinned Valincour's administrative activity until the end of the reign and the establishment of a new pattern with the regency.

Pontchartrain was then at least a friend of the family, if a reluctant friend of the admiral, at the opening of the decade of the 1690s that closed for Valincour with two honors, which crowned his already consolidated credit and consecrated *mérite*. In the second of these, election to the Académie, in which Valincour succeeded his friend Racine on 26 June 1699,[98] Pontchartrain seemingly played a part. Boileau in April had written to Pontchartrain to ask for his support for the candidate, upon whom "all the Academicians had their eyes." Valincour is the worthiest successor to Racine, he adds as much in the tone of Pontchartrain's epistolary style as in his own, because the least likely to offer him a "dull eulogy" ("fade panégyrique").[99] Other support was also forthcoming. Valincour later thanked for it the duc de Noailles, who (while he was still the young comte d'Ayen) had been taken by Valincour to visit Boileau at Auteuil, luckily on a day when La Fontaine appeared.[100] The election was untroubled and the new Academician's eloquence satisfied Boileau's expectation in its praise of Racine. Valincour then and later in the Académie feelingly invoked

---

tier et Président au Parlement; de haut et pt Seignr Mr Arnauld de Pomponne, Secrétaire et Ministre d'Etat et de hte et pte De De Catherine Lavoiar, son épouse; de haute et pte De Charlotte Ladvocat, épouse de M. le Marquis de Vins; de Mr Charles Claude Arnauld de Pomponne, abbé de St Meneur; de Mr César de Vins, Chlr; de Mr Ladvocat, Conseiller du Roy en tous ses conseils, Maître des Requêtes ordinaires de son Hôtel; de Mr Bénigne Le Ragois, Seignr de Bretonvilliers, Conseiller du Roy en ses conseils, Président en sa Chambre de comptes et de De Darroi de St Dier, son épouse; de Jérôme Bignon, Conseiller d'Etat ordinaire et de De Suzanne Phelypeaux, son épouse; de Mr Nicolas du Harlay, Chev Seignr de Bonneuil, Conseiller et de De Marie Françoise Boucherat, son épouse; de Mr Hilaire Rouillart, Chlr Seignr du Coudray, Conseiller du Roy en ses conseils et dans sa Chambre des comptes et de De Marie Coquille son épouse; de Mr d'Aligre, Conseiller du Roy en ses conseils et des Requêtes ordinaires de son Hôtel; de Mr Jean Pierre Dargouges de Reniers, Conseiller du Roy en ses conseils et des Requêtes ordinaires de son Hotel et de Dame Françoise Le Pelletier, son épouse; de Mr Jérôme Bignon, Conseiller du Roy en ses conseils, Maître des Requêtes de son Hôtel et de De Estarte Bellart, son épouse; de Mr Rolland Arnaud, Conseiller du Roy en ses conseils et en sa Cour des aides; de Mr Joseph de Rossambol, Conseiller du Roy en son Parlement de Bretagne; et de Mr Darmoy, prètre principal du Collège de Lyon, amis. De Jean Henry du Trousset de Valincour, Ecuyer, Secrétaire de la Marine, frère; Jean Hocquart, Ecuyer, ancien Secrétaire du Roy, beau-père."

98. See below, chap. 4, n. 53 and text.
99. Letter of 22 Apr. 1699. *Œuvres* (ed. Adam), 807.
100. Letter of July (no day) 1717, *RHLF* 12 (1905), 487.

his long personal friendship and professional association with Racine. Receiving Valincour on behalf of the Académie, La Chapelle leaves no doubt that that friendship directly and indirectly was itself a strong recommendation of Racine's successor. The irresistible recommendation had come with Valincour's first honor of the year—appointment as royal historiographer. La Chapelle incidentally excuses the new man from assiduous attendance at the Académie's working sessions in the interest of the more glorious and important enterprise of chronicling the glories of its sovereign protector.

Valincour's historiographical activities, perceptible as early as 1693 in the perhaps then purely pleasurable activities of observation, narration, and the company of Racine, had been brought to the king's notice with a recommendation from Boileau and an arrangement that drew sarcasm from courtiers already doubtful about the extent of his exertions in the charge.[101] The yearly register of the king's gifts records that Valincour was to aid Boileau "with memoirs" but that Boileau alone was to "hold the pen";[102] to serve, as one observer quipped, as Boileau's "resident at court."[103] No pension for Valincour's services is mentioned in the register.

A second recommendation is also evident in La Chapelle's greeting; indirectly, since Valincour's historiographical apprenticeship began on his campaigns, and directly as his secretary, it was Toulouse and service to him that were recognized as a "title" for membership in the illustrious company. Valincour is invited to join an already long and distinguished line of tutors to the royal household, which included his friends Bossuet (with whom he enters into an important correspondence in 1703) and La Bruyère. The new Academician may have recalled his old friend whose sudden death (1696) had moved Pontchartrain to a final compliment:

... ce pauvre La Bruyère, qui a pris congé si subitement de la compagnie! J'en suis, je vous assure, fort touché; car outre qu'il avoit beaucoup d'esprit,

---

101. B.N. MS. fon. fr. 7665, p. 16: "mai. Le Roi choisit Valincour. Il est Secretaire des commandemans du comte de Toulouse, & Secretaire general de la marine. Pour aider à des Preaus qui par la mort de Racine se trouvoit seul chargé de l'Histoire du Roi. Des Preaus l'ecrira seul, mais Valincour lui aidera à avoir des memoires."

102. Dangeau, *Journal* (1856 ed.), 74. Repeating the division of labor, he adds "et c'est Despréaux qui a prié le roi de le lui donner pour l'aider." See also Raymond Picard, *La Carrière de Jean Racine* (Paris: Gallimard, 1961), 556–57.

103. Vuillart to Préfontaine, letter of 6 May 1699 adds to the bon mot that "M. de Vallincourt a beaucoup d'érudition et beaucoup de politesse." *Lettres de Germain*

il estoit fort honneste homme, et, qui plus est, anti-Perrault. Je suis persuadé que M. l'abbé de Fleury remplira dignement sa place; je luy donne ma voix expectante.[104]

If one old friend was missing, Valincour still had many in the company into which he entered; and had he died shortly after election, many of them would have paid the same compliment that Pontchartrain does La Bruyère. Valincour the "honnête homme" had been pre-known, was re-known, and was often talked about, beginning with Boileau, who in 1701 displayed the cultural ideal/object by dedicating his "Satire XI" on honor to M. de Valincour.[105] "Un épître [*sic*] que Boileau lui dédia fit toute sa fortune," Voltaire hastily wrote in the appendix to *Le Siècle de Louis XIV*.[106] Although Boileau did favors for his friend, and commemorated their long friendship as well as Valincour's academic election in his dedication of "Satire XI," Valincour's fortune was already made before 1701 with the help of many others and principally by the work, devotion, and principles of the "honnête homme" himself.

The letters exchanged by Pontchartrain and Valincour, from 1694 through 1698,[107] offer some unique personal glimpses of the man and of the work habits that must have been repeated in scores of like

---

Vuillart, ami de Port-Royal, à M. Louis de Préfontaine (1694–1700) (Geneva: Droz, 1951), 225.

104. Letter of 22 May 1696 to abbé Renaudot. Georges Depping, "Lettres de Phélypeaux," *Bulletin du comité historique des monuments écrits de l'histoire de France* 2 (1850), 82.

105. On the satire, begun in September 1698, see A. Adam *Œuvres complètes* (Pléiade, 1966), 81–86; 940–44. Boileau's "maîtres ici … Bossuet et Pascal" are shared with Valincour, as is the praise for the integrity of Henri-François Daguesseau and Jérôme Bignon (lines 103–4).

106. Voltaire's friend abbé François-Bénigne d'Héricourt, Valincour's nephew, objected to what he thought a too-rapid treatment of his uncle in the catalogue of writers appended to the early printings of *Le Siècle de Louis XIV* (Letter to comte d'Argental, 8 Sept. 1752, *Œuvres*, ed. Moland, 27:483). Voltaire added praise of his academic eloquence but left in slightly attenuated form a nest of insinuations (taken up by Foisset in 1827 for the *Biographie universelle*). "Une épître que Despréaux lui a adressée fait sa plus grande réputation. On a de lui quelques petits ouvrages: il était bon littérateur. Il fit une assez grande fortune, qu'il n'eût pas fait s'il n'eût été qu'homme de lettres" [*Œuvres historiques*, ed. R. Pomeau, (Pléiade, 1962), pp. 1211–12].

107. Thirteen are preserved in archives: Valincour to Pontchartrain in B.N. D'Hozier, P.O. 2890, 64,220, pp. 18–27: 1 June 1694; 1 Oct. 1696, 12 Nov. 1698, 10 [Dec.] 1698, 10 June [1695], 18 June 1696; Pontchartrain's, somewhat anomalously in A.N. Marine B^2 95, pp. 15–17, 23–25, 48, 69, 74–75: 12 June, 5 July, 15 July, 7 Aug., 11 Aug., ? Sept. 1694; 7 June 1695. Depping published the first two of Pontchartrain's, loc. cit. (above, n. 104).

circumstances. The letters begin and end with Valincour at Bourbon, taking the waters, ill enough in 1698 to alarm Pontchartrain and to elicit his advice about melancholy,[108] likely to have been the by-product of the work-filled war years. But it is an element of Valincour's personality that unexpectedly surfaces in some of his verse and in letters from St. Cloud.

The first letter in the series, written from Bourbon on 1 June 1694, mixes business with friendly exchanges, as hundreds of letters before and after it, sharing pleasures of writing that set the stamp of urbanity of the secretary-letter writer who is not to be thought to be just any secretary. The "honnête homme" banters that he feels like the parasite of Plautus, when asked to write two letters a week, as Pontchartrain had requested while traveling on one of his early tours of naval installation in Brittany and the south. He would rather, Valincour quips, tar a vessel of the line, and assures the minister that if he were to take up the tarbush he would doubtless be as good with it as Pellisson could be. Indeed, he continues, it might well be in the public's interest if the forty of the Académie were all set to the task. Emerging from all this is a serious matter of lost papers, including the appeal to the admiral's justice by a lieutenant at Boulogne (Saint-Luc), which had been sent to Pontchartrain through Bignon and apparently has gone astray. Valincour pleads for justice and adds some fairly sharp banter about ministers who must be obeyed when *they* are in a hurry, even if it means fitting out two ships a day, but leave a Saint-Luc to wait in frustration at the end of four years' procedures. The matter in point had to do with rights of gathering *varech* (kelp). In January, Valincour had written to Du Houlley, *lieutenant général* at the admiralty of Rouen to check his own information on *varech* gathered from the *Coutume de Normandie* and asked for further clarifications before presenting the matter to Toulouse's council (revealingly referred to as the "conseil de S.M.").[109] Conscientious background work, prolonged procedures, lost papers: the bureaucratic drama was a familiar one that the secretary did his best to plot by marshaling the resources of his style.

The minister assured speedy investigation of the matter, took the banter in good part, and returned as good as he had gotten with

---

108. Letter of September 1694, pp. 74–75: "Je vous pardonne votre mélancolie. C'est neanmoins le plus dangereux de tous les maux, et il me semble qu'elle fait desja sur vous de terribles effets. ... Croyez moy, revenes icy au plustost et voulant eviter un mal prenes garde de tomber dans un pire."

109. *Normandie* 10 (1895), 204.

some irony that is perhaps more than an accidental foreshadowing of Valincour's election to the Académie. After answering the *raillerie* about tarring a ship (12 June 1694) with the compliment that he would surely be as good as any Academician, he adds "de même que vous estes meilleur escrivain que beaucoup de ces illustres messieurs." Complaining of another stylized profession of the difficulty of letter writing, Pontchartrain prophetically responded (5 July 1694) with the question: "And what would you do if you were obliged to write a dedicatory epistle for the Académie's dictionary?" When Valincour was faced with the task in 1718, he rose to the occasion on his own terms,[110] just as he did to the advice on letter writing offered ironically by Pontchartrain to the author whose *Lettres à Mme la marquise* had recently been reprinted (1691), whose epistles in verse had more recently been anthologized by Bouhours (1693), and who as secretary continued epistolary battle on behalf of Toulouse. Pontchartrain was delighted by a now lost satirical work, "Le Grand Négus," apparently a mock-heroic piece on a skirmish in the "*war* of the ancients and moderns," as Valincour called it;[111] "You couldn't do better," the minister declared also on 5 July, and dispenses both esthetic judgment and the award for "good sense" with the authority of a Boileau. The more reason to wonder, he insists, that a man "who knows his Marot and Voiture so thoroughly" has so much trouble writing a letter or two to a friend; enough *exordia* (15 July [1694]) on the topos of difficulty, he proposes, and enough of this padding with Latin tags ("What would you have a sea captain do with your quotation of Catullus?"). Valincour never lost his Latin, in response to Pontchartrain or many others, nor the ironic self-mockery of his own writing that overran letters into his verse. But some lessons, added to those already learned about the same time at Auteuil, about corresponding (or conversing) with ministers may have been welcomed. Others were perhaps also gained from the prickly exchanges with Pontchartrain, as the relationship became increasingly strained and the friendship spoiled. In a very plain letter, off his guard it would seem, Toulouse's secretary indiscreetly revealed to Pontchartrain in passing the price Toulouse had paid for the duchy of Penthièvre; a slight indiscretion, it could be thought, since the

---

110. See below, chap. 6, pp. 195–96.

111. Pontchartrain, in addition to the quip about La Bruyère "anti-Perrault," mentions a "dispute" Valincour has had with La Loubère "touchant les anciens," as he does with Charles de Sévigné (5 July 1694), and by antiphrasis to "votre bon ami Alary."

minister surely had other access to the information if he wished it. But it is the only time in all the extant letters Valincour wrote that he went beyond oblique referénces to the comte's affairs in writing to anyone except members of Toulouse's immediate circle (like Noailles). That discretion in the earlier years of Valincour's career had been one of the best parts of "honnêteté."

Pontchartrain's final advice was a lesson Valincour had long learned from Bouhours. "Je veux," the minister asked as Bouhours often had in his manuals of style, "quelque chose d'aisé, de simple, d'enjoué, qui ne soit point affecté." "En un mot," he concluded, "je veux que vous escriviez comme vous parlez; car vous ne sçauriez mieux faire" (7 June 1695). In the same year as Boileau's dedication (making 1701 surely the highpoint of Valincour's literary reputation) Bouhours added in his revised anthology of verse a compliment to Valincour in terms that almost precisely repeat the qualities Pontchartrain had prescribed. Bouhours went on to certify the "honnêteté" of their writer and to praise it in his other writings.[112] For Cardinal de Noailles, who shortly thereafter found Bouhours frivolous and an improper translator for Scripture,[113] this certification would carry no weight (as Boileau's emblematizing of Valincour's honor would not for common enemies in the "war of ancients and moderns"). But both the archbishop of Paris and certain moderns found in Valincour's writings and conversation an "honnête homme" they did not disdain as an interlocutor.

Both writings, other than letters, and conversation that had played a considerable part by 1701 in exhibiting Valincour's *mérite* may seem like shadows in my foregoing outline of his career. Turning, in the three chapters to follow, first to the poetry that Bouhours praised, then to Valincour's criticism and historical writing, I wish to review their modesty. The shadows of the "honnête homme" responsible for that modesty have, I believe, an effect described by La Bruyère: "La modestie est au mérite ce que les ombres sont aux figures dans un tableau: elle lui donne de la force et du relief" ("Du mérite personnel," 17).

112. The text is cited in full below, chap. 2, n. 19 and text.
113. See Lucien Ceyssens, "Autour de l'Unigenitus: le Cardinal de Noailles," *Lias* 11 (1984), 193–94.

Part II

Writing *honnêteté*

Chapter 2

The Pleasures of Poetry

Early Poetry

Valincour's first verse to be published, under the name du Trousset, appeared in stylish company. Two airs and a rondeau were included in Guillaume de Luynes's elegantly produced 1680 continuation of the Pellisson-La Suze anthologies of the "plus beaux airs mis en chant." His lyrics take their place beside those of undisputed masters of the craft, Benserade and Quinault, from which they are by and large indistinguishable.

The highly stylized and polished airs, traditional lovers' complaints of gallant verse, address their sighs to an ethereal Iris, that "Iris dans l'air" of which Boileau made sardonic sport.

> Vous croyez que vos soins et vostre complaisance
> Me pourront à la fin chacer vostre froideur;
> Mais de quoy sert-il d'augmenter mon ardeur,
> Si vous n'avez pour moy que de l'indifférence?
> Hélas, cruelle Iris, est-ce un plaisir si doux
> Que de tromper un coeur qui s'abandonne à vous?
>
> Ah! Du moins si mes feux n'ont pû toucher vostre âme
> Laissez-moy pour jamais oublier mes malheurs,
> Et ne rallumez point par vos regards trompeurs
> Les restes mal éteints d'une inutile flâme:
> Hélas, cruelle Iris, est-ce un plaisir si doux
> Que de tromper un coeur qui s'abandonne à vous?[1]

1. Full bibliographical description that is given in the bibliography of Valincour's writings is not repeated here. Except for the first three, all texts of Valincour's published poems are quoted from the Goujet-La Morinière anthology (1745). A number of stylistic variants suggest revisions of earlier published texts by Valincour himself.

The rondeau is a single admonitory sentence. Its rhythm and brevity artfully mime the kind of naïveté Boileau observed as proper to its form.[2]

> Avant qu'il soit peu, la Belle,
> L'un de nous deux changera;
> Vous cesserez d'estre cruelle,
> Ou vostre Amant se lassera
>   D'estre fidelle:
> Avant qu'il soit peu, la Belle,
> L'un de nous deux changera.

The poet had before these published lyrics already offered other verse that, like them, would have presented a salon with the young poet's "pierre de touche du bel esprit." A manuscript note to the earliest extant, two "Requestes," describes their author as Parisian and not yet twenty-five and identifies the Olimpe for whom they are written as Mme Poncet, wife of the intendant of Berry.[3] The speaker in the first, "Requeste de Lisette à Olimpe" in fourteen octosyllabic *sixains,* is the intendante's dog, in the second, the young poet; his voice firmly differs from those of both the La Suze lyrics and this first "Requeste," which Cazes found in questionable taste even if "worthy of Voiture" (Bernard Pingaud heard it quite differently as an "odelette grâcieuse").[4]

The "Requeste de Lisette à Olimpe" is a parodic piece at the expense of the popular vogue of verse letters from pets to their owners or each other launched by Mme Deshoulières's spaniel Gas (and only at a long distance reminiscent of Tibullus).[5] Valincour's pastiche, the complaint of a bitch in heat to a humble kitchen "turnspit," transforms the poetess's pastoral diction. His Lisette would prefer the kitchen to the salon, a mate to an apotheosis there. Mme Deshoulières's "Apothéose de Gas mon chien" had opened with a goad to this kind of mockery: "Plus d'un murmure / Contre mon illustre chien." Lisette confesses:

> On dit partout qu'il est si doux,
> Olimpe, de l'Estre auprès de vous.

2. *L'Art poétique,* Chant II, v. 140. Ed. Adam, p. 166.
3. B.N. fon. fr. 19144, p. 90. This information allows for a dating between 1673 and 1677.
4. Albert Cazes, "Introduction," p. 26; B. Pingaud, "Pages oubliées: un critique de salon: Valincour," *Les Lettres nouvelles* 7, no. 2 (25 March, 1959), 49.
5. The "Gas" poems appeared in the *Mercure Galant* 1 (1672), 268–71; others, at the moment of Valincour's verse. For the collection of fifteen, see *Œuvres* (1704 ed.), 1:10–14, 50–77.

> Mais cela, s'en dit sans reproche,
> J'aimerois bien mieux pour longtemps
> Estre chien de Tournebroche
> Que perdre ainsi mes jeunes ans. (vv. 25–30)

Comic canine preciousness ("Oui l'Amour se fourre en tous lieux, / Argus même avec ses cent yeux, / En vain se mettroit à l'attache.") alternates its ornaments with a burlesque ribaldry, whose simpering makes the parodic intention of the verse unmistakable.

> Ce n'est pas que vostre Doudou
> Voulust courir le Guilledou . . .
> Je voudrois choisir un époux
> Qui sût me faire des toutous . . . (vv. 31–32, 55–56)

The conclusion, in the manner of a ballade envoy, strikes a pseudo-sly tone that both suggests the kind of humor Mme Poncet and her friends enjoyed and recurs in some of the poet's later private verse recreations with close friends.

> Belles qui plaignez mon tourment
> Faittez-moy trouver un amant.
> Ainsi l'Amour vous soit en aide
> Et dans cet accident fatal
> Vous fasse esprouver le remède
> Avant que vous sentiez le mal. (vv. 79–84)

And another piquant ingredient may have been added. The philosophical quarrel about the soul of animals, far from over,[6] is perhaps playfully echoed in Lisette's downright defense of her virtue—in effect, that she is a dog being a dog, whatever else may remain undisclosed.

> Contre un tel adveu ma Vertu
> Assez longtemps a combattu,
> Mais enfin le besoin l'emporte.
> C'est lui seul qui me fait parler;
> Nature est toujours la plus forte,
> Quand il luy plaise de s'en mesler. (vv. 13–18)

If this first piece offers the first blush of a kind of wit that will remain one of Valincour's cachets in moments of badinage, the second

---

6. Henri Busson notes that Mme Deshoulières referred to her dog Grisette as "la machine aboyante." "Introduction" to *Discours à Madame de La Sablière* (Geneva: Droz, 1967), 16.

"Requeste" sounds in a heightened fashion a satirical register that will remain no less characteristic. It may become muted and modulated in public utterances but in private seeks all the resources and effects of the high eloquence of the "sublime."

After a compliment and the requisite formulas of poetic modesty and creative trepidation (vv. 1–43), the poet, who is charged with legal work for M. Poncet, is interrupted in his poetic flight by that task.

> Tu veux louer Olimpe avec tous ses appas.
>> C'est tout ce que je pourrois
>> Si je n'avois point d'Embarras.
>> Ayant un procès sur les bras,
>> Va, crois-moy, songe à ton affaire.
>> Tu ne peux rien de mieux.
> Presse les Eschevins, fais enrager le Maire,
> C'est là le seul dessein qui t'amène en ces lieux,
> Présente à l'Intendant requeste sur requeste,
>> Mais j'en ay desja présenté
> Et je crains à la fin de luy rompre l'adresse
>> Et de fatiguer sa bonté.
>> Non, si le prétexte est honneste,
> On peut estre importun avec impunité
> Quand il s'agit de pareilles affaires
>> Et pour les choses légères
>> Il seroit souvent tourmenté.
> A ces fascheux discours, qui m'oste le courage
> Je quitte malgré moy l'Enterprise de l'ouvrage
> Et passe tout le jour, dont assez me deplaist,
> A faire une requeste ou relire un arrest.   (vv. 22–42)

The rhythm of the dialogue is unmistakably reminiscent of Boileau, and the musings of the young poet specifically recall Boileau's emergence from "la poudre de la greffe," to take flight "loin du Palais errer sur le Parnasse" ("Epître V"). In his own voice, Valincour launches an almost full scale Juvenalian satire, denouncing the machinery of so-called justice from the special point of observation that made such denunciation also a prominent strand in the first collection of Boileau's satires. Continuing to appear in 1677, with his attack on Racine's detractors ("Epître VII") in February, Boileau's epistles and satires were fresh in Valincour's mind at the moment of writing what in effect becomes his own "Satire I." Through that poetry more than any other he found and distilled his own poetic voice.

Valincour's "Satire I" owes much to Boileau's greatly revised adieu to Paris, "Satire I." Its Juvenalian anger was eventually much attenuated but was still amply audible in the 1674 (or earlier) text Valincour read. If rhyme is identical,[7] so is the shaping of the reason of denunciatory anger: "Maudit soit le premier dont la folle manie / Changeant mal à propos ce doux genre de vie / S'avisa de bastir des bourgs et des hameaux" (vv. 58–60). A catalogue of civic villainies, almost embarrassingly high pitched rhetorically (vv. 77–115), transforms the "indiscreet youth" whose poetic trepidation prefaced the poem. He seems in it to have taken literally the counsel of righteous indignation given by Boileau's Juvenalian paraphrase—"La colère suffit, et vaut un Apollon" (I, 144)—and ends it with a personal expression of horrified repugnance before the deplored spectacle: "Et je m'en sens hérisser les cheveux" (another formula familiar to readers of Boileau's satires).

But there are two telling departures from the model of Boileau's "Satire I" in Valincour's imitation of it. Unlike Boileau's second persona in that satire—the destitute, silly, but honorable poet Damon who flees Paris with the satirist's exemplary blessings—Valincour the poet turns away from his denunciations without turning from the city and those responsibilities in it that first interrupted his poetic flight. He turns from poetry and its privileged, private, and special justice to the necessity of attending to matters at hand and, in their justice or injustice, out of the poet's hands. That gesture typifies a great deal. Important in itself at the moment, and a prelude to similar later poetic enactments, it will be the principal subject also of much of the moral meditation that is the substance of his later verse. Here, without development:

> Mais que sert-il de le tant dire?
> A vostre illustre espoux je m'en plains tous les jours
> Peut estre si souvent qu'il est las de l'entendre.
> Qu'y fasse, c'est de luy que je dois tout attendre,
> C'est à luy seul que j'ay recours.
> Olimpe avec vostre secours
> Que ne pourrois-je prétendre! (vv. 115–21)

Again unlike Boileau, Valincour gives place to a vision of the Golden Age. For Boileau in his first satires the topos, in the shape of an "age of innocence," is rare and purely rhetorical: the idyllic garden envisioned by other satirists as an alternative to the corrupt city, it seems, did not present itself to his mind or sensibility. Valincour's

---

7. Boileau, "Satire I," vv. 37–38: "Que Jacquin vive ici, dont l'adresse funeste / A plus causé de maux que la guerre et la peste." Cf. Valincour, vv. 104–5: "On vit des assassins et le poison funeste / Emporter plus de gens que la guerre et la peste."

evocation of the Golden Age, lyrically overflowing the rhetorical antithesis that summoned it, remains a poetic topos in the grand poetic
tradition, as he wanders through a familiar happy landscape of the
"bella età de l'oro" paraphrased freely from Tasso's well-known choral
celebration of it in *L'Aminta*.[8] The poet who turns away from poetry
on the one hand recovers it on the other, remaining both a satirist and
a lyric poet. In the writing of poetry he finds—perhaps more than the
"bel esprit" of the salon poet—both a place of expansive respite and
one of circumscribing judgment.

Valincour's most frequently reprinted poem, a paraphrase of Horace's "To Leuconë" (*Odes* I, 11), brings together, through a special irony,
the strands of his earliest poetry. A free rendering of the ode, the kind
of "belle infidèle" he later commended to the Académie,[9] Valincour's
elegant badinage seems of a piece with the poems of the 1680 Luynes
collection and was not surprisingly lauded by Ménage (before being
anthologized as a model by Bruzen de La Martinière).[10] As Jean
Marmier has shown, citing Valincour's poem among others, such
paraphrases were as likely in salons as among more bookish persons.[11]
Indeed, a very French "Philis" is introduced and with her the diction
she might expect. The starkness and severity of the Latin poem's
rhythm, imagery, and tone are in consequence transformed by fluid
alexandrins into a more tactful and wistful *carpe diem,* sometimes
conveying skillfully in its own way (as in stanza three) the sense of
Horace's *invidia aetas.*

> De la fin de nos jours ne soyons point en peine.
> C'est un secret, Philis, qui n'est que pour les Dieux.
> Méprisez ces devins, dont la science vaine
> Se vante follement de lire dans les cieux.
>
> Attendons en repos l'ordre des Destinées;
> Prêts à leur obéir, à toute heure, en tout tems;
> Soit qu'il nous reste encore un grand nombre d'années,
> Ou qu'enfin nous touchions à nos derniers momens.

8. Vv. 44–51 are very close to a translation of *L'Aminta,* Act II, Coro, vv. 1–11.

9. "Mémoire sur les occupations de l'Académie française." *Œuvres de Fénelon* (Paris:
Lebel, 1824), 21:153.

10. In the *Ménagiana* (1729 ed., 2:216) Valincour's version is awarded the prize
over another identified as Bouhier's by Charles Des Guerrois, *Le Président Bouhier*
(Paris: Ledoyen, 1855), 136.

11. Jean Marmier, *Horace en France au XVIIe siècle* (Paris: PUF, 1962), 47, 353 and
passim.

Ne songez qu'aux plaisirs que donne la jeunesse:
Nos jours durent trop peu pour de plus grands desseins.
Le tems, cet heureux tems se dérobe sans cesse,
Et fuit loin de moi pendant que je m'en plains.

Profitez en ce jour des douceurs de la vie:
Songez bien qu'il s'en va pour ne plus revenir:
Et qu'après tout, Philis, c'est faire une folie
Que perdre le présent à chercher l'avenir.

The ironic twist, which took the poem out of the salon, was given by Donneau de Visé, who seemingly without its author's knowledge published it for the first time in the *Mercure Galant* of February 1681. Profiting as he had for his play *Les Devineresses* from public enthusiasm for astrology, newly fanned by the recent appearance of a now-famous comet, the publicist de Visé offered Valincour's poem as an appropriate and agreeable pendant to a learned theological treatise on the vanities of astrology by Commiers d'Embrun. The poet may have resented the liberty (though other factors later prompted him to call de Visé a scoundrel). He might rather have been grateful for the poem's new context. It points up a critical spirit, in keeping with the parodic nature and the satirical thrust of Valincour's other early verse. Significantly, from the historical perspective, it also puts Valincour for the first time for later readers into the company of a kindred spirit, Pierre Bayle, whose critique of superstition shortly to appear in the *Pensées sur la comète* has become a landmark in the seventeenth-century Enlightenment.

Parnassus: Compliments of a Master

The small group of published poems that gained Valincour a modest place in the Parnasse Français, granted to him by its architect, Titon du Tillet,[12] were all written before he was forty and all published by his mentor, Père Bouhours. In the first edition of his anthology of 1693, four poems by Valincour were included—two fables ("Le Printemps" and "Le Rossignol en cage"), a slightly revised version of the Horatian paraphrase, and a lengthy verse epistle ("De Daphnis à Damon"). In the augmented second edition (1701), the gayer "Le Printemps" was dropped in favor of a very Malherbean "Consolation à Damon."

12. See above, Introduction, n. 11.

"Le Printemps" is a fable only in the sense of being a fiction. It is a high-styled, allegorical compliment in which the poet offers Olympe the poetic explanation for a chilly spring. After receiving Spring's complaint, Apollo was not moved, and spring has retired to a place where it is possible to reign the year around.

> Alors, sans tarder davantage
> Il vint se retirer dessus vostre visage.
> C'est là qu'il nous fait voir les plus belles couleurs,
> Et qu'il fait éclore mille fleurs. (vv. 76–79)

The wit articulated by an easy rhythm is by 1693 a characteristic one of irregular alternation of *alexandrin* and octosyllabic lines punctuated by the occasional shorter line. And here it makes the poetry of yet another complaint to another Olympe seem an untroubled development of earlier verse. But its elaborate prosopopeia and a high style reminiscent of Malherbe's (as in the closing conceit of his sonnet to the vicomtesse d'Auchy) suggest a poetic effort on an entirely different scale, perhaps addressed to no ordinary Olympe:

> Olympe, de qui les appas
> Font tant de méchans coups dont on n'ose se plaindre
> Et qui sçavez vous faire adorer, aimer, craindre
> Par tel qui ne s'en vante pas . . . (vv. 1–4)

If the *destinataire* here is in fact Mme de Montespan, the Olympe addressed in 1678 by La Fontaine,[13] the sense of the allegory and its undercutting irony might seem a signally tactless poetic offering to the women who, in waning royal favor, could have found with her Apollo any of the springs from 1679 through 1683 chilly. But the poet's closure of unsentimental consolation, with its cynical final turn to display of its artifice and ineffectiveness, in short its defining style, may be successfully pitched to the legendarily sardonic Mortemart wit. The final gesture of an ironic smile at defeat includes self-parody, of the elaborate poetic trappings of the verse itself.

> Mais par malheur, le Dieu qui préside aux saisons
> Ne goûta fort ces raisons;
> Et du pauvre Printemps la harangue inutile,
> Fit aussi peu d'impression,

---

13. "A Madame de Montespan," as Olympe, vv. 11, 129. *Fables,* ed. Clarac (Pléiade), 1:155–56. On Valincour's relations with Mme de Montespan, see above, chap. 1, nn. 37–38 and text.

> Qu'il eut exhorté le Maire d'une ville
> A faire une imposition.
> Il eut beau dire, il eut beau faire,
> Tout alla comme à l'ordinaire. (vv. 58–65)

In 1693, when Mme de Montespan had long been in eclipse and "retreat," "Le Printemps" would have made its private—or semi-private—gesture of friendship to a woman whose protection had meant much to the young du Trousset a decade and more earlier. Courtiers, moralists like Saint-Simon often recall (as he does when citing Valincour's loyalty to Mme de Montespan as an exception), more often have shorter memories.

"Le Rossignol," a fable in the traditional genre, courted the more immediate literary danger of comparison with La Fontaine's fables,[14] of which "Le Soleil et les grenouilles" and "Le Juge arbitre, l'hospitalier, et le solitaire" first appeared in the same volume. From Valincour's first lines, narrative techniques and tones of La Fontaine's style are caught by the poet. His fable's rapidly paced *vers variés* move from the nightingale's first complaint (vv. 1–20), with a delicate if commonplace evocation of pastoral scene, through a quick transition to the second episode of the miniature drama that unfolds as rapidly (vv. 21–45) as did the first. The moralist's unifying voice in the narrative concentrates the focus of the two episodes in two lines—"Toute nouveauté paroît belle" (v. 24) and "Mais comme avec le tems il n'est rien qui n'ennuie" (v. 32)—that point toward the solemn detachment of the epimyth's moral.

> Un Rossignol, dont le ramage
> Effaçoit les plus belles voix,
> S'ennuya du séjour des bois,
> Qui lui paroissoit trop sauvage.
> Quoi, disoit-il en son langage,
> Moi qui suis des humains & le charme et l'amour
> Je m'amuse en ces lieux à chanter, nuit & jour,
> Tout ce qu'on peut ouïr de plus doux, de plus tendre:
> Mais de tous mes airs nouveaux,
> 10   Quel fruit ici puis-je prétendre?
> De charmer des hiboux ou bien des étourneaux,
> Ou tout au plus quelque jeune Bergère,

---

14. Like the Horatian paraphrase, imitations of La Fontaine were frequent and often mediocre salon performances during the 1680s. See F. Gohin, "Les Imitateurs de La Fontaine." *La Fontaine: études et recherches* (Paris: Garnier, 1937), 212.

Qui bien souvent encor sur la tendre fougère,
    Aime mieux s'en faire conter
    Par son amant, que m'écouter.
    Aussi-tôt ce chantre peu sage,
    Quitte son bois, vient à Paris:
    Il se laisse prendre; il est pris,
    On l'enferme dans une cage;
20 On le porte aussi-tôt dans un palais doré
    Il y chante, il este admiré;
Chacun vient l'écouter: il se sait fort bien gré
    De sa condition nouvelle;
    Toute nouveauté paroît belle.
La fille du logis le vient tous les matins
    Appâter de ses propres mains;
Personne n'oseroit y toucher qu'elle-même,
Le Rossignol rend grâce à ses heureux destins,
Ne désire plus rien dans son bonheur extrême,
30   Que de le voir durer toujours;
    Cela dura bien quinze jours.
Mais comme avec le tems il n'est rien qui n'ennuie;
    Malgré ce doux genre de vie,
    Dont il avoit été charmé,
Il vint à s'ennuier de se voir enfermé!
Tous les admirateurs vinrent à lui déplaire:
    Il n'aimoit plus à chanter
    Quand on venoit l'écouter.
Sans cesse il regrettoit son séjour solitaire
40 Mais ce furent autant de regrets superflus;
Dans ces bois désirés il ne retourna plus;
    Il mourut enfin de tristesse.
    La prison la plus charmante,
    Est toujours une prison;
    Et souvent ce qui nous enchante
    N'a rien d'amiable que le nom.

The moral generalization of the fable is self-contained. But the "gilded cage" immediately suggesting the courtier's, the poem becomes more personal when one recalls the younger poet's complaint to Olympe of encumbering paperwork that had greatly proliferated for him on the threshold of his forties and perhaps imposed sacrifices. A moment of resignation to the demands of a life in which poetry was not to have the full part of a younger poet's expectations might be heard in the fable. The bleak final tone in any event, echoing the resignation of the earlier complaint to Olympe, sounds a Pascalian note that is amplified by the meditation of the persistent poet of the "Lettre de Daphnis à Damon."

A scene of a late night storm is quickly and lightly recounted in the opening of the letter in a manner recalling the opening of Boileau's "Satire VI" ("Les Embarras de Paris"). Playful debunking of high style, in an overdetermined "poetic" periphrasis calling forth three goddesses (vv. 3–4) when none is strictly necessary after a precise telling of the hour, is followed by an image of hungry cats in the attic (with the tongue-in-cheek rhyme "Proserpine / sabbatine / cuisine"), then by a nervous plea for divine protection. A more gentle self-parody than that of "Le Printemps" reduces the poet's inspiration, in this cultivated "style marotique," to the circumstances of sleeplessness, or simply to wind.

> Il est une heure après minuit:
> Je suis négligement étendu sur mon lit;
> Diane, Hécate, ou Proserpine,
> A fait la moitié de son tour;
> Nos chats dans le grenier ont fait leur sabbatine,
> Et n'attendent plus que le jour,
> Pour se ranger à la cuisine.
> Quoique je dûsse, cher Ami,
> A pareille heure être endormi,
> Et que j'en eusse même une assez forte envie,
> Y penser seroit folie ...
> Les thuiles en tous lieux volent avec grand bruit,
> Et sans la divine assistance,
> En qui j'ai grande confiance,
> J'appréhenderois, cette nuit,
> De faire une terrible danse. (vv. 1–11, 20–24)

Rapid dialogue, opening a subject easily arising in the circumstances, broaches with some hesitation the subject of man's composition that will occupy the body of the letter. There are echoes of Boileau's "Satire IV" and of Pascal's exploration of diversion ("divertissement") in the transition.

> Ma foi, l'homme est bâti d'une étrange façon,
> Il ne sçait bien souvent s'il est chair ou poisson.
> Entraîné d'une humeur inquiète, inégale,
> Il court sans savoir où, retourne sur ses pas;
> Rejette ce qu'il a, cherche ce qu'il n'a pas.
> A quoi bon mettre ici toute cette morale?
> Est-ce à propos du vent qu'il fait?

Direz-vous ... Non pas tout-à-fait,
Réspondrai-je; mais patience
Et vous verrez où va tout ce raisonnement
Si vous voulez me donner audience
Un moment. (vv. 28–39)

The poet retells the nightingale's story, this time beginning with a city dweller who yearns for the philosophical solitude of the countryside (vv. 44–51). A Horatian "verse character" gives voice to the aspiration in language that proves to be self-deceived (vv. 52–62), empty wisdom exploded as the first touch of autumn chill drives the self-styled sage back to the city (vv. 72–91). From the exposé of philosophical posturing the poet-satirist moves to pastiche of pastoral style.

L'homme donc sans former aucun désir utile,
N'a que de vains emportements:
Quand il est à la ville, il voudroit être aux champs:
Est-il aux champs, il veut être à la ville.
Au milieu de Paris le grand bruit lui déplaît,
Il n'aime que la solitude;
Et le milieu d'une forêt,
Où l'on peut sans inquiétude
Donner carrière à son cerveau,
Lui paroît plus beau
Que le plus grand palais de la plus belle ville.
Heureux qui peut dormir sur le bord d'un ruisseau,
Au bruit de l'eau,
Libre des soins fâcheux qui troublent notre vie,
Sans crainte, sans désirs, & surtout sans envie!
J'aimerois mieux vivre un seul jour
De la sorte,
Que de passer dix ans au milieu de la Cour.
Dans tous ces beaux discours un homme se transporte,
S'estime, & s'applaudit de son raisonnement:
Pense qu'il a tout seul la sagesse en partage:
Des malheureux mortels il plaint l'aveuglement,
Et regarde en pitié tout autre sentiment. (vv. 40–62)

After an inner monologue of hestitation in which this "fausse suffisance" gives way to the comfort of a return to the city (vv. 72–91), the satirist breaks in with a denunciatory lesson nourished by the wisdom of both Horace and Boileau.

... Malheureux, reconnois ton erreur:
Cet ennui que tu fuis est au fond de ton cœur;

Tu ne sçaurois le fuir, qu'en te fuyant toi-même;
　Change de lieu, si tu veux, tous les jours,
Cours la terre & la mer dans ton chagrin extrême,
　Ton ennui te suivra toujours.[15]
En vain, pour excuser ton bizarre caprice,
Tu veux injustement en accuser les lieux;
Il n'en est point pour toi qui ne soyent ennuyeux;
　Ton pauvre esprit a la jaunisse,
　Et tout paroît jaune à ses yeux.
　Le repos que tu te proposes
Ne s'acquiert point à force de courir.
Apprends, apprends à te souffrir,
On vient à bout par là de souffrir toutes choses. (vv. 91–105)

"You have a portion of the soul of M. Pascal," Daguesseau later wrote to Valincour,[16] and the poet shows it as his meditation on capriciousness moves toward his own evocation of the "cœur plein d'ordures." Seeking no special effects of versification, he is far from "elegant banter."

　Certes notre plus grand malheur,
Et ce qui met toujours notre esprit à la gêne,
　C'est que nous ne saurions sans peine
　Voir le dedans de notre cœur.
Il est toujours rempli d'espérances déçûës,
De haines, de soupçons & d'amours mal reçuës,
D'impossibles désirs qui n'ont jamais d'effet,
Et de cent faux chagrins que soi-même se fait.
Nous ne pouvons souffrir cet objet qui nous tuë
En vain, pour s'y contraindre, on fait quelques efforts;
Notre esprit, malgré nous, se répand au dehors,
Et sur d'autres objets cherche à porter sa vûë.
De là viennent ces jeux, ces divertissements,
Que tout le monde cherche avec des soins extrêmes,
Et qui ne sont au fond que des amusements,
　Dont tous les divers changements
Sçavent nous empêcher de penser à nous-mêmes. (vv. 105–21)

15. Goujet-La Morinière first noted the parallel of vv. 91–95 with Horace, "Ode III, i" vv. 37–40: "sed Timor et Minae / Scandunt eodem quo dominus, neque / decedit aerata tiremi et / post equitem sedet atra Cura." Also Boileau, "Epître V": "Un fou rempli d'erreurs, que le trouble accompagne, / Et malade à le ville, ainsi qu'à la campagne, / En vain monte à cheval, pour tromper son ennui, / Le chagrin monte en croupe, et galoppe avec lui."

16. "Sur les Dialogues de M. de Valincourt [sic]," Œuvres de Daguesseau (1819), 16:290.

When in later times, from his rustic retreat at Saint-Cloud, Valincour indulged with his correspondents in various rhetorical and poetic celebrations of his setting and theirs, it was done with the lingering sense of diversion. But it also followed from an abiding belief, foreshadowed in his poetry, in the art of a way of life including poetry to refresh and to clarify. The evasive and empty pastoral formula, sounded here in the earlier part of the epistle—"Heureux qui sur le bord d'un ruisseau"—is complemented by another, a concluding profession of faith in the reasonableness of that art counseled by the wise men (Horace and Boileau) chosen as patrons of the poem.

> Heureux qui peut souffrir une règle fidelle,
> Qui tient tous ses désirs à la raison soumis,
>   Et ne faisant rien que par elle,
> Ne veut rien qui ne soit & possible & permis!
>   Toujours d'accord avec soi-même,
>   Toujours dans un repos extrême,
> Il se tient dans la place où son destin l'a mis;
> Il ne forme jamais de dessein ridicule.
> Le nain n'affecte point de paroître un Hercule,
> Le Bourgeois ne veut point faire le grand Seigneur,
> Ni sans avoir rien lu, s'ériger en Docteur:
> Pour lui chaque pays est un séjour tranquille;
> Aux champs, il veut les champs; à la ville, la ville. (vv. 133–45)

The "Consolation" of the 1701 anthology is a worthy companion piece to this "Lettre," enhancing its wisdom by specific application of its principles of resigned moderation. If the "Lettre" may easily be read as a response of poetic gratitude to Boileau's "Epître V," in which the poet seems "weary and hesitant,"[17] it is tempting to read the "Consolation" as a tribute to deepened friendship offered to Boileau on the death of his favorite sister. But no evidence for that attribution can be found. As it stands, the "Consolation" is a successful imitation, at some cost. Less at home with the tightly constructed Malherbean couplet and stanza than in more discursive freedom of *vers variés,* the poet strikes a compromise by the relative brevity of thirteen stanzas (a12b6a12b6). Skillful in his imitation, as elsewhere following other models, the poet's good ear for style, expressive rhythm, and sound make the "Consolation" a successfully performed "morceau de bra-

---

17. "On le sent las, hésitant." Antoine Adam, *Histoire de la littérature française au dix-septième siècle* 3 (1962), 124.

voure."[18] Its burdens are lightened, if only slightly, by a simplicity of diction that appears less commonplace in sympathy for grief, suggesting personal context, as when it evokes those harsh souls who, never weeping, "Ne sçavent ce qu'on sent quand on perd ce qu'on aime, / Et n'ont jamais aimé" (vv. 27–28).

This "Consolation," the last signed poem published during Valincour's lifetime, in several senses brings a fitting end to the poet's public career. Only shortly after his Malherbean imitation, the critic becomes dominant, as Valincour participates with his new colleagues in the Académie in an examination of Malherbe's sonnets. But even more appropriate, a lengthy compliment by Bouhours in the preface of 1701 memorializes, as it were, the poet's talent—and career—in full flight. Answering a purist who had objected to a hiatus discovered in the "Lettre à Damon," Bouhours praises the poem for "je ne sais quoi de poli et d'honnête dans cet air du monde, dans cette teinture d'urbanité que Cicéron ne sait comment définir."[19] It is a description that might be extended to the group of poems by which Valincour had over two decades become known, with their mixture of *raillerie* and compliment, badinage and moral highmindedness. Bouhours, the acknowledged authority on style, complimenting "cette *molle atque facetum* qui règne d'un bout jusqu'à l'autre avec le solide et le moral," makes the master's final gesture of acknowledging another "one of our masters," he confirms, "as able in poetry as in eloquence and no less talented in composing a poem than in writing a history."

Another Nightingale

Somewhat unexpectedly, but in another long and illustrious tradition (that included Malherbe), Valincour wrote the kind of verse his contemporaries commonly called "licentious." Narrative artistry and wit in the most distinguished contemporary teller of such "contes en vers," La Fontaine, had not saved his published collection of tales from withdrawal from circulation by a police order describing it as "remply de termes indiscrets et malhonnêtes et dont la lecture ne peut avoir d'autre effet que celuy de corrompre les bonnes mœurs et d'inspirer

18. For Cazes ("Introduction," p. 28), "on croirait [le poème] signé de Malherbe." On Valincour's later criticism of Malherbe, see below chap. 8, n. 51 and text.

19. Quoted in F. Lachèvre, *Bibliographie des recueils collectifs* 3 (1904), 120–21. The line defended, "Toujours il s'ennuye où il est," has disappeared in the 1745 text.

le libertinage."[20] Source books of the tradition—Petronius, Aretino, Boccaccio—met the same fate. Valincour nonetheless set his hand to ribald verse, circulated privately until it unexpectedly surfaced. It runs the full gamut from refined paraphrase of Boccaccio in "Le Rossignol" to unprintable grossness in a satirical broadside, "Le Devoir nuptial." Titon du Tillet undisguisedly enjoyed this vein of Valincour's talent, as the teller himself may well have, since there are several indications that he happily indulged in this pleasure more often than the few identified examples of it would suggest.[21]

For more than a century and a half, Valincour's "Le Rossignol" was included among La Fontaine's tales. Despite evidence to the contrary, Paul Lacroix remarked as late as 1863 that it "could well stay there."[22] The author doubtless enjoyed the compliment that crowned another successful imitation when the tale first appeared with La Fontaine's to pad out an edition by an enterprising Dutch publisher (1710). But there was a further joke to be enjoyed, entirely in keeping with the ironic debunking of the poet's own performance that formed a distinctive part of Valincour's early poetic discourse. His lively updated Parisian version of the fourth story of the *Decameron*'s fifth day plays ironically against his earlier fable of "Le Rossignol en cage." In a deft retelling of Filostrato's cheerful tale of the maiden who tricks her parents and succeeds in enjoying the nightingale's song with her lover, the "oiseau," of course, is the phallus. Read retrospectively, the earlier sober fable reads more like the culinary double-entendre of La Fontaine's tale of "Pâté d'anguille" (IV, 11).

Fontenelle alludes to some of Valincour's poetry that the poet might have disavowed,[23] seemingly verse like this other nightingale. But this tale and the pleasure it gave its author were not quickly abandoned. The first text appeared in a curious, doubtless clandestinely assembled collection of ribald and libertine pieces published by Schouten in Utrecht in 1699. A lengthy justificatory prologue (vv. 1–83) presents the tale as the diversion of an exclusively male audience, a group of men awaiting the outcome of a treaty negotiation, to whom it is

20. The Moetjens collections were regularly suppressed in France between 1694 and 1701. See Anne Sauvy, *Livres saisis à Paris entre 1678 and 1701* (The Hague: Nijhoff, 1972), p. 293. La Fontaine's collected *Contes* also was.

21. See Bibliography I, A, nos. 10, 23 and notes.

22. Paul Lacroix, *Contes et nouvelles de La Fontaine* (Paris: Bibliophile Jacob, 1863), p. 454n.

23. "Eloge de Valincour," *Eloges* (1825 ed.), 2:151.

dedicated in Schouten's table of contents ("A Messieurs les plenipo-tentiaires").[24] Shorn of its prologue by 1710, the tale had also undergone extensive revision still visible in manuscript, esthetically profitable to the point of bringing it convincingly into the company of La Fontaine's tales.

Valincour's adaptation, like La Fontaine's, is primarily one of embel-lishment—by movement and rhymes of *vers variés,* ornamenting details of translation into contemporary French settings, and dramatization through dialogue. His version of the discovery of the sleeping lovers by the maiden's parents, capped by a variant on one of La Fontaine's characteristic framings of such scenes of voyeurism—"Qui fut surprise, fut la mère" (v. 219)—is a representative example of the joyously nuanced embellishment of Boccaccio. The *polissonnerie* of veiling (vv. 165–79), of an "intimate eroticism" as Auerbach described it in later scenes,[25] is punctured by parody of the pastoral and especially by a blunt jibe at "ce qui plaît aux dames" (according to Catullus), which prepare the frankly comic ribaldry of the tale's denouement and a final dialogue invented by Valincour (vv. 210–20).

> De dire ce qui s'y passa,
> Combien de fois on s'embrassa
> En combien de façons l'amant & la maîtresse
> 165 Se témoignèrent leur tendresse,
> Ce seroit tems perdu: les plus doctes discours
> Ne sçauroient jamais faire entendre
> Le plaisir des tendres amours;
> Il faut l'avoir goûté pour le pouvoir comprendre.
> Le rossignol chanta durant toute la nuit:
> Et quoiqu'il ne fît grand bruit
> Catherine en fut fort contente.
> Celui qui chante aux bois son amoureux souci
> Ne lui parut qu'un âne auprès de celuy-cy.
> 175 Mais le malheur voulut que l'amant & l'amante
> Trop foibles de moitié pour leurs ardens désirs
> Accablés de grand chaud d'amour et de plaisir,
> S'endormaient tous deux sur le point que l'aurore
> Commençoit à s'appercevoir.

24. This cadre may allude to deliberations concerning the Treaty of Ryswyck or to the moment of June, 1693 when Valincour was in the field at Hargmont and Dinant (see above, chap. 1, n. 59 and text). If the latter, the year of the appearance of Bouhours's anthology including "Le Rossignol en cage," the intertextual play would be the more apparent.

25. *Mimesis* (Princeton: Princeton University Press, 1953), 351, 356.

> Le père en se levant fut curieux de voir
>   Si sa fille dormoit encore.
> Voyons un peu, dit-il, quel effet ont produit
> Le chant du rossignol, le changement de lit.
>   Il entre dans la gallerie,
> 185   Et s'étant approché sans bruit,
>   Il trouva sa fille endormie.
> A cause du grand chaud nos deux amans dormans
>   Etoient sans drap ni couverture,
>   En état de pure nature
> Justement comme on peint nos deux premiers parents,
>   Excepté au lieu de la pomme,
>   Catherine avoit dans sa main
>   Ce qui servit au premier homme
>   A conserver le genre humain;
> 195 Ce que vous n'oseriez prononcer sans scrupule,
> Belles qui vous piquez de sentiments si fiers;
> Et que vous regardez pourtant très volontiers
>   Si l'on croit le bon Catulle.
> Le bon homme à ses yeux à peine ajoûtoit foy;
> Mais enfin renfermant son chagrin dans son âme,
> Il rentre dans sa chambre et réveille sa femme:
> Levez-vous, luy dit-il, & venez avec moy
>   Je ne m'étonne plus pourquoy
> Cathos nous témoignoit si grand désir d'entendre
> 205 Le rossignol, vrayment ce n'estoit pas en vain,
>   Elle avoit dessein de le prendre
> Et l'a si bien guetté qu'elle l'a dans la main.
>   Voyez la belle rêverie
>   Que nous vient conter celuy-ci,
> Dit la femme: Non, non, ce n'est point raillerie,
> Suivez-moy seulement dedans la gallerie,
> Dit l'époux, vous aurez du plaisir de cecy.
> Le mère se leva pleurant presque de joye.
> Un rossignol … vrayment il faut que je le voye;
> 215 Est-il grand, chante-il, fera-t-il des petits?
> Hélas! la pauvre enfant, comment l'a-t-elle pris?
>   Vous allez voir, reprit le père,
>   Mais sur tout songez à vous taire,
> Si l'oiseau vous entend, c'est autant de perdu,
>   Vous gasterez tout le mistère.
>   Qui fut surprise, fut la mère.

"Le Devoir nuptial" more literally belongs to the setting of the prologue to "Le Rossignol." It is a pseudo-fabliau recounting the wedding-night misadventures of an inexperienced simpleton. Its sub-title, "Sur le mariage de L'Empereur," baptizes the piece as an anti-Imperial broadside,[26] but no pointed expression or directing satirical intent transforms the coarseness of its lesson in anatomy.

Any hint of real misogyny that might be suggested by Valincour's more wayward verses is dispelled by a fugitive piece composed in 1701 in a setting more typical of the poet's poetic pleasures. The occasion, a manuscript note explains,[27] was a grand dinner given by Mme de Maintenon in honor of the duchesse de Bourgogne. Valincour, having the misfortune to be seated humbly in a *garde-robe,* with the others there was perishing from hunger. He was called upon literally to sing for supper. His response to Mme de Saint-Géran's request to do so, immediately delivered to the hostess, was twelve stanzas improvised "Sur l'air la foridondaine, la foridondon." Upholding his old repu-tation, the salon poet incidentally reassures us that he had not yet come to sound like Molière's Gros-René or even yet like his Alceste.

> Estre juste et pour son prochain
> Officieuse et tendre,
> Et leur faire mourir de faim,
> Le pourroit-on comprendre?
> C'est Françoise d'Aubigny
> La Faridondenne, la faridondy,
> Que cela se trouve aujourd'huy, biribi,
> A la façon de Barbarie, mon amy.
>
> Ny vos bisques, ny vos ragouts
> Ne nous font point envie;
> Mais nous vous prions à genoux
> De nous sauver la vie;
> Envoyez nous donc du roty,
> La Faridondenne, la faridondon:
> Et nous vous dirons grand merci, biribi,
> A la façon de Barbarie, mon amy. (vv. 41–48; 72–80)

26. The most probable event of an imperial marriage to have prompted this outburst was Joseph I's to Wilhelmenia Amalia of Brunswick Lüneberg in 1699.

27. B.N. fon. fr. 12625, p. 49.

Chapter 3

The Pleasures of Criticism

C'est pour me quereller donc, à ce que je vois,
Que vous avez voulu me ramener chez moi?

Celiméne to Alceste, II, i

Pleasures Divers and Disparate

Valincour's *Lettres à Madame la marquise *** sur le sujet de la Princesse de Clèves* appeared anonymously in mid-June of 1678 and was an immediate success.[1] A book-length criticism of a contemporary novel, much less one at the height of its first success, was in itself a publishing novelty if not a first. But it is the unique publishing event that *La Princesse* had proved to be that the critic evokes repeatedly in his letters. Even before its appearance (in mid-March) it was avidly awaited, he reveals:

Jamais ouvrage ne m'a donné tant de curiosité. On l'avoit annoncé long-temps avant sa naissance: des personnes tres-éclairées, & tres-capables d'en juger, l'avoient loué comme un chef-d'œuvre en ce genre là: enfin l'on peut dire, qu'il est peu de livres, qui ayent aprés l'impression, une approbation aussi générale, que l'a eûë celuy-cy, avant mesme que d'avoir esté veû du public.[2]

---

1. Mme de Senneville announced to Bussy as early as 25 April 1678 after an inquiry about *La Princesse de Clèves* that "on nous en promet la critique" and on 24 July Mme de Montmorency reports a "critique de ce livre, que tout le monde trouve admirable." Bussy, *Correspondance*, ed. L. Lalanne (Paris: Charpentier, 1858), 4:98, 162. Since the "privilège" is 17 June, something of a "publicity campaign" seems to have been conducted, perhaps with the "pirated" printing leading the way to the several issued by Cramoisy before the end of the year (see Bibliography I, B, 1).
2. References are to the facsimile ed., by J. Chupeau, et al. (Tours: Université François Rabelais, 1972). On the "campagne de presse," Roger Duchêne, *Madame de Lafayette* (Paris: Fayard, 1988), 332–43.

As the fictional conversations of the letters show, since its publication the book is being discussed everywhere. "Le moyen de n'en pas parler?" the writer of the letters concludes after a walk in the Tuileries, where he found "des femmes de la Cour, des femmes de la ville, des Provinciales" (386) discussing it. Since the writer professes not to be himself a "faiseur de livres," he was fortunate also to meet a grammarian who offered him the substance of the third letter: a long series of remarks on style in the tradition of Vaugelas (285–370).

The letters themselves are presented as private pleasures, a record of the forming of a considered opinion of the novel that involves a select group of friends, solicited or encountered (sometimes comically, Panurge-like) by the writer as he goes intently about the business of his pleasure of responding to a request for enlightenment from his marquise. In the closing of each letter, he reminds her that her inquiry started the whole enterprise and that she has promised to keep the opinions ("sentiments") secret—if she can:

Adieu, Madame, Je vous ay tenu parole, en vous écrivant ce que vous desiriez de moy: tenez-la-moy à vostre tour, en ne publiant mes Lettres, & sur tout en ne me nommant point à celles de vos amies à qui je sçay que vous ne vous empescherez jamais de les montrer. (372)

The fiction of a leak and the anonymity of the writer plays into the moment of curiosity about the anonymous author of *La Princesse* and discussion widened by the forum on the novel run by the *Mercure Galant*[3] as the writer of the *Lettres* enters into and at the same time keeps his distance from them.

The self-professed amateur apologizes for the results of his private pleasures of writing. There is some disorder, he admits, for various reasons. Meeting the grammarian as he had, some of his remarks have been misplaced. This sometimes amusing representation of the encoding of the amateur spirit of literary "honnêteté" becomes elaborate enough to push the limits of the code. The writer apologizes, for example, at the end of the second letter, for overlapping in the treatment of the subjects chosen to give order to the first two letters— "conduite" (1–200) and "sentiments" (121–285)—betraying himself as the possessor of the specialized (Aristotelian) knowledge of plot-structure and character as linked critical concerns. With an ironic turn, also

3. "L'Extraordinaire" of April 1678, continuation in Oct. A résumé and table of responses are given by Maurica Laugaa, *Lectures de Mme de Lafayette* (Paris: Colin, 1971), 26–40. Fontenelle's letter appeared in the May issue (Laugaa, pp. 22–25).

at the end of the second letter, the writer apologizes for another "negligence," like his ordering, in fact an essential part of his essays in definition. All the opinions of friends and others, directly and indirectly cited, have merged with his own to the point that "je ne sçay ce que vous penserez d'une lettre de cette sorte, & si vous ne direz point comme Monsieur de Voiture, que je vous écris sans vous écrire" (282).[4]

The movement of epistolarity in fact both dissimulates as well as displays, by an irony fundamental to the *Lettres,* essential formal features of Valincour's criticism. Gérard Genette's elegant formulation of Valincour's critical practice, without identifying it as neo-Aristotelian, clearly discloses that *techne,* which unifies the first two letters and in a looser manner extends through the third.[5] A dialogic principle also functions at several levels, including in my reading a problematizing of system, a dialogue that goes beyond the rhetorical functions of interlocutors within the text. The fiction of reading is finally the most inclusive critical context, since its order coordinates esthetic principles.

The text of Valincour's three letters is framed by an initial evocation of the breaking of an individual esthetic response and, in conclusion, the reconstitution of that experience in new terms. A first reading held the reader completely under the spell of illusion. Only reluctantly, in critical rereading, he comes to acknowledge "mille difficultés." At the beginning of the analysis, the writer displays his awareness that the changes in framing, or aspection, will bring present dangers both to himself and to the text. "Suffisance," or the self-satisfied pleasures of criticism as a self-justifying spying out of faults—what Valincour's contemporaries typified as the bookish scholar's way with the text—is the principal trap that he wishes to avoid. After evoking his first, fully admiring reading, the critic continues:

Je vous confesse, avec la mesme sincerité, que je l'ay un peu moins admirée la seconde fois que la première, *soit* que je me suis laissé emporter, au *plaisir de critiquer* un ouvrage généralement estimé, *soit* qu'en effet ce livre ait quelques légers défauts, & qu'il suive en cela la *destinée des choses les plus parfaites de ce monde,* qui ne laissent pas d'avoir les leurs.

J'y ay trouvé mille difficultés en le relisant; peut-être ne sont-elles pas

---

4. Valincour thus closes on a textual rapprochement with Voiture associating his letter writing with the very definition of urbanity that Voiture represented. On the particular letter, to "no one," and his style, see C. G. S. Williams, *Mme de Sévigné* (Boston: G. K. Hall, 1981), 40–41. Bouhours also found Voiture "inimitable," e.g., *Remarques nouvelles sur la langue française* (Paris: Cramoisy, 1675), 386–95.

5. "Vraisemblance et motivation" (1968). Rpt. *Figures II* (Paris: Seuil, 1969), 88–98.

raisonnables, mais *il suffit qu'elles me soient venuës dans l'esprit, pour m'obliger à ne vous les pas cacher.* Vous les corrigerez, si vous le jugez à propos, & je vous prétens bien, qu'aprés vous avoir dit mes sentiments sur la Princesse de Cleves, vous me direz vostre avis sur mes sentiments. (3–4; my emphases)

At this outset here, criticism is posed as dialogue, tentative and exploratory in nature. After the double identification of difficulties for the mind (para. 1), the invitation to follow and respond to the portrait/ perspective of this particular search for truth is given in a Cartesian spirit, surely a new criticism in the context of the novel for a newly critical time.[6] The three series of linear scannings of the text that follow are thus introduced without invocation of a priori authority. The principal assumption, of genre ("en ce genre-là"), appears simply as common sense attention to evidence at hand. The genre, early on identified as "histoire" or "petite histoire"/"historiette" presents two defining qualities, both observable and fundamental to the critic's response: a restricted length and an historical context passing as memoirs, the critic eventually clarifies.

Justification for criticism is then empirically identified as any break in the "spell" of reading. As the beholding "I" takes charge, in analysis and articulation of the private individual response, it does so with continuing meta-commentary that—within the code of "honnêteté"—reiterates warnings against misappropriations of the text. They are needed as the conversations/letters tend to slide toward monologue/ treatise, to digress or repeat in the interest of personal argument or to indulge in wit, all at the expense of the text being examined and in the process being rewritten. The fullest elaboration of this guarantee of fair dealing comes, again strategically, at the close of the second letter, in an apparently complete (if perhaps reluctant) subordination of the critic to the intention and invention of the author.

Quand un Auteur fait un Roman, il le regarde comme un petit monde qu'il crée luy-mesme; il en considere tous les personnages comme ses créatures,

---

6. The claims made at the expense of Valincour's *Lettres* for the forward-looking method of Du Plaisir may be distorted; e.g., César Rouben, "Valincour, Charnes et la querelle de La Princesse de Clèves," *French Literature Series* 4 (1977), 62, 64. It is not a question of an exclusive ancien inflexibly using normative models and rules; Philippe Hourcade's description of Du Plaisir's "modernity" (despite some rigidity) though differently enacted by Valincour's text could also be applied to it. See Du Plaisir, *Sentiments sur les lettres et sur l'histoire avec des scrupules sur le style* (Geneva: Droz, 1976), 5–6, 12, 45. A specific Cartesian parallel text would seem to be *Discours de la méthode*, Part I, paragraph 3.

dont il est le maistre absolu. Il leur peut donner des biens, de l'esprit, de la valeur, tant qu'il veut; les faire vivre ou mourir quand il luy plaist, sans que pas un d'eux ait droit de luy demander compte de sa conduite: les lecteurs mesmes ne peuvent pas le faire, & tel blasme l'Auteur d'avoir fait mourir un Heros de trop bonne heure, qui ne peut pas deviner les raisons qu'il en a eû, ni à quoy cette mort devoit servir dans la suite de son histoire. Je me soûmets donc à la providence de l'Auteur de la Princesse de Cleves: & sans murmurer contre cette mort précipitée qui a fait parler tant de monde, je me contente de l'admirer, & d'apprendre par cet exemple terrible, qu'une femme fort vertueuse peut faire mourir de jalousie le plus honneste homme de tous les maris. (258–60)

From the first "countercriticism," which accepted invitation to dialogue in unexpected ways, historical judgment of Valincour's criticism has depended predominantly on interpretation of the ways in which his criticism as a whole enacts this position. In context, which will be a fully emergent pattern of interlocutors, the critical position symbolized here with its Augustinian tinge and tendency to exemplification of character will be problematized. The status of the general principle of creative freedom will also be, in Valincour's last pages, as will be the résumé of the reader's procedure (lines 7–11), which amounts to an epitome of Valincour's own critical practice as it is defined by his critical system. The critical reader in those final pages will indeed ask for an accountability, though not on "conduite" at that point, and in exchange offers his own as a central, founding act of criticism focused as an individual act of judgment.

The entire passage is worth the hearing, before moving to consider system in a narrower sense, since these closing pages extend Valincour's system to his whole text, speak directly to its success with first readers, and perhaps finally indicate the origins of his project in writing the *Lettres*.

Je n'ay entrepris celle-cy [this criticism] que pour vous obéir, & pour me convaincre d'une chose que j'ay toujours crûe, qui est qu'il n'y a point d'ouvrage si excellent, dans lequel on ne rencontre quelque defaut: mais l'on auroit grand tort de décrier un livre pour cela.

Cependant, la pluspart du monde ne sçauroit demeurer là-dessus dans une juste médiocrité. L'on ne peut concevoir qu'un livre soit bon, & qu'il s'y trouve quelques fautes. On est toujours dans l'exces; on l'admire tout entier, ou on le condamne tout entier. Un méchant vers dans une tragédie, un incident moins bien préparé que les autres, une phrase obscure dans un bon livre, suffisent souvent à bien des gens pour leur faire dire que tout le reste ne vaut rien. Au contraire, ceux qui par interest, ou par préoccupation, sont une fois engagés à défendre quelque ouvrage, soutiennent aveuglément tout ce qui s'y rencontre; & ne peuvent convenir qu'il se puisse trouver mauvais mot, ou une phrase obscure, dans une composition qu'ils croiront admirable, & qui le sera effectivement.

Les uns & les autres, à mon avis, sont injustes. Les defauts d'un livre ne doivent pas empescher qu'on ne remarque, & l'on n'admire ce qu'il a de beau. Mais aussi l'on ne doit pas se laisser éblouir par ce que l'on y admire, jusques à estre incapable d'y reconnoistre les fautes que la negligence d'un Auteur, ou la foiblesse humaine, que l'on trouve partout, y auront pû laisser échapper. Il y a longtemps qu'un grand Maistre nous a appris que ces sortes de taches n'ostoient point le mérite d'un ouvrage qui estoit excellent d'ailleurs.[7] (266–68)

On one level, these pages are a recapitulation (still recognizably maintaining a Cartesian order of discourse) and a crystallization of the preceding textual activity that sets its own margins of the "honnête." The authority invoked here transparently is Horace,[8] the "grand maître," in authority much beyond Voiture and provider of an unexceptionable and expected legitimation of critical activity. These pages thus lead, with their basic suggestion of the transcending pleasures of an enlightening rationalism, directly toward the kind of harmonization of that critical practice that both La Motte and Fontenelle (despite his own different earlier commentary on the novel) provided in their Academic eulogies of Valincour. Both consecrate the "honnêteté littéraire" Valincour sought to represent. Some fifty years after the writing, then, the *Lettres* have within the critical tradition become emblema-

7. Horace, *"De arte poetica,"* 351–53 (identified by all editors), is the master here; the passage, part of the longer one ending with the "dormitat Homerus." This allusion is linked to a second (p. 90: vv. 9–13) in which the innovation of fantastic creatures-figures leads to the limit of a prescriptive "natural compatibility of the parts created." Valincour would seem thus to be laying the groundwork for limit setting to the principle of the unshakable authority of a priori rules, if not of rationalism. See C. O. Brink, *Horace on Poetry: the 'Ars poetica'* (Cambridge: CUP, 1971), 2:347–60, 91; on *vitium* as a kind of esthetic *felix culpa*, Maurice Cunningham, "Ovid's Poetics," *The Classical Journal* 53 (1958), 256.

8. The "ne quid nimis" topos (whether from Terence and/or Horace) is not an adequate description of his esthetic principles, especially as concerns esthetic experience/response; before and after the *Lettres* were in agreement with Saint-Evremond that poetry "demande un génie particulier qui ne s'accommode pas trop avec le bon sens" and that "il faut nécessairement avoir quelque connoissance des défauts que l'on trouve dans les auteurs les plus parfaits." ["De la vraie et de la fausse beauté des ouvrages d'esprit." *Œuvres* (London: Tonson, 1735), 6:153.]

tized as a model, a "modèle d'une critique raisonnable" (La Motte) perfectly balancing by discriminating taste, it is implied, the negative and the positive, the normative and the descriptive.[9]

If time and conventions made, by 1730, a harmonization possible for the like-minded rationalists that looked back in the Académie at Valincour's critical experiment, it also blunts the originality of the *Lettres*, which was first "framed" publicly by an angry partisan spirit— the abbé de Charnes—fully typifying one of the types of criticism characterized in Valincour's final pages from which he had wished to dissociate himself. The pleasures of the critic were in fact not so easily harmonized, as they depend more on the less-evident allusion to Horace (designated in note 7) than the obvious *ne quid nimis* common-place, and are various enough to remain disparate. The pleasure of wit, first evident, is perhaps less compromising, since the text, not yet canonized, was still fair game for some irreverencies at the expense of its devices. The pleasure of analysis, of examining the working of the text, takes place over the *raillerie* (which a different taste may aim back at its perpetrator), just as the final pleasure of admiration displaces it and remains, more satisfying once analysis has been done.

System

Although Valincour had the Greek to read the *Poetics* in the text, and spent a lifetime puzzling at moments over it,[10] it would be fanciful to suggest that the order of the letters directly reflects the *Poetics'* ordering of *muthos*, *ēthos*, and *lexis*. What is evident is that the only critical text directly cited in the *Lettres* is Castelvetro's commentary on the *Poetics*, fittingly by a "savant" who offers the critic in search of the truth his longest conversation (85–121). The relevant section of Castelvetro, once it has been located, is "Plot and its Eight Requirements."[11] That section may be seen to furnish an adequate if not

9. La Motte, "Réponse au discours de M. de La Faye," *Recueil . . . de l'Académie* (1730), p. 12: "il censure avec modération . . . il approuve sans hésiter, & pour ainsi dire, jusqu'à l'admiration. Qui ne sent pas le beau comme il doit être senti, n'est ni digne, ni capable de reprendre les fautes." Fontenelle, "Eloge de M. de Valincour," *Œuvres* (Paris: Salmon, 1825), 2:251–52: "non pour s'opposer à la juste admiration du public, mais pour lui apprendre à ne pas admirer jusqu'aux défauts, et pour se donner le plaisir d'entrer dans les discussions fines et délicates."

10. See below, chap. 8, pp. 284–85.

11. *Lettres*, 109–10: Identified only as Castelvetro. See Andrew Bongiorno, trans., *Castelvetro on the Art of Poetry* (Binghamton: Medieval & Renaissance Texts and

complete theoretical horizon for the first letter's consideration of "conduite" (as plot-structure), which Valincour understands as Racine does in his commentary on Aristotle (or most recently in the preface to *Phèdre*).[12] Tellingly, he also turns to the well-established textual tradition of critical writing on tragedy, intellectually superior in his century to that on narrative fiction, which is in the process of a first consolidation of founding texts that will include the *Lettres*. Rather than to Huet, whose recent *Traité sur l'origine des romans* (1672) may be satirized under a jubilant paraphrase of Montaigne on pedantry (20–21), the critic turns for a model to the Académie's criticism of *Le Cid*, which he later re-recommends to the Académie itself.[13] The order of that criticism, itself neo-Aristotelian, may also have confirmed his own and the logical and esthetic priority of plot-structure. But there are also other indicators of the reasons for his choice of this order/method as most appropriate in the expression of his perceptions of the novelty of the text that he is examining—which in fact differs from the older *romans à dix volumes* and the newer *nouvelle historique* as he knows it[14]—and of his first sense of the power of a new use of narrative. Both length (not yet the worn subject of perennial debate on how short a short story should be) and historical context pointed the reader to an analogy with the best tragedies. How long should the narrative be, when it does display a dramatic structure readily perceptible by analogy to classical dramaturgy? The answer may well be, about as long as the playing time of the performance of a well-made tragedy. How much history it should have may be similarly considered: enough to afford adequate exposition and "stage setting" for a strong sense of place.

Studies, 1984), pp. 72–118; Werther Romani, ed., *Poetica d'Aristotele vulgarizzata e sposta* (Roma-Bari: Laterza, 1978), 1:219–339 (3a Parte, 5–11).

12. "Conduite de l'action," Préface, lines 1–3, is among the first concerns of the commentary as "l'âme de la pièce." See E. Vinaver, ed., *Racine: Principes de la tragédie en marge de la Poétique d'Aristote* (Paris: Nizet, 1951), 14–15.

13. For the Académie's special interests, Valincour reverses the third and first terms. "Mémoire sur les occupations de l'Académie" (1714), *Œuvres de Fénelon* (Paris: Lebel, 1824, 21:151). Laugaa's remarks on the classical divisions of rhetoric and previous critical approximations to them do not seem to me to lead to his conclusion on "contamination réciproque des deux premières catégories" in the *Lettres* (loc. cit., pp. 59–60), necessarily linked in Aristotelian theory.

14. Textual allusions are only to Voiture's unfinished "Histoire d'Alcidalis et de Zélide" (p. 78) and the "Seconde Partie" of Mme de Villedieu's *Les Désordres de l'amour* (1675), p. 216, without posing either as a generic model. On the red herring of the latter (in part from Valincour's "une histoire qui a *quelque rapport* . . ."), see Micheline Cuénin, "Introduction," *Les Désordres* (Geneva; Droz, 1970), xv, n. 6; xvi–xix.

Following the analogy to which perceptions of "originality" in the genre have led him, the critic uses the Aristotelian tradition then to clarify and to challenge both the text and the articulation of his own feelings.

Unity of organic form is thus logically for Valincour, as it would be for Racine, his first concern. "L'esprit qui se fait un plaisir de voir la suite d'une histoire," he begins empirically, "se haste d'aller jusqu'au bout, & souffre avec impatience, & quelquefois mesme avec dégoust tout ce qui le retarde dans sa course, & qui luy paroist étranger à ce qu'il cherche" (19). The alien here is "36 pages" of historical introduction that might have been compressed into a speech given by Mlle de Chartres's mother (and could have been better placed in earlier instruction than that which does come, too late). Objections to the initial framing are thus extended to the entire text, launching the term "digressions" (22–24) for the four intercalated narratives that recent critics have wished to read otherwise.[15] The stories of Mme de Tournon, of Anne Boulen, like that of the "old court," and to a lesser degree the Vidame's lost letter are all de trop, although admittedly not extremely long and always *agréables*. Becoming more exigent, since the author of the narrative has shown no need for this kind of ornament—in fact a narrative device reminiscent of the older narrative form of the *romans à dix volumes*—the critic disqualifies the narrative device with his dismissal of these "ornements." "Ces sortes de digressions ne sont point de véritables ornements. Il me semble que celle-ci ne sert qu'à embarrasser le corps de l'ouvrage, & à le rendre moins regulier; à moins, comme je l'ai déja dit, qu'ils ne soient *absolument* necessaires, pour faire entendre le reste" (my emphasis, on what is added rather than repeated from the first formulation). The Vidame's story may pass, since it is more directly linked to the main action. But it too will be faulted for overplotting ("le génie qui préside aux aventures").

Feeling teased, the desiring subject will tease back, but more significantly rejects with his criticism of historical textual sequences an allegorical reading of history. The "digressions," he remarks, may have some secret ("mystérieuse") liaison with the development of the plot; it seems unnecessary to force the reader into this indirection. In his own historical writing Valincour will be clear enough about the historical

15. For a systematic demonstration of the inadequacy of Valincour's remarks, see J. W. Scott, "The Digressions of the Princesse de Clèves," *French Studies* 2 (1957), 315–22; more in his spirit of the reading effect they cause, John Lyons, "Narrative, Interpretation and Paradox: *La Princesse de Clèves*," *Romanic Review* 72 (1981), 383–400.

consequences of the death of Henry II. But here (57–60) he makes nothing of an historical fragmentation that may be seen to mirror the shattered private world of the characters and professes himself needlessly distracted by the setting of the scene of the king's death. Similarly, he cannot find—or refuses to discern—any use for the textual sequences or adventures, as he persistently calls them, occurring after the death of the Prince de Clèves. The finding, in short, of the inquiry of Part I (i.e., the first letter) is that the power the text already possesses would be heightened by cutting away the historical introduction, the digressions, and everything following Clèves's death scene. Undoubtedly, *La Princesse de Clèves* would thus be rewritten. In Valincour's view, that rewriting would only serve the best that is already there by making the "body of the work" more visible, more accessible to the desire of the reader, say in a manner analogous to the series of scenes from Act I, scene iii, that show Phèdre, and inform us about her in her absence, up to the final climactic scene of the play.

A series of quibbles at the beginning of the first letter, the kind of mixing of considerations of psychological verisimilitude with remarks on plot-structure for which the critic apologizes, has obscured the fact that in the first letter Valincour identifies a series of focal scenes— from the scene at the jeweler's shop through Clèves's death scene— that for him constitutes the armature of the dramatic[16] structure. Scenes omitted from the first letter will be covered in the second, but the essential has been laid down in the first. Part I of the narrative is implicitly considered as an exposition, Part IV as denouement, with

16. Valincour's outline with discussion divisions of text:

Part I	–Frame: court of Henri II	
	1. "aventure du joailler italien"	8–14
	2. "aventure du bal"	17–18
	–"grande conversation: Mme de Charters ('digressions')"	19–24
Part II	3. "aventure du portrait"	24–27
	4. "conversation particulière: Nemours"	33–38
Part III	5. "aventure du pavillon"	41–48
	6. "aventure de la chambre de la Dauphine"	52–55
	–"spectacle de la mort d'un grand roy"	57–60
Part IV	7. "retour au pavillon"	61–71
	8. Clèves and his "gentilhomme"	71–76
	9. Clèves: "cette manière de mort"	78–79
	10. "aventure du marchand de soie"	80–81
	11. "aventure hors les fauxbourgs"	81
	12. "Première conversation": Mme de Clèves and Nemours	86
	–Frame: retreat of Princesse, Nemours	

the intervening parts linked by the adventure of the Vidame's lost letter embodying what would be Acts II–IV of a well-made tragedy. From the first, with the jeweler's shop, the mixing in of remarks on characterization serves a function. Before consideration of characterization is systematized in the second letter, largely in rhetorical terms, Valincour has discretely examined character in action. A vivid and clear image, he feels, of the *ēthos* co-ordinated by the plot-structure is needed, if the princesse, and other principal characters in relation to her, are to be felt and finally remembered with pity *and* admiration.[17] As another, later neo-Aristotelian critic has said of another text, the problem is "the construction of a central action that would organize successfully all the materials ... and the creation of a protagonist who would at once be a true focal point of the spectator's ... truly tragic emotion."[18] If one begins with a young prince who acts like a ninny (in and after the jeweler's shop) and a young lady in a most unladylike place and blushing like a provincial lass, there is a way to go to achieve the formal success imaginable of the writer, especially when this awkwardness is repeated by both characters at other peripeteia of the action, to the point of soliciting the unwelcome interference of comic paradigms. The critic reflects, after it is suggested to him, that there is indeed something of Molière's Agnès in Mme de Clèves after the ball scene and the first meeting with Nemours. Unable to give in entirely to the effects of the "coup de foudre" of love passion, the reason for this break seems to the critic to be the discrepancy between the time of this new knowledge and that of the old ignorance on love: a flaw in dramatic pacing.

This critique of agency centers Valincour's dispersed remarks on particular episodes at the same time that his critique of plot eliminates everything but the heart of the action (his episodes 3 through 9), beginning in Part II with the adventure of the portrait (24–27) and the private conversation with Nemours (33–38), then continued in Part III with the adventure of the pavillion (the confession scene, pp. 41–48) and the revelation of the scene in the dauphine's apartment (52–55). Nowhere is the critic more trenchant than in his criticism of the

17. Beginning with my assumption that *vraisemblance* for Valincour is principally a concern of structural coherence, therefore of the intelligibility of plot-structure, and on *ēthos*, I have profited from Stephen Halliwell, *Aristotle's Poetics* (Chapel Hill: University of North Carolina, 1986), 150–52.

18. Bernard Weinberg on *Phèdre*. *The Art of Jean Racine* (Chicago: University of Chicago, 1963), 255.

episodes that subsequently prepare Clèves's death; the return to the pavillion and the two spies—Nemours and Clèves's man (51–71) and the last interview of Clèves and his spy (71–76). A dumb show, in more than one sense he infers, this last scene culminating the sequence sets up the critic's difficulty with the poetic symbol of the prince's death (quoted above as a stumbling block yet in the concluding pages). Treatment here is especially revealing of the kind of reading Valincour pursues throughout his letters. The death of Clèves is given the special status of a metabasis. Reading for the plot, it appears that the critic has also been looking for the Aristotelian ideal of complex plot, for reversal and recognition in one culminating scene that will embody the fragility of human fortune.[19] Reading his wife's guilt on his spy's face, and condemning himself to death before "sa femme ouvre sa bouche" (265) is the act of a *sot*, the critic finds, as surely as his actions in his first appearance typed him as an "étourdi du comique." "Un honnête homme peut être amoureux comme un fou, mais non pas comme un sot," La Rochefoucauld had put it in a recently published maxim.

With Clèves's rapid change to guilt-ridden self-condemnation, once his wife is heard, the critic attempts a final promotion that falls short of the tragic grandeur of what he may have found in the Thésée of Act V of *Phèdre*. "Cet éclaircissement sert à rendre l'histoire plus tragique et plus touchante," he feels, "une belle chose ... fort difficile de lire sans être *un peu* attendri. Il y a un certain air vif & naturel" (265–66; my emphasis). Just as the preparatory episode with the Gent might have been fine on stage, as formally similar scenes are in *Iphigénie* or *Le Cid*,[20] so is Clèves's death; but again, as in the instance of Thésée, living on rather than being eliminated in so apparently contrived a fashion could have provided the artistic triumph.

In the same frame of reading, the critic rejects the princesse's "renunciation scene." Valincour finds something of the "héroisme cor-nélien" Mme de Lafayette apparently wished to represent, but he does not find the "gloire" forcefully enough represented to carry Mme de Clèves through to the conclusion of her life. The heroine seems to him like Sappho reborn, a reincarnation from *Le Grand Cyrus* (127), or in the phrase of an interlocutor (a woman)—"la prude la plus coquette, & la coquette la plus prude." As the ending stands, her solitary retreat

19. See Halliwell, *Aristotle's Poetics*, pp. 209–14.

20. *Lettres*, p. 262: allusion to *Iphigénie*, 5, 5; *Le Cid*, 5, 5.; Clytemnestra's fear/ Chimène's on death of Iphigénie/Rodrigue before announcements to the contrary.

to a "pays perdu," like her retreat to religious houses "sans dévotion" (276), seems a renunciation by "pur caprice." On the other hand, sacrifice made to guilt assumed for the death of Clèves earlier, motivated by her desire for peace of mind, "semble tres-belle, interrompis-je brusquement, & digne du courage, & de la vertu de Madame de Clèves" (173). If Clèves seemed not to live on long enough, the heroine would seem to linger and fade compromisingly. But compromise is mainly the flaw of Nemours, or of his agency, created by overplotting and overexposure.

From the introduction of this "chef-d'œuvre de la nature," the critical reader is prompted to snigger over a too-recognizable "héros de roman." Only a storybook character can wander the woods a full night without contracting a cold, he quips, or can explore a pavillion and discover its secrets without first securing his horse. "Angusto vase é debil core / A traboccante amore," the reader hums (48)[21] over "Nemours amoureux." As if the staging of the first pavillion scene were not contrived enough, the second adds nothing ("inutile") except a blackening of Nemours's character, finally accomplished by his fatal divulging of what he has seen to the Vidame. "Pour estre Héros de Roman, il faut du moins estre au dessus de ces petites démangeaisons de parler" (54), Valincour judges, without sympathy for this potentially tragic error. Idealized virtue is not expected, he insists, even for a "paragon de toute chevalerie"; but for credibility, both his own and Mme de Clèves's imaginary transformation of him, something more of the "honnête homme du commun" (233) is required if the actions of the sequences in which Nemours appears are not to leave us with the final impression of an ineffectual seducer who merits his loss (and final incriminating fading from the text). Although there is not a critical judgment by a prior paradigm, Nemours is never really fully forgiven for Mme de Lafayette's transformation of Brantôme's swaggering captain (204–5).[22] Ambivalence within character, not in itself proscribed, must nonetheless be controlled if a proper balance of reaction is to be kept in the reader's mind: "ni tout à fait innocent, ni

21. *Lettres*, p. 49. The imagery epitomizes Valincour's interpretation, while performatively the lines are analogous to La Rochefoucauld's, "il y a des gens qui ressemblent aux vaudevilles, qu'on ne chante qu'un certain temps" (211).

22. *Lettres*, 194–95. Near the end of his life, Valincour was delighted when Bouhier's reference to Brantôme brought back pleasures of reading that dated to an early reading of the *Hommes illustres* (1st pub. Leyden, 1665–66). Letters of 12 Dec. 1729, *RHLF* 31 (1924), 402.

tout à fait coupable"—Racine had recently described that balance with deceptive simplicity.[23]

In final summary of the second letter's investigation of characterization, Valincour concludes from his evidence that all the characters are flawed, this conclusion following logically and esthetically for him from a similar finding in his first letter: that the plot-structure is episodic, "peu regulière." Despite this evidence, he would see *La Princesse de Clèves* as a success. "Les faiseurs de nouvelles croyent avoir beaucoup fait, lors qu'ils ont affectionné leur lecteur à quelqu'un de leurs personnages: dans celle-cy il n'y en a pas un pour qui l'on ne s'intéresse. On admire Madame de Chartres; on aime Madame de Clèves; on plaint son mari; on estime Monsieur de Nemours; on est mesme touché de l'affliction de Sancerre, quoy-qu'elle soit hors d'œuvre; enfin il n'y a rien qui n'y fasse sentir" (277). The critic has vaulted from argument into another register of judgment, which has seemed faint praise, outweighed as the feeling here is by the amassed evidence of contraries spied out by the mind's quest for flaws. The tribute, however, is clearly to Mme de Lafayette's originality; the situation within the tradition of the *nouvelle* as Valincour knew it finally affirms his now-qualified first impression that there is nothing in that tradition worthy of comparison with this narrative, which opens new perspectives for the genre. For this final moment of "harmonization" to carry conviction, its appeal to the senses needs a grounding in the inquiry that led to it. That grounding Valincour provided in his representation of a series of episodes that, despite formal flaws, nonetheless powerfully engage the critic in an experience in which the reader feels "élevé, transporté, ravi." This feeling consecrated by Longinian description of the sublime in discourse[24] may be, the critic would have it believed, at least as illuminating as formal analysis.

Poetic Subject(s)

If Aristotle's *Poetics* was a lifetime preoccupation for Valincour, Racine's tragedies were, from his adolescent experience of *Britannicus* to a final exaltation of Racine's "sublimity" to Bouhier,[25] the love of a lifetime and its companion to critical judgment of other literary texts.

23. On the relation to choice (*prohairesis*), Halliwell, *Aristotle's Poetics*, pp. 150–51.
24. Preface to the 1674 ed. (Pléiade, p. 383); on its esthetic/critical significance, see W. G. Moore, "Boileau and Longinus," *French Studies* 14 (1960), 56–61.
25. See chap. 8, below. p. 290.

A reference to Pradon in the *Lettres*, as well as some contemporary perhaps militant parody in Valincour's unpublished verse,[26] suggest that admiration for Racine had recently been rekindled by *Phèdre*, which functions as intertext in the *Lettres'* measurements of interpretation and judgment of formal aspects of *La Princesse*. If the results of this analogy seem largely negative, a positive presence of the Racinian model is explicitly evoked in reference to *Iphigénie*. Textual moments of sublimity are represented also within a specific dialectic—presented for the most part in the second, longest letter—of speech and silence, at the center of the tragic dramatic structure of *La Princesse* for Valincour as surely as it is in the "tragédie de la parole" *Phèdre* has since been read to be.[27]

A moment of sublimity is felt archetypically when silence is represented as "plus beau que toutes les réponses" (228). Valincour comments at length on the scene in which Clèves recoils from the discovery that Nemours was the name withheld from his wife's confession. The "s'attendrir" that would control response to the moment does move the reader, from Clèves's faltering voice to the mute embrace it inspires, with husband and wife "pénétrés et fondant en larmes." The author has surely and admirably imitated, the critic remarks, that great painter who veils the faces of a mother and father whose grief could not be depicted. His allusion to Timanthes's "Sacrifice of Iphigenia," designating the sublime, is praise grounded in Quintilian, who used it as an example both of expression of the inexpressible and more generally of discrimination of innovation in art from rigid norms.[28] Valincour sends his reader back to a similar moment he had evoked in his first letter, to Mme de Clèves's grief ("de se voir abandonnée") at her mother's death. In this instance, which for him compensates a faulty exposition, it is impossible to remain detached from the heroine's human drama. With the perspective already in view of Clèves's failure to live up to the new "amitié" needed from him by his wife—resulting in her moral solitude even in the later moment of intimacy—poignancy

26. If Mme Deshoulières did figure in the cabal mounted against *Phèdre*, the parody of her verse (see above, chap. 2) may have been implicated by this "betrayal"; ridicule of Pradon's "Phèdre du faubourg," p. 109. See for the cabal, R. Picard, *La Carrière de Racine*, p. 103.

27. Roland Bathes, *Sur Racine* (Paris: Seuil, 1963), 118.

28. *Lettres*, p. 231. *Institutio oratoria* (ed. H. E. Butler, Loeb, 1930), Lib. II, 13 (1:295). The preliminary question is art "in qua vel praecipue laudabilis est ipsa illa novitas ac difficultas" and the last development poses distrust of rules of art as "ruts made by others."

expands to sublimity. Simplicity, the critic underscores, is its textual means: "Et combien y a-t-il d'histoires au monde qui toutes ensemble ne valent pas ces quatre mots, 'il luy sembloit qu'à force de s'attacher à luy, il la défendroit contre M. de Nemours'?" (158)

Imbedded within objections to the exposition is a similar unqualified admiration for another moment of eloquent silence. When the mother is for the first time not taken into the daughter's confidence, after "inclination" for Nemours has been felt, this dissembling seems to the critic the first instance of a truth of passion whose expression can be universalized as the poetic subject of the narrative. The dialectic of language and silence, thematized in the second letter's examination of dialogue (some forty "conversations"), commands the reader's admiration from this moment of evoked desire throughout the narrative concatenation of those scenes that the critic's formal analysis situated at the heart of Mme de Clèves's tragedy. There is nothing more "agréable" and "naturel" than these openings onto the "nature de certains mouvemens qui se ferment dans nostre cœur, que nous cachons à nos plus intimes amis, & que nous taschons de nous cacher à nous-mesmes, de peur d'estre obligéz de les combattre" (16–17). The first stirrings of jealousy, here and later (176–77), are similarly admired; as in Stendhal's first crystallization of love, they seem to Valincour to give new eyes for discovering "les sentimens les plus cachez" and at the same time blinders to a reality transformed by desire. The non-verbal communication by which the mother sees what has been withheld by her daughter, and which moves the mother to verbal intervention meant to save the daughter socially, is another moment similarly felt to be "tendre et naturel" (146). The mother's failure, this time in "discretion inutile" (153), to direct her daughter as both might wish again raises poignancy to sublimity. It is with praise both for knowledge of passion's tenacity and for language's failure to contain it that the critic then generalizes an achievement of perfect accord of thought and style in *La Princesse de Clèves*. "Il faut penser bien juste ce qui se passe dans le fond du cœur, & sçavoir bien exprimer ce que l'on pense, pour faire des portraits de cette sorte" (176). The new eyes opened within the narrative can thus see new possibilities for the genre. Commenting on representation of jealousy, Valincour again generalizes:

Il n'est rien, à mon avis, de si naturel, que tout cet endroit, ni qui fasse mieux connoistre le cœur humain. On se retrouve dans cette peinture; & un simple recit de cette sorte, qui vous met, pour ainsi dire, les choses devant les yeux, touche, à mon avis, bien davantage, que de grandes réflexions, qui disent la mesme chose, mais d'une manière plus abstraite, & moins sensible. (141)

Narration, whatever its flaws, does progress through these sharply etched and unforgettable scenes. In and after the scene of the stolen portrait, which marks a progression in Nemours's certainty of shared inclination and in the princesse's self-incrimination, the "embarras de Madame de Clèves est parfaitement bien exprimé." That the heroine is not pictured as a woman of the world capable of extricating herself verbally from this situation is precisely the point of its expressive power, not a fault of the writer. The requisite universalizing in this instance—"Je suis seûr que de toutes les femmes, qui se sont trouvées en l'état ... il n'y a pas une qui ne se reconnaisse icy, comme si on l'avoit dépeinte elle-mesme"—is insistent. It becomes more so as the critic strives with more expansive eloquence to express the reader's increasing involvement with the princesse's disarray as it grows through a series of similar scenes. "Agréable" as a qualifier tends to fall away by the time Valincour considers the scene of the forged letter, when the fact of shared passion becomes fully understood, negating the heroine's prior resolutions to self-constraint and transforming this virtuously motivated encounter into something other than the innocent "plaisir qui ne peut estre combattu d'aucun scrupule raisonnable." The shattered identity of the heroine, "ces retours sur elle-même," which she felt in silence after the scene, is evoked in lengthy paraphrase (199) and once again generalized: "Il n'y a rien de plus beau que toutes ces réflexions, & il faut avoûër que l'Auteur est admirable, lors qu'il entreprend de faire voir ce qui se passe dans nostre cœur." This moment belongs at the very center of the narrative (Act III, as it were) and is immediately linked, after two critical comments, to the pavillion scene ("aveu") that raises to its highest point the drama of the failure of control ("résolution/défaillance"). Many have found, the critic summarizes, that this is the finest moment of the *histoire*; and he agrees with them that "en effet il n'est rien de plus tendre, ni de plus touchant, que tout ce que dit Madame de Clèves à son mari." Critical reservations in fact turn in favor of the power of scene, which elicits the first juxtaposition with Iphigenia. Shortening the actual moment of confession in his consideration and attentive as he generally is to the gestural code, the heart of this heart of the novel is the more powerful for the vain exchange of speech that prolongs it and forecasts the future of husband and wife.

After the "confession" the critic noticeably draws closer to the heroine, anticipating the highly significant verb selected to formulate his final statement of successful characterization: "on aime" Mme de Clèves (whereas "on admire Mme de Chartres"). It is the revelation of the supposedly secret confession to her husband that draws the reader closer to this final investment of feeling. Her disarray again is "une chose qu'on ne peut payer." By this time, this "priceless" art has diminished almost to its disappearance any sense of fictional distance: one feels and would like to intervene as a friend. "En lisant cette aventure, l'on entre dans les sentiments de Mme de Clèves; l'on souffre avec elle; et il n'y a rien que l'on ne fit pour la tirer de la peine où l'on la représente" (54). After Clèves's death, finally, "il n'y a personne qui n'aime Mme de Clèves." An explicit retrospective glance at this moment back through the dialogues analyzed minimizes in résumé the "petites irrégularités" due to novelistic contrivance or staginess: "Il y a un certain air vif & naturel dans toutes ces conversations, qui se fait sentir jusqu'au fonds du cœur." This time, in conclusion, the critic-historian goes beyond the genre and places among the greatest the tragic fiction that reaches its denouement here: "Je crois qu'il y a peu de livres en nostre langue, qui soit plus capable d'attacher le lecteur, & de faire impression sur son esprit" (266). The successful enactment of tragedy within the genre and its proper (essential) means is then formulated, prefacing regret that what follows textually compromises this beauty. "Tout ce qu'elle pense est si généreux, & si digne d'une femme de grande vertu, qu'on ne peut s'empescher de plaindre son malheur, & de luy souhaiter une meilleure fortune" (267). Expressing his regret in hyperbolic terms ("je suis au désespoir"), and attempting to find reasons for the author's failure to stop here, the critic settles on a partial explanation and discloses openly the *moraliste*'s frame of reading already suggested in a series of passing reflections on the imperfections of this world.

"Man's strongest resolutions are but little," Valincour glosses, "and the slightest thing can cause the greatest of disorders in the wisest and best-ordered minds." The structurally useless episodes subsequent to Clèves's death seem thus to continue the pattern of broken resolutions discerned early on and increasingly called upon in the critic's commentary to exemplify the tragic limitations of the fact of humanity. A Pascalian echo here, as in Valincour's contemporary verse, is again audible, as the commentary reconciles itself to the vanity of wishing the heroine's release, after Clèves's death, from continuing reversals of moral grandeur and physical wretchedness (suffering). The reader, who has so fully come to feel through and for her, is left dissatisfied in body (desire) and mind and with nothing but imaginary transcendence (in the last scene with Nemours) and a flight without devotion from the world. The brilliance of the novel's setting gives relief to the shadows that surround this progression of scenes of moral solitude. Within this world of incessant diversion, education—that is, telling stories or casting maxims—is futile; the imagination, all powerful in shaping "fantômes du devoir." Devotion aside, the critic remarks in one of his earliest comments, on the jeweler's shop as the scene for the first eruption of passion into a previously well-ordered world, a church would have been preferable. But why a church? it may in turn be asked, as Charnes does with a ready-made answer. Religion suppressed, it seems, in an appropriate response to a "nouvelle historique" in which it is not expected to figure, returns as the *moraliste* shares the reader's feeling and recoils before the spectacle he perceives as the imprisonment of a loved one by "misère de l'homme sans Dieu."

The resonant questions asked by the critic who had found his way in Longinus (and to be heard in Boileau's recent rendering of the text)[29] are in the nature of "which would you prefer, small perfection or supreme greatness?"—to be Ion of Chios with his impeccable art or Sophocles with his sometimes great faults? Valincour's preference is evident, once a reader's predisposition to fault his criticism for "chicane" and the critic's details are set aside momentarily and the "picture" of his reading is put into perspective. Horace, too, shortly after the *vitia* passage, was concerned with painting as a clarification of poetic *virtus*, in a manner that puts his treatment into contact with the Longinian sublime.[30] Through a series of rhetorically charged evocations, "pictures" of moral disarray that reflect and maintain his first appreciative reading of *La Princesse*, Valincour seems to pay

29. Fourteen printings of the *Traité du sublime* had already appeared since 1674; the pertinent questions are in ch. 27: "Si l'on doit préférer la médiocrité parfaite au sublime qui a quelques défauts" (Pléiade ed., pp. 386–87).

30. See C. O. Brink, op. cit., 2:92. Horace's 9–13, cited by Valincour, is linked by Brink to Longinus, ch. 33 (Boileau's ch. 27). The inference is then finally that the *Lettres'* entire system of allusions to classical critical-esthetic texts converges in a meditation on the sublime.

tribute to *La Princesse de Clèves* in this manner; then, in his last pages, he offers a final portrait/perspective of his own critical enterprise.[31]

Dialogue

"I am for the truth wherever I may find it," the critic insists to the Savant, and seeks it in the spirit of Socratic dialogue in the *Lettres*. Particularized in varying detail, from a single trait to a full character sketch, a score of interlocutors personifying opinions are distinguished by social standing, intelligence, temperament, and gender (about equal in number). The typology and patternings of these personifications point up the overall significance the critic writer wished to give to his critical enterprise: that of an inquiry open, complex, and synthesizing. No one interlocutor offers the full truth of a fully adequate approach to the specific achievement of *La Princesse de Clèves*. Furthermore, some, if not all of them, by single-minded adherence to their "views," may positively threaten to obstruct rather than to illuminate the ideal conditions for judgment. The Savant of the first letter, by the length at which he sets forth his views and their reflection of the reader-critic's own previously expressed formalism, is the first and most important of these "fâcheux." But like the first letter, the two that follow select a broad and specialized critical perspective. The second does so through a concluding series of moralizing reservations, one reader's insistent reservations about the effects of the novel on young women readers. Finally, the grammarian of the third letter has the stage all to himself until the critic-reader re-emerges with the synthesis of his last pages.

In navigating his way around these global contexts, each with a partial claim as means to an end that transcends any one of them, Valincour puts to good use his appreciative reading of and reflection on Molière's *Critique de l'Ecole des femmes*, which was much more

31. My insistence on portrait/perspective has derived from discussion of d'Aubignac, Du Bos, and in general on the sublime and "legitimation of reason by aesthetic theory of the period that does not occur without a paradoxical counter-nurturing of spectatorship and its psycho-political idiosyncrasies" by Timothy Murray. *Theatrical Legitimation: Allegories of Genius in Seventeenth-Century England and France* (New York: Oxford University Press, 1987), 167–74, 201, 210 and passim. The interest of Valincour's usually dismissed "theatricality" is much heightened by this innovative discussion.

influential than has been acknowledged in shaping the *Lettres*.[32] The savant of the first letter is, in the more subtle epistolary presentation, still unmistakably akin to the Lysidas of Molière's *Critique*, obsessed with rules, and led on by the critic-letter writer (as others will be) to replay Molière's representations of caricatural thinking.[33] The Savant is dogmatically assertive, to the point that his interlocutor must heighten his own tone of objection in response to the claim that there is little if anything more in this new novel than Horace's poetic monsters. Supporting himself with a fully accepted authority (Castelvetro), and especially concerned with historical invention and verisimilitude (to which I shall return presently), the Savant changes tactics when he meets resistance in the cause of keeping a more open mind ("I am for the truth *wherever* . . ."). Softening demands, it would seem, but only by the nature of his analogy, the Savant argues (119–20) that in a perfectly harmonized concert ensemble one does not listen to the individual parts. The burden of bearing an "esprit de système" may seem lighter, and the interlocutor pauses in seeming agreement with this formulation that in fact continues the passages of the first letter in which he called for formal unity with increasing demand; but the Savant's seductive rhetoric with its partial truth has not changed the nature of his position. In his own résumé at the end of the letter, the critic reflects some agreement with the Savant, as he must, but casting himself in the role of Molière's Dorante—opposite his marquise as Uranie—he echoes Dorante's famous meditation on "the rules." Esthetic rules may or may not work, for esthetic success or in judgment of it; intuition or discernment alone, on the other hand, may either hit the mark or go astray. The two in combination constitute the surest esthetic and critical stance.[34]

32. Cazes (p. 141, n. 1) pointed out the similarity of Valincour's text with *La Critique de l'Ecole des femmes*, scene vi. Similarly, Laugaa, op. cit., p. 51 (with a dismissal, continued p. 53).

33. The caricatural nature of a good number of Valincour's interlocutors' thinking has been suggested to me by David L. Rubin's treatment of Molière's techniques: "Image, Argument, and Esthetics in *La Critique de L'Ecole des femmes*." *Romance Notes* 15, Supplement No. 1 (1973), 98–107.

34. Dorante's later more provocative remarks on rules to the pedant Lysidas are ballasted by this position stated to the marquis: "il y en a plusieurs qui sont capables de juger d'une pièce selon les règles, et que les autres en jugent par la bonne façon d'en juger, qui est de se laisser prendre aux choses, et de n'avoir ni prévention aveugle, ni complaisance affectée, ni délicatesse ridicule." *Œuvres complètes*, ed. R. Jouanny (Paris: Garnier, 1962), 1:494.

The comic presentation of the increasingly angry and aggressive Savant, bent on his desire to win the argument, is a warning remaining for the rest of the text, since a significant point is being made about dialogue itself. Effort is required to keep it functioning properly, it is suggested, with something like a pastiche of the "atmospherics" of Plato's *Cratylus*.[35] The message is that dialogue must be kept going, against obstacles (including a rush to name), obstacles that from this exchange on extend throughout the *Lettres*, as well as in its continuation beyond the text. The performing grammarian's response, to those who would silence him, is also calculated to keep dialogue functioning. In a turn of wit, as characteristic of Valincour as scoffing at storybook characterization or comic ambiguities of plot, the grammarian answers those who would silence him for nit-picking that philosophers may claim that animals think, but it is certain that they do not converse. Therefore, "l'homme ne sçauroit assez cultiver un avantage assez prétieux qu'est celuy d'exprimer ses pensées."[36] This grammarian well met will be neither a Lysidas nor a Trissotin.

In complicity with his correspondent, marquise***/Uranie, the letter writer leads on with a proper conversational urbanity a number of interlocutors (of both genders) who could be cast as Molière's Climène ("prude façonnière de théâtre"). The pleasure of being listened to, of having center stage, leads more than one "pousseur de beaux sentiments" into amusing contortions of thought, ironizing and problematizing tendencies or particular points of this kind of critic's fault-finding as well as Valincour's own. One of these contortionists is given, for example, the analogy of Mme de Clèves and Molière's Agnès, an insight of some critical value, it is inferred, until it blocks all others. The concerned moralizing critic at the end of the second letter is no Climène. But by that moment in letter writing when her point of view appears, it seems to be secondary if not eccentric, primarily because of the decidedly less conventional tone and different focus of analysis adopted and adapted by the letter writer/Dorante with his marquise in mind. Their ethical concern has been concentrated within rather than beyond the esthetic context. The lightly censorious voice of the

35. Cf. "Cratylus' attack on the foundations of dialectic," discussed by Rudolph H. Weingartner, *The Unity of Platonic Dialogue* (New York: Library of Liberal Arts, 1973), 23–26.

36. *Lettres*, p. 286. The play on "prétieux" here with the theme inevitably recalls the art ("canine *préciosité*") of Valincour's verse parody of Mme Poncet's "Lisette." See above, ch. 2, nn. 4–6.

moralizing interlocutor, deserving consideration but only up to a point, seems to join a chorus of women interlocutors who fall short of what the ideal reader in the marquise had been constructed to be.

Insisting on their experience as women of the world, "mondaines" sure of their own verbal skills in conversation, the "professionals" as Maurice Laugaa labels them[37] in the art of savoir-dire are by no means presented in the *Lettres* as the best guides to critical competency. That interlocutor who finds the episode of the stolen portrait lacking in verisimilitude, because a woman of the world like herself could have saved the moment verbally, has missed the embarrassment that Valincour from his special appreciative angle has admired. The mistress of the one-line verbal put-down, who has made it a specialty for avoiding or exposing emotional involvement, does not have the heart ("tendresse") to feel Mme de Clèves's silent moments with Nemours.[38] These readers, with their impatient assumptions of possessing *the* truth, are liable to miss *a* truth that is not part of the reflected portrait sought in the mirror of the fictional text. A prosecution of supposedly essential faults often is mounted thus on the basis of circumstantial evidence. Men are of course also guilty of this referential fallacy,[39] which has so clouded Valincour's text that dialogue and its problematizing irony have been forgotten by hunters of "chicane" wishing to assign all remarks on external verisimilitude to Valincour directly. A curious interlocutor, a bachelor who particularly feels the Prince de Clèves's tragedy and objects to fun-making at the character's expense, may also in part figure Valincour's explicit but complex response. Unlike that response, the interlocutor's is fragmented, distorted, and not open to

37. For Laugaa, who refuses the dialogue, this code is disembodied rather: "écto-plasmes du texte romanesque" (p. 49).

38. *Lettres*, pp. 127–28, 153, 192, generalizing this type of response, exemplified for example by p. 168 (on the portrait scene), 177 (on letter writing), then after others in this line by the moralizing final woman-interlocutor, pp. 277ff: "un peu farouche." This sustained line of criticism, as a part of the investigative coupling of hyperbole/understatement across the text of all three letters, which is not gender-specific in its referents nor linked to a textual paradigm of *préciosité* that is, leads me to interpret ellipsis differently from J. De Jean. Ultimately, however, her presentation of the problems of Valincour's criticism (shared by Bouhours's esthetics of language, I would suggest) acutely points up both a "resolutely conservative poetics and economics" of the text and a limiting perception of the "economic potential of Lafayette's 'écriture féminine'" (p. 890). See "Lafayette's Ellipses: The Privileges of Autonomy," *PMLA* 99 (1984), 884–902.

39. Or "illusion réaliste" (Genette, p. 90). Cf. S. Halliwell on this shift that to him represents the trivialization of the Aristotelian sense of verisimilitude: *Aristotle's Poetics*, p. 298.

modification by dialogue.[40] The critic of the letters is, was, and ever will be "Socrate en bonne humeur." And so is his grammarian. Presented with a touch of *raillerie*, he is far from a grimacing pedant. Without the mistaken priorities and mock-heroic quibbles of Molière's caricatural pedants, he accepts his place with an ironic bow. It befits a judge of style in the narrow sense and can be gracefully assumed when the judge is quick to point out (as was Bouhours) that faults he corrects may not destroy the essential beauty of a passage, much less that of an entire work.[41]

Dialogues sourds, dialogues sonores

By December of 1678, Bayle had read the *Lettres*, which "m'a plu infiniment,"[42] and reported a countercriticism in the making. The new critic, Jean-Antoine de Charnes, was, like Bussy and Mme de Sévigné, sure that the real author of the *Lettres* was Bouhours. With the appearance in May of 1679 of his *Conversations sur la critique de la Princesse de Clèves*, printed by Mme de Lafayette's publisher Barbin, that attribution became a mixed blessing. Valincour preferred to continue the exchange privately, the "honnête homme" feeling, in the circumstances, bound to assume responsibility for authorship but disinclined to public polemics. When Charnes learned of his mistake, he apologized for the publication.[43] There was good reason. Charnes, a respected but little-known

40. *Lettres*, pp. 213–14. He is finally classed among the "chagrins, & qui disent les duretez."

41. The Tours editors' marginally cited passages from Bouhours and Vaugelas demonstrate the consistency of these remarks both with Bouhours's own texts and with the tradition Valincour continues elsewhere (see below, chap. 6, n. 36 and text). Importantly, the *vitium/virtus* principle is quoted in one passage from the "Avertissement" of the 1675 *Remarques nouvelles* (p. 366). There are examples of the grammarian's being as good as his word (e.g., on redundant epithets, p. 347, that mar but do not destroy the power of the much-admired textual moment of the Princesse's "identity crisis"). For a different interpretation of the grammarian's function— dominance over the text and foreclosure, see J. De Jean, loc. cit. (above, n. 38).

42. The order of Bayle's remark is interesting: "La critique de la *Princesse de Clèves* m'a plu infiniment, et la *Princesse de Clèves* aussi. On imprime une *Réponse* à la *Critique*." Letter to Minutoli, 15 Dec. 1678. *Lettres choisies* (Rotterdam: Fritsch and Böhn, 1714), 1:117.

43. "Il fut fâché d'avoir écrit contre lui et il en fit une espèce de satisfaction," the Tours editors (see n. 44 below) report from a note (Appendix I) in Bouhier's copy, indicating Valincour as source for this information published in the *Bibliothèque du Richelet* [*Dictionnaire de la langue françoise ancienne et moderne*. Lyon: Duplain, 1728. v. 1, p. xcviii]. A fuller confirmation occurs in a letter to abbé Laurent-Josse Leclerc,

scholar specializing in Italian literature,[44] had taken a schoolmaster's pen to the text of the *Lettres* and a stick to its author. Sure of his own readings of ancient and modern texts, the "dialogue de sourds" that resulted in large part took shape with his ad hominem attack on Bouhours the Jesuit. The fictional frame of the *Conversations* simply reproduces the marquise***, who denies her part in the genesis of the *Lettres,* and adds an interlocutor from Barbier d'Aucour's recent attack on Bouhours.[45] Pascal is said to have animated the *Lettres* (as a *mauvais génie* it is more than implied), and the textual allusions to Voiture are ignored. Charnes nonetheless himself felt justified in seeking his own guide in the *Provinciales*,[46] "as though defending a bad cause," however, Fontenelle judged.

Once the fictional cast is assembled in the first part, the conscientious defender of the honor of the princesse and her creator proceeds in three conversations to contest Valincour point by point. Judicial process is Charnes's model of critical practice, set in the first part by the witnesses for the prosecution produced to testify to the inadmissibility of the *Lettres* as dialogue. With this indictment of fraud, irony loses any hearing, and with it any recognition of the reflexive and reflective dimension of the *Lettres* that makes its subject criticism as well as *La Princesse de Clèves.* Consequently, the defamer may be convicted for rigidity on the one hand and irrelevantly impressionistic taste on the

editor of the revision: 12 May 1726 (B.N. MS. fon. fr. 24413, p. 590). "Il est seur qu'il [d'Aucour] n'est pas l'Autheur des conversations sur la Princesse de Clèves, qui lui ont été attribuées, et qui ne sont dignes de lui. Elles sont de l'Abbé de Charnes, auteur de la Vie du Tasse, lequel l'a avoué à Mr de Valincourt (de qui je le tiens) en lui demandant pardon d'avoir lancé ces Conversations contre lui. Car elles ont été composées contre les Lettres sur ce Roman, qui ont été attribuées par le P. Lelong au P. Bouhours, & qui sont de Mr de Valincour certainement, quoique je ne doute pas que ce Jésuite n'y ait mis la main."

44. Biographical information on J.-A. de Charnes (1641–1728) and bibliographical precisions are much supplemented beyond any previous notices by the excellent introduction to the facsimile ed. of the *Conversations*. [Ed. F. Weil et al. (Tours: Université François Rabelais, 1973).]

45. The link, leading to the mistaken attribution to d'Aucour (a friend of Port-Royal), is made by introduction of the Cléante of the *Sentimens de Cléante sur les Entretiens d'Ariste et d'Eugène* (1671), acrid denunciation of Bouhours's thought, "precious" style, and uses of citation. The suggestion of the Tours eds. is of a masking pastiche (ii–iii). For the context of Bouhours's polemics (from 1668) and the conditions of a "Jesuit" reading of the *Lettres'* absolutions of faults and protests against the author's cruel "providence," see G. Doncieux, *Bouhours* (Paris: Hachette, 1886), 45–79.

46. *Conversations*, p. 20.

other, as on a final charge of "purist" grammatical pedantry. This partial reading, resulting historically in a failed debate and a replay of the "quarrel of *Le Cid*,"[47] nonetheless forces issues important for the future of both criticism and the historical novel. In a concentrated focus on innovation, Charnes insists on the creator's freedom to shape the fictional world. He thus hastens an emancipation from the "rules," an anti-Aristotelian movement underway but by no means accomplished either in Valincour's *Lettres* or in the historical moment shared with Le Bossu and Rapin.[48] Fundamentally, and most significantly in historical context, Charnes presents the claims for intentionality against the text-based criticism Valincour preferred by inclination, stated as the critical presuppositions of his method, and had adopted by necessity since ignorance of the true author of *La Princesse de Clèves* was not for him a purely textual strategy.[49]

The responses of Fontenelle, Bussy, and Mme de Sévigné indicate that among contemporary readers, only Charnes, in his angry imagination, perceived in Valincour's *Lettres* a literal attack on *La Princesse de Clèves*. But the fact that Charnes focused his criticism on intentionality at least suggests that the author of *La Princesse de Clèves* herself may have contributed to that anger. Biographers of Mme de Lafayette from Emile Magne to Duchêne, as well as the Tours editors of Charnes,

47. Genette develops the parallel at length. Of special interest from the point of view of similarities in critical terminology and the inadequacies of Valincour's terminology to his insights, see Noémi Hepp, "Esquisse du vocabulaire de la critique littéraire de la querelle du Cid à la querelle d'Homère," *Romanische Forschungen* 69 (1957), 332–408.

48. Rapin, who found Valincour's criticism "pas mal" (letter of 24 July 1678 to Bussy, *Correspondance*, ed. Lalanne, 4:161) may speak for both in the Preface to his *Réflexions sur la poétique* (2nd ed., 1675): "Sa Poétique n'est à proprement parler, que la nature mise en méthode, et le bon sens réduit en principes: on ne va à la perfection que par ces règles"; therefore, "Aristote: qui est l'unique source, d'où il faut prendre des règles, quand on se mêle d'écrire." [Ed. E. T. Dubois (Geneva: Droz, 1970), 9, 10.] On Aristotle and the moment, Annie Becq, *Genèse de l'esthétique française moderne* (Pisa: Pacini, 1984), 1:43–46, 49–53, 121ff. The characterization of Valincour's freedom from "rules," as well as the theoretical/methodological situation of *vraisemblance* set by the first *Lettre*, consequently seem to me overstated and distorted by Jean-Pierre Dens, *L'Honnête homme et la critique du goût*, pp. 129–38 (especially, pp. 129–30).

49. Before and after the *Lettres*, Bouhours is Valincour's only known link with Mme de Lafayette's circles and source of Valincour's knowledge about her. It is not certain moreover that Bouhours knew the true author, from his "Il faudroit que je fusse bien hardi pour critiquer ce qui vient de cet endroit-là." [Quoted by Bussy, letter to Mme de Sévigné, 14 October 1678. *Lettres* (ed. Duchêne, 1974), 2:634.]

have carefully but unsuccessfully searched for conclusive evidence to link them.[50] Charnes's defense appears to be strengthened by privileged information seemingly available only from this mystery witness. On Mme de Lafayette's historical background readings, for example, but also on the timetable of composition, and especially on Corneille's Pauline as a model for the princesse, he has evidence that will rectify, he insists, the mistaken impressions of Valincour's reading.[51] More generally, he also insists upon confirming and heightening Valincour's repeated compliments to an author who "knows the court." Although there is no extant record of Mme de Lafayette's response to the *Lettres*, her irritation and a desire to set the record right seem all the more probable in the light of her often-quoted reflections on *La Princesse de Clèves* to Lescheraine. She expresses two strengths, with an author's satisfaction: the fiction gives a finished illusion of historical memoirs and does so by an equally finished representation of the speech of the court; in the spirit of that speech she then admits one qualified weakness: the language is "correct mais peu soigné."[52] Almost preternaturally, Valincour's letters respectively questioned the strengths and heavily confirmed the weakness.

Bussy, who had his own ideas on historical style, seems in his reading of the *Lettres* to be pleased to find doubts that would support his own.[53] Refusing to be drawn more than she wished into this negative discussion of *La Princesse de Clèves*, Mme de Sévigné responded more in the spirit in which the *Lettres* was addressed to its fictional marquise. As invited to do, she keeps her own opinion about the novel's real

50. The Tours eds. (p. xi): "Aucun témoignage ne nous assure que Charnes ait été en relation directe avec Mme de Lafayette ni qu'il ait eu mandat de répliquer aux *Lettres*." Same opinion in R. Duchêne, *Mme de Lafayette*, p. 339. Magne had reached this conclusion also: *Le Cœur et l'esprit de Mme de Lafayette* (Paris: Emile-Paul, 1927), 237. Specific links remain hypothetical.

51. Pp. 149–50 point out more sources than just Brantôme; p. 231 suggests the anteriority of *Les Désordres de l'amour*; on Pauline, p. 234. Confirming the first, see the article by Chamard and Rudler cited in the bibliography; on the genesis, M. Cuénin, loc. cit. and G. Mouligneau, *Mme de Lafayette romancière?* (Brussels: Eds. de l'Université, 1980, pp. 161–67); for Pauline, see Harriet Allentuch, "Pauline and the Princess de Clèves," *Modern Language Quarterly* 30 (1969), 171–82.

52. Letter of 13 Apr. [1678]. *Correspondance*, ed. A. Beaunier (Paris: Gallimard, 1942), 2:63.

53. On a style he would have, "noble mais simple," see César Rouben, "Un spécimen d'histoire royale," *Revue des sciences humaines* 148 (1972), 516–32. On 24 July the "critique m'a paru admirable; j'y voudrais pourtant trancher quelque chose, mais fort peu" (Lalanne ed., 4:163); with Mme de Sévigné, on 12 Aug., preferring what the two cousins could have written, he is less laudatory (Duchêne ed., 2:620).

power, while enjoying the representation of conversational discussion that to a degree mirrors her own pleasures.[54] Her judgment of the *Lettres* then is that it is not a "pièce à désavouer en qualité de bel esprit" (12 October 1678).

The marquise***, who remains prudently "mystérieuse, sans doute fictive" for the Tours editors,[55] is doubtless, like Bouhours's interlocutors, constructed as an ideal reader—and conversationalist—functioning as an *arbitrix elegantiarum*. But there are intertextually a striking number of traits common to the marquise and the Olimpe to whom Valincour addressed his almost exactly contemporary verse "requestes," the first salon performances of a "bel esprit" that continue in much the same fashion in the *Lettres*. And the performing grammarian of the *Lettres*, with his turn on the "souls of animals" controversy, as I have suggested, is also associated with those verse diversions. The marquise is a mature woman, with one daughter at least (educated with special attention to coping with society). She has a taste for *raillerie*, especially when the subject of conversation turns to *galanterie*. She may once have been attracted to the older, heroic novel, but now is sarcastic about its narrative techniques and its personifications of love. If she is generally unsentimental about fiction, and love itself, she has shed tears over Racine's *Iphigénie*, which moved her deeply. She enjoys hearing some Italian verse, has read Horace, and is indeed a devoted reader who enjoys ancient and modern history as much as or more than novels or verse. If more were known of Mme Poncet, and the guests she received in the rue des Francs-Bourgeois, than her reputation for "agréments," and a circle that did include Bouhours,[56] an identification of the recipient of the *Lettres* might be possible.[57] But the connections already make possible some inferences that are more interesting than the simple identification of an historical subject of Valincour's portrait of the marquise ***, "honnête femme."

54. On Mme de Sévigné's personal reading of *La Princesse de Clèves*, see C. G. S. Williams, *Mme de Sévigné*, pp. 135–36.

55. *Lettres*, p. 1. No attempts have previously been made to suggest an identity for the marquise.

56. Bouhours had collaborated as editor on Pierre Poncet's *Considérations sur les avantages de la vieillesse dans la vie chrétienne, politique, civile, économique et solitaire* (Paris: Cramoisy, 1677), 590 pp. See G. Doncieux, *Bouhours*, p. 65.

57. Née Marie Bétault (?–11 Feb. 1723), daughter of Louis, président in the *chambre des comptes*, sister of the Présidente Molé (née Louise Bétault), wife of Mathias II Poncet de la Rivière, comte d'Ablis (1626–93), then of Ambroise Ferrand (1702). The marquis de Trichateau praises her *agréments* to Bussy on 19 March 1679 (*Correspondance*, Lalanne ed., 4:331). Her daughter married the comte de Chamilly.

Whether or not the *Lettres* were planned to recapture the conversation of a specific circle, beyond the individual writer who is a part of
it, Valincour's letter writing figures a dialogue at a different level from
that considered above. This dialogue is the intersection of continuing
discussion with Bouhours and "Mme Poncet," who is invited to be the
final arbiter or at least to correct the assumptions made about her
response during the inquiry. The Tours editors have convincingly
argued that the grammatical remarks of the third letter are Valincour's
rather than Bouhours's directly.[58] Writing him into them, like practicing the "bel esprit" taught by the essay of Bouhours's *Entretiens d'Artiste
et d'Eugène*, [59] is an act of mastery, acknowledged by the attributions
of the text to Bouhours. However great that influence, the final gesture
of the text, prepared throughout as the portrait of the marquise ***
emerges, is a bestowal of final authority of judgment upon the "honnête
femme" who provides the new harmonizing setting for both the
grammarian and the young wit who would shine by a "bel esprit" that
was not synonymous with mindlessness.

Valincour's *Lettres* were neither championed nor disavowed by their
author. Authorship, which was doubtless known to friends long before,
was not revealed in print until 1723.[60] When they were reprinted in
1691, possibly to aid the widow of his publisher, Cramoisy,[61] the *Lettres*

58. See above, n. 41.

59. Furetière's *Dictionnaire* (1690) cites Bouhours in defining the positive value of
"négligence" as "qui ne gâte rien, qui plaît même, et qui pare le discours." The model
for conversation was first set by *Entretiens*' fourth section, "Du bel esprit": "Chez
Bouhours le bel esprit doué pour la conversation possède toutes les qualités requises
dans une conversation parfaite: le caractère . . . est de parler bien, de parler facilement
et de donner un tour plaisant à tout ce qu' ils disent. . . . Pour peu qu'on les excite,
ils disent mille choses surprenantes; ils savent surtout l'art de badiner avec esprit et
de railler finement dans les conversations enjouées; mais ils ne laissent pas de se bien
tirer des conversations sérieuses; ils raisonnent juste sur toutes les matières qui se
proposent et parlent toujours de bon sens." See Christoph Strosetski, "Les Types
idéaux du 17e siècle comme paradigmes de la conversation," in *Rhétorique de la
conversation* (Tübingen: Biblio 17, 1984), 127–28. The citation is *Entretiens*, pp. 289–90.

60. The Tours eds. (p. iv) give the *Bibliothèque du Richelet* (1728) as the first public
"revelation" of Valincour's authorship. It had previously been made in vol. 2 (1723)
of the *Bibliothèque françoise ou histoire littéraire de la France* (Amsterdam: J.-F. Bernard), 20: Quoting the *Segraisiana* on Mme de Lafayette: "Elle a méprisé, . . . de
répondre à la Critique que le P. Bouhours a faite de la *Princesse de Clèves*. M. de
Segrais ne se tromperoit-il point en attribuant cet Ouvrage à l'ingénieux Jésuite? Il
passe pour être de M. de Valincourt."

61. The widow Cramoisy underwent bankruptcy in 1690 and was closely linked
to Bouhours (according to Minutoli: see A. Adam, *Histoire* 5:78, n. 1). The 1678 text
is unaltered.

remained anonymous, as the history shortly to come would be. No subsequent reference is made to the book in the author's correspondence, either by him or by his friends. After his first experience of literary polemic, and the capital discovery of the extent to which an author's intentions are uncontrollable, the pleasures of literary criticism remained private until special circumstances involving friends brought them back into print under the writer's signature in the last year of Valincour's life.[62] That late return to criticism was not concerned with fiction. Valincour did remain, however, interested as a reader of novels after *La Princesse de Clèves*. Without commentary he announced to Pontchartrain, for example, in 1696 that Catherine Bernard's new novel (*Inès de Cordoue*), dedicated to the prince de Dombes, was the publishing event of the summer.[63] Near the end of his life, Valincour agreed with Bouhier (and Fleury) that Montesquieu's *Lettres persanes* was "in fact an abominable work."[64] His reasons have little if anything to do with its technical aspects and a great deal to do with the ethics of writing. Their satire of the *Unigenitus* controversy, for example, at a moment Valincour was convinced silence should be observed on the matter, was quite enough to motivate his judgment. Problems of the referentiality of historical fiction, ethical as well as esthetic, may also have been in the critic's mind as he examined the fictitious "historical memoirs" Mme de Lafayette offered her public.

The exchanges between the critic-reader and the savant in the *Lettres* may illuminate Valincour's past and future as well as that of the historical novel. The discussion already engaged the issue that Charnes will take up and formulate as a full creative freedom to rewrite the past. The history on which the two interlocutors agree for the novel, over the text of Castelvetro, is one known to them both from tragedies, the "histoire secrète" that will discreetly integrate invention without distorting or tampering with widely received knowledge. If Charnes's free invention has a more brilliant posterity for novels of other worlds or the re-creation of the past, Valincour's also has a solid one, which Sainte-Beuve found in the novels of Sir Walter Scott.[65] Beginning with the new current of "nouvelles historiques" (Mme de Villedieu begins *Les Désordres de l'amour* with a story involving Guise) and continuing in 1678 with *La Princesse de Clèves*, Valincour was on the side, as it

62. See below, chap. 8, pp. 290–92.
63. Letter of 18 June 1696. B.N. D'Hozier MS., P.O. 2890, 64, 220, p. 27.
64. Letter of 28 Jan. 1728, *RHLF* 31 (1924), 391.
65. "Madame de Lafayette," *Portraits de femmes* (Paris: Garnier, 1845), 279.

were, of the creators, intrigued by a new use of history. By 1681, when he has found his way as a writer of history through a careful examination of the historical truth of documents on Guise, he will have little use for fiction posing as historical truth (or even passing as historical memoirs). Just beginning in the *Lettres* is a tendency to prefer history to the novel and with it a desire, which will grow more insistent, for both clear historical relativism and differentiation of historical fact from fiction.

The "bel esprit," who did show off his mind as well as his wit in the *Lettres*, in his demonstrated talents of letter writing and conversation, had the resources to continue those talents in circles and with problems that neither needed nor wanted a Voiture. His first critical remark, inserting a qualifier into Mme de Lafayette's first sentence that pitches her historical setting, is an emendation that points ambiguously toward the writer's future. "La magnificence & la galanterie n'ont jamais *encore* paru en France avec tant d'éclat que dans les dernières années du règne de Henri II," he corrects (5), with the comment that the author had doubtless forgotten he was living in the reign of Louis XIV. Stylistically, this remark is the first of a sustained line exploring in Mme de Lafayette's fiction the interplay of hyperbole and direct statement (or understatement) so characteristic of her. Historically, in anticipation of the grandeur to come, while waiting for a peace near at hand in the summer of 1679 that will end with an explosion of exaltation of Ludovicus Magnus/Bellérophon, Valincour indulges in a display of devotion to his time that might be taken as a dubious omen for the future historian. At the moment of beginning a lifelong career of service to the king, his gesture may be read otherwise. At the beginning of his remarks, intended for a new time and new minds that can interpret it if they make an effort, Valincour rejects a nostalgic view of the past and gives notice that past and present glories should be distinctly and clearly differentiated.

Chapter 4

The Responsibilities of History

Valincour's appointment as royal historiographer, it has been seen, solidified his place within the Republic of Letters and at the same time gave him personally an avenue of advancement not entirely dependent on the comte de Toulouse and service in his household. Historical writing remained nonetheless in Toulouse's service: memoirs like those responsibly composed for the comte's first education continued almost to the end of Valincour's life.[1] History, like verse and criticism, was for him a means to an end—of gaining charges and fulfilling them; but history, like verse and criticism, was also an activity freely sought, a source of pleasure as well as a discipline.

History, grounded in pleasures of writing enhanced perhaps by certain responsibilities, became in fact the central coordinate of Valincour's writing. In advancing age, it redirected the nature of his poetry, once the Académie in part replaced the salons frequented by the younger poet. And it continued to shape and frame his thinking on literary matters. The critic of literature, of the past and the present, is first an historian; the historian is always first a critical reader. In his earliest historical writing, the life of Guise, the same independence of mind was at work that considered the *Princesse de Clèves* and ensured the history's success with readers as diverse as Bossuet and Voltaire, Bussy and Fontenelle. Writing the *Vie* centered the intellectual pleasures and responsibilities of the craft of historian in the life of the still-young man with ambitious plans.

1. See chap. 5, note 142.

Vie de François de Lorraine, duc de Guise (1681)

The specific nature of Valincour's ambitions is disclosed in a letter to Du Cange that accompanied a gift of the recently published *Vie* to the distinguished lexicographer and historian. In this letter Valincour reveals his plan of an extensive series of similar works, later abandoned but already underway with a life of the Connétable de Bourbon. Mabre-Cramoisy in similar terms had already promised in his notice to the *Vie*, "de cette manière la Vie de tous les grands hommes du siècle passé & de celuy-cy," in large part (it would thus seem) by the ambitious if anonymous author, who continued to mine the historical reading and knowledge of principal sources gained during his examination of *La Princesse de Clèves*.

But the letter to Du Cange reveals more than this joint publishing venture. The single known direct commentary on the *Vie*, this letter reveals a central concern for documentation, in good part responsible for the *succès d'estime* the *Vie* enjoyed with first readers like Bussy (a hard judge of the efforts of men of letters to write military history),[2] then with Voltaire, and yet with nineteenth-century historians that maintain the *Vie* among their sources.[3]

A Paris, le 10 avril 1683

Les personnes, Monsieur, qui sont aussi utiles au public que vous l'estes sont souvent exposées à estre importunées par les particuliers. Mais comme ces importunités sont des marques de la confiance que l'on a en la science et en la bonté de ceux à qui l'on s'adresse, elles sont en quelque façon excusables. Ainsi, Monsieur, sans avoir l'honneur d'estre connu de vous, je ne fais point de difficulté de vous supplier d'accepter la Vie du duc de Guise qui vous sera rendue avec cette lettre et de vous demander vostre avis sur les moyens de continuer le dessein, c'est à dire, la vie de tous les grands hommes du siècle passé. Vous trouverez dans celle-cy beaucoup de choses qui ne sont pas assez expliquées et quelques unes mêmes qui ont esté omises, faute d'avoir eu des mémoires assez particuliers. Je voudrois corriger ce défaut dans cet ouvrage et l'éviter dans la vie du connétable de Bourbon qui est presque achevée et dans quelques autres. Comme je ne puis consulter personne qui ait une connoissance plus parfaite que vous, Monsieur, de tous les livres et de tous les manuscrits où je puis trouver ce que je cherche, je vous prie de vouloir bien

2. Bussy attributed the *Vie* to Saint-Evremond. He warmly recommended it on 1 Jan. 1686 to Catherine de la Madeleine. *Correspondance* (ed. Lalanne), 5:486.

3. E.g., Hippolyte La Porte, *Biographie universelle* 19 (1827), s.v. "Guise"; René de Bouillé, *Histoire des ducs de Guise* (Paris: Amyot, 1849), 1:314, 411, 435, 466; 2:38, 57, 88, 107, 184, 218, 237, 239, 267, 285–86; Henri Forneron, *Les Ducs de Guise et leur époque* (Paris: Plon, 1877), 1:i.

me marquer les lieux où on peut trouver aisément ces auteurs entre autres Oronville et Fanyus que vous citez sous le mot *allen* dans le l[er] tome de vostre incomparable ouvrage. Je regarderay comme un grand plaisir l'obligation particulière que j'auray à une personne à qui toute l'Europe est si obligée. Je suis de tout mon cœur, Monsieur, vostre très humble et très obéissant serviteur.

M. Trousset[4]

If the historian at the beginning of his career had not yet had access to the Bibliothèque du Roi (and to Guise's own memoirs still there in manuscript), documentation was nonetheless central to his concerns for the *Vie*. It is not deployed and noted in the fashion of contemporary erudition, but it is continually kept in focus, along with a line of evaluation that appeals to the intelligence of a reflective reader. The dissatisfaction expressed to Du Cange is in fact not a disavowal of the earlier work. To the contrary, it affirms the fundamental approach of the historian as documentary and suggests that his future way was to be a refinement of the critical method already in place in the *Vie*. Fontenelle, in the fullest description by anyone with direct knowledge of the historian and his method, gives prominent place to Valincour's desire for evidence, among a cluster of qualities that suggest the *Vie*'s prefiguration of Enlightenment historiography (and in turn its adumbration of nineteenth-century positivist method). This

short historical work . . . fulfills everything that may be demanded of a good historian; research that, although done with much care and sometimes in out-of-the-way sources, does not exceed the limits of a reasonable curiosity; a well integrated and animated narration, which carries the reader along naturally and always holds his interest; a noble and simple style, which draws its ornaments from the nature of the matter, or from elsewhere, very acutely; *no partiality for the hero, who could well inspire passion in the writer of his life*.[5]

To read the "no partiality" of the tribute as "objectivity" in a nineteenth-century sense, however, oversimplifies the appeal of the *Vie* to a special community of readers: Bayle, Fontenelle, and Voltaire, who recommended it to his friend Fawkener among the twenty "best books I know in regard to history produced by Frenchmen."[6] More importantly, it displaces the real interest of this aspect of Valincour's writing: that it exists in tension with the "beauties of History" he

4. B. N. MS. fon. fr. 9502, pp. 119–20.

5. "Eloge de Valincour," *Œuvres* (Paris: Salmon, 1825), 2:252–53. My translation and emphasis.

6. Letter (in English) of 25 Mar. 1752. *Correspondance*, ed. Besterman (Geneva, 1954), 10:264.

appreciated and cultivated in the long humanist tradition of historical writing. Like his masters at Clermont and the learned friends he sought as a young man, and from strongly humanist inclination and convictions, Valincour made himself a moral judge in his reading of the "lessons" of history. And as a convinced believer in history as "wise counselor" for the present (ultimately of a prince but basically for every thinking person), he writes accordingly a life of Guise that becomes an exemplary study in fanaticism. The "passion" to which Fontenelle tactfully alludes is unmistakably, if by indirection, Valincour's central subject. Voltaire's recollection of the *Vie* as late as 1752, from readings pursued as background for *La Ligue*, most probably resulted from this focus on fanaticism that he surely must have felt to be a kindred project.[7] And rather than implying a kinship in "objective" historical method, Bayle's use of the *Vie* in his *Dictionnaire* (art. "Guise") may suggest another shared concern, again from an earlier period. Bayle's denunciation of fanaticism, in his *Contrains-les d'entrer*, and the genesis of Valincour's *Vie* share the same moment—the years from 1679 to the Edict of Fontainebleau, the period of what Elisabeth Labrousse has characterized as the death throes of a coexisting Reformed Church of France (R.P.R.).[8]

What most probably began as a publishing venture and pure enjoyment for the man of letters almost certainly underwent thoughtful genesis as Valincour became increasingly mindful of at least three kinds of violence against the R.P.R.—written polemics, a wide gamut of negatively predisposed public opinion, and the coercive force of royal justice. Exacerbation of any or all of these threatened the peace of the church and in particular the spirit of irenism that the young writer doubtless shared with many of his fellow humanists.[9] In these circumstances the writer must have felt with growing concern that a life of Guise was unavoidably a political act with incendiary potential. As will be seen, Valincour as a fledgling Academician was to celebrate the king's zeal in affirming "true religion"—a unified Catholic king-

7. In his 1724 Academic discourse, which Voltaire admired (see below chap. 6, n. 63), Valincour again alludes to "les fureurs de la Ligue."

8. *Une foi, une loi, un roi? La Révocation de l'édit de Nantes* (Paris: Payot, 1985), pp. 167ff. ("L'Agonie de la R.P.R.: 1679–1685"). See also Jean Orcibal, *Louis XIV et les protestants* (Paris: PUF, 1951), 104.

9. See Labrousse, loc. cit., 86–88: "Ultime avatar de la *Respublica christiana*, la République des Lettres ... les cercles lettrés s'accommodèrent on ne peut mieux de l'Edit de Nantes." Jean Queniard, *La Révocation de l'édit de Nantes. Protestants et catholiques français de 1598 à 1685* (Paris: Desclée, 1985), 77–78.

dom. And it will become evident that ideologically he believed, with the vast majority of his contemporaries (including the generally hyper-gallican R.P.R.), that "subjects rising against their sovereign can never have right on their side. Since we are not in the Republic of Plato, whoever says king and subjects affirms on the one side the right to command and on the other the necessity to obey. . . . That is the only good decision to take at all times and especially in troublesome times."[10] The younger man certainly felt in 1679–81 much the same and believed that right, a century before his own youth in the aftermath of the civil war of the Fronde, lay on the side of François de Lorraine and the "cause" of the Triumvirat.

But the story in 1681 is not so simply told. Following the critical spirit that is always a mark of his writing, Valincour renounces in his *Vie* all explicit propaganda, dogmatism, or pragmatism that could be construed as an apology for violent destruction of "heresy" by power. Like d'Aubigné and De Thou, before Bayle and Voltaire, he regrets that for the sake of "bons Français" Guise's last words to his son— "Souvenez-vous de moy, sans désirer de venger ma mort, puis que Dieu nous commande de pardonner à nos ennemis."—fell on deaf ears. The *Vie* ends with the facts of a contrary reality: "Jamais une seule mort n'a tant fait couler de sang, ni entraisné un si grand nombre d'illustres victimes" (174).[11] With this reality in mind, Bayle later described in the Guises "un mélange de bonnes et de mauvaises qualités . . . propre à bouleverser un état." Valincour had already found this mixture dramatically presented in a more than rhetorical question asked by La Renaudie, which De Thou had transcribed:

Demeurons d'accord que le Duc de Guise a fait glorieusement toutes choses dans la guerre; mais les choses qu'il a faites sont-elles de si grande conséquence, qu'elles puissent récompenser & les pertes & les deffaites qu'on a reçues dans le Royaume par sa funeste ambition, & qui ont ouvert le chemin aux maux qui estoient déjà prêts d'y entrer, & que ces Princes y ont appelez?[12]

It is this question that the historian explores and focuses in his biography of François de Guise.

In form Valincour's life of a great soldier seems to offer few

10. Letter to Bouhier, 19 Aug. 1725, *RHLF* 31 (1924), 374–75. Valincour is speaking of parlements and significantly qualifies the duty of obedience with the right to remonstrance: "le devoir et même la nécessité d'obéir après avoir remontré."

11. References are to the first Mabre-Cramoisy printing. See Bibliography I, B. 2.

12. J.-A. De Thou, *Histoire des choses arrivées de son temps*, trans. P. Du Ruyer (Paris: Courbé, 1659), 2:90–91.

surprises. "Ce n'est pas l'histoire que j'écris, mais une vie," he asserts, echoing Plutarch.[13] The humanist adopts an outline traditional to the genre—of life, works, portrait—and concentrates his narrative on battles and diplomacy. But his account of the soldier's soldier "born" at Metz and extinguished at Orléans moves toward final eulogy in its own terms. The traditional miscellany of the final portrait begins with a description of popular reaction to Guise's assassination. "Les Catholiques disoient qu'ils avoient perdu leur protecteur, & regarderent sa mort comme un Martyre qu'il avoit souffert pour la défense de la Foy." To the popular mind, kept in constant focus, the historian juxtaposes his own reflection on the evidence: "Il eût toutes les qualitez qui ont jamais fait les plus grands Heros" (164). Rather than the heroism of a martyred knight of the church cut down, in his pre-destined mission of defense of the faith, by a fanatical "heretic," Guise is finally eulogized as "le Seigneur le plus honneste de son siecle" (146)— the same picture of the soldier of honor and humanity and the "bon Français" that radiates from Brantôme's life of Guise.

But in Valincour's history we are not in the rhetorical realm of Bossuet's funeral orations, describing a Le Tellier for example as *"toujours* semblable à lui-même, *toujours* supérieur à ses emplois." Rather, Valincour insists: "il faut avoûër que tous les temps de la vie des grands hommes ne se ressemblent pas," specifically when he faces the follies of Guise's Italian campaign, "une guerre qui paroissoit manifestement injuste."[14] When it becomes a matter of civil war, he declares: "On ne peut lire sans horreur ce qui fut dit en ce temps-là, & ce qui a esté escrit depuis." Valincour's contemporaries in polemical writings were quick to liken the present with the time of the Ligue;[15] but he distinguishes the two, in a final qualification of his method as historian that is neither apologetic nor defensive. "Si ses ennemis luy [à Guise] ont reproché quelque chose, *c'estoit moins* à luy qu'il s'en falloit prendre, qu'au malheur de son siecle, & aux desordres qui sont

13. Cf. "Life of Alexander," trans. J. and W. Langhorne (London: Tegg, 1825), 484. Other ornaments are discreetly drawn from Plutarch—p. 9: Montmorency and Guise are compared to Craterus and Hephaeston; p. 134: Guise's tactics at Dreux, to Philopoemen's at Mantinea. (Montaigne makes similar comparisons.)

14. The description of the Italian campaign (pp. 53–60) typically rejects the virulent anti-papal propaganda of Régnier de La Planche [See "A Legendarie, Containing an Ample Discourse of the Life and Behavior of Charles de Guise" (Geneva, 1577)] for the more sober lines of De Thou (1:977).

15. See Labrousse, loc. cit., pp. 73, 110, 116.

arrives durant son temps" (165; my emphasis). Personal interventions by the historian accordingly call for understanding of particular circumstances and stress the fact that sources distorted by personal jealousy, popular idealization, and partisan passion render even more elusive any real understanding of the already complex matters of human motivation and historical causation. The historian does not ask for total absolution (as the words emphasized above indicate). Nor does he claim to have the final truth of this life. His combative tone instead issues a claim to have gone beyond polemic and to have moved toward the truth of this life in itself and within its time.

In these terms Guise's career is made to indicate an evolution, three distinct phases, within the span of eleven years of changing perspective that must be viewed before the significance of the life may be seen and judged. First military glory (13–71) from Metz to Calais, redeeming Italy and establishing Guise's reputation, consecrates the lieutenant-général as "Conservateur du Royaume." With the death of Henri and accession of a pathetically depicted François II, the scene changes (71–121), as the man embroiled in court life and civil administration emerges. New position and power for the Guises, likened to the medieval Mayors of the Palace, require a new perspective when events lead to the formation of the Triumvirat in opposition to Condé. As Guise moves (122–64) from the "signal de la rebellion" (that is, Condé's possession of Orléans) by way of Blois, Tours, Bourges, Rouen, Paris, and Dreux to his death at Orléans, the skills and qualities of both soldier and "courtier" are viewed against the reality of civil war.

Two-fifths of the *Vie* is given to what had become for men of letters by 1681 the fine art of description of military art.[16] The armature of the *Vie* is the series of battles already enumerated by Brantôme, with first place in praise given to Metz. The thirty-two page description of Metz is as precise and pertinent as that to be found in later "scientific" accounts (for example, in Lavisse). The eye-witness account usually sought (here the diffuse *Mémoire* by Salignac)[17] is reduced to clear chronology and narrated with scarcely less animation than is Bossuet's famous account of Rocroi. Appreciating Brantôme's expansive tribute to Guise, Valincour follows to the letter its concluding remark: "Bref,

16. On the art, Roger Zuber, *Les "Belles infidèles" et la formation du goût classique* (Paris: Colin, 1969), 208–10.

17. Bernard de Salignac, *Le Siège de Metz* (Paris, 1552). Rpt. Collection Petitot-Monmerqué, vol. 23 (1823).

qui voudra bien mettre en ligne de conte tout ce qui s'est faict en ce
siège, dira et conffessera que ç'a esté le plus beau siège qui fut jamais."[18]
After elaboration he confirms this judgment soberly: Guise "fit une
infinité d'autres reglemens, qui peuvent servir de modele à ceux qui
se trouveront en de pareilles occasions."

The "model" serves a complex function in the *Vie*. Careful technique
in "model" military description shows Guise's "model" art of war—the
thoroughness of reconnaissance; strategic deployment and maneuver;
and post armistice reconstruction that with Metz came to characterize
his military genius more than did incisiveness and speed of attack and
withdrawal. Technical precisions are accompanied by other generalized advice for the commander—delegation of subordinate command,
treatment of mercenaries in combat and negotiation, as well as treatment of civilians facing the trials of war. But description is not purely
technical and pragmatic. The chef-d'œuvre also reveals the presence
of a powerful man. In place of the myth of Providence's special favor,
which Guise's "miraculous" victories and recoveries suggested in the
popular mind and beyond,[19] Valincour visualizes Guise's control and
natural command as causes explaining successes. Nothing is beyond
him in planning, nothing beneath him in work necessary to implement
it. For all involved at Metz, Guise is the ideal and, as Roger Zuber
sees it, an historical paradigm of "un égal, mais un égal d'un prestige
supérieur,"[20] both for the soldier who wished to feel a superior mind
in charge of his action and for subordinate commanders who desired
proper opportunity and recognition for those qualities of *courtoisie* that
Brantôme most admired.[21]

As Valincour felt and presented it, war is for men like Guise what
it was for Brantôme—a superior mode of life, conception of existence,
and source of morality. "Jeunes guerres" reveal personality and character that do not change in "normal and natural" circumstances. Brantôme agreed with La Brosse that "qui a faict parestre son courage et
valeur en la chaleur de la jeunesse, il ne le perd jamais, quelque vieil

18. "M. Guyze le Grand," *Œuvres de Brantôme*, ed. P. Mérimée (Paris: Jannet,
1858), 5:103.

19. Physical recovery as "quelque chose de miraculeux," pp. 6, 167, following the
Mémoires de Martin et Guillaume du Bellay, ed. Bourilly (Paris: Renouard, 1908–19),
4:313–14.

20. Cf. R. Zuber, loc. cit., pp. 208–9; also, Michelet, *Histoire de France* (Paris:
Calmann-Lévy, 1879), 15:188.

21. See Robert D. Cottrell, *Brantôme: The Writer as Portraitist* (Geneva: Droz, 1970),
123–49.

aage qu'il face, si ce n'est par une grand' disgrace." For him, Guise was "très-bon en sa jeunesse, très-brave, très-courageux et très-généreux; bref, telz en jeunesse que sur l'aage, et telz sur l'aage qu'en jeunesse."[22] Part of Guise's prestige at Metz, the qualities of "*clémence, courtoisie, douceur & miséricorde*," Brantôme found greatly promising for the remaining career. The whole series of anecdotes recounted by Valincour in his narration of the battle of Metz, and in that of military activity throughout the *Vie*, exemplify these different manifestations of a soldier's noble code that unaltered deserves in final eulogy "à faire connoistre le caractere de son esprit & de son humeur."

The qualities of heart and mind seen in the observance of the soldier's noble code, as they are described by "honorable men," serve as criteria for judgment, both of actions in the last phases of Guise's career and of the verisimilitude of their description by other historians. It is not only in the enthusiasm of Brantôme or the celebratory verse by Michel de l'Hôpital that the historian found the exemplary qualities of the hero of Metz; "clémence" and "douceur" he found acknowledged in one of the most likely, responsible sources of contradiction, d'Aubigné.[23] Valincour will thus be able to see Guise acting during the civil war with concern for injury to his countrymen (as when precautions against looting were taken to spare the Rouennais) because he had seen Guise's documented concern for the material and spiritual well-being of the citizens of Metz. A massacre at Vassy then is a psychological improbability. Facts can be adduced to illuminate it in terms other than the armed charge against unarmed Huguenots that had been evoked by some Protestant writers. And when it is a question of public proclamation that soldiers demanding further favors after the death of Henri II will suffer death, Valincour will no more than Brantôme consent to believe Guise directly responsible, for what appeared to him to be the Cardinal de Lorraine's violent policy.[24] Valincour had seen too vividly from Metz to Calais the soldier's *courtoisie*, and the respect it offered and received, to believe in its subordination to fiscal necessity. Similarly, he will not give as the truth a self-serving ambition that allegedly motivated Guise's fatal slowness in aiding Thermes at Gravelines. "Je ne puis croire ce que dit un Auteur célebre qu'il [Guise] affecta ce retardement pour donner lieu à cette défaite qu'il regardoit comme l'augmentation de son autorité" (70). Again, typically insisting

22. Brantôme, "Vie" (Mérimée ed.), pp. 279–80.
23. *Histoire universelle*, ed. Ruble (Paris: Renouard, 1886), 2:143–44.
24. P. 77; cf. Brantôme, "Vie," pp. 223–25.

on evaluation of evidence as well as psychological verisimilitude, when Guise is said to have plotted the assassination of Condé, Valincour judges that "quoy-que le seul recit de cette histoire la fasse paroistre incroyable, principalement à l'égard de Guise qui n'estoit pas capable de conseiller un assassinat; j'ay cru estre obligé de la rapporter icy comme je l'ay trouvée écrite dans les Historiens de ce temps-là" (97).

The historian's critical sense gives value to accounts by others that are not restricted by a single point of view. Consequently he reacts negatively to anonymous broadsides, partisan exposition, and generally dismissed foreign sources[25] because he wishes to gain both a reasonably true view and a hearing for it. But he also opposes "un Auteur célèbre," De Thou, although Valincour owes him much in method and in critical procedure. The table of contents of Du Ruyer's translation[26] of De Thou's *Histoire* contains almost an exact outline for Valincour's *Vie*, which distances it from Brantôme after the adoption of his armature of military events and portrayal of Guise's noble code. Brantôme's *cursus honorum* had scarcely changed focus with the reality of civil war, while his "socioeconomic defense" of it as demographic control (if serious) is totally outside Valincour's humanist orientation.[27] Forever the paradigm for Brantôme, Guise remains the "diamond of *courtoisie*," the standard against which the merits and faults of a Coligny, a Condé, or any other commander may be set off. Brantôme consistently denies any ambition in Guise that might suggest the taint of self-interest. De Thou's *Histoire* constitutes a middle ground between this praise and vituperation to be found elsewhere. Valincour discovered in De Thou (for example, in the transcription of La Renaudie's deposition at Nantes) a steady focus on the infamous ambition of the Guises and the movements of power politics. And in a presentation of evidence thus similar to his own he also found indirectly a justification to reexamine the *Histoire* itself critically. His finding, like Mézeray's, was "l'historien De Thou que les bons Français ne doivent jamais nommer sans préface d'honneur."[28] For the hearing he wished on Guise, the historian, who proceeds in this manner, might have described his method as Voltaire

25. E. g., pp. 12, 52.
26. See above, n. 12.
27. "Vie de l'Amiral de Chastillon." *Œuvres* (Mérimée ed.), 4:328–34.
28. Quoted by Sainte-Beuve, *Causeries* (Paris: Garnier, 1857), 7:224. Valincour's criticism may well have resulted from some sense of the "histoire plurielle" and of textual strategies employed to reconcile service to the monarchy (Henri IV) and truth telling. See Jean-Louis Bourgeon, "Une source sur Saint-Barthélemy: *l'Histoire de Monsieur de Thou*, relue et décryptée," *BSHPF* 134 (1988), 506–10, 534–37.

does his in a characteristic passage of *Le Siècle de Louis XIV*, a method also sometimes similar to Bayle's tactical preparation for his own point of view.[29] Valincour opposes De Thou, d'Aubigné, and Bèze, sources that a hard critic in 1681—say a Jurieu—might admit, to those like Brantôme or Lancelot de Carle, for example, which he would not.

Guise's dramatic career as it is shaped by the *Vie* is not unlike the drama of Corneille's Horace. Already in "Act I" the seeds of ambiguous "natural ambition" are planted, in the historian's account of the Italian campaign, which after decisive peripeteia will become compromising at a later high point of Guise's career. Again more in keeping with Corneille's dramaturgy than the heroic novel, Valincour leaves personality and motivation complex as extraordinary virtue is tested by extraordinary circumstances that force an ambiguity in human response. The king's favor, the consecration as "Conservateur du Royaume" by Parlement and Parisians after the national crisis of Saint-Quentin, the transformation of the soldier's soldier of Metz thus into the national hero of 1558–59—all crystallize the Hero. And the event that brings final consolidation of that power—the death of Henri II—closes "Act II" of the drama.

The dramatic high point of the last phase of Guise's career, an "Act IV" for a classical dramatist, is brought about by the extraordinary circumstances and "testing" by the reality of civil war. Along with the expository preparation for this moment sought in the Italian campaign, Valincour makes one telling event at Metz premonitory. Guise ordered there a general procession "pour rendre graces à Dieu; & pour achever cette cérémonie par un Sacrifice agréable, il fit brusler publiquement tous les Livres de Luther qui se trouverent dans la ville." Valincour, without commentary and, significantly, following De Thou, omits Salignac's observation that this ceremony took place "sans scandale d'aucun."[30] By the time of the ambivalent last phase of Guise's career—its "Act IV"—the questions that will create its dramatic ambiguity have been implied. Ambition of the king's man and "le seigneur le plus honnête de son siecle"—or the demagogue's drive to power and

29. Voltaire, *Œuvres historiques*. Ed. R. Pomeau (Paris: Pléiade, 1957), 889–90. Cf. the critical evaluation of method by J. H. Brumfitt, *Voltaire Historian* (Oxford, 1958), 23, 188; Jacques Solé, *Bayle polémiste* (Paris: Laffont, 1972), 19. "Histoire raisonnée" may be the most apt designation for Valincour's method, as its features are defined by Phyllis Leffler, "The *histoire raisonnée*, 1660–1720: A Pre-Enlightenment Genre," *Journal of the History of Ideas* 37 (1976), 219–40.

30. P. 44; cf. *Le Siège de Metz*, coll. Petitot, 23:401 and De Thou, 1:628.

pretensions to a crown? Piety from *miséricorde* and humanity—or fanaticism in an outward show of the kind Bayle was shortly to denounce in his *Pensées diverses sur la comète?* With these questions there is also the incrimination of men swayed by fear and the prestige of power to support violence, the "peuple trop crédule," "peuple furieux," that are so frequently a part of the denouement of Corneille's later plays.[31] Are they not endorsing that disorder which they wish to prevent? "A Paris, le Prevost des Marchands & les Eschevins allerent au-devant de Guise, & le peuple le receût *comme un homme envoyé du Ciel* pour conserver sa Religion" (117, emphasis mine). But these men also included the *parlementaires.*[32]

When the field is left for the court, there are always threats of that disgrace Brantôme imagined only for others, never for Guise. First in the misfortunes of the Italian campaign, then after Henri II's death, Valincour's narrative establishes a basis for the judgment of at least one twentieth-century historian who found that "François de Lorraine was not a politician. The type of the pure soldier, he had the genius and the temperament of his art and a kind of naïveté in nonmilitary matters."[33] His talents and true glory are the soldier's; and ambition and thoroughness do not work in the same ways in the context of power struggle. When Catherine and Montmorency, Coligny, Condé, Navarre—and Cardinal de Lorraine more than anyone—exert wills of their own determined by other codes, Guise is forced into a different position and light. There is no doubt that true military glory is "*souillée*" in Valincour's narration; and, beginning with his account of Metz, this stain is implied to be the result of what Voltaire would see as intolerance or prejudice. Polemical, impassioned evidence is, from the death of Henri II on, given more hearing. The spectacle of Guise being manipulated and of his lapse from former virtue was felt by outside observers. With this loss of control come loss of admiration and division of

31. Or by Voltaire, e.g., *La Henriade*, 2:26–28. Valincour also, pp. 38, 62, 78, 88–89, 113, 131.

32. Implied here is the same judgment of Parlement explicitly passed after its letter following Amboise declares Guise "Conservateur de la Patrie" (p. 88): "la reconnoissance du Parlement parut extraordinaire, & un peu au dessous de la dignité d'une si grande compagnie." On Parlement's "persistent hostility" to Huguenots and Guise's use of it, see J. H. Shennan, *The Parlement of Paris* (Ithaca: Cornell, 1968), 211–12, 225–27.

33. Lucien Romier, *Les Origines politiques des guerres de religion* (Paris: Perrin, 1913–1914), 2:119.

opinion in polemics that may derive only from jealousy of the great but still have additional justification and significance for the historian.

With the accession of François II there is a dramatist's "suspension agréable" before the last actions and denouement. "Jamais les Guises ne s'estoient veûs si proche de leur ruine, & jamais ils ne se virent si élevez. Il sembloit que toutes choses eussent conspiré pour les rendre maistres du Royaume" (74–75). The figures around Guise remain suggestively shadowy, and thereby vaguely conspiratorial and menacing, as though abstract terms in a struggle that could be seen simplistically as the good (fighting for king and church) against the bad (rebels fighting for themselves). Only the personage of Cardinal de Lorraine, to emphasize his importance, is given some fullness. Yet this simplicity of interpretation, partly the result of Valincour's political orientation and partly that of classical economy in composition, does not leave Guise, in his ideals and *gloire*, any the less compromised in the ambiguous contests of power struggle and civil war. Lorraine is not the "fiend from Hell" (nor is Catherine the "Italian dissembler") excoriated by d'Aubigné. He is shown rather as the timid man Brantôme describes,[34] acting from weakness with a brash and aggressive violence presented by Valincour as compensatory, misguided emulation of his brother. Emulation in the field by men of arms may have noble results, but this rivalry brings nothing but compromising ignominy when, as Brantôme admitted, the man of ambition in the cardinal takes precedence over the churchman. Valincour does not, however, simply follow the line of chroniclers, from Villehardouin on, who absolve leaders of responsibility and compromise through the presence of bad counselors. As men commanding admiration and hatred, Guise and his brother are antithetical. But eschewing the lengthy antithesis that could constitute a rhetorical "beauté de l'Histoire," it is more subtly the similarity of the hero and "anti-hero" of the same blood that Valincour suggests. The cardinal is the incarnation of the infamous ambition of the Guises, shared by François, legitimately directed in the field by the soldier's qualities, but darkened in the spheres of the cardinal's actions. Rather than an absolute antithesis to Guise, the cardinal is the embodiment of his worst quality. A similar function is given to the rebels. Their use of religion as a pretext for seizure of power and seemingly blind indifference to injury done thereby to sovereign and countrymen

34. Pp. 55, 72; Brantôme, pp. 229, 276.

represent the temptations and ambiguous reality of Guise in his most questionable moments.

After all the psychological probing and interpretation, there remains at the center of the drama the image of François II. The historian who sparingly indulges in the invented speeches of humanist history here does so pointedly by making the king ask the Guises pathetically: "Qu'ay-je donc fait à mon peuple pour l'obliger à me vouloir tant de mal? . . . Ne seroit-il point à propos que vous retirassiez?" (83). However "right" their defense of king and church, the facts remain of disorder, of a suffering France, of a king doubtfully served by them in life and neglected scandalously in the honors of burial.[35]

It is in recounting the details of an alleged plan by which the Guises sought supreme affirmation of power by liquidation of the entire royal family that Valincour specifically records his own general feeling of horror over confrontations of power using religion as a pretext. "On ne peut lire sans horreur ce qui fut dit en ce temps-là, & ce qui a esté écrit depuis. Que les Guises craignant les ressentimens du Roy de Navarre, & jugeant d'ailleurs que leur autorité ne seroit jamais tranquille ni assûré tant qu'il resteroit un Prince de Sang pour la contester, ils avoient entrepris de s'en défaire" (95). The historian of Metz knows a Guise "doux et modéré," incapable of such action, who "eut toûjours une affection tres-pure & tres-sincere pour la Religion Catholique" (104). But it is precisely because he was "doux et modéré," the historian acknowledges, that Guise "se rendoit complice des violences & des emportmens de son frere, en ne les empeschant pas, & souvent en l'aidant à executer des desseins auxquels il auroit deû s'opposer" (78). What is true of Guise's passive responsibility in seconding his brother's pretensions (to the papacy in the Italian campaign, as Valincour interpreted them from anti-Guise and antipapal sources) is also true of Vassy and more generally for events leading to the First War of Religion.

Primary responsibility at Vassy may be that of the rabble, hangers-on of the great, "qui ne témoignent jamais l'attachement qu'ils ont à leur Religion qu'en outrageant ceux qui n'en sont pas" (113). In this outbreak of violent intolerance, insults are fast followed by rocks as "domestiques" of Guise avenge an accidental blow he had suffered. It

35. On pp. 99–100, Valincour repeats the famous Tanneguy du Chastel, "où es-tu," seemingly following De Thou, 2:175. In the pathos of his depiction of François II, among other devices he gives to the king the famous account of the impact d'Aubigné felt at Amboise (*Histoire universelle*, Book II, chap. 17).

is the Guises' doubtful fortune to arouse passionate admiration and hatred, in the fickle crowd, "aisé à effrayer [et] qui pour l'ordinaire se consolent aussi aisément qu'ils s'affligent."[36] But clearly the historian asserts that men of arms, at Vassy or in *dragonnades* that began to be feared in 1681,[37] should not allow their code of honor to be debased by the modes of feeling and violent intolerance of lesser men who all too soon become a rabble.

Even though he has the misfortune of being a catalyst of this kind of violence, a man like Guise, faced with this "malheur et désordre," has the same passive responsibility in loss of control that he has to bear in tacit consent to the cardinal's violent actions. For this responsibility there will be the repentance of final general confession. But the historian suggests that something more efficacious might have preceded it. Active participation in the cardinal's violence is made more precise in the historian's account of the Conjuration d'Amboise and its aftermath. He deplores the violence of recriminations following Amboise that so moved the young d'Aubigné, whose emotions Valincour transfers dramatically to François II. But he also deplores the design of the princes to assume power and the dissimulation of Condé. "La liberté de conscience qu'ils demanderent ne leur servit que pour couvrir leurs intentions d'un titre specieux & pour grossir leur parti, en y attirant les Huguenots, qui haïssoient mortellement les Guises, *dont ils avoient toujoûrs esté persecutez*" (79, my emphasis). The fault lies on both sides and incriminates both parties in the causes of war. And once again, of importance for the fanaticism to come, the blame must be shared by the "public qui dans ses malheurs ne cherche qu'à trouver de qui se plaindre" (78). Both sides lose, as they well might in 1681, if violence in a political struggle replaces any reasoned mediation of real issues of religion troubling France.

After Amboise, Valincour states, the Guises could not shift responsibility to others. Nor could they keep the king from hearing of the hatred with which they were blamed (83). As for Condé, "sans doute le Chef des conjurez, s'estant plaint avec cette audace qui imite si bien l'innocence de ce qu'on avoit voulu donner au Roy de méchantes

---

36. Valincour opposes the allegation of a formal charge by Guise at Vassy [Bèze, *Histoire ecclésiastique*, ed. Baum, (Paris: Fishbacher, 1883), 1:807 or d'Aubigné, 2:6)] and like Brantôme refuses the term "massacre" in a literal sense ("Vie," p. 153). On the "goujat" topos, see above, n. 31.

37. See, in particular, Orcibal, *Louis XIV et les protestants*, pp. 72–74; Labrousse, loc. cit., pp. 70–71.

impressions de sa conduite, ... il s'offroit de le démentir à la pointe de l'épée." In Valincour's account this is not a ritual challenge to a duel of honor. It is a gross ruse that Guise tactically counters with another. Smarting yet from this and dissatisfied with Montmorency's report that the Conjuration "ne regardoit point la personne du Roy comme ils [les Guises] le vouloient faire croire," the Guises are justified by him to Parlement in what may seem to be terms of pure violence: "Si les Seigneurs particuliers ne pouvoient sans honte souffrir qu'on fist insulte à leurs domestiques ... il n'estoit pas étrange que le Roy eust pris une vengeance exemplaire de l'entreprise qu'on avoit osé faire contre les premiers Ministres de son Estat" (87). The ally of policy, always presented as more violent than Guise, already puts into question the very existence of the Triumvirat—"Act IV" of Guise's drama—formed in part, the historian makes it clear, as a safeguard of personal power vis-à-vis the princes and Coligny. There is no doubt that Valincour lauds the principle of this alliance of 6 April 1561. But he takes care to show that the reconciliation of Guise and Montmorency at Chantilly, where they remained until the coronation of Charles IX, did not put an end either to personal ambition or to the tension of factions. With the detail of a Saint-Simon, he recounts a quarrel over precedence at the coronation, and reflects: "Ne pouvant plus souffrir le mépris public qu'on faisoit de la Religion, *ni peut-estre la diminution de son autorité*, Guise se retira chez luy, après s'estre plaint à la Reine de la protection qu'elle donnoit aux Huguenots" (110, my emphasis). The Triumvirat, Valincour concedes, was an "entreprise qui a conservé la Religion Catholique" (122); but because of it, civil war, "très funeste à tous les deux partis," is the final reality, compromise, and denouement of the drama of the *Vie*.

In his account of Guise's death Valincour, insisting on his documentation, reports—without rhetorical display of his own—what he found to be in Guise an easy, natural eloquence. "Je rapporteray icy quelques-unes de ses dernieres paroles, non pas telles que je les auray imaginées, comme font la pluspart des Historiens, mais comme elles ont esté écrites par l'Evesque de Riés, qui l'assista jusqu'au dernier soupir."[38] But there is a significant reordering of his source. Guise is made to turn first to Catherine with the most important counsels the *Vie* has to offer "bons Français" of 1681.

38. Lancelot de Carle, "Lettre de l'Evesque de Riez au Roy," (Paris: Keruer, 1563 without pagination), near beginning. Prior to this, for Orléans as elsewhere when

Il luy conseilla d'employer toutes choses pour faire la paix, que c'estoit le seul moyen d'appaiser les troubles qui divisoient la France, qu'Elle sçavoit bien qu'il ne luy avoit jamais donné d'autre conseil; que dans le temps mesme où il croyoit se devoir rendre maistre d'Orleans, il avoit esté d'avis qu'on fist de nouvelles propositions d'accommodement aux Huguenots; et qu'enfin tous ceux qui conseilloient la guerre, n'estoient ni bons François, ni bons serviteurs du Roy. (158)

With the probity of method that Fontenelle describes, (the *honnêteté* in historical writing that we have followed in practice), Valincour adopted the traditions of humanistic history and adapted its formal devices to his own ends. Still well within the tradition, he refuses to take sides and to make his examination and dramatization of fanaticism either pure denunciation or simple doctrinal exposition. His concern in exposing the abuse of power and its pretexts is consistently and forcefully to display the flawed process of reasoned action. In the events, this failure is the breakdown of mediation, of dialogue, in the face of some form of human violence. Valincour's message reflects consideration of events since 1679 that included the barrage of royal edicts harassing places of worship, ministers, and the faithful of the Protestant community; the hardened rhetoric of the *Assemblée du clergé*;[39] the historian Maimbourg's use for one of history as apology for power, or another extremist's antithetical recommendation of separation from Rome.[40] Valincour's message also issues from a spirit he had found in Bossuet and that in turn recommended him to the prelate. The irenic direction taken by Bossuet,[41] in the attempt of his *Exposition* (1668–71), *Conférence avec Claude* (1678), and the *Histoire des variations* (begun in 1681), may by 1680–81 have been a dead letter. But Valincour

possible Valincour has followed the account by Castelnau, *Mémoires*, chap. 9 [Coll. Michaud-Poujoulat, vol. 9 (s.d.), 483–86].

39. The harassment is exhaustively detailed by Elie Benoist, *Histoire de l'Edit de Nantes* (Delft: Beman, 1693–1695), vol. 4; On the Assemblée's developing rhetoric and its constant of opposition, Michel Péronnet, "Les Assemblées du Clergé de France et la révocation des édits de religion (1560–1685)," *Bulletin de la Société de l'Histoire du Protestantisme français* 131 (1985), 469–79.

40. The former extreme, Maimbourg, "Epistre au Roy" of *Histoire du luthérianisme*, 2nd ed. (Mabre-Cramoisy, 1681). On his uses of writing as apology for power, see Bernard Dompnier, *Le Venin de l'hérésie* (Paris: Centurion, 1985), 111–12; the latter extreme: *Moyens sûrs et honnestes pour la conversion de tous les hérétiques* (Cologne, 1681).

41. See Alfred Rébelliau, *Bossuet, historien des protestants* (Paris: Hachette, 1892), 70–73, 76–77; A.-G. Martimort, *Le Gallicanisme de Bossuet* (Paris: Eds. du Cerf, 1953), 280; Jacques Truchet, *Politique de Bossuet* (Paris: Colin, 1966), 22, 46, 88.

could not have discerned what the direction of the court's policy, of strict legalism, was in the process of doing with its edicts, which finally made the Revocation itself redundant.[42] He remains in good faith in solidarity with this tradition he shared with others who had the courage to separate themselves from events of 1681.

The deployment of the first *dragonnades* as pressure to abjure implemented by Marillac in Poitou in the first months of 1681 seems too close to the appearance of Valincour's *Vie* to have played a part in its conception or genesis. But these tactics are one of the possible outcomes of violence that he may have feared and foreseen at an extreme point where any suggestion of "conferences" for the purpose of mediation on "concessions" would put an end to any real possibility of reasoned confessional reunion or continued coexistence. Mme de Maintenon, Valincour's future friend at court, for one protested the general policy of harassment and expressed, also in 1681, the belief that in the matter of Protestant conversions "il faudroit ne rien oublier pour les gagner par douceur."[43] Henri Daguesseau, of whom Valincour later wrote an admiring prose portrait, wrote from Languedoc that "le zèle de la Religion ne doit pas aller jusqu'à l'injustice."[44] But this moderation, if nothing more, was not shared by all zealous ladies of piety, intendants with force of arms at their disposal, or *parlementaires* (among whom, Valincour knew, a good number of strict constructionists wished to iron out the legal anomaly that the Edit of Nantes remained). As "Bulletins de victoire" began to appear regularly in the *Gazette de France* in February, publicly recording the body-counts of forced conversions, it may well have seemed to Valincour that he had his audience. Men of arms who might be given to violence, pious ladies more rigorous than Mme de Maintenon, magistrates less enlightened than Daguesseau—all these persons responsible for both force of opinion and its violent direction, and likely to be caught up in it themselves—

42. The focus on legalism is one of the leading arguments of E. Labrousse, loc. cit., especially pp. 120–22, also 135–40, 166–72. For accompaniment: *Recueil des édits, déclarations, et arrests du conseil, concernant les Gens de la Religion Prétenduë Réformée, les quels ont été Registrez en la Cour de Parlement depuis l'année 1664.* Dernière edition (Rouen: Besongne, 1721).

43. E.g., letter of 28 sept. 1681. *Correspondance*, ed. M. Langlois. (Paris: Letouzey & Ané, 1935), 2:405. The "mauvaise fée" role (according to Labrousse) is the casting of the Protestant La Beaumelle.

44. Daguesseau, often instanced, is also cited as exemplary by E. Benoist, *Histoire* 4:383.

are among the most likely audience for the kind of book Valincour was writing and seem to be precisely those persons for whom its method and message were intended.

Long before Voltaire wrote to the Swiss pastor Vernes that the *dragonnade* "a fait le malheur du siècle,"[45] Valincour may have been among the "honnêtes gens" scandalized by the dragooning that was only beginning. If Elie Benoist could credibly record, by the end of 1681, that those "honnêtes gens" of the court unanimously condemned Marillac's policy for its treatment to the integrity of men of arms and the violence of the man himself,[46] Valincour's life of Guise may have played some effective part in influencing the direction of that opinion. But whatever the reality of its effectiveness, the *Vie* is an act of faith in the efficacy of history, "wise counselor of princes," by a humanist who makes his history a political act conceived with intellectual probity.

There is no known evidence that in writing or other public utterances Valincour joined Fontenelle in celebration of the Revocation's victory over "heresy," which won Fontenelle the Académie's prize for eloquence in 1685, or that he joined others in the majority of the Republic of Letters that lauded the victory in verse and in prose.[47] Silence is here of course ambiguous. But another may be less so. If Valincour's life of the Connétable de Bourbon and others in the sixteenth-century series of lives announced in 1681 did not appear, the reason may at least in part be due to events after 1681, up to and including the Revocation. After the letter to Du Cange, Valincour entered into other charges and a different career from that announced (and perhaps angled for) by the writer.[48] Although it had been a recommendation to Bossuet in the past, history as Valincour conceived it might in the event not continue to be in the future if he pursued subjects similar to Guise. What may have been a prudent sacrifice could also have ensured integrity. But the historian Valincour wished to be would not abandon the kind of history exemplified in the *Vie* in favor of the merging of historical memoirs and fictional narrative that had become the popular vogue (and is fully represented in the

45. 22 Sept. 1766, *Correspondance*, ed. Besterman, vol. 62 (1961), 232.

46. Benoist, *Histoire* 4:503; see also Orcibal, pp. 73–74, on the general reaction, Louvois and the arrêt of 19 mai.

47. A census is done by Orcibal, pp. 113–14; see also N. Ferrier-Caverivière, *L'Image de Louis XIV*, (Paris: PUF, 1981), 188–92.

48. See above, chap. 1, n. 43 and text.

fictionalized, pseudo-historical life of the Connétable that appeared at the moment Valincour's might have).[49] The refusal of that kind of popular alternative may have been accompanied by another refusal (in keeping with the historical *honnêteté* of 1681): namely, the writing of tracts, of history regularized by power.

Without his having to abandon the writing of history, since it presented itself shortly among his charges with Toulouse, or what was with the *Vie* the beginning of a lifelong concern in the affairs of the Church of France, Valincour's prudence was repayed. Contemporary events, however, in the demands of the Académie, put the historian of the *Vie* to a new testing. It was no secret to anyone that the history of which the Académie was the custodian was a monument to the glory of Louis XIV, already inscribed there as Ludovicus Magnus. The new Academician was expected to weave his part into that "tissu de la gloire."[50] With his acute sense and enjoyment of irony and the active critical spirit of which it was a part, this kind of eloquence might be expected to go against Valincour's grain. When Boileau recommended Valincour to Pontchartrain as the candidate most likely not to offer a dreary panegyric,[51] he doubtless enjoyed a private joke about the personal "difficulties" this accomplishment would entail. But the more obvious and immediate difficulty was to offer Racine, Valincour's mentor, colleague, and friend, a tribute worthy of him and of the Académie he had taken very seriously. For this task there could be no question for Valincour of marking his discourse of reception with a personal irony, as Voltaire later did,[52] which would distance the speaker

49. Anon. [Nicholas Baudot de Juilly], *Histoire du connestable de Bourbon*. Paris: Luynes, 1696, 12°, 324 pp. A pirated printing also in 1696 (La Haye: Foulque).

50. A variant among many, the expression is abbé d'Olivet's describing the history of the Académie. On its sublime mode, there was a good deal of sarcasm, notably Bayle's: "Pourvu qu'il n'y ait que les harangues de Messieurs de l'Académie Françoise, qui soient toujours dans les exclamations, toujours dans les figures les plus outrées, le mal ne sera pas grand." *Lettre à M. L.A.D.C. touchant les comètes* [Cologne (Rotterdam): Marteau, 1682], 245.

51. Letter of 22 Apr. 1699, *Œuvres* (Pléiade ed., 1966), 807. Boileau's own discourse of reception (1 July 1684, ibid., 606–10), while offering the ritually traditional praise, gives as its central development an historical manifesto, principally on the style "sans artifice se contentant de rapporter fidèlement les choses, et avec toute la simplicité de témoins qui déposent," which can be offered, he adds defensively, by an "homme sans fard, et accusé plutost de trop de sincerité."

52. Voltaire's well-known definition of the Académie's discourse as a fixed tripartite ritual of praise, in *Les Lettres philosophiques* [ed. R. Naves, (Paris: Garner, 1962), pp. 139–40], has obscured the serious intentions of reshaping it visible in his discourse of reception (9 May 1746—"un discours utile . . ."), similar to those Valincour will be

from the eloquence, the genre, and their history that the new academician continued.

The Académie of Louis le grand

For the assembled academicians and others, Valincour's discourse of reception on 27 June 1699[53] successfully rose to the highest standards of the Académie's eloquence. The last Academician to be received in the century of the Académie française's foundation, Valincour prudently chose to shape his discourse in all ways in terms of its traditions. In its form he follows the tripartite eulogy already traditional: first, of the academy in its present disposition, with a fittingly humble expression of gratitude for election into the illustrious company (pp. 465–67);[54] centrally, of the deceased academician (467–73); finally, linking all three parts, a peroration exalting the royal protector and host of the Académie and the Republic of Letters it symbolizes (473–76). The *Journal des savants'* report on the events includes a specific compliment to Valincour's success with the form. "There is nothing to be extracted or cut," it commented on 27 July. "The entire piece is to be read and repays the efforts."[55]

Compliments on the style by Jean de La Chapelle, who greeted the new academician officially on behalf of the Académie, are for several reasons worth a rehearing. He greets Valincour, as has been seen,[56] primarily as royal historiographer, and his own discourse properly has much more to say about Racine than his successor. Valincour's opening compliment to the company had invited this order of priorities, in a deft *propositio* that places service to the king at the point of origin of all activity implicated in this academic ritual, past, present, and future. Presenting his own claims, such as they are, on the one hand in terms of the grandeur of the task, the highest to which a man of letters may aspire (". . . l'employ le plus noble qui puisse jamais occuper des gens de lettres"), he emphasizes on the other the arduousness of the work

---

seen (ch. 6) to undertake from 1711. See Karlis Racevskis, *Voltaire and the French Academy* (Chapel Hill: University of North Carolina, 1975), 51–55. Even so, is it only Cicero who "laiss[e] aux petits esprits leur constante gravité, qui n'est que le masque de la médiocrité"? (perhaps a paraphrase of La Rochefoucauld, Maxime 257).

53. *Les Registres de l'Académie française, 1672–1793* (Paris: Firmin-Didot, 1895–1906), 1:350–51.

54. The text quoted is *Recueil . . . de l'Académie française,* 1699 (Paris: Coignard).

55. 3 Aug. 1699 (Amsterdam, 1732), 585.

56. See above, ch. 1, p. 43.

on which he has been the "associate" of the "illustrious writer" who preceded him. For these reasons, since the Académie is zealous in attending to the glory of the king, he is worthy of reception into a company where he may receive the benefits of its occupations (the statutory business of lexicography, grammar, and poetics), in effect continuing his apprenticeship. He is therefore rightly "touché de ce qui fait l'objet de vos exercices, & digne peut-estre d'y d'estre admis, par le désir sincère que j'ay tousjours eu d'en profiter" (466). There can be no question of *replacing* Racine, the speaker continues in his *captatio*; to the contrary, his successor will be happy if the Académie finds in him only the memory of the man with whom he was long attached by an intimate ("étroite") friendship.

The tone that Valincour has established, "natural" on the rhetorician's scale, La Chapelle compliments and further sets off by his own orotundity. His style is more typical of academic eloquence than is that of Valincour which was modeled astutely on Racine's eulogy of Corneille.[57] Here is the period:

> Avec les talents nécessaires, avec la douceur & l'élégance d'un Tite-Live, avec la force & la majesté d'un Thucydide ... Vous avez parlé, & nos doutes se sont dissipez.... Quelle grandeur! quelle majesté! quelle sublimité de pensées et de style éclatèrent dans cet éloge magnifique dont vous nous avez fait souvenir! Il est tel que quand tous les Ouvrages de ces deux Auteurs incomparables seroient perdus, échapé de l'injure des temps, seul il pourroit rendre leurs deux Noms immortels.

In these apostrophes and periphrases and in the ornamental syntax there is a trick of perspective that is central to that of the eloquence of academic discourses. The compliment here is in fact to Racine's eulogy of Corneille, which, in its proper place, Valincour had evoked (and incidentally provided a note to his own "source"/model). Valincour's part, after the seemingly omnipresent honorific parallels with the great figures of antiquity, is reduced to a clause ending one apostrophe ("dont vous nous avez fait souvenir"). But the whole redounds to Valincour since it is his "douceur" and "élégance" that have forcefully

---

57. "Discours" (1685), *Œuvres complètes* (Pléiade ed.), 2:344–47. Nicole Ferrier-Caverivière points out the "ampleur" of this discourse on Louis; but here as in other "discours" there is a modulation of tone levels and not a single, unrelieved line of *amplificatio*. See *L'Image de Louis XIV dans la littérature française de 1660 à 1715* (Paris: PUF, 1981), 209. Rollin in fact cites the discourse as "un modèle achevé de cette Eloquence noble & sublime, & en même tems naturelle et sans affectation." *De la manière d'enseigner et d'étudier les Belles-Lettres* (Leyden, 1759), 96.

summoned up for La Chapelle and other auditors Racine's "grandeur," "majesté," "sublimité." These three affects are the goal of all Academicians' eloquence; they are similarly requisite for that of the royal history, whose style Valincour explicitly celebrates as it is embodied in Racine's historical writing: "un stile simple & sans fard . . . où la vérité toute pure sera encore plus merveilleuse que la fiction mesme soustenuë de tous les ornemens de la Poësie" (473). Striving for this, all Academicians, Valincour included, work, in the closings of their discourses, an arabesque in perspective. This is the requisite blaze of glory, tribute in the sublime mode, to the sovereign. However grand, even majestic, the career of the deceased Academician, that which follows its representation has also preceded it. LOUIS (regularly in raised type)—his glory, of presence, patronage, example . . .—has allowed it to flourish. La Chapelle's compliment then not only crowns a successful performance of academic eloquence in the genre; it also acknowledges positively the capability of the official historian.

In his tribute of friendship to Racine, Valincour tailors his chronology of Racine's career to accommodate it and the qualities it displays, by gradation and transition, to his final development on Louis. Racine's appointment as royal historiographer and its fruits as described are the last terms in the chronological outline, both an apotheosis and a "conversion" to the "emploi" of historian (from the "métier" of playwright).[58] This moment is directly preceded by a celebration of the biblical plays, separated from the earlier ones on secular themes, the triumphs—*Andromaque, Mithridate, Britannicus, Iphigénie, Phèdre*[59]— through which Racine's "graces sublimes et touchantes" gained an admiration equaling that for Corneille. The first part of Valincour's account, and its evocation of genius and education (especially in Greek)—two in the trinity of qualities of the perfect poet[60]—concludes

58. Bossuet in *Maximes et Réflexions sur la comédie* had already spoken of conversion. By 1677, Racine himself spoke of his earlier plays in terms of God's grace leaving him "peu sensible au bien et au mal qu'on en peut dire." See R. Picard, *La Carrière de Jean Racine* (Paris: Gallimard, 1961), 292–93, 491.

59. Valincour is re-affirming an already existing canon (and at the same time pointing to what is still in the theatre). Omissions of any doubtful successes are expected except perhaps for *Bérénice*. Its omission probably responds to Bossuet's emphasis on "conversion" to "sujets plus dignes" after *Bérénice*.

60. The idealized perfect poet is especially particularized by youthful Hellenic enthusiasm evoked poetically—"charmé des beautés . . . seul dans un bois"—that will later become explicitly a tribute to Port-Royal. "Qui n'a pas présent à l'esprit cette poétique image," Paul Mesnard remarked quoting Valincour, (*Œuvres de Racine*, GELF ed.), 1:20.

with this moment of "renonciation des Muses profanes" (470), signifying spiritual progress. Yoked with the historical "conversion," the
superior "grace" of this writing overflows into the decision/"conversion" to the way of the special history with which Racine was charged.
Discipline, the third attribute of the perfect writer, representing the
"second part" of the career, has, in what follows, heightened multiple
significance. This complex moment of transition fully justifies La
Chapelle's praise, as the ascending movement of the discourse, by
theme as well as device, reaches for representation of the moment and
beyond it ultimately toward the final section of peroration.

> Mais lorsque renonçant aux Muses prophanes, il consacra ses Vers à des
> objets plus dignes de lui, guidé par des conseils[61] & par des ordres que la
> sagesse mesme avoüeroit pour les siens, quels miracles ne produisit-il pas
> encore?
>
> Quelle sublimité dans ses Cantiques, quelle magnificence dans Esther &
> dans Athalie, pieces égales ou mesme superieures à tout ce qu'il a fait de plus
> achevé, & dignes par tout, autant que des paroles humaines le peuvent estre,
> de la Majesté du Dieu dont il parle, & dont il estoit si penetré!
>
> En effet, tous ceux qui l'ont connu sçavent qu'il avoit une pieté tres-solide
> & tres-sincere, & c'estoit comme l'ame & le fondement de toutes les vertus.
> (470)

Within this representation, generally significant as a search for
perfection, Valincour's parallel of Corneille and Racine remains historical, though he exhibits what one exigent Racinian scholar, Eugène
Vinaver,[62] has called "fine sagacity" in the critical focus of his remarks.
An admirer of both, Valincour awards the "first prize" to neither
and is content to juxtapose the historical moments when the specific
geniuses of both tragic playwrights imposed themselves. It was a new
era in the history of the French theatre when Corneille's "grandeur
Romaine" gave to the stage "figures plus grandes que le naturel, mais
nobles, hardies, admirables dans toutes leurs proportions" (468–69);
and spectators seemed as though swept away, "n'avoir plus d'âme que
pour admirer la richesse de ses expressions, la noblesse de ses senti-

---

61. If R. Picard has effectively destroyed the myth of a "conversion" in 1677 (loc.
cit., 307–12, in résumé), he gave little attention to direct "conseils" on retirement; one
would like to know to whose advice Valincour alludes.

62. *Racine and Poetic Tragedy* (Manchester: Manchester University Press, 1955), 27.
"New roads" is Vinaver's phrase for Valincour's perception, in effect the Hellenic
inspiration, or what W. G. Moore once called the "recovery of tragedy"—"not tragedy
itself so much as a vehicle for tragedy: the tragic style, the tragic tension, the concentration. ... " *French Classical Literature: An Essay* (Oxford: Clarendon, 1961), 70.

ments, & la maniere imperieuse dont il manioit la raison humaine"
(469). New too was the moment when Racine "ne songea qu'à se faire
des routes nouvelles." The insistence on Racine's "new ways," and the
description of his recovery of the tragic form and emotion Aristotle
discussed in the *Poetics*, like the qualities of the perfect poet that Racine
exemplifies, remain articulated by generalization and idealization. But
unlike some earlier and later contributors to the proliferating genre of
parallels of the two great playwrights, Valincour avoids the simplifi-
cation for both of representing Corneille as "precursor" or Racine
explicitly as the agent of progress in the art of tragedy who brings it
to perfection.[63] Valincour sought to harmonize his own parallel on the
one hand with Racine's tribute to Corneille, on the other, with La
Bruyère's more famous parallel, against which Racine evoked to the
Académie—like Corneille's *grandeur romaine*—strikes some familiar
resonances.[64] Thanks to a "public équitable," which can admire both,
the French theater is "au comble de sa gloire" and is now entitled to
the topos of final honor in the history of the theater, comparison
with the age of Sophocles and Euripides, both different and both
incomparable, Valincour again stresses. It was only much later in the
privacy of a letter to d'Olivet, not well received when made public,
that Valincour would trouble any of these harmonizations.[65] They may
adapt and idealize, but they have not sacrificed the independent critical
spirit of the younger critic. Here at length is the historian:

Monsieur Racine entra, pour ainsi dire, dans leur coeur & s'en rendit le
maistre, il y excita ce trouble agreable qui nous fait prendre un veritable
interest à tous les évenements d'une fable que l'on represente devant nous; il
les remplit de cette terreur & de cette pitié, qui selon Aristote, sont les
veritables passions que doit produire la tragedie: il les arracha ces larmes qui
sont le plaisir de ceux qui les répandent, & peignant la nature moins superbe
peut-estre & moins magnifique, mais aussi plus vraye & plus sensible, il leur
apprit à plaindre leurs propres passions & leur propres foiblesses, dans celles
des personnages qu'il fit paroistre à leurs yeux.
Alors le Public équitable, sans cesser d'admirer la grandeur majestueuse

63. The tendency of eighteenth-century criticism fixed by Schlegel. See Robert J.
Nelson, *Corneille and Racine; Parallels and Contrasts* (Englewood Cliffs: Prentice-Hall,
1962), v–vi.
64. Valincour attributes to Racine's tragedies (see next quotation) the Aristotelian
tragic emotion, which La Bruyère had held to constitute the common ground of all
tragedy. Roman grandeur is, as Corneille's "pathétique du héros," something else for
Valincour (who later will be much preoccupied with the concept of catharsis).
65. See below, chap. 8, pp. 290–92.

du fameux Corneille, commença d'admirer aussi les graces sublimes & touchantes de l'illustre Racine.

Alors le Theatre François se vit au comble de sa gloire, & n'eut plus de sujet de porter envie au fameux Theatre d'Athenes florissante: c'est ainsi que Sophocle & Euripide, tous deux incomparables & tous deux tres-differens dans leur genre d'écrire, firent en leur temps l'honneur & l'admiration de la sçavante Grece. (469)

It is not the expected link of this moment of glory to Louis's illustrious patronage that forms the transition to Valincour's set-piece of final sublimity. Piety, which has been coupled with proper historical style, forms the link. Piety was much the order of the year, figuring in the topics set for the Académie's prizes both in eloquence and in poetry. Valincour shrewdly chose to elaborate on the subject set for the prize for eloquence: "Sur la piété du Roy & sur l'attention qu'il a eue aux interests de la Religion dans le dernier traité de paix." The peace is that established by the Treaty of Ryswyck, with special attention to its article on religion; the history, one may fear, is to be "local," an unhappy compromise for the historian of 1681 who had struggled with historical perspective, and indeed with piety. Idealization and willful rhetorical harmonization again tailor somewhat the narration of facts, generally only sketched for an audience that had no need for precise designations. But once again the story, as in 1681, is not so simply told. Like the modified humanist devices used to his own ends in the life of Guise, the demands of the new discourse and its eloquence are accommodated to Valincour's own views, rather than the contrary that might appear to be true.

The historian who had closed his life of Guise with an exhortation to the sovereign for peace, and had celebrated its qualities in different realms in his verse could have few difficulties with that peace, restored by the treaty after ten years of war. Valincour evokes that war as a struggle that pitted France against an alliance that brought together practically the whole of Europe. Keenly aware of the possibilities for shifts of power; aware as well of the precariousness of the Church,[66] the new Academician praises Louis's aggressive policy, which in 1687 led to frontier fortifications and the following year to invasion of Germany. He celebrates a defensive action, where others saw aggression deriving from "visions of a universal empire with a Bourbon

66. The signing of the League of Augsburg, of course, in July 1686, but also the anathema launched against the king and his ministers by Innocent XI in November 1687.

prince crowned in Madrid, Paris, and Frankfort." James II for one saw an infringement of the Treaty of Nymwegen.[67] The justified action, Valincour maintains, was subject to cessation whenever the League would agree to mediate a new treaty within the framework of existing ones. The word "Ligue," combining with the context of troubled mediation, seems here enough to raise old fears in the historian who had long meditated on the sixteenth century. Valincour speaks forcefully to an opinion, concentrated in the Académie, that had favored Louis's entry into the war and with him had lauded French courage at Philippsburg as well as the real, if temporary, victories of Tourville in the Channel and Catinat at Staffarde (which Valincour had doubtless followed carefully with Toulouse). The new Academician's rhetorical display resembles the "feux d'artifice" that after the capitulation of Mons and Nice in April of 1691 had "portrayed the figure of Hercules on a mountain with the League of Augsburg buried under an avalanche."[68] As in that display Valincour keeps the king ever illuminated:

Le Roy anime tout, soutient tout, par son courage & par sa prudence, tantost tranquille au milieu de son Royaume, il fait sentir sa force à ses Ennemis sur toutes les frontières et jusques dans leur propre pays; tantost à la teste de ses Armées, il s'expose à tous les dangers comme le moindre de ses Soldats, & voit blesser à ses costez un jeune Prince, qui tout occupé d'un si grand exemple ne s'apperçois pas luy-mesme de sa blessure. Ainsi le fills de Jupiter estoit un Héros dès le berceau. (475)

The final ornament aside, it is evident here that Valincour's eloquence has drawn in several important ways on his own experience, which may add persuasiveness for those who could hear its particular individual authority. On the one hand, this development is a transformation of Valincour's own tribute to the thoroughness that characterized Guise's military genius and emblematized his heroic command. After the death of Louvois, as the Academicians had seen, the king had in fact assumed responsibilities for the overall direction of the war. On the other hand, as many of his audience knew, Valincour had been able to observe directly some of the war of which he spoke, thus being

---

67. See John Wolf, *Louis XIV* (New York: Norton, 1968), 440–41, 444 and n. 19.

68. "Explication du feu d'artifice dressé devant l'Hôtel de Ville . . . le 25 avril 1691" (Paris, 1691). Cited by J. Wolf, loc. cit., 461; a similar display for 1697, ibid., p. 487. It is, however, La Chappelle's rhetoric in 1699 that has been signaled as a part of the fixing of the king's "corps imaginaire" (indeed "astral body") for the collective consciousness and at the same time "le grand siècle." See J.-M. Apostolidès, *Le Roi-machine* (Paris: Minuit, 1981), 145.

himself the "eye-witness" the historian had characteristically sought in his earlier history. During the years 1690–91, as has been seen,[69] he had accompanied Toulouse, and the royal historians, to observe the king's actions. At home too, he had observed what is characterized as the king's "tranquillité si difficile à conserver" in facing "stérilité imprévue," an evident allusion to the bad harvest and economic disorders of 1693, which Louis and his coordinated ministers had dealt with in a variety of new ways.[70] If he had not heard personally the king's expressed desire for a treaty, he had heard it repeated, if nowhere else than in its grandiloquent and providential articulation that opened the king's letter to the Congress of Ryswyck. That desire was thwarted, the Academician asserts, by the Spanish in 1696, when Spain's "ancienne jalousie de valeur, plus forte que la haine se réveille" (476). As this passion stalls the machinery of reasoned process, the narrative mapping is familiar from the life of Guise. And before the happy denouement, brought about by the king, the audience is left suspended there as "toute l'Europe suspendue attend avec frayeur le succès d'une si grande entreprise."

In the denouement of peace, Valincour enters rhetorically once more into public celebration. Louis XIV had written to the archbishop of Paris a letter stating that "God, favorable to the designs that He has always inspired in me, has opened the eyes of the allied powers ... disabused of their false hopes, and touched by their veritable evils." Hercules was once again in the sky, standing triumphant over the League, this time with religion depicted at his side. The historian who had managed to use Corneille's dramaturgy in his dramatization of Guise's life, as he fulfills the highest academic ideal—"célébrer les actions immortelles de vostre auguste Protecteur"—he reminds the audience, seems to move from heroic testing like Horace's to the triumph of Auguste.

C'est ainsi que toute la Chrestienté voit succéder un calme heureux à cette guerre effroyable, dont les plus habiles Politiques ne pouvoient prévoir la fin:

69. A letter from Le Peletier de Souzy to Le Bret, exactly on 24 Apr. 1691, refers to Valincour's return from Mons, thus in time for the "feux d'artifice." (B.N. MS. fon. fr. 8840, p. 38.)

70. Louis XIV's central place in coordination of command after Louvois's death and at home have been positively refocused by François Bluche, as have been victories previously often considered only "temporary." See *Louis XIV*, pp. 645, 651–56, 660–62, 675–80, 682, 724–27. Consequently, a revision is due of the consideration of Academic language, considered too quickly perhaps as pure topoi; e.g., the heroic presence of

& c'est pour offrir à Dieu des fruits dignes d'une Paix qui est elle-mesme le fruit de tant de miracles, que le Roy n'est occupé jour & nuit que du soin d'augmenter le culte des Autels, de procurer le repos & l'abondance à ses Peuples, & *d'affermir de plus en plus la véritable Religion* dans son Royaume, par son exemple & *par son autorité.* (477)

Even fifteen years after the Revocation, this message sounds at best ambivalent (in the words I have emphasized). But what was heard in the Académie is complex, different in its range of signification from the simple meaning heard perhaps by a later reader unfamiliar with the *Actes et mémoires des négociations de la paix de Riswick* (in a Dutch printing that had not yet reached France at the moment of Valincour's discourse).[71] Two of the ambassadors to the Congress (Callières and the comte de Crécy) were in the audience, and others like Bossuet with them knew a complex account of what had transpired at Ryswyck concerning the king's piety. Valincour had followed the negotiations, indirectly with Toulouse, who was involved by the treaty's stipulations concerning the normalization of commercial shipping specifically in his domain, perhaps in part directly.[72] Thus both he and a significant part of his audience may have known what was published concerning the principal remonstrances on religion made in October 1698 through the imperial ambassador at The Hague.[73] It had been demanded of the French ambassador that an explicit statement be made ensuring that Protestants in lands newly acquired by France be allowed to retain their religion and not be forced to conversion. Allowing for this, and in fact for similar treatment of Huguenot sailors captured on British ships,[74] was a triumph of diplomacy by Valincour's friends which, as it were, succeeded in having things both ways. According to the published report, the French ambassador "n'y accorda que la liberté

---

the king listed predominantly with other features of "pièces de circonstance" by N. Ferrier-Caverivière, op. cit., pp. 209 and passim, pp. 208–12.

71. 4 vols. Amsterdam: A Moetjens, 1699.

72. Toulouse, and Valincour in his entourage, were visitors to the deliberations in 1697. See above, chap. 1, n. 60 and text.

73. *Actes et mémoires*, 3:382: "En vertu du 3 Article de ladite capitulation [Sept. 1681], ils [the Strasbourgeois] jouiront à l'avenir comme auparavant de la liberté de conscience, & que la France leur laissera le libre exercice de la Religion suivant la Confession d'Augsbourg, avec le pouvoir de disposer librement de leurs biens Ecclésiastiques, & des revenus qui y sont annexez."

74. Ibid., 3:130–53: "Traité de commerce, navigation et marine" (20 Sept. 1697), with the Formulaire des passeports and Formulaire de l'acte contenant le serment. Signé Loüis, comte de Toulouse, p. 173: "Protestants françois, pris sur des vaisseaux anglois, les François promettent de les relâcher."

de retraite que nous avions demandée, & une promesse de bouche qu'on n'y feroit *aucune violence* dans les affaires de Religion, & rejetta généralement tout ce sembloit faire la moindre restriction."[75] To ask for more, the ambassador retorted (and Valincour might well agree), was hair-splitting ("vouloir séparer un cheveu en quatre parties").

To Valincour this promise must have seemed an enormous progress of and victory for reason, rational problem solving fully justifying his private meaning in lauding the king's piety. In the last instance, that celebration is not much different for him from the victory the Swedish court found in the peace, from its special angle a "signal triumph of pacific diplomacy."[76] To see Valincour as endorsing violence, either in the past or to come (in the Spanish Succession question), is to rob him of a part of the success of his first performance with the Académie's rhetoric. For the uninformed who read him, however, an endorsement of violence could be heard, just as a compromise with the principles of the historian of 1681 can be interpreted in the idealization that at forty-six catches the "honnête homme" in a shift corresponding to that of the term itself: from "homme de probité" to stylist.[77] It may be no accident that this specific example of academic high style is never duplicated in Valincour's subsequent discourses. From their future modifications of his eloquence, it may become possible to see that with time the royal historiographer will become hesitant, if not sceptical, about "official" history—"d'un stile simple et sans fard, où la vérité toute pure sera"—beyond this privileged place, which, being the "Sanctuaire des muses," was its sanctuary.

75. Ibid., 4:333.

76. R. N. Bain, "Charles XII and the Great Northern War." *The Cambridge Modern History* (New York: Macmillan, 1908), 5:584.

77. Although the theme of Louis XIV's piety is central and some rhetorical features may seem to be harbingers, Valincour's discourse seems in my reading only super-ficially a part of the development to come of courtiers' "pièces de circonstance" performed around the theme of piety traced by N. Ferrier-Caverivière. Loc. cit., pp. 232–37.

Part III

The Shape of a Career

Chapter 5

The King's Servant (1701–1726)

In the summer of 1701, Valincour wrote to Noailles that he had set aside three hours a day for his historiographical tasks.[1] And in the autumn quarter he participated regularly in the working sessions of the Académie. Service for and with Toulouse, however, often interrupted the pleasures and responsibilities of the historiographer and Academician in the first decade of the new century. Toulouse's activities again expanded and grew more complex. Those of his secretary, by choice as well as necessity, kept pace and brought adventure and enterprise into the career of the man who had already begun to regret the loss of the quiet days he had planned to pass in his new house at St. Cloud.[2]

In the new war, Toulouse had the chance to command, which he eagerly sought and accepted. He was made a commander of the Spanish fleet by Philippe V and of the galleys of France by Louis in May of 1702. The secretary was dispatched to Toulon to make preparations, which proved to be lengthy, for the admiral's maiden voyage. They then set sail together on the Foudroyant at the head of six vessels. Renaudot informed Noailles that Valincour, once freed from "longues despeches,"[3] had written from Malazzo, where the fleet had stopped (after calling at Rome). "He is so delighted with the ceremonial at Palermo," Renaudot then reports, "that he writes of nothing else save it and the extravagance of Avignon."[4] The traveler

1. Letter of 27 June 1701, *RHLF* 10 (1903), 672.
2. So quoted by J. -B. Racine, letter of 24 Aug. 1700, *MLN* 54 (1939), 179.
3. Renaudot, letter of 4 Sept. 1702 to Noailles, *RHLF* 7 (1900), 636.
4. 14 Sept. 1702, *RHLF* 7 (1900), 637. Renaudot is tantalizing in his allusiveness; according to Saint-Simon, *Mémoires* (Truc ed., 2:72), Toulouse was extravagantly received.

obviously had an eye for ritual and protocol, which was already well trained and as keen in spotting its "ridicule" as in appreciating its beauty. From Malazzo he accompanied the comte on to Messina.[5] In all, it was seven months before Valincour reappeared in the Académie, for the reception in December of the duc de Coislin.

From July 1703 through January of 1704, Valincour was again posted to Toulon and charged with still slower preparations, lasting from July until November,[6] for Toulouse's first battle command. There was enough time for him to exchange letters with Bossuet on biblical prophecy that amount in themselves to a small treatise. And he had the equanimity to do so: "J'y attends l'ordre pour mon départ, sans le désirer ni le craindre,"[7] he wrote phlegmatically, attending to business but allowing his mind some time elsewhere. Toulouse's Mediterranean excursion with the maréchal de Cœuvres (d'Estrées) was prepared with, as Saint-Simon put it, the comte commanding the maréchal, as admiral not as bastard of France, but nonetheless "soumis à son conseil."[8] The waiting was in vain. As Valincour foresaw, no encounter with the Anglo-Dutch fleet commanded by Shovell occurred.

The following summer more delays ensued. Two months were spent at Brest for the assemblage of the fleet before setting sail for Toulon. Valincour sent an account of the voyage to Noailles. It is not eloquent, he admits, but it is "exacte et sincère" and in that will be valuable as a corrective to other relations already in circulation. Confidentiality of information is requested; trust need not be, since the writer is sure that Noailles does him "l'honneur de me croire sur ma parole." Also revealed are the ordinary obstacles that attended the admiral and, more importantly, his decisiveness and largesse in dealing with them. To accomplish the armament, Toulouse financed it himself, at high cost. The secretary allows himself some excitement now, only slightly dampened by the final report of another delay.

Monseigneur le comte m'ordonne de vous dire que sans l'embarras extrême où il est pour l'armement que l'on fait ici, il vous aurait écrit luy-mesme, mais qu'il s'en remet à ce que j'ai l'honneur de vous mander. Nous devions trouver icy quinze vaisseaux armés pour ressortir aussitôt. Il n'y en a pas un de prest: on dit que c'est manque d'argent. Et afin d'en trouver, s'il est possible,

5. 24 Sept. 1702. Ibid.
6. Renaudot to Noailles, letters of 6 July and 22 Aug. 1703, *RHLF* 7 (1900), 642, 644.
7. 5 June 1703, *RHLF* 10 (1903), 676.
8. *Mémoires* (Truc ed.), 2:262.

Monseigneur le comte de Toulouse a envoyé l'ordre d'emprunter cent mille escus à Marseille sur ses billets. Dès que nous serons en estat de ressortir, nous ne perdrons pas un moment de tems; et si nous trouvons les ennemis, il y aura de la poudre bruslée de part et d'autre. Je prévois que nous serons icy assés longtemps pour que j'y puisse recevoir votre réponse.[9]

Monseigneur le comte directs me to tell you that he would himself have written you were it not for the confusion about armament here, but he entrusts me with the honor of informing you about it. We were to find fifteen vessels armed for immediate departure. There is not one ready, it is said for want of money. Monseigneur le comte, to find some if possible, sent orders to borrow 100,000 écus in Marseilles on his notes. As soon as we are in order for departure, we won't lose a minute; and if we face the enemy, there will be some powder burnt on both sides. I foresee that we will be here long enough to receive your answer to this letter.

Having left Brest on 6 May, the fleet of twenty-three ships arrived at Cadiz on the twenty-fifth. After discharging troops and munitions, it proceeded into the Mediterranean and menaced the English vessels commanded by Rooke drawn up for an assault on Barcelona. Taking advantage of their dispersal and favorable winds, Toulouse adroitly commanded an escape from their pursuit and landed his ships at Toulon (where he was to meet Duquesne). With forty-nine ships of the line and accompanying galleys, he embarked on 24 August to pursue the enemy. Met at Malaga, and outnumbering him, the British fleet gave fight an entire day without breaking the French line, suffering the heavy loss of 3,000 men and two ships, then was forced to fall back to Gibralter. Saint-Simon spoke for general opinion when he praised Toulouse's command, especially for its "calm courage" and the resulting decisive tactical skill.[10] Louis's approval was followed by Philippe's bestowal upon Toulouse of the *Toison d'or*. Rewards to the secretary were of course less grand and more indirect. While in the company of his master, Valincour had been wounded at Malaga, and that highly publicized wound[11] became a new, dramatic proof of the devotion of his service, particularly impressive in the Republic of Letters. He may too have felt a special gratification when after Malaga

9. 4 June 1704, *RHLF* 10 (1903), 677–78.
10. On Malaga see Charles de La Roncière, *Histoire de la marine française* (Paris: Plon, 1932), 6:349–64; Saint-Simon, 2:368–69.
11. Public proclamations abroad: e.g., "A Relation of the Sea-Fight near Malaga on 24th August, 1704. N.S. as it was writ from on Board the French Fleet" (Beinecke Library B0108.063). See also Piganiol de la Force to Villemont, letter of 28 Aug. 1704, cited by Jal, *Dictionnaire*, p. 970.

a frigate was named "The Valincour." And it was doubtless with some sense of reward as well as relief that he heard the decision permitting him to remain at home during the campaign of 1706, thereby sparing him the rendez-vous with Admiral Leake's forces that proved to be Toulouse's last (and less successful) command.

Valincour does not figure in the detailed description of Toulouse's staff for the Italian excursion recorded in the annual register of the king's gifts.[12] But his place is again marked in the plan remaining in Toulouse's papers for the admiral's "tables" aboard the Foudroyant in July of 1702.[13] All in all there were 243 persons to be victualed, including a "table de la musique" of fifteen musicians (with a "Couperin au clavecin"), four chaplains, twelve pages, and twenty-three guards of S.A.S. The galley staff included a chef borrowed from Mme de Montespan. There was a separate table for the secretaries, but Valincour was seated at the admiral's, the only man of the eleven there who was a non-officer.[14] He himself had two *commis* in addition to a valet. Conversation at the admiral's table and the naval excursion generally became a special fund of experience for Valincour. It was later tapped by the Academician in his discourse of 1711. When the secretary of the comte de Toulouse evoked for the Académie a high ideal of service embodied by the comte d'Estrées, he was acknowledged to know whereof he spoke and was himself associated by his audience with that ideal of "service of letters" he represented to them. And more personally, but with similar persuasiveness since it gained him an invitation to Rome from Cardinal Gualterio, Valincour nostalgically invoked the sights and conversations of his all too brief stay in Rome.[15]

Enterprises at home followed adventures abroad. Armed with the admiral's first successes, Valincour mounted and stepped up a campaign on behalf of the admiral's rights and incidentally the prerogatives of

12. B. N. MS. fon. fr. 7666, p. 42. A short account is given of the Italian voyage. D'O, *chef d'escadre* was detached (perhaps accompanied by Valincour) to compliment the pope. At Palermo, greetings were extended by the viceroy of Sicily, Cardinal del Giudice. After arrival at Messina (20 Aug.), the *bailli de Lorraine* was sent to compliment the *grand maître de Malte*. Toulouse returned to court on 6 November.

13. A.N. 300 API: 90. A cahier of 10 pp.: "Etat des personnes qui composent les tables de S.A.S. Monseigneur Lamiral abord le Foudroiant le 1er juillet 1702." Valincour figures on p. 11.

14. Also listed besides d'Estrées and D'O are "Relingues [*lieutenant général*]; D'Aubo, *intendant;* St. Pierre, *capitaine;* Beaujeu, *capitaine et commandant des gardes;* le chevalier de Cominge; La Longuere and E. [name erased], *ingénieurs.*"

15. See below, chap. 8, n. 10 and text.

his own charge. Combined with the usual work of the councils, these efforts took a year and a half to reach their conclusion if not their goals. The decree of the council of 9 March 1695, which had restored proper functioning to the *conseil des prises* had maintained the secretary—Valincour—as recorder (*greffier*) and it was as such, with consultative but not deliberative voice in the council's decisions, that he countersigned and stamped as the admiral's ordonnances. By a decree of 13 August 1707, the secretary regained the deliberative voice his predecessors had had before the reforms of 1669;[16] no doubt Valincour felt, as he did when requesting Toulouse for the reinstatement of privileges in 1689, that this restitution was a matter of the "honor of the charge." Although the minister Pontchartrain for his part may have been annoyed with this measure, it was in fact part of a settlement with the minister after an extended series of procedural confrontations that had elicited more than his impatience.

Late in 1703, then concertedly in 1704, Toulouse himself[17] challenged the minister's right to convey (and indeed to speak for and thereby interpret) "orders" from the king that should come directly from him to the admiral by *lettres de cachet*. The admiral in no manner claimed autonomy from the king's justice but, in a test case at Toulon in 1707, sought to affirm the principle that his own justice could be exercised where he was—that prizes in fact could be judged by him in ports or on ship without convening the *conseil des prises*. Advised against a power that seemed to the minister a reversion to that of the old masters of navigation, which the administrative reform of 1669 had suppressed and reassigned, the king acceded and charged Henri Daguesseau with the decree of 1707, which maintained the minister and the constituted council as the intermediary and venue of the admiral's judgments/ justice.[18] The secretary may have won for his charge a limited victory. The admiral had not. The disillusion he suffered, it would seem, together with ill health (Toulouse was afflicted by the stone), began to figure in his decision later taken to withdraw from active service as admiral and/or to curtail his ambitions. That decision was much

16. See Sylvain Lebeau, ed., *Nouveau code des prises, ou recueil des édits, déclarations, lettres patentes sur la course et l'administration des prises depuis 1400 jusqu'à présent* (Paris: Imprimerie de la République, An VII–IX), 1:49 (lettres-patentes for 1695); 1:337 (for 1707).

17. A.N. Archives de la Marine, C⁴ 230, no. 1: "Mémoire présenté par le comte de Toulouse, en 1704, au sujet du conseil des prises"; also F²20, p. 199: Letter of Pontchartrain to Toulouse, 19 Sept. 1703.

18. See Auguste Dumas, "Le Conseil des prises," p. 255.

regretted by Saint-Simon, who subsequently saw Pontchartrain as Toulouse's personal enemy and his self-interest as responsible for nipping in the bud a career as advantageous to the realm as it was promising for the commander of 1704.[19] There were henceforth no hard feelings between Valincour and Daguesseau. But with Pontchartrain it was another story.

Whatever the limited triumph, Valincour's courage of his convictions in 1707 put him at risk. The confrontation with Pontchartrain had become a subject of gossip and concern with others beyond administrative circles besides Saint-Simon. Mme de Maintenon wrote to Noailles that she feared (as she later would) for Valincour caught between "two masters,"[20] then seemingly intervened with the king to offset whatever report was given to him in 1707 by the minister. Valincour made a special point of thanking her a last time for that intervention needed at a moment when he—never a servant of two masters—imagined "ma ruine totale" for "having too strongly maintained the interests of the prince to whom I am attached."[21] Earlier in the decade, about the time he amused Mme de Saint-Géran by singing for their suppers at Mme de Maintenon's banquet for the Bourgognes, Valincour had also sought her aid (through Noailles)[22] in placing his brother Héricourt.

Bénigne d'Héricourt, after "serving twenty-two years under four controllers" with "probité et capacité"[23] (evidently his own definition of the "honnête homme" defined through service to king and realm), had not lost his position with the resignation of Claude Le Peletier

---

19. *Mémoires* (Truc ed.) 2:410–11: "La peur qu'il eut de succomber sous la gloire ou sous la vengeance d'un amiral fils du roi le détermina à perdre lui-même la marine." The composite portrait of Pontchartrain is one of Saint-Simon's most venomous and subject to emendation from recent revisionist studies of his considerable administrative abilities.

20. Quoted by Auguste Geoffroy, *Madame de Maintenon d'après sa correspondance authentique* (Paris· Hachette, 1887), 2:37.

21. Letter of 4 Sept. 1715, *Mémoires et lettres de Mme de Maintenon* (Maestrich: Dufour et Roux, 1789), 8:163–64.

22. Noailles had married Mme de Maintenon's niece Françoise d'Aubigné in Toulouse's apartments in 1698. Valincour vividly evokes favor seeking from Mme de Maintenon on 27 June 1701, then on 16 August his 7:00 a.m. rendez-vous with her that ironically ended in her asking him a favor for Fathers Tiberge and Brisacier, of the Missions étrangères, seeking 1,000 liv. from the Etats de Bretagne. See *RHLF* 10 (1903), 671–73.

23. Letter of 27 June 1701, ibid., p. 673. On Héricourt, see chap. 1, nn. 4, 33 and text.

from the controller-general's office in 1689. As might be expected from his personal ties with Pontchartrain, he remained until Louis de Pontchartrain left the department. Whether he did not wish to remain there, after Chamillart's arrival, or was not welcome, by 1701 he was looking elsewhere. It was Toulouse who profited from the occasion and took on Héricourt as a second to his brother at the moment of Valincour's posting to Toulon, with the prospect of his continuing absences from the household while in the comte's entourage.[24] After 1704, Héricourt remained, as his unfailing signatures in the minutes of the household council beside his brother's thereafter attest. As was so often the case with Toulouse's staff, whose loyalty the comte seems to have inspired, Héricourt remained for his lifetime (and it was he who noted Valincour's successor's name in the registers in 1730). His name remains also in a plan of Toulouse's household for 1709 that offers a striking comparison with the more modest "project" of 1693 and the added information of the "gages" and "pensions" of his retainers, including the household council.[25]

In 1709, Toulouse's establishment was five times what it had been in 1693. The lands and residences themselves demanded extended attention. Upkeep, renovations, sometimes just overseers, were needed for the duchy of Penthièvre and lands held from Albert and Damville; the residences at Versailles, Marly, and Fontainebleau, as well as a concierge at Saint-Germain; and most costly of all (at 29,378 liv. 16s.8d.) the château at Rambouillet, where the king was to be entertained in 1712.[26] Now *grand veneur* of France, Toulouse's expenses for the *vénerie* and its studfarm weighed in at 56,320 liv. 5s. per annum (with 20,600 livres for the kennels and 10,880 livres for uniforms provided by the comte for the nineteen *seigneurs de la vénerie*). All in all, 225 horses (at a cost of 1,917 liv. 16s.8d. each) required some sixty-one grooms. In the total expenses of 625,209 liv. 1s.8d. the stables at 188,421 liv. 19s.2d. outdistanced "chambre et bouche," the former including wardrobe, "menus plaisirs" (an entry of 50,000 livres that is of course un-itemized), and gratifications, given the respective subtotals of 112,228 liv. 16s.8d.

24. Valincour refers to "une seconde charge de Secrétaire des commandements" in his circular letter (29 Jan. 1703) to the *officiers des amirautés* joined with Héricourt's provisions. (Bibliothèque de La Rochelle MS. 73, no. 14.)

25. A. N. 300 API: 89: "Etat general de la maison de S.A.S. Monseigneur le comte de Toulouse, année 1709."

26. The terre de Rambouillet was purchased in 1705 and later expanded. See Saint-Simon, 2:509; 4:82–83.

and 99,415 liv. 15s. If artists or paintings, musicians, men of letters, or books were pensioned or purchased they must have figured among these "menus plaisirs" (or under "furnishings"), since there are no line items elsewhere for them.

The total annual expense for the council of 34,150 livres (24,550 livres gages, 9,600 livres pensions), although approached by kennel expenses and far below "menus plaisirs," is relatively important within the overall budget and in size. It figures ninth in categories, followed only by "external pensions" at 20,540 livres (a mixed matter of indemnities as well as charitable benefactions).[27] In the nature of such things, the staff needed elsewhere outnumbered the enlarged household council; but it seems after 1693 to have grown less even proportionately than other departments. Including three "enfants de cuisine," there were, for example, thirty-two in the kitchen staff under the *contrôleur de la bouche*, Choquet (2,104 liv. 10s.), and the head chef Pandoix (836 livres); twenty-five valets de chambre under the premier valet Valentin (1,347 liv. 10s.); sixteen valets de pieds, with fifteen more for the *vénerie;* twelve pages under the governor M. Piganiol (1,712 liv. 10s.), with two valets and a staff of masters (for arms, design, geography, mathematics, and dance); a modest honor guard of five, and two "trompettes" as well as Gilles de Hautefort (5,000 livres) as *premier écuyer* and the *seigneurs de la vénerie.* An approximate total, excluding the caretakers in Brittany, is some 350 persons directly in service to Toulouse.

The council of 1709, which probably was similarly constituted throughout the war years, with secretaries numbers seventeen persons. Its constitution suggests that Toulouse believed in the assistance of a few trusted and long tried men. Brossard continues long service as treasurer with the assistance of two *commis.* Héricourt and he both have wages of 6,000 livres. Benoise, listed in 1714 as *conseiller d'honneur au Parlement,* another long-serving member has remuneration of 4,000 livres in pension. Chardon, *avocat,* serves with two law clerks (all at 1,150 livres). Louvet is charged with the archives (1,200 livres wages, 600 livres pension) and allotted 200 livres for expenses. Two secretaries (De Vaux and Bailly) double as masters for the pages. Not included in the council are the almoner (abbé Picard, who had also accompanied

27. Of the twenty external benefactions of 1709, the two largest (to the marquis d'Antin, 10,000 liv. and Mme d'Epinoy, 3,000 liv.) are indemnities from the contested price of land purchased by agreement of 1705. Others averaging 300 liv. in this list and 1708 are by the large majority to widows and orphans, the latter occasionally as novices at St. Joseph (founded by Mme de Montespan).

Toulouse on the Foudroyant) and the estates manager (*contrôleur-général* in the original plan), Martine, who had one son a *commis* in the stables and another successively page and *gentilhomme* in the household. One personal physician, Paillet (1,000 livres), and an apothecary (Laserre at 1,700 livres) round out the medical staff. From the original diners and officers of 1693 finally there remains M. d'O, unremunerated as *premier gentilhomme* (pace Saint-Simon) except for two valets.

In the council, Valincour is the most highly remunerated at 2,000 livres wages and 5,000 livres pension. He continued to have the services of his *commis* Vauerin (900 livres), at least on his sixteenth year of employ, and three others (the above-mentioned De Vaux and Bailly and additionally, perhaps from loyal attachment to the past, a Le Peletier). His remuneration (not counting the perks of the office of *secrétaire général de la marine*) equals that of any "department head" in the overall household. The pattern of signatures on minutes over the preceding years, together with this payment, suggest that he was de facto "chef de bureau" and that Héricourt's high wages (for a relatively recent tenure) reflect the assumption of that function, freeing Valincour for the specific duties of the admiral's correspondence and memoirs, travel arrangements and liaison between 1704 and 1709. And he continued to relieve Valincour of some duties that had once fallen to him; when Toulouse acquired the sumptuous Hôtel de la Vrillière in 1712, for example, it was now Héricourt who verified its reappointing and oversaw the complicated mechanisms of the financial negotiations. Valincour's own work continued, however, to be demanding. The usual work of the *conseil des prises,* without addition of the special efforts of 1704–1707 negotiations on the admiral's charge, although not in the present state of the documentation quantifiable (either in volume or frequency), is visible enough from archival records to leave no doubt about the sustained efforts needed for meetings that had multiplied beyond the usual Monday sessions and increased the needed coordinating preparations for them. Among the papers filed was a thick dossier labeled "differences of M. de Valincour with M. de Pontchartrain," withdrawn from the comte's archives for reasons that I shall later clarify. A welcome aspect of the "victory" in 1707 was most probably, then, the arrival on the scene of a surely useful *greffier.* It is with undisguised weariness, and not surprisingly, that Valincour confessed with regret to Noailles in 1709 that he had not "set foot in the Académie in three years."[28] The three hours set aside daily for historiographical

28. 20 Sept. 1709, *RHLF* 11 (1904), 143.

work, for which an accounting was shortly to be asked, most likely with similar regret had to suffer the same abandonment.

When Mme de Lambert opened the doors of her drawing room in 1710 to a select company, those who could celebrate the thaw of the "grand froid" of 1709 in verse or discuss its causes more philosophically, Valincour may not have been among the first to frequent the gatherings now thought of as the first of the great Enlightenment salons. He is invariably listed among the guests by those who have reconstructed the assembled group and its topics of conversation.[29] And from the first he would have been welcome and have found interlocutors, had he wished.[30] But in 1710 a good part of his time and concentration was otherwise engaged. In 1710–11, he returned to projects concerning the admiral's function and proposed a general reform that in scope surpasses the memoirs of 1704. Valincour's "Mémoire sur ce qu'on pourroit faire pour rétablir la course" ("On the Business of Shipping" could be its title),[31] put into motion in June of 1709, is in spirit similar to the administrative reforms enacted by his friend Daguesseau during the emergencies of 1709. If Daguesseau's measures to reform grain distribution nationally, like his later projects for reshaping certain domains of private law, are based on humane principles, they, like Valincour's, are first of all practical. It is not simply the admiral's rights that are now in question; the realm's needs in wartime and the king's rights to the best service he may be given in these circumstances are the animating concern of the new "Mémoire."

During the seventeen months in which the "Mémoire sur la course"

29. E.g., as résumé of the current, Bernardine Melchior-Bonnet, *Dictionnaire des Lettres: XVIIIe siècle* (Paris: Fayard, 1960), 32. See also C. G. S. Williams, "Mme de Lambert," *Dictionary of Continental Women Writers* (New York: Garland, to appear). On the salon and its setting: Robert Dauvergne, *La Marquise de Lambert à l'hôtel de Nevers* (Paris: Albin Michel, 1947).

30. The spirit of the salon, best described by J. P. Zimmerman, "La Morale laïque au commencement du XVIIIe siècle. Madame de Lambert," *RHLF* 24 (1917), 42–64; 440–55, also catches very well the evolved *honnêteté* Valincour represents by 1710: "Le premier devoir d'un honnête homme est de savoir s'adapter à la société dans laquelle il vit, *de s'y rendre utile* ... des considérations qui dépassent l'individu" (p. 52; my emphasis). Although Valincour had a number of friends among the "mardistes" and "mercredistes," others were not and are slightingly referred to in a letter to Noailles: 12 Sept. 1716, *RHLF* 12 (1905), 485.

31. Two copies, the first in Valincour's hand, are in A.N. G144, nos. 8 (28pp., unpaginated), 9 (63pp., unpaginated). The preliminary correspondence is B.N. MS. fon. fr. 16731, pp. 47–64v, 67–75v. "Course" in the technical sense means "expédition des corsaires," "aller en course" (Littré).

was elaborated, Valincour, with Toulouse's blessing and collaboration, elaborately maneuvered to circumvent the minister and, through Harlay and other members of the *conseil des prises,* to arrive at a new procedure that might win the king's assent directly. The eight letters from Toulouse and Valincour to Harlay in 1710[32] have more than a suggestion of "conspiracy," as Valincour quips with the magistrate about the precedence of councils over the pope. Having learned from the past, Valincour had the first memoir he sent to Harlay forwarded also to Henri Daguesseau and to d'Argenson, both members of the council, who are requested to give their opinions this time to Toulouse himself, "sans qui," the secretary carefully avers, "je ne dois proposer la moindre chose dans ces sortes d'affaires" (73v). The comte then exactly supports his secretary's position in a letter of 6 June. "I do not know what Monseigneur le comte de Toulouse will think," the secretary had begun, "about the changes in the form of the council, in which the judgments will no longer be in his name, and the suppression of appeals that will take from him the honor of entering the Conseil Royal, for it is not apropos to speak with him about all this until I know whether it can happen."[33] With this political caution, Valincour voices his own opinion that these changes are for the good of the realm. Toulouse in fact will voice almost verbatim the secretary's justification:

S'il me fait l'honneur de m'en demander mon advis, je luy dirai, monseigneur, comme je vous le dis à vous qu'il n'est pas question d'autorité particulière ny de prerogatives de charges, mais du bien de l'Estat, et de rendre les armements aussi utiles qu'une armée navale.

If he does me the honor of asking my opinion, I shall say to him, Monseigneur, as I say to you, that it is not a question of personal authority or of the prerogatives of charges, but rather of the good of the state and of rendering armoring as useful as a naval force.

The first means to this end, and the cornerstone of the reform, is to make the council a court of last instance, so that all who use it will be assured both just and conclusive dealings on all pertinent matters. This heightened power should inspire no jealousy, Valincour reasons, since that power will remain "l'autorité du Roy dont le conseil ne sera que dépositaire."

32. B.N. MS. fon. fr. 16731, pp. 48–64v: letters of 20, 25(2), 29 Aug.; 3, 8, 13 Sept.; 3 Nov. 1710.
33. P . 73v: "Je ne sçay ce que pensera Monseigneur le comte de Toulouse sur ce changement de la forme du conseil, où les jugements ne seront plus en son nom, et

Valincour 's solemn oath on his handling of funds, in the placet of 1711 quoted earlier,[34] is preceded in the negotiations for this reform by a similar accounting, valuable in its turn for the information offered about the functionary and the personal reasons for his initiatives. Unlike the placet of 1711, whose accounting is preliminary to a request for a charge and the king's largesse, Valincour's testimony in this instance reveals a striking absence of self-interest in a different way.

Depuis vingt ans il m'a passé par les mains plus de trois cent millions d'affaires de prises. J'ay tousjours dit aux armateurs, et leur dis tous les jours, que le premier qui viendra se plaindre à moy de quelque sorte de malversion que ce soit dans le bureau de S.A.S. je commenceray par tirer de ma poche la somme qu'il croira luy devoir estre restituée que je la luy rendray sur parole, et le quadruple ensuite quand le fait sera vérifié, apres quoy je m'engage encor à luy procurer une récompense de S.A.S.[35]

In twenty years more than three hundred millions have passed through my hands in the prize affairs. I have always told armorers, and tell them every day, that the first person to complain of any sort of malversation whatever in the office of S.A.S. will have on his word from my pocket the sum he feels necessary in restitution, four times that when the fact is verified, then my undertaking to secure compensation from S.A.S.

Thus sure of the trust of investors, Valincour proposes practically to set up an office in Paris to deal with them. Three or four clerks (at 1,500 livres to 2,000 livres) will suffice, and part of this expenditure is recoverable from licensing fees. The experienced "chef de bureau" offers his own services of running this office for only the expenses of bi- or tri-weekly journeys to Paris (suggesting Valincour's primary residence in 1710 was St. Cloud). "Pour moi, je ne demanderay rien que l'entretien de deux chevaux pour aller à Paris deux fois la semaine, et trois fois s'il est besoin" (74v).

The proposal for this consolidated office, coordinated with a council that has final authority, speaks to the crisis Valincour conceives to be at present endangering the course of the war. It is not a matter of capital, he assures, but of confidence: "L'argent ne se peut trouver qu'en regagnant la confiance publique que l'on n'a pas eue jusques à présent." Efficient management and effective public relations, we

---

la suppression des appels qui luy oste l'honneur d'entrer au Conseil Royal, car il n'est pas apropos de luy parler de tout cecy que je ne sache si cela peut avoir lieu."

34. See chap. 1, n. 68 and text.

35. Letter [3 Nov. 1710] to Chancelier Pontchartrain, B.N. M.S. fon. fr. 16731, p. 73.

would now say, combine in the solution Valincour proposes. "Il faut songer à armer d'une manière qui ne soit onereuse ny au public ni aux particuliers, et qui les invite à apporter leur argent."

With the new consolidation, Valincour cites seven abuses that would be remedied by his propositions and no longer impede investment. Obstructions by port commissaires slow to provide seamen with requirements would be avoided, as would excessive demands for caution money that had been the case of recent abuses in Toulon and Dunkirk. Of capital importance, excessive legal costs (estimated at up to fifty pistoles for a quarter of an hour's paperwork) and delays caused by it could be avoided. Vexations concerning the domestic sale of seized goods, recently especially irksome to a number of investors at St. Malo, and delays in liquidation could be controlled—both responsible for freezing capital and the diminution of investment (for perishable goods). Finally, delays in communication between the local *amirautés* and the council, now sometimes a full month, would cease. With these abuses gone, Valincour foresees that the king's vessels and officers now idled in port could be in action by the end of the year—"des Escadrons en estat de croiser à Dunkerque, à l'ouest de la Manche au cap Finistère, et dans la Méditéranée qui payeront plus que leur dépenses, et qui fatigueront les ennemis et troubleront leur commerce."

Colbert might have been pleased by this consolidation of administration and even of ordonnances (Valincour alleges that the ordonnance even of 1694 is difficult to find and those from the war of 1688 are scattered). A year's delay, before both Toulouse and Valincour push harder—through Harlay and the council—suggests that, as Valincour had predicted, difficulties in discussion, namely, contestations of operations and jurisdiction, had intervened. Meanwhile, as he observed, "toutes les affaires vont de travers, et la course est perdue, il n'est que trop aisé de le voir." The difficulty he had foreseen from one sector may have played a predominant part, more insistently than was foreseen in the secretary's planning to minimize it. By including Daguesseau and d'Argenson in the planning stages, he had apparently wished to include but also to contain the part to be taken by the *conseil du commerce* in the new "*règlement*" (and henceforth for that matter). As he wrote to the chancellor, "On pourra mesme admettre dans ces sortes de conferences un ou deux des gens de la Chambre du commerce"; but, he adds, "pas davantage pour les exciter à faire des objections" (74). In the pressing correspondence of 1710 with Harlay, he thus begins with a report of d'Argenson's approval and a request for Harlay's support in the form of a letter to Toulouse, recommending a steering committee and setting a schedule of meetings specifically for drafting the *règlement*. A sense of urgency and conspiracy animates the correspondence: "Je say que l'on songe à nous traverser et qu'il n'y a pas de temps à perdre," he writes, then jokes that Escobar would not disapprove of the expedient being used—"et cela le rend du moins probablement bon et me met en sureté de conscience" (53v). The new council, he continues in the same vein when Harlay has agreed, will be acknowledged as "infaillible. Ce sera comme les conciles généraux qui sont maîtres du Pape" (50v). Harlay is invited to stop at St. Cloud on his way to Versailles (51v–52). But the letter was not properly delivered, and a second meeting is missed. Valincour writes again to Harlay with the king's endorsement of the project to force the issue; on 3 September, "J'ai passé, Monsieur, ce matin à vostre porte pour avoir l'honneur de vous dire que le Roy est fort entré dans tout ce que lui a dit Mg le comte de Toulouse. Il a ordonné que l'on travaille sans perdre de temps au projet de règlement pour le nouveau tribunal" (57). Toulouse will himself send along the king's order to proceed, within twenty-four hours, Valincour adds on 8 September, before returning to other business that Harlay will be representing in the comte's council on the 13th. A draft has already been sent, which Valincour regrets he had less than a day to review, since several items in Harlay's exposition seem to him "impossible to implement in relation to the secretary of state and even to the king himself."

One of the matters, an impediment not previously listed by Valincour himself, is the admiral's tenth. The point, he informs Harlay, is not negotiable, as he continued to provide some now valuable information on the collection of the admiral's privilege, which the king rather than Toulouse himself would not allow to be diminished. The tenth was, however, discretely negotiable. Toulouse himself, having wished to encourage commerce, had exempted ships of the *Companie des Indes* from it under certain conditions decreed by an *arrêt du conseil* of 26 November 1707.[36]

Pour ce qui est du 1/10, j'auray l'honneur de vous répéter qu'il est inutile de rien proposer sur cela, car ce sera sans aucun succès et d'ailleurs je prens sur moy de faire avouer à tous les armateurs qu'il ne leur est et ne leur a jamais esté à charge. Bien plus il est certain que faisant la reformation qui se propose

36. A.N . B⁵ 2: "Contentions entre le comte de Toulouse amiral de France et la Compagnie des Indes ... ," no. 4: "Extrait de arrest ... le 26 novembre 1707."

il n'y aura pas dans 4 mois un Vaisseau capable d'estre armé en course qui ne le seroit. On trouvera de l'argent et des hommes, preuve certaine que ce n'est pas au dixième qu'il tient ainsy. J'ose vous dire si vous me le permettez que jusqu'à ce que l'on voye de contraire il paroist qu'il soit utile de ne point s'élever contre, à l'heure qu'il est, parce que cela estant sans succès peut produire des mouvements. (62–62v).

Concerning the tenth, I shall have the honor of repeating that it is useless to propose anything about that, for it will have no success, and moreover I take it upon myself to swear to all armorers that it is not and never has been at their expense. It is certain, to go further, that in effecting the proposed reform there won't be a ship capable of being armed that will not be a-sail in four months. Money and men will be found, a certain proof that it is not the tenth that prevents all that. I dare say, if you permit, that until evidence to the contrary is forthcoming, it seems useful not to raise any opposition to the tenth for the time being, because it could not possibly be successful and might set off countermeasures.

The reactions feared, which could sink the whole enterprise, are seemingly the king's own opposition.

On 3 November, with a new report on disorders at Marseilles that seem incapable of being corrected, Valincour adds that "notre conseil des prises" seems in the same shape. Nonetheless he is optimistic after two hours' conversation with the chancellor, since Pontchartrain "y est entrée avec bonté et comme un homme qui a une véritable envie de faire le bien." He has been asked to draw up a larger memoir on the matter, which he has done with an elaboration of his seven points, a preamble, and a cover letter sent to the chancellor that morning. In the attached letter, he repays the chancellor's candor and apparent good faith with an answer to a source of difficulties standing in the way of "notre réforme." Whether it had already been an objection, or is merely foreseen, Valincour raises the matter himself of his own past service and "titles," specifically the pride to which I earlier referred in having come up through the ranks without purchasing a charge and the frank allegation that nobody's been the worse for all that. On the contrary, the evidence of service and ability is on record and, for that matter, lies before the chancellor's eyes. While the claims are doubtless valid, another interpretation could well be put upon the status of the "honnête homme" so clearly evident in the reform enterprise of 1709–10. In the new council, Valincour, who had a deliberative voice, would be the only member who was not a "maître des requêtes" or a "conseiller": to the "honnête homme" the titles are an issue of nominalism; to a legal mind, rightly or wrongly, one of metaphysics. Legalistic or simply professionally oriented, this opinion would judge that the "hon-nête homme" had reached his limits.

The irony of the final memoir to Pontchartrain, whether or not it was in itself a delayed tactic on his part, is that it came too late. The war's end shelved the reform, just as it ended the council's work (except for the aftermath of accounts due). However much this outcome of seventeen months' efforts may have disappointed Valincour, he surely preferred the end of the war. In the letter of 3 September to Harlay, he had reiterated his misgivings about Spain as an ally: "On a envoyé ordre à M. de Goësbriant de se rendre les armées bien-tost. L'Armée du Roy d'Espagne est de 18 à 19,000 effectifs. Celle du duc de Noailles se forme. On dit qu'il faut que la France se sauve par l'Espagne. C'est un adage politique fait à la haste ... pour [le] faire on vend à present toutes les affaires. Il n'est qu'extinction d'ancienne négotiation avec la Hollande et l'Angleterre" (63v). In letters to Cardin Le Bret, intendant in Provence, Valincour is equally glum in review of the costs of the Succession war.

Voilà la paix faite et toute l'Europe ruinée par deux guerres de vingt ans, et la France plus ruinée qu'aucun autre royaume. Quel en est le fruit ? de faire roi de Sicile le duc de Savoie, qui fera enrager tout le monde, et d'avoir enrichi en France, aux dépens du roi et du peuple, cinquante coquins qu'il faudroit pendre le jour que la paix sera signée. ... [37]

Here we are with peace declared and all of Europe ruined by two wars having lasted twenty years—and France more ruined than any other kingdom. And what is the fruit of all this? To make a king of Sicily out of the Duke of Savoy, who will infuriate everyone, and to have enriched in France, at the expense of the king and people, fifty scoundrels who should be hanged the day that peace is signed.

The letters addressed regularly by Valincour to Noailles in 1709–10 (while the latter fought in Spain, languished there from want of funds to mobilize his troops, or retired to the spa of Plombières) are not just the newsletters literary friends often provided and sometimes were payed to supply in such circumstances. They are a friend's letters, with reminisences of past pleasures, gossip of the court and Paris, and the kind of wit Noailles had long enjoyed (as in the wager of a copy of Terence bound as handsomely as a financier—before Chamillart's taxes—over who could win the greater favor from Mme de Main-

37. Letter [Apr. 1713] quoted in *Catalogue des autographes provenant du cabinet de M. A. Martin* (Paris: Merlin, 1842), p. 48, no. 297. The date of the publication of the Peace of Utrecht is 10 April 1713.

tenon). The correspondent self-consciously also plays Cicero to the commander he would have be a new Caesar. In response to a *lauréatam epistolam* announcing a military victory, he confesses that he "feels disposed to write a letter in the style of Voiture ('Haud etenim tali me dignior') or at least in that of Montreuil or Le Pays."[38] But enthusiasm is dampened by the times—"Les affaires du dedans sont encore plus tristes que celles du dehors." The first duty consequently that the letter writer assumes is to keep his friend well informed on the progress of the war and peace, from his angle and information, on conditions and opinion on the home front, and finally on the king's coping on all fronts with the challenges of these darkly trying years. Thanking Noailles earlier for a portrait of Louis XIV, Valincour had remarked that as royal historiographer he should have his subject always before his eyes;[39] and so he does in the letters. "Practicing to be among the sage and serious,"[40] he turns a critically practiced eye to reports on the "misère du temps" and its "cruels jeux."

On the war, as it is reported in dispatches at Versailles or by military men returning there, Valincour has excellent informants. He quotes Mortemart's arrival, for example, with the capitulation of Douai on the day of the event, in this (and often) as quick and well-informed as is Dangeau in his journal.[41] He promises news from Harcourt, then delivers it after dining with him at Pontalie.[42] He indeed has a personal line of communication with Harcourt,[43] which is shared from a private letter on the fall of Aire on 12 November 1710. And in the same letter he reveals others received from Flanders that provide an accurate description of the political situation of the Marlboroughs in England. Intelligence of this quality, as it continues, allows Valincour some shrewd predictions, including the final costs of the settlement of Utrecht.[44]

38. 20 Sept. 1709, *RHLF* 11 (1904), 143

39. 27 June 1701, *RHLF* 10 (1903), 671.

40. 7 July 1709, ibid., p. 687.

41. 29 June 1710, *RHLF* 9 (1904), 151; Cf. Dangeau, *Journal* 13:194, 190.

42. 27 July 1710, ibid., p. 155.

43. In a letter recounting the exclusion of Courcelles from the Bourgogne household on 10 Nov. 1710 (*RHLF* 12 (1905), 474) Valincour refers to having been personally embroiled because Courcelles is "beau-frère de M. d'Harcourt." It has not been pointed out that the same relationship links him to Valincour's brother Héricourt. Pélissier, editor of the Noailles letters, professed no knowledge of Héricourt (see *RHLF* 10 (1903), 673, n. 1: "frère inconnu"). Valincour's direct link to the Bourgogne household through Courcelles is also of interest (see below, n. 66).

44. See letter of 16 June 1709, *RHLF* 10 (1903), 683: "Marlborough perdra son

Torcy himself was Valincour's informant, directly and indirectly, on peace negotiations. Certainly since the time of his ministry, Torcy—who in a sense had "inherited" Valincour's loyalty—had been a visitor at St. Cloud, as Valincour would later be to Sablé.[45] Although there seems to have been no sustained patronage on Torcy's part, or of service on Valincour's,[46] favors were exchanged. Special attention was given to Toulouse's mail,[47] for example, and Valincour conveyed certain information. Matthew Prior wrote engagingly of the two men's company, and the easy enjoyment of some banter they also shared in verse: "Going to Chanille this afternoon, Monsieur de Torcy and Madame, Monsieur Dalincourt [sic], Secretary of the Admiralty, in the coach; Monsieur de Torcy read, and gave us to read the Dutch Gazeteer, and upon a passage in one asked me, if it were true that at the Secretary's office, passports were sold for six pounds each."[48] Valincour would have laughed at this gazeteer with Torcy; but over others he shared the minister's anger.

Commenting on the "malheureuse guerre," most often qualified as "ruineuse," Valincour follows Torcy's negotiations and public response to them with enthusiasm and concern. He reports the "insolent and unreasonable" conditions with an indignation that should be shared by all "bons Français." "Renewed war there must be," he responds; "but how and with what? 'O navis, referent in mare te novi / Fluctus!' There is no heart that doesn't complete the lines. And I speak for all good Frenchmen."[49] While he would not have Spain and Philippe V

crédit en Angleterre où il est haï, et le peuple de Hollande voulant la paix, on pourra la faire . . . à des conditions moins onereuses."

45. "M. de Torcy, sage en bastiments comme il l'a esté toute sa vie en toutes choses, s'est contenté de faire à Sablé un bastiment très modeste," Valincour reports to Gualterio, 19 Jan. 1710, then describes an evening there on 25 June. (B.M. Add MSS. 20395, pp. 36–36v; 41–42v.) Frequent references appear between 1716 and 1727 to Torcy's visiting St. Cloud.

46. Research on Torcy's pamphleteers has yielded no evidence of Valincour's direct or indirect collaboration on "propaganda." See Joseph Klaits, *Printed Propaganda under Louis XIV* (Princeton University Press, 1976).

47. On 15 Sept. 1702, d'Argenson acknowledges Torcy's intervention to free some of Valincour's goods from customs (A.A.E. Mem. et Doc. France, 1106, pp. 113–14); on the other hand, Torcy requests release of mail held by the *greffier* of the *amirauté* at Dunkirk (ibid., 117, pp. 41r–v).

48. Letter to Bolingbroke, 10 Oct. 1712. Henry St. John, Viscount Bolingbroke, *Letters and Correspondence* (London: Robinson, 1798), 3:134. On Prior and Boileau, see below, chap. 6, n. 33.

49. 2 June 1709, *RHLF* 10 (1903), 682. The citation is Horace, *Ode* 1:14. Torcy arrived from Rotterdam on 1 June (Dangeau, 12:427).

abandoned, he cannot resist wishing that the king of Spain emulate Diocletian and find happiness in planting cabbages.[50] But his mind moves from Phillip, "unhappy in his happiness," to the man who must be king: Louis XIV.

Valincour is soberly moved by the circular letter of 12 June 1709 that Louis XIV sent to his bishops. It invited a new rallying to the king, a new kind of patriotism, and has been seen to exhibit a new opening of the monarchy.[51] But with dissention evident ("sédition vive" at Rouen), fears of invasion that had brought the court to anticipate withdrawal to the Loire valley, and dissatisfaction over scarcity and inflation, this opening seems to the old servant of the king a real risk. He deplores the fact that the king's "policy" should become the talk of every household and street corner (13 June), then waxes indignant over men of letters who act no more wisely. "A great and important question has been agitated here," he continues on 14 June, "namely, whether the king, according to divine and human rules, may proceed to make war on the Spanish in order to give peace to his realm. Fine dissertations on one side and the other have appeared. But the matter seems to me not only too high to discuss, but also beyond reporting on." Actions are called for, however, and the letter writer undertakes them with the pen in the same way he had with his *François de Lorraine* and would later in response to *Unigenitus*. Writing to Noailles as he does is one action. Valincour persistently punishes unethical and frivolous writers with sarcasm on the one hand and on the other engages in a leit-motif of warnings about the real state of economic affairs. "Suffering is great," he insists, and emphasizes the cost to the realm: "When one thinks that we are perhaps about to undertake a battle that will decide the fate of the realm, or better, its ruin, and cannot effect its salvation!"[52] And these accusations and warnings do not remain in the realm of generalities.

M. de Visé, Valincour reports (7 July 1709), has seen fit to publish a book entitled *Les Préliminaires de la paix rejetés par le Roy;* "on l'a fait supprimer sur le champ, et le roy a esté sur le point de faire mettre

50 . 20 Mar. 1709, *RHLF* 10 (1903), 680; again, 16 June, p. 683. That Diocletian is in his mind is an interesting indicator that Valincour has been meditating on his famous fiscal reforms of A.D. 301 in which the emperor attempted to fix maximum market prices.

51. On the "appel du douze juin" see F. Bluche, *Louis XIV,* pp. 798–801.

52. 27 June 1709, *RHLF* 10 (1903), 685. The battle feared in the event would surely be Malplaquet.

l'autheur aux Petites Maisons." The letter writer leaves no doubt that he has had a personal part in this suppression of the special issue of the *Mercure* in question, which seemed to compromise Torcy's progress in peace negotiations.[53] "M. de Torcy has experienced at The Hague the effect I have often remarked on; namely, that the *Mercure,* opera prologues, and the stupid inscriptions of M. Peltier on the gates of Paris have created the king more enemies than his power has,"[54] Valincour concludes, sounding more than a little like Boileau. Twice while announcing Visé's death, the letter writer does not relent in his condemnation of the impertinence of the *Mercure.* "Notre siècle est destiné aux grands événements," he remarks when a new editor succeeds Visé—"Uno avulso non deficit alter / stultior." Not revealing the fact that he has intervened with Toulouse to get the needy Visé a pension,[55] he concludes with the *imperatoria brevitas* habitually sought for such announcements: "L'Armée de Flandres n'a pas de pain pour quinze jours, et il nous reste quatre mois de campagne."

The case against Cardinal de Bouillon is even clearer. Parlement's condemnation of his letter to the king is merited, but Valincour judges the letter to be simply the act of a madman (27 May; 15 June). He has little more sympathy for Baluze, whose scholarship in defense of Bouillon in the *Histoire généalogique de la maison d'Auvergne* is "ridicule en ce qui peut estre jugé par un homme de bon sens." Baluze's disgrace moves him, however, by the human irony of the situation; devoted service has been paid with disgrace and is "bien triste pour un homme de quatre-vingt ans qui n'est ni évesque d'Ostie ni doyen du collège sacré."[56] When Bouillon's manifesto is published at Douai (14 July 1710), Valincour rises tellingly to the challenge and wishes he could serve the king directly: "I would not be displeased if the king were to desire me to answer it. I'm sure I could do better than Callières, even though he is my senior in the Académie."

53. Letter, n.d. [Aug. 1709], *RHLF* 11 (1904), 140. On Torcy's anger and the suppression, see J. Klaits, *Printed Propaganda,* pp. 69–73.

54. Ibid. Torcy wrote similarly to Petkum, 18 July: "A foolish writer does more harm to those he intends to praise than a man of wit does to his enemies by attacking them with the pen." Cited by Klaits, pp. 71–72.

55. 27 July 1710, *RHLF* 11 (1904), 155. The pension list for 1709 (A.N. 300. AP1: 89) contains an entry of 240 liv. to M. de Visé. On his final penury, see Pierre Mélèse, *Donneau de Visé* (Geneva: Droz, 1936), 237–41.

56. 15 July 1710, *RHLF* 11 (1904), 153. Baluze's letters in exile have been published: see *Bulletin de la Bibliothèque de l'Ecole des Chartes* 76 (1915), 259–62; 82 (1921), 272–75.

There may be some good things issuing from the Republic of Letters, say Massillon's panegyric of the prince de Conti, which Valincour mentions (but revealingly has not had the time to read). Sarcasm extends far enough into the territory, however, as to seem to permeate it. Bulletins from these lands of genres, authors, and performances all in some way share in the kind of frivolity—a scandal to the mind given the war and its seriousness—Valincour holds up to ridicule in his narrative of J. -B. Rousseau's legal brouhaha and subsequent exile. Told as one of two "great matters" dividing the court and city, his case is incriminated by its companion anecdote, the explusion of Courcelles from the Bourgogne household. In that matter—since "les plus petites choses lui sont présentes aussi bien que les grandes" (an observation that will have great fortune in Valincour's Academic discourse of 1711)—His Majesty was forced to take part, as though he had nothing better to do. By analogy then, the Rousseau affair encumbers the king's justice:

Rousseau devient un personnage par la protection des femmes, qui couchent au Parlement pour séduire les juges en sa faveur et pour protéger l'innocence opprimée et bastonnée. On dit qu'il se fait dévot, et je prévois qu'il fera une grande fortune s'il ne devient point janséniste. Et c'est à quoi je ne lui ai jamais vu beaucoup de disposition. Or vous savez, *jucundissime domine,* que nous avons tous en ce pays-ci, comme dit Rabelais, le cœur embrasé de l'Amour de Dieu et de notre prochain, moyennant qu'il ne soit pas hérétique.[57]

Rousseau is becoming a personage through the protection of women who sleep in Parlement in order to seduce judges in his favor and to protect innocence oppressed and defamed. It is said that he is making himself into a devout man, which will make him a great fortune, I predict, if he does not become a Jansenist. And I have never seen much inclination to that in him. Now you know, *jucundissime domine,* that in this country we all have, as Rabelais said, a heart aflame with the love of God and our neighbor, provided that he is not a heretic.

Playing satirically off Boileau's censored verse on love of God, with which Valincour will be especially concerned, his final remark here aims at another territory as heavily bombarded with sarcasm as the Republic of Letters it borders: controversy in the Church as frivolous as any secular squabbles. If the war effort had as much artillery as the Jesuits have used in the Chinese rituals matter, it would be further

57. 12 Nov. 1710, then more charitably on 1 Jan. 1711. *RHLF* 12 (1905), 463, 477. On the exile see Dangeau, 13:311 and on the whole affair: H. A. Grubbs, *Jean-Baptiste Rousseau* (Princeton, 1941), 74–93.

154 • Shape of a Career

advanced;[58] their friend (and Fénelon's) Maulévrier, has stirred up the *Assemblée du clergé* in such a way that the letter writer again fears for the realm. The reference to this latter affair sets the rhetorical stage for later writings in the "malheureuse affaire" of the *Unigenitus*, steeped in the language used against the "malheureuse guerre" of 1709–10.[59] St. Paul will more temperately be cited in place of Rabelais. But the vividness of accusation and the sting of satire will scarcely be lessened, in later attacks, from the charge already made in his final turn on the Rousseau affair and—more importantly—the first personal reference to Cardinal de Noailles. Noailles has been badly goaded, he writes, and the insult has caused

assés de bruit icy. Vous connoissez mieux que personne la douceur et la bonté naturelle de M. le Cardinal, mais il y a des fripons, et peut estre mitrés, qui cherchent à l'aigrir mal apropos, et qui abusent de la créance qu'il leur donne. Le roi n'a pas voulu prendre connaissance.[60]

a great stir here. You know better than anyone the gentleness and the natural goodness of M. le Cardinal, but there are scoundrels, and perhaps mitred ones, who seek to embitter him improperly and abuse the faith he has in them. The king has not wished to know all this.

When Noailles, on a much grander scale, is embroiled by the enmity Valincour identifies here, the king will have "to know." Fearing a new bull (a replay of *Vineam domini Sabaoth*), and as prophetic about *Unigenitus* as about Malplaquet, Valincour assumes the voice of d'Aubigné's baron de Foeneste here, which will be scarcely disguised in later judgments of Clement XI: "Sua Santità reniega Cristo."

Preoccupied as he is with inflation (bread, he repeats, is at 8s. the pound), and with scarcity of funds as much as food, Valincour's sarcasm does not penetrate so far into the territory of financial administration. He had, after all, been making his own reforms with the expressed desire of improving the economy. His sense of ridicule is momentarily awakened by the spectacle of Desmarets and Voysin asking each other for funds when neither has them. But he is already working with

---

58. 24 Oct. 1709, *RHLF* 11 (1904), 146: "Cependant les Jésuites et les missionnaires se mangent les yeux sur les cérémonies de la Chine. Les livres pleuvent tous les jours. Je voudrois bien que nous puissions faire la guerre de même contre les Anglais." "Querelle, qui fut aussi vive que puérile," Voltaire also judged. *Le Siècle de Louis XIV, Œuvres historiques* (Pléiade ed.), 1105.

59. E.g., the often-repeated "scriptural" formula "illum quam dare, pacem sed poscimus omnes." 24 Oct. 1709, ibid., p. 146.

60. 15 June 1710, *RHLF* 11 (1904), 149.

Desmarets, approves of his appointments as "bon sujets," follows his proposal of a "dixme royal" with tacit approval, and finally regrets that he is no longer "in place."[61] Quite characteristically, he also remains loyal to Michel Chamillart, with whom he had also worked and whose guest he had been at L'Etang.[62] He has nothing to say about the alleged incompetence that precipitated the minister's fall. Praise instead comes for the wisdom in adversity the ex-minister has shown. In comments on it, similar to those concerning the king of Spain, Valincour includes himself, with the suggestion that retirement may be beckoning him also. "I can assure you, for having experienced it," he advises Noailles, "that such good soups may be made from herbs that any man of good sense who has the wherewithal to have them when he wishes can easily give up Versailles" (13 July 1709). When Noailles later became president of the regency council on finance, he received from his old correspondent a similar, long familiar kind of letter complimenting him.[63] Recalling old pleasures together, at Auteuil, Valincour regrets that the new charge will keep Noailles from simple pleasures (reading, chess, music) and will replace them with a horde of favor seekers. The only favor Valincour would ask is one already asked by his prior letters' insistence on "misère": that the minister not forget to look down at his new height. In the meanwhile, another compliment summarizes, as it were, the letters of 1709–10 and already signals a future that will not soon include retirement. Complimenting Noailles on the victory of Girone (6 February 1711), Valincour wishes he could summon up Horace and Virgil, Malherbe and Voiture, to give the victory its fitting celebration. The sad reality, he reckons, however, is that there is now no one capable of rising to the challenge. But Valincour offers a compensation. "Si par le malheur du siècle, il ne se trouve personne qui puisse vous donner des louanges dignes de vous, il y a un Roy de France capable de vous donner des récompenses dignes de vous et de luy." [If by its misfortune our time has no one who can give you the praise you deserve, there is a King of France capable of giving you

61. Valincour to Desmarets, 17 Dec. 1709 on affairs in Brittany. A. de Boislisle, *Correspondance des contrôleurs généraux des finances avec les intendants des provinces* (Paris: Imprimerie Nationale, 1897), 3:353; on appointments, 21 Aug. 1709, *RHLF* 11 (1904), 141; on loss of place, 12 Sept. 1716, *RHLF* 12 (1905), 483; on the "dixme," 11 Sept. 1710, *RHLF* 12 (1905), 472 and F. Bluche, *Louis XIV,* pp. 817–18.

62. 25 May 1703, *RHLF* 10 (1903), 675. On Chamillart's fall Mme de Maintenon declared: "M. de Chamillart ne nie pas qu'il ait laissé les affaires bien gâtées." Cited by F. Bluche, *Louis XIV,* p. 779.

63. July 1717, *RHLF* 12 (1905), 487.

recompenses worthy of you and of him.] And a second compensation is offered: the old letter writer, who no longer dances, he admits, will offer the violins for Boileau (and abbé Renaudot) to dance a celebratory minuet, if they are so minded. Offering the violins for Boileau, and sometimes in the company of Renaudot, will be done more than once after his friend's death, scarcely a month later. And a minuet at least will be danced to a victory of his own.

On 17 February 1712 the king rewarded Valincour with the appointment of *secrétaire du cabinet,* citing the "connoissance particulière que nous avons du mérite personnel et de la profonde érudition."[64] The following day at Marly he issued a "brevet de retenue" that allowed the new secretary full disposition of his charge and to raise through it, by four loans, the 200,000 livres needed to purchase it (with 140,000 livres to be paid immediately). Thereby the king wished to "grattifier et honorablement traiter le sr Valincour secretaire general de la marine et secretaire de la chambre et du cabinet de Sa Majesté, eu considération des services qu'il luy a rendus dans ledtes charges et de ceux qu'il continue de rendre."[65] After the war of 1688, the king's servant had been indirectly rewarded by Toulouse; near the close of the War of the Spanish Succession, by the king directly, with the influence of a new powerful patron—the duc de Bourgogne.[66] But the emergence of the new protector did not mean, as has been alleged,[67] that Toulouse had withdrawn from the proceedings. Nor could he, in his own interest as well as Valincour's, in the near future. On the very day of the issue of Valincour's brevet, Bourgogne died, and with him hopes for the future that Toulouse and Valincour seemingly had shared with many others.

After Boileau's death, two placets had been addressed to the king. With the announcement of his friend's death to Noailles, in an elegantly simple, "Il est inutile de vous dire combien j'ai de raisons d'être affligé," Valincour explained the circumstances in which the placet enclosed[68] had been written: Toulouse had literally pushed him to the writing table and had insisted on seconding, himself, Valincour's request to

64. Transcription in B.N. MS. D'Hozier, P.O. 2890, no. 64, 220, p. 34.

65. Notarized transcription, ibid., p. 35. 20,000 liv. was borrowed from Héricourt; 30,000 liv. from his mother's estate; 1,000 liv. from Jean Hocquart; 60,000 liv. outstanding to d'Andrezelle.

66. Letter n.d. [late 1716 to Mar. 1717] to Noailles. *RHLF* 12 (1905), 486: "M. le duc de Bourgogne me la fit achepter."

67. R. E. A. Waller, *The Relations between Men of Letters and the Representatives of Authority in France, 1715–1723* (D. Phil. Diss.: Oxford, 1971), 426–27.

68. See *RHLF* 12 (1905), 480–82. The letter is 15 Mar. 1711.

continue alone the work of historiography begun with Racine and continued with Boileau. A second later placet was sent to His Majesty (via Mme de Maintenon)[69] requesting permission to acquire the charge of *secrétaire du cabinet* that d'Andrezelle at the moment wished to sell. In this second placet, to which I have several times referred for its accounting of funds Valincour handled, Valincour, under the rhetorical mask of Diogenes, is straightforward in another kind of accounting. He has not built a large personal fortune, he insists, and has been deterred from previous requests because of fear of the kind of debts others have not acquitted in their lifetimes, the more so as he has "une grosse famille" (good indication that Valincour felt his brother's family his own).[70] Nonetheless, he maintains, becoming a "domestic" in His Majesty's household has always been his fondest desire. Louis and his advisers apparently having seen no reason to doubt this wish and much evidence supporting it, the bestowal of the new charge in the event answered the two placets. Although Valincour was not always to consider it so, the new secretaryship was a sinecure (held by 204 persons in 1704).[71] The new "charge," which might answer some objections made over titles if not qualifications Valincour possessed in 1710, did not demand a change in the scene of his letter writing. It rather added to the old occupations and service to Toulouse new access and space in which to accomplish the historiographical tasks. Valincour had earlier asked repeatedly, and unsuccessfully it would seem, for space at Versailles for his papers and a *commis;*[72] in his first placet, he had reiterated that request in a special language that at the same time renewed his commitment to his own conception of the historiographer's responsibilities.

In his request to assume alone the task of historical writing previously shared in apprenticeship with Racine and Boileau, which is presented as his strongest qualification, Valincour pays tribute to twenty-five years' collaboration and friendship spent without the "slightest dispute" and properly marks the "infinite distance" separating him

69. See *Lettres de Mme de Maintenon* (Maestrich ed.), 8:157–58.

70. In addition to Bénigne-Jérôme, *intendant des galères,* and Voltaire's friend abbé François-Bénigne mentioned above (chap. 1, nn. 95, 106) there were two other sons: Louis (1694–1738), *lieutenant du roi au Cap Français,* and Charles (1708—?), *contrôleur général de l'Artillerie,* whose pranks as a page are recounted to Bouhier by Valincour [Feb. 1727, *RHLF* 31 (1924), 388].

71. Information cited by Waller, *Men of Letters,* p. 426.

72. Letters to Noailles, 27 June 1701; 27 Aug. 1705 (from Toulon), *RHLF* 10 (1903), 672, 679.

from the "grands personnages" with whom he has been associated. No matter how like-minded authors may be, he reasons, the kind of historical enterprise in which they were engaged, with its demand for a sustained unity of composition, can logically be the work of only one writer, just as the central figure of a great canvas can be that of only one painter. The man who later revealed his pleasures in watching Le Brun at work, and of discussion with him,[73] thus caps his logic with the request for privileges of observing his subject's "slightest actions and words." He remains true in the terms of this request to the documentary and Plutarchian conception and method of his own earlier history. Practical as always, the would-be historian also promises to deliver his work quarterly. In promising this, he directly, if tacitly, faces the worst of the past record of the historiographers, whose delivery of their prose had been subject to highly noticeable and much-remarked interruptions (twelve years, in fact, for Boileau). Again to strengthen his case, he separates himself from his friends, thereby running the calculated risk of the kind of accusations of ingratitude and opportunism later made by J.-B. Racine.[74] Both Racine and Boileau, he alleges, expressed their frustrations with the writing, "contraire à leur génie," which "n'était que pour les vers." Putting himself forward on the contrary as a man of prose, of which the king in fact had recently read a large sampling,[75] he pointedly reminds the king that the record of past nonproduction was not his responsibility, simply by recalling that it had in 1699 been the king's wish that Boileau alone "hold the pen." The whole truth about Racine may have been sacrificed. It may well have been to the end of saving Boileau, who had frequently expressed for himself the reservations Valincour repeats. On the one hand, Valincour may have hoped to do the kind of historical work for which he had wished opportunities since the early 1680s, thereby also accomplishing the service to the king as his "writer" that he professed himself keen to do in the polemics of 1710. On the other hand he, in clear conscience, by continuing work left undone by Boileau, could compensate if not cover for his friend and serve that friendship so

73. See below, chap. 8, n. 73.

74. On the anger of 1729 that spoiled their friendship, see below, chap. 8, n. 50 and text.

75. To Noailles, 1 Apr. 1710, Valincour alludes to a work that may be a version of his reform of "la course" but cannot be definitely identified: "Le roy a eu la bonté de lire deux fois d'un bout à l'autre l'énorme mémoire dont j'ai pris la liberté de vous envoyer la minute; il a dit qu'il en estoit content et qu'il y penseroit." *RHLF* 11 (1904), 147.

valued in his past that it dictated a series of battles on Boileau's behalf after his death.

As I shall show (Chapter 6), Valincour's academic euology of Boileau is a highly charged defense of an esthetic and of a way of life centered in the ethics of writing. In it, Valincour also solidified an esthetics that he had shared and which fully crystallized in conversation with visitors and in intellectual challenges at Auteuil. It was there the young salon wit had really served his apprenticeship. One dialogue from Auteuil, memorialized by an appreciative transcription,[76] suggests, as the 1709–11 letters frequently have, that Valincour practiced to be "sage and serious" specifically in the vein of Boileau. After 1711, his academic eloquence and memoirs for the Académie, public pronouncements and private verse, all continue to broadcast the messages about writing that had commanded his assent at Auteuil. In 1713, according to a privilege to print granted at the moment of the discourse of 1711, Valincour with Renaudot again supplied the violins. The edition of the collective works of Boileau they co-edited provided the "pièces justificatives," as it were, for the discourse of 1711 reprinted with it.[77] The full record of Boileau's controversial last years for the first time became available in this truly collective edition of his writings, which includes all the texts previously censored or suppressed.[78] The editors' annotations, unlike those of Brossette that Valincour judged impertinently obtrusive,[79] were kept minimal, clarifying rather than interpreting the texts that were presented in the spirit of Boileau's "favorite edition" of 1701.

It was a man very different from Boileau, however, who dealt with

76. See Bibliography I: B, 14. Among other topics Henri Daguesseau maintains the necessity of the study of letters for young magistrates; Boileau attacks Perrault. The date is not later than 1695.

77. See Bibliography I: B, 5 and B, 4, and notes 26, 27. In conversation, the late René Jasinski agreed that, although there is no demonstrable proof of Valincour's editorship (see his article, cited, n. 27), there is also no conclusive evidence to disprove it. Contemporaries attributed it to him: e.g., J. -B. Rousseau to Brossette, 11 May 1733 and 11 Jan. 1737. *Correspondance,* ed. P. Bonnefon (Paris: Cornély, 1910–11), 2:146, 215. In addition to the date of the *privilège,* the new "Avertissement touchant la dixième Reflexion sur Longin" (1:xli–xlvii) supports probable authorship by the similarities with Valincour's posthumously published poem attacking Huet and abbé T. (see chap. 6, nn. 83–84 and text).

78. Most importantly, the full text of "Satire XII sur l'équivoque" and accompanying "Avertissement" (see A. Adam, Pléiade ed., p. 946), the full Epître XII (dedicated to Renaudot), the full series of "Réflexions sur Longin." The copy I have used is Indiana University Library PQ 1719.Al. 1713. v.1–2.

79. Letter to Bouhier, 1 Dec. 1729, *RHLF* 31 (1924), 401.

problems raised for Valincour during the last two years of the reign, difficulties especially in 1714 that I shall consider later (Chapter 7) with his active and public entry into the *Unigenitus* controversy. An accusation of Jansenism shook the king's faith in him, which in 1712 had seemed beyond question, and left Valincour needing to justify himself in order to recover favor. For this maneuvering, both new and old patrons were needed. Badly shaken himself, Valincour wrote to Mme de Maintenon that at the moment he could do no better than he already had with one of her requests about Brittany and "will never succeed in doing so as long as I am believed to be a Jansenist. I remember that once when Lully had a lawsuit that much concerned him hanging over his head, he sent a message to the king by way of M. Colbert that he could not write a note until it was judged and won."[80] Mme de Maintenon took the broad hint and, with others, intervened. Valincour combined repeated expression of his gratitude with condolence sent to her after the king's death.[81] She wrote in turn to Mme de Caylus, on 25 September, with a judgment of Valincour's behavior and letter that was by then familiar: "Your friend M. de Valincour has tried to be obliging in this time and has written with a great *honnêteté*."[82] The following year she wrote again to Mme de Caylus, once more expressing her concern that "your friend M. de Valincour" might yet again be in difficulties because of his loyalty to Toulouse.[83] At this date, however, she could no longer intervene in his favor. Valincour's world had in the interval changed drastically; and, as he might have said: "O navis, referent in mare te novi / Fluctus."

Regents and First Ministers

With the regent's conciliar experiment in government, declared on 14 December 1715, the *conseil de la marine* became one of seven permanent councils coordinated by and responsible to the Regency Council, whose members replaced the former secretaries of state. Toulouse, named president of the *conseil de la marine*, with comte d'Estrées, served also on the Regency Council and was thus in place to report on

80. Letter, n.d., *Lettres de Mme de Maintenon* (Maestrich ed.), 8:152–53.
81. Letter of 4 Sept. 1715, ibid., pp. 163–64.
82. Letter cited by comte G. P. O. d'Haussonville and G. Hanotaux, *Souvenirs sur Mme de Maintenon* [Paris: Calmann-Lévy, n.d. (1904)], 3:12.
83. Letter, 24 Feb. 1716, cited ibid., 3:91. The friendship between Valincour and Mme de Caylus dated at least from a soirée of the comtesse de Gramont in 1693. See letter from Racine to Bonrepaux, 28 July 1693. *Œuvres* (GELF ed.), 7:105, n. 15.

and guide its business (on Tuesdays). It might seem that much of what the admiral and his secretary had wished, recommended, and worked for had come to pass; and initially they must have felt considerable enthusiasm for the new working conditions and optimistic about their future utility. Naval affairs would henceforth be, as they had wished, the responsibility of a standing committee; Toulouse's place now effectively did away with the intermediary bureaucracy and gave authority to his council's decisions; and finally, officers with specialized knowledge were included in decision making.[84] Valincour was not at the beginning or ever an appointed member of the *conseil de la marine*. But once again elaborate paperwork and coordination for Toulouse fell to him; and until 1718 he accompanied the comte to sessions.

In addition to this changed pattern of governance, Valincour, by a fortune he surely did not expect, possessed with Toulouse a new working network of relations with great promise for effective service. Noailles, his continuing correspondent, headed the council on finances. The chancellor, Henri-François Daguesseau, already a friend and linked by family ties,[85] remained among Valincour's closest friends; d'Argenson, too, an old working associate, remaining as *lieutenant général de la police* was a sometimes useful friend.[86] Torcy also remained, charged with the post office and consultant in papal and English diplomacy. Finally, all the members of the *conseil de conscience* were personal friends.[87] Best of all, perhaps, Valincour had known the duc d'Orléans literally since his nursery, and by all indications both liked him personally and respected his politics as regent. The regent reciprocated and was responsible for new honors bestowed on Valincour. It was Orléans, also an amateur scientist, who personally was responsible, Valincour revealed to Gualterio, for his honorary membership in the Académie des Sciences.[88] That honor gave Valincour great pleasure,

84. On conciliar organization, Michel Antoine, *Le Conseil du roi sous le règne de Louis XV* (Geneva: Droz, 1970), 43–101; J. H. Shennan, *Philip Duke of Orleans* (London: Thames and Hudson, 1979), 33–50.

85. Only after Valincour's death, however, were there family ties: his nephew Louis II Dupré's daughter Françoise married (1736) J. -B. Paulin Daguesseau de Fresnes.

86. E.g., in the imprisonment of the chevalier d'Assurini, of interest to Gualterio. Letters of 10 Oct. 1723; 30 Jan. and 24 Mar. 1724. B.N. Add MSS. 20395, pp. 152, 175v, 187.

87. Cardinal de Noailles, Joly de Fleury, abbé Pucelle, Armand Bazin de Bezons (archbishop of Rouen). On the last, "ami particulier depuis plus de 20 ans," Letter to Gualterio, 12 Oct. 1721, loc. cit., p. 152.

88. Letter to Gualterio, 12 Oct. 1721 (loc. cit., p. 104): "Je crois devoir avoir l'honneur de dire à Votre Eminence que S.A.R. m'a fait l'honneur de me donner une place d'honoraire dans l'Académie des Sciences." He reports to Bouhier having forwarded

as would have a similar membership in the reformed Académie des Inscriptions, had he not been conscientiously moved to relinquish it after a brief tenure in favor of a candidate (Lancelot) with more time to serve that Académie.[89] Toulouse, too, had of course excellent early personal relations with the regent. First campaigns were shared, as were once upon a time rôles in Molière's *Précieuses ridicules*. Although he was never one of Orléans's companions in revels, Toulouse did not scruple over selling the duchy of Damville to the regent's mistress, Mme de Parabère (at 300,000 livres).[90]

On the one hand then, Valincour emerges with the regency as one of a significant number of civil servants—from *premiers commis* to ambassadors and former ministers—who provided, indeed made possible, an effective change in the day-to-day workings of government. On the other, Valincour's continued ascension (since 1711) gave him somewhat unexpectedly a privileged and influential position not unlike that which the duc de Saint-Simon expected as his birthright. It was in fact the duc who more often sought out Toulouse's secretary, cultivating him for the pleasure given by the raconteur and for information, which for the analyses of their society that would become the *Mémoires* was already the duc's raison d'être. And in the noble causes the *Mémoires* champion, including a campaign on behalf of Toulouse's reputation, the secretary and the duc became allies.[91]

As though to prepare for the increased action of the councils, Valincour again relocated in 1716. For almost four years, and for the only sustained period, he took up residence in the Hôtel de Toulouse. In that splendid house, where the council met, Valincour was the more readily available for ordinary work and contingencies. These included correspondence with impoverished Breton *gentilshommes* who could not pay the *dixième* and sent their petitions to Toulouse.[92] Perhaps for

a note on inoculation, 29 July 1725 [*RHLF* 31 (1924), 374]. For listings and dates, see also C. B. Paul, *Science and Immortality: The Eloges of the Paris Academy of Science (1699–1791)* (Berkeley: University of California, 1980), 113, 126.

89. Valincour, listed among the "associez" in 1717, seems to have made no contributions to the proceedings before his demission of 1719. See *Histoire de l'Académie royale des Inscriptions et Belles Lettres* 1 (1717), p. 37; 5 (1719), p. 10.

90. J.-C. Petitfils, *Le Régent* (Paris: Fayard, 1986), 259.

91. Georges Poisson dates the friendship from 1699, the entry position of the portrait of Valincour in the *Mémoires*. [*Monsieur de Saint-Simon*, rev. ed., (Paris: Mazarine, 1987), 128, 426.] The first letter dates from 1718; "Valincour que je connaissait fort," he wrote for the same year (*Mémoires*, ed. Truc, 6:124).

92. Toulouse sometimes offered to pay for them himself. On his generosity, see Leclercq, *Histoire* 3:130, quoting Dangeau, 18:120.

the same reasons of being ready for new action, Valincour also began in 1716 to negotiate the sale of his charge of *secrétaire du cabinet*. It had been a disappointment. There is first no known indication that Louis XIV ever took up the promise of the historiographer's first placet of 1711 to provide him with quarterly installments of his history. Nor had Valincour apparently been asked to do other work. In late 1716 or early 1717, when Callières was in failing health, Valincour unsuccessfully tried to "upgrade" his secretaryship and become one of the four secretaries really involved in the king's writing; he could write a letter as well as another, he wrote testily to Noailles, who surely knew it. With a request for support he also complained of Callières, whom he had long disliked, at least since 1710. (His dislike surfaced in the Academic discourse of 1717 but remained unclear in its origins.)[93] There were several other more pressing reasons for either disencumbering himself of the charge or upgrading it to put him closer to the king in his entourage.

In August of 1716, Valincour wrote to Noailles—this time on business of his own—with a placet requesting that actions be taken on unpaid wages. Quarterly interest payments are burdensome, he reminds Noailles, for a man with a "fortune médiocre."[94] Fully aware that his are far from the only unpaid wages, he apologizes for presenting accounts "dans un temps comme celui-ci" and would not "si je n'estois pas cruellement tourmenté moi-mesme." A month later he returns to the matter in a more pressing tone, declaring that he will have to sell his house at St. Cloud and his books and would have done so if he could have found a buyer. That buyer would now have to be a Swiss colonel, he adds sarcastically, since at the moment no businessman in France could take the risk of this outlay of capital.[95] Callières has more income than he himself has capital, the complaint continues. Later in the year or early in 1717, he tallies up other figures; eight months have elapsed since Noailles's promise to do something about the wages, now calculated precisely at the considerable sum of 28,000 livres. Writing from Bourbon, where Toulouse is taking the waters, Valincour reminds Noailles that they have been friends for thirty years

93. The dislike, Boileau-like, may have arisen from his extensive publication of vulgarizing works, especially the *Histoire poétique de la guerre nouvellement déclarée entre les Anciens et les Modernes* (1688). That he was well-to-do is indicated by the "news" of the disposition of his will; e.g., Breteuil to the marquise de Balleroy, *Les Correspondants* (éd. Barthélemy), 1:122.

94. Letter of 16 Aug. 1716. *RHLF* 12 (1905), 483.

95. Letter of 12 Sept. 1716. Ibid., p. 484.

and reiterates his past gratitude. Before ending with the specific new requests, he puts his art of letter writing to use. Having himself no need to bathe, he reveals, Valincour offers himself as a detached spectator at leisure to "exercer ma philosophie sur tout ce qui s'y passe." Like Mme de Sévigné at Vichy, he has intimations of mortality, as he walks about ruined buildings and sees paintings he and Noailles once admired now in need of restoration. The letter writer proposes to buy one for Noailles (if the money can be sent), not so grand as the "St. John" the regent recently acquired but well worth having. Before settling back to read Mme de Lambert's "long letter" to the R. P. Buffier,[96] Valincour wishes someone could give the kind of peace she is offering as a mediator in the War of Homer to other quarrels—the Church's, of course, but also that of the Parlement and the ducs.[97] He proposes to erect a marble statue to Noailles near the fountains if he can achieve any of these; in the meanwhile, he offers an apotheosis in his own gratitude if he will do any one of three things to help him: acquire the different secretaryship, sell his charge, or recover his wages.

In this tactful but direct letter, so typical of the secretary's skills, he discloses as in earlier letters of the year new occupations that made his move of 1716 necessary. "You will understand better than anyone," he confides, "the reasons that I have for not mentioning this matter to Monseigneur le comte de Toulouse in the present circumstances of an unhappy affair in which I would wish that he did not have to answer for himself." This does not seem to be an allusion to the comte's problems with the *fermiers-généraux,* to which he alluded with a jauntily businesslike tone earlier (12 September 1716),[98] but rather to the great question central to Toulouse's fortunes after the setting aside of Louis XIV's will with which the regency began: what are and will be Toulouse's titles and place? Or what more literally may be his fortune, now that Louis XIV is no longer there to protect it?

In 1716 Condé and his allies presented a request demanding a *lit de*

---

96. Valincour may be sarcastic: the letter is quite short. See *Œuvres complètes de Madame la marquise de Lambert* (Paris: Collin, 1808), 361–64. He would certainly have agreed with her that "les querelles d'érudition vont toujours plus loin qu'il ne faut."

97. For a good recount of the affair, Jean-Pierre Labatut, *Les Ducs et pairs de France, au XVIIe siècle* (Paris: PUF, 1972), 407–19. For its "stage" at the moment, Leclercq, *Histoire* 2:90–91.

98. *RHLF* 12 (1905), 483. The difference apparently involved their blocking of sale and shipment of supplies for Toulon during reparations. See V. Brun, *Guerres maritimes de la France* (Paris: Plon, 1861), 1:156.

justice annulling the *légitimés'* right of succession, their status as princes of the blood, for a moment even their name (Montespan was to replace Bourbon). Provoked by the duc de Bourbon's affronts to Maine, Toulouse had chivalrously risen to challenge him with satisfaction by his own sword (since, unlike Maine, he had no children). The quarrel was the more justified, he held, as "le feu roi leur père les avoit l'un et l'autre appuyés de son autorité dans tous les biens et dans toutes les dignités qu'ils possédoient" ["the late king, their father, had with his authority guaranteed all the possessions and dignities they both possessed"].[99] After an active campaign by Bourbon (supported by Saint-Simon, who rallied some ducs) both sides were heard in Parlement from 17 June 1717. Since the Parlement declined to judge, the regent resolved the matter in council: both Maine and Toulouse lost the right of succession but were to retain the privileges of princes of the blood. In the *lit de justice,* which came in August of 1718, Orléans (pushed by Dubois this time, along with the earlier allies) did more. Early on the morning of the day, Saint-Simon aroused Valincour with a warning for Toulouse: "Qu'il soit sage, qu'il va arriver des choses qui pourroient lui déplaire par rapport à autrui mais qu'il compte avec assurance qu'il n'y perdra pas un cheveu; je ne veux pas qu'il puisse en avoir un instant d'inquiétude" ["that he be discreet, that things are going to happen to others that may give him pain but that he be assured that he will not lose one hair; I don't wish that he may have a moment's anxiety"].[100] The council meeting and following *lit de justice* are among Saint-Simon's most famous pages: Toulouse having appeared in the council, despite the warning, the regent took him aside to warn him again not to attend the session. Again undeterred, he left with Maine in protest to the regent's provocation of him. He would also protest with his brother the edict of 1718 that stripped Maine of his privileges but exceptionally maintained his own for his lifetime. On 26 August he was granted them in words Valincour would have felt a "grâce au mérite."

Le Roi ayant jugé à propos de rendre aux ducs et pairs le rang dont ils avoient cessé de jouir, a cru devoir conserver à M. le comte de Toulouse tous les honneurs dont il est en possession, honneurs si justement mérités et dont la

---

99. For the anecdote, see Jean Buvat, *Journal de la Régence* (Paris: Plon, 1865), 1:160.

100. *Mémoires,* 6:124: Valincour's response was, "Nous avions bien prévu qu'à la fin il y auroit un orage. On le mérite bien, mais non pas Monsieur le Comte."

durée devroit être indéfinie si le courage, les services rendus à l'Etat, les vertus du cœur et les talents de l'esprit étoient des titres suffisants pour en perpétuer la jouissance.[101]

The king having judged it fit to give to the dukes and peers the rank they had ceased to enjoy, has believed he must conserve for M. le comte de Toulouse all the honors he possesses, honors so justly merited and whose duration would be indefinite if courage, services rendered to the state, virtues of heart and talents of mind were sufficient to perpetuate them.

These words might seem to be the fruit of Valincour's life's work on Toulouse's behalf, from the spirit of his early instruction through the battles for the admiral's rights, recognized and repaid despite the restriction. Before and after 1718, Valincour had much to say on these matters to Toulouse and others. Mme de Staal's *Mémoirs* disclose his presence at Sceaux at the beginning of the affair, when Louis XIV's will was read and the duchesse du Maine formed her own "council" of Président de Mesmes, Malézieux, and Valincour for advice on future measures to be taken.[102] An unpublished letter-memoir, written in the face of new challenges in 1723 to which I shall return, is of capital importance in its clarifying review of the early advice given to both the Maines and Toulouse.

V.A.S. dit qu'elle n'aura aucune peine à vivre à la campagne et de venir seulement ici [à Versailles] les jours de chasse ... et si vos revenues sont arretez comment viendrez vous à la cour uniquement pour montrer au Roy une vennerie malentretenue et délabrée. V.A.S. me dira que je vois bien noir et je conviens. Mais M. Du Mayne me disoit la meme chose et avec des railleries tres ameres à Fontainebleau lors qu'il envoya au premier President le memoire où je marquois en detail tous les malheurs que l'envie d'estre Princes du sang lui attireroient un jour. Mad. du Mayne me traittoit de visionnaire lors qu'elle se laissoit égarer par les visions de ceux qui trouvoient dans Du Tillet que M. du Mayne et ses enfants devoient succeder à la couronne. Elle se mocquoit des abismes que je lui faisois voir sous ses pieds. Elle y est tombé dans ces abismes à mon grand regret. Tous les malheurs que j'avois predits à M. du Mayne sont tous arrivez tels que je les avois prédits et en la maniere que je les avois predits. Et il n'en est tombé qu'une trop grande partie sur V.A.S. qui n'avoit rien fait pour les attirer.[103]

V.A.S. will say that he will without hardship be able to remain on his lands and come to Versailles only on hunting days ... and if your revenues are

---

101. Cited from Leclercq, 2:183; for Saint-Simon's description of the moment, 6:169–71 and the previous council, 133–36, 146–47. See below, n. 127.

102. Coll. Petitot-Monmerqué, 77:320.

103. A.N. 300 AP1:91, no. 15: "Mémoire de M. de Valincourt sur la conduite qu'il

stopped how will you come to court except to display to the king a venery ill-kept and in ruins? V.A.S. will say that I am very pessimistic and I agree. But M. du Maine said the same to me with very bitter raillery at Fontainebleau when he sent the first président the memoir in which I designated in detail all the misfortunes that the desire to be princes of the blood would one day bring him. Mme du Maine treated me like a lunatic when she allowed herself to be misled by those who found in Du Tillet that M. du Maine and his heirs should succeed to the crown. She mocked at the abysses I pointed out at her feet. She has fallen into those abysses, to my great regret. All the misfortunes that I had predicted to M. du Maine have happened all as I predicted and in the manner I predicted. And only too large a part of them have fallen to V.A.S., who did nothing to bring them about.

Valincour's presence near Toulouse in 1716 was doubtless in part welcomed for assistance in the work of the councils, as in his shouldering part of the household council's financial affairs. These were already complicated by the extent and diversity of the comte's holdings but rendered even more so by the pervasive effects of the failure of Law's schemes and the progressive national dilapidation of the naval infra-structure.[104] More than anything else, however, the most vital and confidential matters of the defense of Toulouse's status and rights demanded Valincour's presence; and to collect, compile, and compose the large mass of documentation still among Toulouse's papers, he appears to have been specially "detached," as it were, from the house-hold council. One extant document outside those archives, surely one of many like it, dates from 1716 and is significantly on the office of *grand veneur*,[105] held to be unique in the memoir of 1723 because "la seule chose où vous tenez au roi." The memoir appears to be simply a

---

estimoit que S.A.S. Mgr le comte devoit tenir avec M. le Duc, lors de son avenement au ministre ... 10 9bre 1723." 9pp., p. 6v.

104. In 1716 Toulouse purchased the "greffes" of Marseilles (273,000 liv. and indemnity of 250,000 liv.); rights on "greffes des amirautés" were already at 550,300 liv. (see D. Dessert, *Argent, pouvoir*, pp. 352, 369). In 1716 he also purchased (682,000 liv.) a group of alienated properties in Brittany, in all then estimated at one-sixth of Brittany (Mme Guenard, *Vie du duc de Penthièvre*, p. 43; also, Dessert, op. cit., 351). In 1711 he financed (75,000 liv.) Duguay-Trouin's successful Rio expedition (E. Taillemite, "Une Utilisation originale des forces navales," p. 214). To pay his dependents in the wake of the Law crash, 181,500 liv. was borrowed from Samuel Bernard (J. St. Germain, *Samuel Bernard*, p. 272). A "bordereau" dated 18 juin 1721 lists his holdings at a total of 6,620,247 liv. (the largest items being 5,000,000 liv. in the Compagnie des Indes; 1,200,000 liv. in "aides et gabelles"). A.N. API 300: 89, no. 10960.

105. B.N. MS. Clairambault 720, pp. 225–28: "Mémoire de M. de Valincour secret. des Commandemens de Mgr le comte de Toulouse. 7 juin 1716."

careful inquiry about the office, culled from genealogical sources, and as such is sent to Clairambault to be vetted. It is also research on the precedents of Toulouse's rank as *légitimé*. Set to the kind of task that had brought about Baluze's disgrace (through an admitted lack of scholarly attention to genealogies), Valincour is typically more cautious. So was he in his advice to Toulouse in the second half of 1718. If he could write in 1723, as quoted above, of Toulouse's innocence and, for the most part, his escape from the abysses into which the Maines fell, it was the result of the caution of both men from that moment. As surely as at Malaga, events in 1718 brought adventure into the secretary's life that gave it some turns worthy of the plots of Courtilz de Sandras's novels. These adventures, in the cause of Toulouse's interests, and more generally the fate of the "bâtards du soleil" (the legitimized children of Louis XIV), rather than his earlier seafaring provided the material for Valincour's first translation into historical fiction.[106]

The year 1719, in which Valincour offered (in July) the Académie's compliments to Louis XV and an eloquent plea for its protection by him,[107] is a watershed in the last stages of his career. The charge of *secrétaire du cabinet* is finally sold (at 200,000 livres) in February to Bosc, *procureur général* in the *Cour des aides*. "Marques de la satisfaction que Sa Majesté a de ses longs et agréables services" came on 3 March in a "brevet" of Louis XV that maintained Valincour's *entrées*: "Que les portes lui en soient ouvertes sans difficulté et que les huissiers de son antichambre ou sa chambre et de son cabinet et tous autres officiers qu'il appartiendra luy en laissent une entière liberté" ["that doors be open to him without hindrance and that the guards of the antechamber, chamber, and study and all other officers permit him full liberty"].[108] He also gained freedom in other ways. Bénigne-Jérôme d'Héricourt, now *commissaire de la marine*, provided liaison work his uncle might

106. Eve de Castro, *Les Bâtards du soleil* (Paris: Orban, 1987), 334. On Louis XIV's will and the provisions of 1714: "Valincour ... fort attaché au prince, résume ses alarmes: 'Monseigneur, voilà une couronne de roses dont je crains qu'elle ne devienne une couronne d'épines, quand les fleurs en seront tombées.'" Then in 1717–18 (p. 386): "M. de Valincour ferait une plaisante Cassandre ... L'Ami a vu juste: de la couronne toutes les fleurs sont tombées." The remark was recorded by Duclos in *Mémoires secrets sur le règne de Louis XIV, la Régence et le règne de Louis XV. Œuvres complètes* (Paris: Fain, 1806), 5:103.

107. See below, chap. 6, n. 45 and text.

108. Transcription in B.N. MS. D'Hozier P.O. 2890, 64,220, p. 36: "Brevet pour conserver au Sr Valincour les entrées dont il jouissoit en qualité de Secrétaire de la Chambre et du Cabinet. 3 mars 1719."

earlier have done,[109] contributing to the extensive and difficult reparations of the port of Toulon, the first large project of the *conseil de la
marine* ably overseen by Valincour's half-brother Hocquart.[110] In the
summer of 1718 and again in October, Valincour had written to Noailles
of other doors, closed to him this time; he was freed from attendance
in the *conseil de la marine*. Sardonically, he speaks of being "un prophane
à l'égard de tout ce qui a rapport au conseil de la marine, et que si
j'avois quelque chose à demander, je serois obligé de chercher des
protecteurs" ["a profane person in respect to everything related to the
marine council and that if I had something to request, I would be
obliged to seek a protector"].[111] Excluded, he sets himself free with
good conscience in a letter from St. Cloud: "Je m'en suis encore plus
exclus moi-même, et je ne me mesle de ce qui s'y fait ni m'en approche,
non plus que les Juifs de celui de l'inquisition" ["I exclude myself and
do not involve myself in or approach the council any more than would
Jews the Inquisition"].[112]

Although the reasons for this exclusion are not entirely clear, Valincour's bitter tone—"la dureté des temps qui semblent oster tout moyen
de bien faire"—would seem to include more than just the economic
stringencies that were already undermining the good intentions of the
council. The moving spirit of its restructuring, or liquidation, as well
as the future master of its concerns, was the abbé Dubois,[113] whom
Valincour would surely consider a prominent feature of "hard times."
The pragmatic Dubois, about whom more is to be said, may well have
found in the "honnête homme" a limit he could not tolerate, any more
than Valincour, after a certain point, could tolerate the *Realpolitik* of
the unscrupulously ambitious self-made man Dubois. He gave up the
council in a disgust that later if not at that moment included Orléans's
old tutor, whom he had known also since Toulouse's first campaigns.
But he retained activities on behalf of the admiral and his establishment
or "freelancing" for friends before the valedictory of the 1725 memoir

109. See V. Brun, *Guerres maritimes* 2:228–29.
110. Ibid., p. 155 and passim. Problems of construction and maintenance of ships,
of reconstruction of the port, of unemployment and worker emigration, even of
hospital conditions.
111. Letter of 27 June 1718, *RHLF* 12 (1905), 488.
112. 7 Oct. 1718, ibid., p. 489.
113. The *conseil de marine* is the last to go (see Leclercq, *Histoire,* 2:205–7),
remaining until 1723. Toulouse is replaced by Fleuriau d'Armenonville in the reorganization of 24 Sept. 1718, but nonetheless "remains influential" (Shennan, p. 44). He
is reinstated on 31 Sept. 1720 and d'Armenonville is excluded (Marais, *Journal* 1:429).

(with which I shall end this chapter). He gladly helped Noailles with the establishment of an *amirauté* in Rousillon; using his long experience with Brittany, which he saw as an analogous situation, he drew up a memoir that Toulouse presented to the council.[114] Public statement, in 1725, is, like his discourse in the Académie in 1719, addressed to Fleury and through him to the new king. Valincour, the servant of his illustrious great grandfather, continues his service to the man who now must be king.

As though to matters neglected but constantly in mind, Valincour's occupations shift in 1718–19, as does his residence once more. At the end of 1719, again as if marking a "new period" in his life, he moved into lodgings of his own in the rue des Bons Enfants, nearby but independent of the Hôtel de Toulouse. He first turned his mind and renewed attention to the Republic of Letters, in which he in fact had been much visible during those years. In the busy year 1716 he had found enough time to drink a special ritual toast to the health of Homer. Mme de Staal reported, as others thereafter did, the festive supper held at St. Cloud in April that brought together in apparent reconciliation La Motte and Mme Dacier, with Valincour, and Mme de Staal as Neutrality.[115] But in 1718–19 he was publicly much more visible, as though basking in the wide discussion and acclaim of his academic discourse of 1717 and, as will be seen, in the successful completion of the second edition of the Académie's *Dictionnaire,* for which he had written a dedicatory epistle. He was also honored by corresponding membership in the Accademia della Crusca.[116] And he began again to write verse that through the preceding decade had already become a new kind of poetry. Like his new academic discourse it bore the marks of meditation, as well as satire of hard times shared with friends. The tragicomedy of Law's fall, which contributed to his own hard times,[117] had ensnarled both Noailles and Daguesseau, the

114. 7 and 12 Oct. 1718 to Noailles, *RHLF* 12 (1905), 489.

115. *Mémoires* (Petitot-Monmerqué ed.), 485.

116. I have been unable to identify the exact date. News is relayed to Gualterio after the appearance of the 2nd edition of the *Dictionnaire:* 25 June 1719, B.M. Add MS. 20395, p. 41v.

117. B.M. Add MSS. 20395: 8 Oct. 1719 (p. 48): "Tout ce qu'on peut vous mander de Paris sur la fureur des François pour la banque est au-dessous de la vérité. On ne voit que des gens qui y vont à genoux demander qu'on recoive leur argent et leur or pour du papier. Et M. Law a accompli à la lettre ce que dit Tertullien *de cultu fructorum.*" 19 Nov. 1719 (p. 51): "Vous auriez peine à croire ce qui se passe à Paris au sujet de l'argent et combien de misérables qui n'avaient pas de souliers à la fin de 1718 se trouvent riches de 7 millions à la fin de 1719. Vous seriez encore plus étonné

former fatally for his public career. With Daguesseau in exile, at Fresnes, Valincour spent considerable time, sometimes in the company of Louis Racine or the Duprés de Saint-Maur,[118] and discussion there led to other writings—philosophical dialogues again related to the times and to Valincour's second renewed activity in 1718–19.

As will be seen (in Chapter 7) Valincour's correspondence with Gualterio[119] and the campaigns he conducted through it greatly intensified from 1719 as it closely monitored and approved both the regent's and the chancellor's principles, politics, and actions dealing with the seemingly eternal problems of *Unigenitus*. At the very moment of emancipation from the *conseil de la marine,* he turned in this direction. He has not been excluded from his church at least, he announces to Noailles, and declares his approval of and solidarity with Cardinal de Noailles's appeal (kept secret from 3 April until publication on 24 September 1718) and at the same time his disapproval and critical distance from the papal letter *Pastoralis officii,* published on 7 September, which excommunicated all who did not recognize the bull.

Il faut pourtant que je l'allonge [cette lettre] encore, pour ajouter que, n'estant pas exclus de l'église catholique comme du Conseil de la marine, j'adhère de bon coeur aux deux appels que Monseigneur le Cardinal de Noailles vient de publier, et à celui de la Faculté de théologie. Et si j'étois à Rome, je répéterois au Pape ce que lui fut dit, il y a quelques années, au sujet de cette faculté par un bon moine en qui il prenoit confiance: "Eh Santissimo! Santissimo! di grazie non la pigliate con questi dottoroni che non sanno più di noi!" *Vale.*[120]

I must yet lengthen [this letter] to add that not being excluded from the Catholic church, as I am from the marine council, I subscribe heartily to the two appeals Cardinal de Noailles has just published and that of the Faculty of Theology. And if I were in Rome, I would repeat to the Pope what was said several years ago by a good monk in his confidence: "Eh Santissimo! Santissimo! di grazie non la pigliate con questi dottoroni che non sanno più di noi!" *Vale.*

de voir combien de ducs, de duchesses et de maréchaux de France sont tous les jours à la porte de M. Law. ... Je me contente de ma petite maison de St. Cloud et de l'apartement que V. E. a eu la bonté de me donner dans celle du Corgnolo." 30 Nov. 1720 (p. 81): "La variation des changes et des monnoyes ... que l'on souffre à Paris. Je suis ruiné de fonds en comble sans avoir jamais voulu prendre part au Commerce ni aux profits de la banque. ... Je pourray dater les lettres ... comme Scaliger *ex Villula Musarum in summa rerum omnium inopia.*"

118. On the gatherings at Fresnes including Valincour, see Oscar de Vallée, "Valincour et Louis Racine à Fresnes," *Moniteur universel* (29 Aug. 1859), 995–96; F. Monnier, *Le Chancelier D'Aguesseau* (Paris: Didier, 1863), 245–50.

119. See below, chap. 7, n. 44.

120. Letter of 7 Oct. 1718, *RHLF* 12 (1905), 489.

The "good monk" of the following letter (12 October 1718) is Rabelais's Friar John, as Valincour reflects on his own experience (of 1714) and fears that controversy—even schism—will greatly weaken the Church and foster disbelief: "Nous sommes dans un temps où l'on va devenir hérétique à bon marché, si Dieu ne nous assiste." So the Gallican Valincour will write to Rome, convinced, as Voltaire would later be, that the "horrors of the Fronde were succeeded by those of *Unigenitus*." (As Bernard Groethuysen has more recently judged, the "malheureuse affaire" was "one of the greatest events to have happened within the Church."[121]) The old servant of a new king, acting for his Church as well as his Académie, strives in both to offer a "service honnête" by safeguarding the best of the past in hard times demanding hard speech.

Mme de Staal's continuing glimpses of Valincour at Sceaux are of capital interest in 1718. On 9 December, he was with her when the news arrived there of the search and seizure of the Spanish embassy engineered by Dubois. The abysses for the Maines to which he later alludes—exposure in the "Cellamare" conspiracy by this event that led to their arrests—open before his startled eyes; in his friend's account the event clearly establishes the innocence of Toulouse (and himself) he also later alleges. "M. de Valincour stayed a long time with me discussing this adventure," she wrote, "which astonished him."[122] Always moved by the spectacle of faithful service, Valincour continued to befriend the duchesse's unfortunate attendant when she was in her turn imprisoned. Quite typically, a complimentary note and copies of "des Epitres de Sénèque, et le traité des Bienfaits traduit par Malherbe" were combined more practically with a purse and news of other letters written to those in authority, including the new keeper of the seals.[123] That he could write those letters indicates that Valincour was not everywhere linked to Cardinal de Polignac as he was in one contemporary judgment that "it was M. de Valincour and Cardinal de Polignac who have fixed the judgment of the court."[124] Clearly, this had not been true in an incriminating sense at Sceaux, where he did hear the cardinal read and explicate his *Anti-Lucrèce* to the duchesse.[125] Polignac

121. Bernard Groethuysen, *Origines de l'esprit bourgeois en France. I. L'Eglise et la bourgeoisie* (Paris: Gallimard, 1927), 100. For a review of older, more limiting interpretations and a revision more in keeping with Voltaire's views, see René Tavenaux, *Jansénisme et politique* (Paris: Colin, 1965), 134–63.
122. Ed. Petitot-Monmerqué, p. 361.
123. On the purse, ibid., p. 383; the new *garde des sceaux* was d'Argenson.
124. J.-B. Rousseau's opinion; see below, chap. 6, n. 57 and text.
125. Mme de Staal recounts Valincour's presence in 1713 at this "docte rendez-

ended the year in exile. But Valincour's and Toulouse's conduct at Sceaux luckily had been directed away from the duchesse's councils by the secretary's distrust of her and Toulouse's "strong dislike"[126] in combination with the blessing that he, to Saint-Simon's relief, "ne ressemblait en quoi que ce pût être au duc du Maine son frère."[127] Thereafter Valincour's advice to Toulouse was to stay clear of the Maines and not to link his fortune with theirs as he previously had done. With Dubois, the course is different and perhaps took both further than they intended into another "conspiracy."

At first some tact and maneuvering existed with Dubois, perhaps less in Toulouse's interests than in those of peace. Dubois coveted both resolution of the *Unigenitus* impasse and peace within the framework of Utrecht that Valincour ardently desired[128](and Toulouse supported with the regent's policy in council on 17 July). His opposition to Dubois, seconding Toulouse's, really began at the moment of Dubois's consecration as archbishop of Cambrai (and his first celebration of the mass) on 4 February 1720. By June, Valincour was actively in opposition to a power he warily watched on the way to a biretta. A first ministry reached its ends as he and Toulouse saw Dubois enter the council as a cardinal on 28 February 1722 (once Rohan had been sent to clear the way), assume the place of first minister on 23 August, and finally receive adulation as the "new Richelieu." The letter to Saint-Simon of 9 June 1720, which celebrates the recall from exile of Daguesseau and his new alliance with the regent "pour le bien de l'Etat," at the same time "groups the recruits" to check Dubois.[129] Following the liquidation

vous." *Mémoires* (ed. Petitot-Monmerqué), 315. Saint-Simon places them together in 1718: *Mémoires* 6:192. On his implication in the Cellamare conspiracy, see Pierre Paul, *Le Cardinal Melchior de Polignac* (Paris: Plon, 1922), 258–62.

126. "Des caprices d'une folle qu'il abhorroit," according to Saint-Simon, *Mémoires* 6:194. See the development by W. H. Lewis, *Sunset of the Splendid Century* (New York: Anchor, 1963), 301–2.

127. *Mémoires* 2:262. Saint-Simon's politics in 1718 depends on the difference he wished to see. Toulouse's early solidarity with Maine continued in their joint protest in 1718; thus what he sees of Toulouse may be read differently, i.e., "que le comte de Toulouse sentoit moins sa distinction que le malheur de son frère," was in fact true, with the result for Saint-Simon: "il fut très froid" (ibid., 4:195).

128. Leclercq, *Histoire* 2:15. Valincour remained faithful to Torcy and did not, on Dubois's initiatives in 1717–18, share discontent over "selling out" (e.g., Daguesseau, Saint-Simon). See H. Carré, *Louis XV (1715–1774)* (Paris: Hachette, 1911), 48–52.

129. Leclercq, *Histoire* 3:63; for the letter, Emile Bourgeois, *Le Secret du Régent et la politique de Dubois* (Paris: Colin, 1909), 1:198. Saint-Simon's answer (13 juin) is the second in a series of four letters [the first a "blind," destined for Bourbon(?)] that confirm the existence of the cabal: *Correspondance* (*Mémoires*, Truc ed.), 7:434–43. Y.

of the *conseil de la marine,* Toulouse had formed new political alliances, with the duc de Bourbon he had once challenged and the duc de Chartres.[130] With the participation against Dubois of the maréchale d'Estrées and duchesse de Rohan, the sense of a "new Fronde" was shared and considerable advantage gained when Le Blanc, Dubois's sometime collaborator and secretary of state joined them. Chartres, who entered the council in 1722, had his great moment in January of 1723 when he publicly defied Dubois (with the regent and Toulouse in attendance). After the declaration of the king's majority on 16 February, when the regency and its council came to an end, the advantage turned against the "party" when Dubois joined Chartres, Bourbon, and Fleury in the new *conseil royal.* Toulouse, not a member, learned, as Mathieu Marais put it, that since the suppression of the *conseil de la marine* "he was no longer anything."[131] In February already *lettres de cachet* had exiled Villeroy, Noailles, and Daguesseau. Torcy also had been gotten out of the way. In April Dubois returned to the question of the *légitimés* and pressed the case against Toulouse and Maine further.[132] Toulouse's and Valincour's network had by then

Coirault believes the first letter to be simply misaddressed (*Mémoires,* 1983 ed.), 1:1466, n. 5.

130. Saint-Simon speaks of Bourbon's personal esteem of Toulouse even in 1718. *Mémoires* 6:195. Apropos of the appearance of Louis Racine's "La Grâce," with a dedication to Valincour, Marais notes (*Journal* 2:371) in November 1722 that Valincour "a été exilé." Valincour does not in fact appear in the Académie in 1722 (including its official delegation to compliment Dubois on his ministry) but does reappear on 9 November, then regularly and in time for the delegation to compliment the king on his coronation (3 December). This period then would correspond with Daguesseau's disfavor (from 28 February). Nothing in the letters to Gualterio indicates any "official" exile. On the "frondeur" spirit of 1722, see Leclercq, *Histoire* 2:294–96.

131. Marais, 2:433: The entry begins in bold letters: *"COMTE DE TOULOUSE N'EST PLUS RIEN."* The following reference to Pontchartrain and his failure to consult is revealingly close to Toulouse's and Valincour's, as Marais considers Morville: "Il gouvernera le tout, comme M. de Pontchartrain, si ce n'est qu'il travaillera avec le ministre [Dubois], qui voudroit être surintendant des mers. ... C'est le singe de Richelieu"; he then adds a lukewarm appraisal of Toulouse's popularity: "Il est aimé, chéri, adoré des officiers. Je n'ai pas dit la vérité. ... La marine a été bien payée, et puis c'est tout" (p. 434).

132. The Déclaration of 26 Apr. 1723, the obligatory restatement after Louis XV's accession of the 1717–18 position on the *légitimés,* gave rise to a complex summary of the whole history with pertinent documentation: A.N. AP1 300:91. The two brothers are treated equally. A "Memoire concernant les princes légitimés" places Fleury at the center of the inquiry in December 1723, directly after the regent's death, suggesting that he along with Valincour had been advising Toulouse earlier in the year, specifically against Dubois's blandishments pushing the *légitimés* to renew old claims (and therefore into a compromising situation?). On the declaration of 1723 and its relation to

broken down. But Fleury received the *légitimés'* petitions and defused the new initiative against them. A new alliance had been formed.

In the summer of his seventieth year, Valincour was, then, especially pleased and relieved to be back to St. Cloud and to exert his philosophy at leisure. On 4 August 1723 he wrote to Noailles in exile, asking his opinion on the "revolutions" happening every day (in the event, the arrest of Le Blanc), expressing hopes never to be tempted to accept "high office," and reflecting on the crassness of the times—"taut de gens de condition, qui par les gains énormes qu'ils ont fait, croyent n'avoir acquis autre chose que la license de se porter sans pudeur à toutes sortes de friponneries" ["so many persons of consequence who by the enormous gains they have made believe they have acquired nothing less than a license to conduct themselves shamelessly in all sorts of knaveries"].[133] The letter writer has been quite content for the last two months to look at the court through a telescope. The real revolution, however, came six days later with the death of Dubois, surely included in Valincour's reflections on the living a week earlier. On 12 August, another letter to Noailles persuasively listed the advantages of retirement and bade him not return to public life, even though he is now free to rejoin the regent. Valincour, in a brief, scornful account of Dubois's last confession ("au premier recollet qu'on a pu trouver") and his frantic artifices to stave off last rites, reduced him to an object of black humor.[134]

It was in this reflective spirit of retirement that Valincour wrote his long memoir-letter to Toulouse, on 10 November 1723, advising him on the way to act with the new first minister, Orléans, in the event especially of new measures taken by Maine to attempt to recover his privileges. Reflecting on the power Dubois had accrued, and without needing to do more than suggest their common experience of it, Valincour lists four principles concerning first ministers that are axio-

earlier dispositions see Jean-Pierre Labatut, *Les Ducs et pairs de France au XVIIe siècle* (Paris: PUF, 1972), 350.

133. *RHLF* 12 (1905), 491. A new, self-imposed exile? (Toulouse is at Rambouillet) or simply the usual summer holiday? Special devotion (with the gift of a turkey) is declared on 20 Nov. 1723 to Noailles (ibid., 494), now recalled from exile, the letter replacing a call at Versailles. It appears that in the last quarter of 1723 Valincour is shuttling back and forth between Toulouse's Versailles residence (where the memoir of 10 Nov. was written) and St. Cloud.

134 . Ibid., p. 492; then more philosophically to Gualterio on 19 Sept. 1723: "Je suis persuadé qu'il n'y a guère de premier ministre qui au moment de sa mort ne voulut avoir esté moine de la Trappe toute sa vie" (B.M. Add MSS. 20395, p. 146).

matic: 1) They may have more power in a kingdom than does the king, who may be powerless to undo what they do; 2) For those in office it is a necessity to be an openly declared friend or enemy of the minister. Neutrality is the most dangerous path; 3) The decision to be a declared enemy of the first minister is always fatal; 4) There is no other decision than to be the declared friend of the minister. Valincour's logic is preceded by a kind of ethical political testament in which he distinguishes between moral principles as clear and self-evident as geometers' axioms and counsels/maxims clouded by special circumstances and emotions, whose potential distortions require clarification and subsequent rectification by true principles. Among self-evident first principles, on which the third most evidently but really all of his propositions on the minister depend, is: "Dans les divisions qui troublent un royaume [il n'y a] jamais de bon parti [que] celui où est la personne du Roy et l'autorité royale." Valincour's principle of principles had thus not changed since his *Vie de François de Lorraine* and must have been reinforced by the recent experience of "frondeur" spirit. He uses some of his former historical research in the list of historical examples that follow the first ethical principles and flesh out the pragmatic axioms: Du Prat's violence against the connétable de Bourbon (whose life Valincour once wrote); Richelieu, especially in his actions toward Marie de Medici; Mazarin's alienation of Gaston d'Orléans in the king's affections among his other *friponneries*. The examples are especially chosen to enforce the need he felt for conciliation with Orléans and to discourage Toulouse's involvement with new petitions for privileges that might come from Maine. These petitions, in Valincour's view, would be contrary to good sense and indeed to logic itself.

Valincour's personal concern becomes particularly clear in the second part of the memoir where a double argument is developed. On the one hand, perhaps importunely, since Toulouse's own honor must finally decide, the old servant lists at length the consequences of total cessation of money from the treasury. In the passage cited above, he breaks in familiarly with the whole question: "Mais de par tous les diables, le parquet vaut-il que vous vous exposiez un moment à toutes ces extremités?" (6v). This line of argument according to self-interest has a new forcefulness. Toulouse was no longer the hero whose celibacy permitted the beau geste of fighting for Maine; he had early in the year married Sophie-Victorine de Noailles and a child was expected shortly.[135] The second argument (often underlined by a hand that may be that of the future duc de Penthièvre or his secretary) brings to bear the opinion of "gens raisonnables dans tout le Royaume qui jugent cette distinction [of the princes of the blood from the *légitimés*] necessaire et qui ont été indignés (il faut dire le mot) de ce que les importunitez de Mad du Maine avoient extorqués du feu roi de cet égard."[136] These "gens raisonnables," among whom Toulouse himself must be counted this time, all agree that the Parlement is "the most venerable and authentic" ceremonial of the kingdom, and regret particularly there the disfiguring of it by the exceptional blurring of rank.

To conclude, Valincour sums up his past record of advice, balancing his advice to Toulouse to act for himself (with 100,000 écus on the tenths of St. Malo) in arming his fleet for Malaga against the caution he counseled in the first *lit de justice* after the death of Louis XIV. In both instances he was right. Repeating in a last development the advice he had given to the Maines, the prophetic truth of which had already been emphasized, Valincour urges Toulouse to keep his views "simple but carefully considered" and to check them against possible future events this time. The proof of prophecy, Valincour insisted to Bossuet, depended on its intelligibility: here he is ready to trust his logic and foresight, without the need for corroborating events. But the comte must act according to his own honor *and* his usual wisdom; and he must act quickly.

Valincour was surely prophetic on the last point, since Orléans died less than a month after the memoir, once again making one of his memoirs seem ironically redundant, except of course in relation to the new first minister, the duc de Bourbon, who would seem by

135. Marie-Victorine-Sophie de Noailles (b. 1688), widow since 1712 of Toulouse's nephew the marquis de Gondrin (son of his half-brother d'Antin). Married secretly, with only d'O accompanying Toulouse, by Cardinal de Noailles during the *lit de justice* on 16 Feb. 1723. The public announcement was made only after Orléans's death. See Saint-Simon, 7:290–91, 392; Barbier, *Journal* 1:316; *Mémoires du duc de Noailles* 3:191. Valincour alludes to the godparents of the duc de Penthièvre (b. 16 Nov. 1725), prematurely on 29 Nov. 1723 (*RHLF* 12 [1905]), 495. "Jamais union ne fut plus tendre," says Mme Guenard: *Vie du duc de Penthièvre* (Paris: A. Egron, 1803), 36. A running chronicle of the comtesse's great favor with Louis XV is given by d'Argenson, *Mémoires* 2:150 and passim.

136. Cf. on the édit de Juillet 1714, François Bluche, *Louis XIV*, pp. 871–75. Valincour's arguments here and generally for division in the service of Toulouse's self-interest flesh out the views attributed to him by Saint-Simon in 1718. *Mémoires* 6:194–96.

temperament to justify the admonition to be wary of the power inherent in a first ministry. Letters to Gualterio on Bourbon's assumption of government (largely with those in office) stop just short of a denunciation of brutality.[137] And violence is felt again with the threat of intolerant repression—against the R.P.R. once more—evident in the declaration of 14 May 1724.[138] The Ligue now rather than the Fronde is in Valincour's mind, as it was in the early 1680s, and animates the eloquence of his last academic discourse.

Importantly, Toulouse followed the advice of the memoir of 1723. Accompanying Toulouse now as chancellor, in the reception of Monseigneurs les princes à l'ordre de la Toison d'or, rather than a conspiracy is a pleasure Valincour transparently enjoys behind the banter and modesty of his report to Noailles.[139] Like many others (Toulouse, Saint-Simon), Valincour had missed the coronation of the new king, without a regret expressed; indeed preparations for it were fodder for the satirist.[140] The marriage of Louis XV is quite another matter. To Gualterio, Valincour wrote a letter of private celebration for the reception of a saint in France,[141] as hopeful as his greeting of the successor to Clement XI will be seen to be. The disgrace of the duc de Bourbon on the other hand scarcely engages the letter writer's usual musings on fortune. Some lingering threats of war, which Valincour continued to fear, may have gone with him. But to Valincour they, like all else, had been held in check by Fleury, the new star of his later years, to whom much will be directed, including the memoir of 1725 on the state of naval affairs.

Valincour and Toulouse once again worked together,[142] composing independently memoirs that echo and confirm each other. Valincour's often-cited views, recently praised for their perspicuity,[143] are of course historically framed and could be considered an exercise quite proper

137. Valincour prefers, however, to be optimistic; on 24 Feb. 1724, to Gualterio: "On espère beaucoup icy des soins du nouveau premier ministre. Il est fort appliqué à retrancher les dépenses superflues qui depuis 60 ans ont ruiné le Royaume." B.M. Add MSS. 20395, pp. 181v–82.

138. See H. Carré, Louis XV, pp. 84–86.

139. 23 June 1724, RHLF 12 (1905), 495.

140. 7 Oct. 1725. B.M. Add MSS. 20395, p. 239.

141. 8 July 1725. Ibid., p. 229.

142. Published by Monmerqué, Mémoires du marquis de Villette (Paris: Société de l'Histoire de France, 1844), li–lxiii.

143 . Etienne Taillemite, L'Histoire ignorée de la marine française (Paris: Perrin, 1988), 152: "L'Amiral possédait dans son entourage un conseiller fort lucide en la personne du secrétaire général de l'amirauté [sic], Valincour."

to a royal historiographer if that function were not to be defined simply by the composition of eulogy. The autopsies, both of the seventeenth-century navy (perhaps too often emphasized in readings of Valincour's report) and of the work of the regency's council, in fact take up little space. The history of the navy in the last century, its beginning, apogee, and decline may in fact be summarized in a nutshell, Valincour insists: the names of Richelieu, Colbert and Seignelay, then Pontchartrain, suffice to evoke its outline. The first two, "grands génies" with all the knowledge needed to implement their visions, are followed by Seignelay, who, having instructed himself on all aspects of the navy, "estoit très capable." After this death,

M. de Pontchartrain, qui lui succéda, lui fit bien voir qu'un excellent esprit, joint aux bonnes intentions, ne peut supléer à l'expérience que l'on n'a pas acquise ... M. de Pontchartrain ayant succédé à son père ... le Roy, informé de tout ce qui s'étoit passé fut sur le point de [le] renvoyer, *et depuis ce temps-là il n'y a pas eu d'armée navale.*[144]

M. de Pontchartrain, who succeeded him, made it evident that a fine mind and with it good intentions cannot fill in for a lack of acquired experience. As his successor, Pontchartrain's son was nearly dismissed when the king was informed on all his doings; *and from that time on, there has been no naval force.*

The score with Jérôme Pontchartrain had long before been settled, in the councils in 1715;[145] the criticism here in historical perspective has, with its reference to the king, a more general import. It is the whole structure of administrative relationships, the inadequacies of which the admiral and his secretary had experienced, that is incriminated. Louis XIV is as much at fault as any other, since his knowledge of a defective administrative functioning was not followed by the actions that would reform or replace it.[146]

Oddly, it might seem, Valincour again insists that it has not been the lack of money that has been responsible for the decadence, indeed "anéantissement," of the navy that he deplored to Noailles in 1710 and that is written large across the memoir in the catalogue of 150 vessels uselessly grounded in the mud at St. Malo and the present ruin of the

144. There is obvious exaggeration in this presentation.

145. Toulouse gave a severe appraisal of Pontchartrain early on in the council (1715); it is said, though the text is not extant, that he "ne visait pas l'honnêteté de Pontchartrain" (Maurice Filion, *Maurepas* [Montréal: Leméac, 1967], p. 34). He resigned on 4 November.

146. "Sans blesser le respect qui est dû à la mémoire d'un si grand roy, ne peut-on pas dire que c'est ce qu'il a eu de plus défectueux dans son gouvernement?" (p. lvi).

ports of La Rochelle, Dieppe, Bayonne. "If one were to examine the accounts," he maintains, "one would see that during recent years [ces dernières années] it has cost the king more than it did in the time of M. Colbert and M. Seignelay." Valincour minimizes the sabotaging of the good intentions of the *conseil de la marine* by budget cuts that dropped from fourteen million livres in 1713 to ten in 1719, insufficient to deal with the upkeep of ships (eighty seaworthy in 1713; fourteen, in 1719). Marais's irony about the council's work at the beginning of its existence may seem conclusive: "La Marine est bien réglée, il ne lui manque plus que des vaisseaux."[147] The economic argument used in 1710 again appears, however; problems of scarcity will be lessened by supply, in the extensive but not hopeless activities of required reparation. Minimization of financial problems extended to the "fautes grossières" of Louvois and, now fully declared, the "unfortunate results of the incapability of Chamillart." What is being emphasized by these tactics is a crisis of leadership, of administrative capability wedded to a broad vision (the latter exactly what the *conseil de la marine* was lacking, according to the judicious review of its fifty-odd volumes of minutes by Leclercq and others).[148] It is "l'incapacité des ministres et mauvais gouvernment" that must be attended to in the present if the situation is not to remain the same.

The end of this argument might be foreseeable for anyone who has followed Valincour's long campaign for the admiral. Things will remain the same indeed until he is properly installed and maintained in his functions. "Il est aisé de voir que ce sera toujours de mesme, tant qu'elle ne sera pas dirigée autrement qu'il est," it is said generally of naval administration, then immediately "tant qu'elle ne sera pas dirigée par l'amiral de France avec le conseil des plus habiles officiers." Would in fact Toulouse have been a better choice than Maurepas? The question, which the memoir puts without any ambiguity, may still be asked. Maurepas, in the beginnings of his appointment, is unfairly dealt with by secretary and admiral, who obviously fear a future replay of the past for the new admiral, Toulouse's son and heir, the duc de

147. *Journal* 1:430. These figures are often cited. See, e.g., Filion, *Maurepas,* pp. 40–44 and tables, 143–45. Those on ships are Maurepas's (1732). On funds, E. H. Jenkins, very similarly to Valincour, remarks: "Colbert had spent 216 millions in building up the service, and in roughly the same time the two Pontchartrains had spent more than twice as much in running it down." (*A History of the French Navy.* [London: Macdonald and Jane's, 1973], p. 106). Taillemite ("Une crise," p. 153) notes that Toulouse did protest the duc de Bourbon's budget cuts in 1724.

148. *Histoire* 2:56–60; Michel Antoine, *Le Conseil du roi,* p. 95 and n. 204.

Penthièvre. But to pass over a man of Toulouse's experience for one of twenty-four with everything to learn? This scandal to the mind, Valincour insists, would make an English spy laugh. The full passage merits quotation, as his Englishman is informed of the realities:

Pour traverser tous vos desseins et pour vous attaquer vous-même, on vous oppose un jeune homme de vingt-quatre ans, de bon esprit, qui a de très bonnes intentions, mais qui ne sait pas de quelle couleur est la mer, ni comment est fait un vaisseau, qui depuis qu'il est en place, n'a fait autre chose que d'examiner si d'un écrivain on peut faire un enseigne, et si l'on envoyera celui-cy à Toulon et celui-là à Rochefort; *du reste, il ne prendra conseil de qui que ce soit;* les officiers de guerre seront exclus de toutes les deliberations; mais il s'enfermera avec quatre commis, qui n'en savent pas plus que lui et qui n'ont pas plus d'esprit. C'est avec eux qu'il dressera le projet de la campagne qui va s'ouvrir et les instructions pour la flotte, si on en peut avoir une. (lv-lvi; my emphasis)

To thwart all your plans, and to attack your person, a young man of twenty-four has been set in opposition to you. He has a good mind and very good intentions but doesn't know the color of the sea, nor how a ship is made. And since being in office he has not done more than examine whether one can make an enseign of a writer and who should be posted where. *Moreover, he will not take advice from any one at all.* Naval officers will be excluded from all deliberation; but he will closet himself with four secretaries who know no more than he and are no more intelligent. It's with them that he will draw up the plan for the approaching campaign and instructions for the fleet, if one can be had.

Prophecy, this time based on a realist's evaluation of the capabilities of those in command to solve problems at hand, will remain ambiguous in its fulfillment. The signs (Maurepas's reforms as expressed in the memoirs of 1730 and 1745), come after Valincour's death and remain inconclusive.[149] What is clear is that despite the time lost in providing the minister with pertinent information (enough to justify the memoirs of 1725?) Maurepas came to identify, and to work for the solution to, a good number of the specific problems identified by Valincour in 1725. More than its bitter historical analysis, and beyond the self-interest of its special pleas, these recommendations on what is to be done for the present give Valincour's memoir the value he wished it to have "pour le bien de l'état." Taking the lead for once from England, he recommends both officers' training and a standing admiralty board in

149. On Maurepas, René Jouan for one outlines a great reforming success that would in effect respond to all the issues of the 1725 memoir: *Histoire de la marine française* (Paris: Payot, 1950), 83; Filion is more circumspect.

which those officers would make their experience tell against the inex-
perience of functionaries. Support of the fleet, he insists, means also
continuing much-needed support for commerce in peacetime. Subsidies
to independent companies or private individuals would better be payed
directly to the navy. Finally, to return to the admiral, a minister of the
navy must be a man of vision as well as of proven experience, possessing,
as Lacour-Gayet in fact saw in Valincour and Toulouse, "le sentiment
de la France et des vrais intérêts de sa marine."[150]

When Valincour went to St. Cloud in 1723, for a summer's well
earned rest celebrated as retirement in his letters to Noailles, he took
with him from the comte's archives several *liasses* of papers, the admiral's titles among them and the thick folder of his "differences with M.
de Pontchartrain in 1707."[151] He obviously intended that his leisure
would include work, specifically on his long-nurtured plans for a legally
constituted "règlement" of the admiral's rights, which would once for
all guarantee those rights in law against any king's pleasure or minister's
interpretations. In his catalogue of Toulouse's possible losses in the
memoir-letter of November 1723, he spoke with regret of "droits de la
marine" still not ensured by a "règlement que je n'ai jamais pu obtenir"
and at the mercy of a prime minister who would by fiat make himself
"Maître de la navigation." The memoir of 1725 is the first campaign
directed toward a new government yet to come, of Fleury for Louis
XV; "à suivre," were it not for the fire at Saint-Cloud that opens in
1726 the last period of Valincour's life and by necessity closed certain
dossiers for good in the agenda imposed upon his last years.

150. *Histoire de la marine militaire sous le règne de Louis XV* (Paris: Hachette,
1910), 71.
151. A .N. 300 AP1: 89. "Recipissé de M. de Valincour des Titres & Papiers retirés
des archives de S.A.S. 3 juillet 1723."

Chapter 6

The Responsibilities of the Académie

L'Academie est une espèce de Patrie nouvelle que l'on
est d'autant plus obligé d'aimer, qu'on l'a choisie.

Fontenelle

Je demande son ajournement, jusqu'à ce que son utilité
soit constatée.

Deputy of the Constituant, 1790[1]

According to Dacier's note describing the Académie's session on 13
July 1719, "M. de Valincour explained in few words the subject of this
new convocation and spoke most forcefully on the necessity of its
making resolutions that can be effected to ensure that a company as
illustrious as the Académie française, which had received such glorious
distinctions from Louis the Great, should not become a useless part of
the State."[2] Throughout his thirty-one-year tenure, all Valincour's
activities in and on behalf of the Académie could be summarized by
this note, specifically calling for a renewal of directions after the
completion of the second edition of the *Dictionnaire*. His eloquence
and participation in the business of running the institution both served
to remind the company of the continual need of renewal of commitment to statutorily defined responsibilities, if the Académie wished to
remain worthy of its past and merit continuing respect as an institution.
And in new modulations of his earlier verse, Valincour set his poetry
to express the same convictions. The Académie should be the "Sanctu-

---

1. Cited by Gérard Jaeger, *Qu'est-ce que l'Académie française? à quoi sert-elle? A
propos du rapport de Chamfort sur les Académies (1634–1803)* (Paris: La Pensée universelle, 1978), 42.
2. *Les Régistres de l'Académie française, 1672–1793* (Paris: Firmin-Didot, 1895), 2:79.

ary of the Muses" proclaimed in his public eloquence; but the sanctuary must not be understood to be simply a place of privileged retreat.

Eloquence and Business

The discourse that Valincour composed for the reception of abbé d'Estrées, 25 June 1711, was a melancholy occasion for the speaker. By chance it fell to him to offer in it the eulogy of his friend Boileau, as it had fallen to him twelve years earlier to deliver that of his friend Racine. To commemorate this privilege of friendship, and its responsibilities, Valincour may at first seem to have chosen the same kind of simple but elevated eloquence sought in his discourse of reception as the appropriate expression of his gratitude to Racine, his modest claims to the place of an Academician of his predecessor's stature, and his sense of responsibilities to the Académie's traditions.

Hé: comment pourrions-nous oublier un Homme, que les hommes n'oublieront jamais, tant qu'il y aura parmy eux des vices dignes de censure, & des vertus dignes de louanges.

Je ne crains point icy, Messieurs, que l'Amitié me rende suspect. Elle fourniroit plutôt des larmes hors de saison, que des loüanges exagérées. Ami dès mon enfance, & ami intime de deux des plus grands personnages, qui jamais ayent esté parmy Vous, je les ay perdus tous deux, dans un petit nombre d'années. Vos suffrages m'ont élevé à la place du premier, que j'aurois voulu ne voir jamais vacante. Par quelle fatalité faut-il que je sois encore destiné à recevoir aujourd'huy en vostre nom, l'Homme illustre, qui va remplir la place de l'autre; & dans deux occasions, où ma douleur ne demandoit que le silence & la solitude, pour pleurer des Amis d'un si rare mérite, je me sois trouvé engagé à paroistre devant vous pour faire leur éloge.[3]

As the first periphrasis describing Boileau quoted here already suggests, fulfillment of the personal demands of eloquence before the Académie of 1711 required a higher public pitch of rhetoric than had a eulogy of Racine spoken to a consensus of opinion. To eulogize Boileau in a manner he felt to be personally appropriate meant in fact to mount a polemical defense, since there was among Valincour's auditors no more a consensus that Boileau's writings, career, or person represented "l'honneur des lettres" than there had ever been beyond them on those subjects in gazettes or salons. Scarcely a year after Boileau's death the satirist Gacon, a self-proclaimed disciple, deplored the fact that "little minds" saw fit to censure the master and had treated Boileau before

3. *Recueil ... de l'Académie françoise* (Paris: Coignard, 1711), 301–3.

the "entire Académie" as a "misanthrope who regarded any praise as an affront to truth and by naming bad authors had indulged in personal satire for which he would repent in the next world."[4] In the same spirit, Valincour displayed complex rhetorical strategies, and raised the pitch of his rhetoric to a formality unique in his Academic eloquence. Still within the traditional tripartite pattern of the academic discourse, Valincour's discourse seeks for it the authority of a different model, which he further exploits in later discourses that continue to modify and adapt the fixed form of the genre.

The polemical goal set for the eulogy of Boileau that is the central development of Valincour's discourse is a convincing demonstration that "love of truth" was the determining principle of Boileau's writing. A "higher court" is first sought in the fact of successful translations that may signify an "approbation universelle." Pointing to this truth that demonstrably transcends restricted circumstances, Valincour pointedly reminds his audience that it is only in this kind of transcendence that a truth is to be found in which "tous les hommes se réunisse[nt]" (296). For the Académie assembled, well on its way to including the majority of churchmen it numbered for Valincour's later discourses,[5] this phrase, its central development, and the sonorously periodic sentences that introduce and sustain it inevitably cast the discourse in the form of a secular sermon. In this sanctuary of the muses, the exhortation to seek only the truth, in which all men are one, trades tactically on the supreme model of the speaker of another kind of eloquence, Bossuet in his sermons,[6] adapted for the specific edification of the audience. Personal conviction, rhetorically enunciated and transcending logical demonstration (nonetheless in place), replaces scriptural citation with implicit but clearly discernible recollections of the Académie's original statutes. The first truth set forth, in this secular analogy to the truth of Scripture, is the symbolic integrity of the

4. "Discours apologétique" (1712). Cited by J. R. Miller, *Boileau en France au dix-huitième siècle* (Baltimore: Johns Hopkins, 1942), 104.

5. A list of the "majority party" of churchmen is given for 1713 and discussed by Wladimir d'Ormesson, *Le Clergé à l'Académie* (Paris: Wesmaël-Charlier, 1965), 149. Of the 21 Academicians in the 1711 audience for Valincour: 8 abbés and 2 bishops. On the surface, the constitution and climate change little between 1711 and 1719.

6. Given the generalized movement toward thematics noted (disparagingly) by Lucien Brunel (*Les Philosophes à l'Académie au 18e siècle* [Paris: Hachette, 1884], p. 59), evident in Valincour's development, Bossuet's sermons rather than his *panégyriques* seem the more probative formal analogue to the "discours" as genre; the celebrated "Sermon sur la mort" (28 Mar. 1662) is a model.

institution. The original statute forbidding unseemly criticism of colleagues symbolically safeguarded it as a place of higher harmony in the search after truth.[7] A Platonizing vision of the Republic of Letters, symbolized for Valincour in the Académie as founded, remains a constant of its eloquence in his view and use of it. But like the constants of the humanist tradition of historical writing he had adapted to a specific present,[8] that vision with its related rhetoric must be fittingly accommodated to political reality if the integrity of both discourse and institution is to be preserved. The "sermon" on Boileau, "excellent poet" and "virtuous man" ("homme de bien"), is accordingly linked to an Academic ideal in the humanist tradition emphatically celebrated in the first part of the discourse. This ideal exemplified then by Boileau in the special narrative focus of the eulogy is finally confirmed in the traditional peroration with its Louis/Augustus topos. In 1711 that amplification could not truthfully be, and significantly is not, what it had been in 1699.

Ironically, it may have been Valincour's well-publicized wound at Malaga in service with Toulouse[9] that carried conviction. Without objectionably neglecting the abbé d'Estrées (whose qualification for the Académie is a talent for historical research that in its turn may further the elaboration of the history of the reign), Valincour astutely concentrates on an ideal of humane letters more grandly apparent in other members of the family and associates himself with it. Of the cardinal, a memorable diplomat and the Académie's doyen:[10]

Quelles terres, quelles mers, quelles guerres, quelles négotiations: & pour parler de ce qui nous convient plus particulièrement, quelles Académies peut-on citer aujourd'huy, où l'on ne trouve des traces de gloire de ce nom illustre! Quel amour pour les lettres dans tous ceux qui le portent; & qu'ils ont sçu joindre à tant d'actions éclatantes, & à tant de services rendus à l'Etat. (287)

Moving to the maréchal d'Estrées,[11] a parenthesis of humility only makes more apparent Valincour's own self-presentation, of credentials

---

7. Statute 34: "Les remarques des fautes d'un ouvrage se feront avec modestie et civilité, et la correction en sera soufferte de la même sorte." Quotations from statutes (1635) from Jean-Léon Aucoc, *Lois, statuts et règlements concernant les anciennes académies* (Paris: Hachette, 1889).

8. See above, chap. 4, pp. 116–17.

9. See above, chap. 5, n. 11.

10. On Cardinal d'Estrées's place in the Académie's traditions, see d'Ormesson, *Le Clergé,* pp. 146–47.

11. Victor-Marie, comte d'Estrées (1660–1737), maréchal de Cœuvres (1703), vice-amiral (1684), grand d'Espagne (1704), married to Lucie-Félicité de Noailles.

certified beyond the Académie (like successful translation of Boileau into other languages) yet lying at the heart of its statutory foundation: service to the king and realm that illustrates the essential dignity of letters. A Circeronian ideal of utility and pleasure in study thus serves the cause of defense of Boileau, in the accumulation of apostrophes of the opening period and then in its repetition:

J'ai vu moi-même (qu'il soit permis à un Académicien de se citer ici, puisqu'il s'agit de l'honneur des Lettres); j'ai vu ce frère qui vous est si cher, adoucir les ennuis d'une longue navigation, tantôt avec ce Poëte qui fut l'Ami de Scipion, tantôt avec celui qui fit les délices d'Auguste. Je l'ai vu employer les heures de son repos à chercher dans l'Histoire, non cette connoissance stérile & infructueuse qui ne fait que l'homme savant; mais cette connoissance active & pratique, qui fait l'Homme d'Etat & le Capitaine, la veille d'un grand combat, étudier tranquillement dans les Héros des tems passés, des actions de conduite & de valeur, dont il alloit lui-même donner de nouveaux exemples.

C'est ainsi, Monsieur, que les grands hommes sçavent honorer les Lettres en s'honorant eux-mêmes. (288–89)

D'Estrées was of course the real commander at Malaga. Even without knowing as we now may how much Valincour's portrait of him reflects his own (reading Horace and writing to Bossuet in a schedule of heavy administrative labor), the speaker's privileged access to the truth in this depiction could well dispose his audience to hear favorably the transition to a Boileau, the active man, soldier in his own way and a way that is—or should be—"ce qui nous convient plus particulièrement."

Love of truth, again like a good preacher, the speaker presupposes, is of necessity combat for the truth. That Boileau's satires, alone among his writings, reflect, as Valincour insists, constant battle in the cause of even poetic truth is a profession of faith, as apparently so for the auditors as for later readers of Antoine Adam's study of the genesis of the satires.[12] The speaker repeats Boileau's own assertion that it was the writer, not the man, who was this satiric target. He allows the equivocal distinction of symbol and specific referent to stand. But to offset it, as well as to dispel objectionable suggestions of an idolatry of poetry/writing, Valincour draws up his strategies on two fronts. First,

12. In résumé of earlier work (including gratuitous name changes for rhymes), see *Œuvres* (Pléiade ed., 1966), xi. Cf. Lanson's judgment, however, that Boileau "laissant de côté l'érudition et la diffamation, offrit aux honnêtes gens des jugements sincères, que le goût et un certain idéal de perfection littéraire dictaient." *Boileau* (Paris: Hachette, 1892), 74; Allen G. Wood on maintenance of a "standard of both ethics and reason": *Literary Satire and Theory: A Study of Horace, Boileau, and Pope* (New York: Garland, 1985), 84 and passim.

he orders his narrative chronology in a manner that directly parallels his earlier presentation of Racine's career and evolution. Second, he again seeks transcendent authority, now centrally, by elaboration of a "classical credo,"[13] principles of truth whose acceptability would in the abstract scarcely be questioned by "Anciens" in the audience but which again constitute a profession of faith not so palatable to others (say, La Motte). Purposely tendentious on both fronts (and courageously so) under the standard of the cause of higher harmony, Valincour's public academic discourse remains polemical, combative in the spirit of truth he represents in Boileau.

In repeating the pattern of Racine's eulogy, Valincour replaces what had been the culmination of the biblical plays and royal historiography with Boileau's last religious verse and that celebrating Louis's military achievements. In both domains of Boileau's writings, he had to assume the burden of proof imposed upon him by an audience predisposed to skepticism on both of these claims. Valincour gives the foreground to Boileau's epistles and ode on Namur, strategically minimizing thereby the threat to assent that primary focus on the polemical satires and *Art poétique* would have posed. Among the epistles, he selects that on the love of God (XII, dedicated to abbé Eusèbe Renaudot) to make his case. It is the last piece, Boileau had himself maintained, in defense of true love of God against bad theologians.[14] Boileau's insistence that love of God for Himself is the foundation of Christian life and morality, powerfully expressed in the epistle, transported Bossuet, who had proclaimed the poem "a celestial hymn of divine love,"[15] had found in it echoes of his own treatise (posthumously published, 1736), and read corrections demanded of the author in a controversy that delayed integral publication until the collected works edited by Valincour and Renaudot appeared in 1713.[16] An alleged doctrinal Jansenism with concomitant anti-Jesuit attacks, which triggered and fueled first opposition to publication, remained in the minds of Valincour's clerical audience, incriminating him by the very eloquence of his convictions on Boileau's "true religion."[17] Less dangerously, but more at variance

13. For J. R. Miller, loc. cit., p. 35: "le credo classique tel que l'a prêché Boileau."

14. Boileau to Brossette, letter of 15 November 1709. *Œuvres complètes* (Plèiade ed.), 727.

15. Bossuet to abbé Renaudot, s.d. [Dec. 1696]. Cited by A. Adam, ibid., 982. Cardinal de Noailles also read the text.

16. See above, chap. 5, nn. 77, 78.

17. On Boileau's Jansenism, Henri Busson, *La Religion des classiques* (Paris: PUF, 1948), 30–34.

with his personal inclinations than religious tenets he held unswervingly in accordance with the catechism of Meaux, Valincour condemns the theatre. Again following on Bossuet's traces, he is however less sweeping than the bishop in condemnation and more specifically paraphrases Boileau's criticism of romance as the center and predominant subject of theatrical representation (302).

Boileau's less than zealous dedication to royal historiography was general gossip by 1711 and had reached as far as the Vatican Library according to De Brosses.[18] Valincour leaves a lacuna but places representatively the "Ode sur la prise de Namur" prominently enough to block the vision of the omission. Lightly, he uses the defensive line of Boileau's previous defender, Baillet,[19] that the truth of this kind of panegyric has its best guarantees in a satirist's earlier production (Boileau's own tack initially in fact in addressing the monarch). Once more it is the spirit, that of Boileau's discourse on the ode, rather than the letter that Valincour wishes to speak through him. Attacks on the letter, literal interpretations of the "official" poet's professed hesitancies,[20] were as enduring in the audience as a sense of the doctrinal error of *Epître XII* and the religion of Boileau's later years.

The prestige of the classical credo that Valincour extracts from Boileau's writings, an influential text in the development of an idealized "formation de la doctrine classique," continued its polemical charge as it became through the nineteenth century the most frequently reprinted of Valincour's writings.[21] Continuing the kind of official literary history already sought in the eulogy of Racine, and whose origins in the Académie's own discourses have not been adequately acknowledged, Valincour solidifies by generalization principles already at work in his presentation of Racine. Platonizing is no less obvious here than in his conception of the Republic of Letters and the Académie. Concentrating

18. Letter of 1 July 1748: "Moi-même j'ai ouï dire au Cardinal Passionei qu'il tenait de la bouche de Boileau qu'il avoit connu dans sa jeunesse, que ni lui, ni Racine, n'avaient jamais été assez sots pour travailler sérieusement à l'histoire d'un roi vivant." *Lettres de Charles de Brosses à Ch. C. Loppin de Gemeaux* (Paris: Firmin-Didot, 1929), 186. Officially, Boileau put the appointment at the apogee of his career ("Preface" of 1683. Adam ed., p. 857).

19. *Jugemens des savans* (Amsterdam: Dep. de la Cie, 1725), 4:359.

20. Hesitancy (e.g, "Epître IV," vv. 1–4) become ritualized with praise, an ironic protection that can be literalized for parody. "Incapable peut-être du sublime," Voltaire remarked in his discourse of reception (Moland ed., 23:211). Among parodies was Matthew Prior's "An English Ballad on the Taking of Namur by the King of Great Britain" (1695).

21. See Bibliography I, B, 4 and n. 26.

a long tradition and contributing to a long history to come, of canonized principles of a "classical doctrine," Valincour posits love of truth as its first principle. This first principle founds a system and esthetic with its three corollaries—study of nature, contemplation of the great touch-stones of antiquity, and the guidance of reason.

[1] Comme il [le vrai] ne se trouve que dans la nature, ou pour mieux dire, comme il n'est autre chose que la nature même, Monsieur Despréaux en avait fait sa principale étude. Il avoit puisé dans son sein ces grâces qu'elle seule peut donner, que l'art emploie toujours avec succès, & que jamais il ne scauroit contrefaire. [2] Il y avoit contemplé à loisir ces grands modèles de beauté & de perfection, qu'on ne veut voir qu'en elle, mais qu'elle ne peut voir qu'à ses Favoris. Il l'admiroit sur-tout dans les Ouvrages d'Homère, où elle s'est conservée, avec toute l'innocence des premiers tems; et moins de le paroître. . . . [3] Mais c'est en vain qu'un Auteur choisit le Vrai pour modèle. Il est toujours sujet de s'égarer, s'il ne prend aussi la Raison pour guide. Monsieur Despréaux ne la perdit jamais de vue. (297–98)[22]

In 1717, after the publication the previous year of Terrasson's critical remarks on the *Iliad*, J.-B. Rousseau remarked to Brossette that despite the "efforts of extravagant critics, the court does not fail to be for Homer; it is the Cardinal de Polignac and M. de Valincour who have fixed the Court's judgment."[23] The discourse of 1711 is Valincour's first "public" offensive in the quarrel of the ancients and moderns. It is seconded by his discourse before the company in 1717 and continued meanwhile more covertly both in the edition of Boileau published in 1713 and in privately circulated verse. Valincour has no wish to renew by his own discourse of 1711 what he calls the "fameuse guerre." His project is rather to exhort the Académie to solidarity in the principles evoked through Boileau and his combat in earlier campaigns of that battle of books. Pushing the polemic, he introduces the new champion, Mme Dacier, in the presence of the enemy (La Motte, who in fact

22. Structurally, Rene Bray's "doctrine classique" (1927) is here (*La Formation de la doctrine classique*. Paris: Nizet, 1961); [1] chap. 5, "L'Imitation de la Nature," p. 147, citing Boileau's "Epître IX": "Rien n'est beau que le vrai"; [2] chap. 6, "L'Imitation des anciens," p. 171: ". . . le principe de l'imitation des Anciens est fondée sur le principe de l'imitation de la nature."; [3] chap. 4, "Le Rationalisme classique," p. 122: "Dès l'origine la raison prend le pas. Le culte des anciens est nettement subordonné au culte de la raison." Cf. also Adam's "esthétique de l'expression," *Histoire* 3:49–51.

23. J.-B. Rousseau to Brossette, 28 Aug. 1715: "Malgré les efforts de tous ces critiques outrés, la cour ne laisse pas d'être pour Homère, c'est M. le Cardinal de Polignac et M. de Valincour qui ont fixé le jugement de la cour." *Correspondance*, ed. P. Bonnefon (Paris: Cornély, 1911), 19.

submitted drafts of his own Academic eloquence for Valincour's comments[24]). If in an honorific, figurative way Mme Dacier—Valincour's
close friend as well as companion in arms—is put forward as Boileau's
true successor, Valincour goes further. She may be held to be as fully
worthy of a place in the Académie as she is in its discourse.[25]

Il faut espérer que ceux qui se sont fait une fausse gloire de résister aux traits
du défenseur d'Homère, se feront honneur de céder aux grâces d'une Nouvelle
Traduction, qui le faisant connoître à ceux même à qui sa Langue est inconnue,
fait mieux son éloge que tout ce qu'on pourroit écrire pour sa défense. (298)

The full force of Valincour's exhortation to peace within the Republic of Letters, and to attention to the letter of article thirty-four of the
statutes, is not present until his peroration. With the king's exemplary
efforts to overcome economic disorders, warweariness, and grief over
the death of a royal heir, it is a scandal to the mind that bickering
within the Republic of Letters and the king's Académie should exist.
Putting himself in the place of Boileau, speaking finally as always in
this discourse through agreement with him, Valincour also denounces,
as Boileau had, the vain efforts of panegyrics and medalistic histories.[26]
Time has buried in oblivion more worthy monuments to past greatness.
In the present state of France, some of its past greatness may already
be forgotten, the eulogist of the reign implies and accordingly gives a
final unexpected slant to the obligatory Louis/Augustus parallel, a
change that may be seen to look forward to bolder ones in the form
of the discourses to come.

The portrait presented of Augustus finally remains an incomplete
allegorization of the present in Valincour's penultimate period (305–
6). It is turned toward a past glory, as threatened potentially by disorder
among the true guardians of its preservation within the Académie as
by disorder beyond it. Leading up to a final, ringing affirmation of
Boileau's place among the glories of the reign—"N'en doutons point,
Messieurs, tel & plus encore, la Postérité verra l'auguste LOUIS dans les
Ouvrages de M. Despréaux, & dans ceux de cette illustre Compagnie"
(306)—the historian in fact issues with it a challenge to the audience
to rise to the highest dedication to its ideals. From the act of faith in

24. Valincour to Bouhier, 16 Sept. 1729. *RHLF* 31 (1924), 395.
25. See below, n. 57.
26. Boileau was a member of the Académie (1685–1706) and wrote inscriptions
included in the 1702 *Médailles sur les principaux événements du règne.* He was, however,
highly critical of Charpentier's style in them (see Adam, ed., p. 611) and according to
the *Bolaeana* mocked the activity in conversation.

its ability to do so, expressed with that challenge, Valincour passes on to one more in conclusion. Lowering rather than raising his voice, the Academician's and the royal historiographer's eloquence finally seeks appropriate closing in a rhetorical simulation of prayer. Rather than a false idealization of the realm, the most fitting offering from the sanctuary of the muses is enunciated as a prayer for the king in his personal bereavement, for his guidance of the realm, and for its wellbeing. The last words of this eloquence, which the speaker wished to be heard along with "gloire," are peace and happiness.

Puisse-t-il encore, durant un grand nombre d'années preparer aux siècles à venir de nouveaux sujets d'admiration.
  Puisse la cruelle affliction, qui vient de mettre son courage à une si rude épreuve, être la dernière de sa vie.
  Et puisse une longue & heureuse paix le mettre bientôt en état de procurer à ses peuples un bonheur qui fait le plus cher objet de ses desirs, & qui fera la confirmation de sa gloire. (306)

When not kept from Paris by duties for Toulouse, Valincour did more than participate in the receptions, delegations, and presentations of the Académie's public functions he almost invariably attended. He was a part, from the start, of the smaller working groups that kept the institution functional and reflected practically on their operation. A pattern was established in the year August 1700–September 1701. At a moment since described as "grammatical anarchy"[27] (concerning both the unsettled methods of the imminent work on the grammar and final stages of revision of the *Dictionnaire*), Valincour was named to a committee of four (with Perrault, T. Corneille, and abbé Dangeau) to present matter for discussion during the last quarter of 1700. He duly offered with his colleagues grammatical points drawn in part, the registers note, from d'Ablancourt's writings.[28] After completion of all but compilation of the revisions of the dictionary was announced to Pontchartrain in December and the king of Spain had been complimented on his accession, Valincour was reported to the minister to be among those contributing "dissertations" for the company's discussions. His subject was to be Malherbe's sonnets.[29] At the same time he

27. Thérèse Goyet's phrase. *L'Humanisme de Bossuet* (Paris: Klincksieck, 1965), 1:169.
  28. *Registres,* 1:361–62. Also on Vaugelas. No identified contributions by him can be found in these collected remarks (*Observations de l'Académie françoise sur les Remarques de M. de Vaugelas,* Coignard, 1704; 2nd ed., revised and augmented, 1705).
  29. Ibid., 1:359, 371.

contributed and participated in an ongoing examination of Vaugelas's *Remarques*. On 8 January 1701, then again on 7 and 25 May, he recorded, himself, in the registers continuing grammatical work that was pursued until revisions of the dictionary were resumed in October. In July he helped select the year's prize pieces in poetry and prose (though he skipped their public reading). He attended memorial services in the more capacious new setting of the église des Cordeliers for his deceased colleagues Rose, the bishop of Noyon (Clermont-Tonnerre), and Segrais, and took part in deliberations for and reception of their successors Louis de Sacy, Malézieux, and Campistron. In the second session of deliberations on the latter two, Boileau joined Valincour (but stayed clear of their reception); those two sessions were the only ones Boileau attended that year.

More than a decade later, when this pattern of activity again became possible, replacing the persistent but scattered attendance of the intervening years, Valincour began much more than a new series of delegations, which in 1714 took him with Cardinal de Rohan to offer the Académie's condolences to the d'Estrées on the occasion of the maréchale's death. In February of that year he was named to a commission (with Huet, Renaudot, and again abbé Dangeau) requested to draft a new set of statutes.[30] This charge followed another series of proposals for the Académie's activities while the printing of the *Dictionnaire* was in course. After a generally low attendance in 1712, things had looked up for the future with the succession of Dacier as *Secrétaire perpétuel* in September 1713. Valincour may especially have wished to support Dacier's efforts to renew the Académie's directions when he responded to the request of 23 November 1713 that all Academicians submit a memoir on the subject to the new secretary.

The first of four memoirs received that were printed for the membership and its public deliberations, Valincour's was long mistakenly thought to be a draft of Fénelon's well-known *Lettre*.[31] But in nature and thrust it is a quite different document. Divided into two parts, of which the first, longer section deals with the present schedule, Valincour's memoir is, more than Fénelon's, a true working paper. Much shorter, and much less self-indulgent than Fénelon's musings in reflec-

30. Session of 22 Feb. 1714, ibid., p. 571.
31. For discussion of the circumstances of attribution to Fénelon and conclusive attribution to Valincour: Charles Urbain, "Les Premières rédactions de la 'Lettre à l'Académie.'" *RHLF* 6 (1899), 367–77. The "Mémoire sur les occupations de l'Académie" is quoted here from *Œuvres de Fénelon* (Paris: Lebel, 1824), 21:145–55.

tive solitude, Valincour's concerns seemed to Charles Urbain those of a "laborious member" concerned with everyday business, and in that all the more seriously devoted to "the mission of the Company."[32]

Valincour begins with a brief defense against the bad jokes of the "ignorant" that offers some summary definitions. To provide a dictionary that will be a timeless repository of the changes of the language, he asserts, is itself an unending task by nature imperfect at each stage. The Académie has made a praiseworthy if not perfect start. Changing metaphors as he moves to the matter of the grammar, the writer likens a dictionary to a well-tempered clavier (146). It will render true tones but yet requires a manual of instruction ("art") offered by grammar. To render the utility of that work more compelling, Valincour generally emphasizes its importance for foreign learners of French, then offers the example of Matthew Prior, "peut-être de tous les étrangers, celui qui a le plus étudié notre langue" (147); Prior, he reports, had a "hundred times" expressed impatience over the completion of such a useful volume.[33] Bringing his claims for utility back to France, Valincour extends them in another way. He hopes to include the public more, as has the Académie des Sciences with geometry (which has made such extraordinary progress in society in the last thirty years, he attests); hoping for the public's interest and betterment he proposes something like a newsletter. All will profit if members vary contributions in the form of letters or dialogues as well as the more usual questions (149–50). All Academicians (including those of provincial academies) should submit remarks regularly and promptly, which would be printed quarterly.

For the double advantage of providing foreigners with a commentary on "our good authors" and French speakers with a surer guide to their language, since "le fond de notre langue n'est pas encore parfaitement connu" (149), Valincour recommends a combination of scrutiny of the speech of "honnêtes gens" and good authors, rather than compilation of the work of previous grammarians. In our "good

32. Charles Urbain, loc. cit., p. 370.
33. Valincour most likely met Prior when he accompanied Lord Portland as secretary in 1699 and remained with Lord Jersey. In June, he was a guest of Boileau at Auteuil, where Boileau assured him that he had "more genius than all the Academy." Prior may also have been met through Torcy (see above, chap. 5, n. 48). He returned briefly in 1711, then in 1712. For the quotation and description of Prior's reactions to France, see Charles K. Eves, *Matthew Prior: Poet and Diplomatist* (1939; Rpt. New York: Octagon, 1973), 137, 220–37, 243.

books," attention should be paid to "toutes les façons de parler qui le
mériteront, ou par leur élégance, ou par leur irrégularité, ou par la
difficulté que les étrangers peuvent avoir à les entendre" (148). With
some evident pleasure, after taking part in proofreading of the completed second edition of the *Dictionnaire* (1718),[34] Valincour specifically
enumerates in his preface to it features embodying these earlier recommendations. Words have been "republicanized," he ventures to say,
in that each is given entry only according to alphabetical listing, has
its own cluster of illustrated significations, and is distinguished but not
excluded according to level of style. "Dès qu'un mot s'est introduit
dans notre langue, il a sa place acquise dans le Dictionnaire, & il seroit
souvent plus aisé de se passer de la chose qu'il signifie, que du mot
qu'on a inventé pour le signifier, quelque bizarre qu'il paroisse" (xxiv),
Valincour maintains (and Goujet reports with approval).[35]

Working generally within a tradition of definitions of usage learned
nearly a half-century earlier with Bouhours, Valincour leaves a considerable margin of variation (that is, freedom from rigidly codified
standard usage) for individual speakers.[36] A touch of his own early
freedom, the "raillerie" of the young man who had collaborated with
Bouhours, is set on the dedication of the *Dictionnaire,* which had,
ironically, fulfilled threats made long before in Pontchartrain's admon-
itions to the reluctant correspondent on this most onerous kind of letter
writing.[37] After his own grammatical remarks, Valincour paraphrases
Quintilian on the frivolity of grammatical study: "Il y a des choses si

34. With Renaudot. See session of 4 Jan. 1717, *Registres* 2:18.

35. The Preface's only rhetorical flourish is this analogy: "Il semble en effet qu'il
y ait entre les mots d'une Langue, une espèce d'égalité comme entre les Citoyens d'une
République, ils jouissent des mesmes privilèges et sont gouvernés par les mesmes loix;
et comme le Général d'Armée et le Magistrat ne sont plus citoyens que le simple
soldat, ou le plus vil artisan," Cited in *Dictionnaire de l'Académie,* 7e éd., p. xxiv.
Goujet's detailed critique is in *Bibliothèque françoise* 1 (1741), 203ff; see also, on
"restrictions," G. Matoré, *Histoire des dictionnaires français* (Paris: Larousse, 1968), 94
and passim.

36. See, e.g., Vaugelas, "Préface," 1.3 (facsimile ed., Droz, 1934). For Bouhours,
"bon usage" depends on "bel esprit," but the field of investigation is the same for the
grammarian: "On a beau lire les bon livres, & voir le grand monde; on ne fait rien,
si la nature ne s'en mesle" (*Entretiens d'Ariste et d'Eugène,* 2nd ed., 1671, p. 209).
Bouhours's continuation of Vaugelas is examined by Théodore Rosset, "Le Père
Bouhours continuateur de Vaugelas," *Entretiens, Doutes, Critique et Remarques du Père
Bouhours sur la langue française* (Grenoble: Allier, 1908), 77–160.

37. See above, chap. 1, n. 110 and text.

frivoles dans certaines parties de la grammaire, qu'un Grammarien sage doit se faire un mérite de les ignorer" (xxvi).[38] Concerned causally with what are surely perceived as essential characteristics of the language—clarity, precision, elegance—Valincour is predominantly concerned with "connaissance pratique" both in compilation and use of the dictionary; wise grammarian that he remains, he leaves final proclamation of the universality of the French language (promised to entice the Academicians in 1714), and its intrinsic rights to that place, to the huffing and puffing of the dedicatory epistle by Massieu in 1718 and to the future topics of the Prussian Academy.[39]

In the second, shorter section of the 1714 *Lettre* Valincour, recommending for the future, reminds the Académie that it has in its history a good example that it might again follow, now more temperately, in its remarks on *Le Cid* as well as those more recently done on Malherbe.[40] Observations offered for grammatical scrutiny of the best authors seem a natural preparation for a series of authoritative editions of them, for "honnêtes gens" rather than scholars, on the model of Dacier's translation of Aristotle's *Poetics*.[41] Just as grammatical remarks would lead to the generalizations of a grammar, as well as its founding examples of usage, the series of editions would appear to be the best means of accomplishing "le dessein que l'Académie a tousjours eu de donner au public une Rhétorique et une Poétique" (152). The wisest and most judicious practice of antiquity, after all, had worked this way, Valincour recalls. Voltaire reiterated these recommendations.[42]

Without Fénelon's detail, Valincour's *Lettre* only suggests schematically the contents of the future poetics and rhetoric. The "talents

---

38. The paraphrase of Quintilian has picked up a resonance of Vaugelas's famous principle of the "grammairien sage" (Preface, 5. 2): "En un mot l'usage fait beaucoup de choses par raison, beaucoup sans raison, & beaucoup contre raison."

39. While eschewing a hierarchy and the final term of "perfection" Rivarol and others would see, Valincour like Bouhours ("Entretien sur la langue française") believes in a "precellence" which is "la conformité d'une langue avec la fonction qu'elle doit remplir" and the potentiality for "bon sens qui brille" / "bel esprit." On the term and its currency, Alfred Ewert, "Of the Precellence of the French Tongue" (Oxford: Clarendon, 1957), 6–7, 19.

40. On the Aristotelian orientation of this remark, see above, chap. 3, p. 77.

41. "Peut-être pas si intelligible de son temps pour les Athéniens qu'elle l'est aujourd'hui pour les François . . . accompagnée des meilleurs notes qui aient peut-être jamais été faits sur aucun auteur de l'antiquité" (152). Privately Valincour later called the notes "impertinentes": letter to Bouhier, 19 May 1726, *RHLF* 31 (1924), 381.

42. *Lettres philosophiques*. Ed. R. Naves (Paris: Garnier, 1962), 139–40.

particuliers" of the language, in tragic poetry and epigrams particularly, should be considered, as should versification necessarily invented for "mesures convenables aux mots dont notre langue est composée" (153). The eloquence of pulpit and lawcourt, renewed at least four times in the preceding century, he observes, is proposed as the proper field of investigation for a rhetoric. Differing decidedly from Fénelon on an ultimate model of eloquence, Valincour singles out Bourdaloue, "qui a effacé tous les autres, et qui est peut-être arrivé à la perfection dont notre langue est capable dans ce genre d'éloquence."[43]

Finally, with a different focus from Fénelon's in his extended treatment of the Querelle des Anciens et des Modernes, Valincour makes only passing allusion to that war of polemics while elaborating his views of the nature of the editorial function of Academicians in their future work:

Or cela ne se fera pas en se contenant d'assurer avec une confiance peut-être mal fondée, que nous sommes capables d'égaler et même de surpasser les anciens. Ce n'est en effet que par la lecture de nos bons auteurs, que nous pouvons connoître nous-mêmes et faire ensuite sentir aux autres ce que peut notre langue et ce qu'elle ne peut pas, et comment elle veut être maniée pour produire les miracles qui sont les effets ordinaires de l'éloquence et de la poésie. (152)

Minimizing reference to the quarrel, in his eagerness for an efficiency of operations that disharmony lessens, it remains the "ordinary miracle" of humanist training and its vision that takes precedence over the specialist's expertise. Paraphrasing Æschines this time, Valincour forcefully concludes with a warning against disharmony and dilatoriness (which, as the speaker himself revealed, had already made the Académie the stuff of popular gossip and learned wisecracks). The tones might have been even more portentous had the speaker known that these sentences were among the last of his public utterances in the Académie of Louis le grand before the king's death. His plea, all the more needed during the uncertain times of a regency (and interim protector) to come, is for exact discipline and attention to the statutes, in order to preserve the most precious of Academic privileges—"l'indépendance et la liberté que nous procure la glorieuse protection dont nous sommes honorés." "Eschine disoit à ses concitoyens qu'il faut

43. Valincour's judgment follows Boileau's: e.g., in "A Madame la présidente*** sur le portrait du Père Bourdaloue," first published in the contemporary 1713 edition.

qu'une république périsse lorsque les lois n'y sont point observées, ou qu'elle a des lois qui se détruisent l'une et l'autre,"[44] Valincour conclude, adding for the company by statute a republic that "il seroit aisé de montrer que l'Académie est dans ces deux cas" (154).

Regency and Fleury

It seemed to Dacier entirely fitting that it fell to Valincour, on 22 July 1719, to offer the Académie's compliments to the young Louis XV, on the occasion of his unique (first and last) visit. It was a date, the aging Academician promised, that would be engraved in golden letters in the Académie's annals. "Meeting public expectation, accustomed to see only chefs-d'œuvres from him," Dacier in fact recorded, Valincour's compliment was "very noble, very wise, and marvelously sustained the reputation of the Company."[45] In an exchange with his fellow Academician, the maréchal duc de Villeroy, the king's governor who accompanied him, Valincour offers the boy a gentle admonition to apply himself to the study of letters, indeed to enjoy the fruits of his realm and his Académie's labors.[46] With a personal prestige derived from it, Valincour simply pledges to the new king the same devotion of service the Académie had offered his "auguste Bisaïeul."

By a new situational irony (providential it might seem to some of the clerical majority of the regency Académie) it had also been Valincour who had received the first Academician elected after the death of Louis XIV. The unusually large number of twenty-seven Academicians had attended the reception, 23 June 1717, in which Valincour welcomed the bishop of Fréjus, André-Hercule Fleury, future cardinal, first minister, and de facto protector of the Académie, at the time principal tutor to the king (by testamentary wishes of Louis XIV) and

44. Æschines is within the rhetorical pantheon and would be familiar to readers of Scaliger (see M. Fumaroli, *L'Age de l'éloquence* [Geneva: Droz, 1980], p. 412); he infrequently appears in 17th-century French rhetorical manuals. The passage Valincour paraphrases is given by Demetrius as an example of anaphora ("On Style," ed. W. Rhys Roberts. Loeb ed., p. 463), which Valincour likes in his own higher style. The paraphrase here suggests his reminiscence and emphasis on the subject: repeated focus on law/statutes and equality in their ordered observance.

45. *Registres* 2:81.

46. Paul Mesnard belittles the exchange, with Villeroy, as "le plus touchant échange de bienveillante condescendance et de respectueux hommages." *Histoire de l'Académie française* (Paris: Charpentier, 1859), 58. But the real exchange is the subtext between Valincour and Fleury, whom he received in 1717 and will later compliment by sustaining (between the tutors) the garden metaphor.

member of the regency *conseil de conscience*. It was Du Bos this time who recorded the Academicians' special gratitude to Valincour for "the honor done the Académie by his fine discourse," again subject to much discussion in the Republic of Letters.[47]

With authority by now well established, Valincour greets Fleury with a discourse that takes noticeable liberties with its traditional form. François de Callières, his predecessor, is given only the most formal brief eulogy,[48] and, in place of its expected elaboration, the central section of the discourse is devoted to issues that consequently seem the more pressing, even urgent, for all assembled. After an exordinum placing Fleury in the succession of royal preceptors that have distinguished the Académie by their utility, Valincour launches upon a full-scale remapping of the *sanctuaire des muses*. With a bold stroke, for an established *Ancien,* he sacrifices the "marvels of Amphion and Orpheus" among other ingenious fictions dear to the Greeks ("qui ont tousjours esté des enfants"). He demythicizes the muses, presenting them simply as personifications designating a common process of reason shared in different mediums.

Il ne faut pas les chercher sur le Parnasse, ni en faire des Déesses; les Muses en effet ne sont autre chose que les différents moyens dont la raison s'est toujours servie pour s'insinuer dans l'esprit des hommes, tantost par la simplicité des discours, ou par la majesté de l'éloquence; tantost par la sublimité de la Poësie, ou par les charmes de la Musique. (268)[49]

For Paul Hazard, this development was one harbinger of an era of triumphant rationalism, one more indicator through promotion of prose of an oncoming "époque sans poésie."[50] The context and the content of Valincour's discourse suggest a different interpretation. A critical exposé of the present decadence of French poetry would surely

47. *Registres* 2:30; J.-B. Rousseau and Brossette agreed, loc. cit. (above, n. 23), 115–16.

48. *Recueil,* 1717, p. 265: "La mort de M. de Callières nous a privéz d'un Académicien dont le mérite avoit paru dans plusieurs Employs illustres, & que son amour pour les Lettres, & son assiduité à nos exercices avoient rendu fort cher à l'Académie." On animosity, see above chap. 5, n. 93.

49. Valincour's demythicizing is also in keeping with the "classical" principles and their rationalism outlined above, n. 22, For what I take to be Valincour's "reflective equilibrium," see also Jeanne Haight's remarks on the expansion of the concept of reason "to meet the needs of the classical writer" and the more pragmatic aspirations of the empiricist: *The Concept of Reason in French Classical Literature, 1635–1690* (Toronto: University of Toronto Press, 1982), 152.

50. *La Crise de la conscience européenne* (1935; Rpt. Fayard, 1961), 318–19.

have been a doubtful means of eliciting the favor and protection the Académie needed and desired.

In the Académie's interests, as Valincour represents them, the Republic of Letters in itself and the Académie as symbol of its present are portrayed as vital. An idealized historical harmony of the social utility of poets, historians, philosophers,[51] and public speakers is first presented, then in central development embodied within the Académie and its recent past. The initial description of orators, which is elaborated in a compliment to Fleury in 1726, by implication both includes Valincour's present efforts and suggests the expanded public role he would have Academic eloquence generally display. That role is a heightened commitment to contemporary affairs; if it may prove not to be a literal adherence to the original statutes, which paradoxically stipulated the non-political nature of Academic discourse,[52] its spirit is warranted by fundamental responsibilities that must be assumed to protect the institutional stability and continuity in moments of uncertainty and transition. Orators of the right sort know how to join "les règles de la morale aux raffinements de la politique, & dans le cabinet des Rois, ou dans les Assemblées des Peuples, ils sçurent par des raisons solides appuyer des conseils salutaires, & montrer les différents avantages & les droits différents de la Paix & de la Guerre" (270). In the form and tone of secular sermon already assumed in 1711, Valincour in his high humanistic seriousness at the same time would in his discourse temper change and open accommodatingly to it. Verbally in this discourse the ancient is displaying the compromise of ancients and moderns that he ritually presided over elsewhere.[53]

After giving first place to the Académie's successes in its primary

51. Poets incite men to "actions généreuses de la Guerre & aux travaux pénibles" (269); historians and philosophers serve statesmen, "les historiens marquant avec soin l'origine et l'établissement des Loix et des Coustumes de chaque pays, & tenant un Registre fidelle des actions bonnes et mauvaises, qui méritoient d'estre transmises à la postérité, donnèrent lieu aux Philosophes de déterminer les bornes du juste & de l'injuste, & de faire voir en quoy consiste la difformité du vice et la beauté de la vertu" (269–70). Orators join "les règles de la morale aux raffinements de la politique, & dans le cabinet des Rois, ou dans les Assemblées des Peuples, ils sçurent par des raisons solides appuyer des conseils salutaires, & montrer les différents avantages & les droits différents de la Paix & de la guerre" (270).

52. Paradoxically it may seem from the point of view of current studies of ideology: Statute 22: "Les matières politiques ou morales ne seront traitées dans l'Académie que conformément à l'autorité du Prince, à l'état du Gouvernement et aux lois du royaume."

53. See above, chap. 5, n. 115 and text.

concerns with the language, in this instance "à la Langue Universelle de tous les Siècles, de tous les Pays, de toutes les Sciences & de tous les Arts" (275), Valincour attests evidence of the present vitality of eloquence, poetry, and history. As Fénelon and he himself had in 1714, Valincour extols judicial and legal eloquence, now shaped for "auditeurs qui ne se laissent plus esblouîr par de vaines paroles, & qui n'ont plus d'attention que pour les choses qui peuvent les rendre plus sages ou plus heureux" (276).[54] Turning to poetry, Valincour paints a picture in which the living legacy of the immediate past brightens the hues; without undue neglect of what might to some seem a diminished place in the real world of letters, poetry is noticeably expanded. Compensation for the always lacking modern epic is sought with a repeated (indeed insistently present) praise of the translation of the *Iliad* by Mme Dacier that has made Homer French. In poetry, as in eloquence, the high goals of wisdom and happiness are deemed present and determine the presentation of "high" genres (religious odes J.-B. Rousseau perhaps heard as praise of his poetry, Polignac's *Anti-Lucrèce*, tragedies continuing in the forms of Corneille and Racine); but among these "sublimities" satire is also admitted.

La Poésie reprenant des sentiments dignes de sa première origine, entreprend aujourd'huy de confondre l'impiété de l'Epicure par les mesmes armes dont on avoit abusé pour l'establir & dans les miracles de la nature qu'elle explique avec des grâces nouvelles, fait voir toute la sagesse & toute la majesté de celuy qui en est l'auteur. Elle nous donne des Odes où la Noblesse du style se joint à la pureté de la Morale;[55] des Satyres qui vengent le bon sens outragé dans des ouvrages ridicules, des Tragédies égales ou supérieures à celles d'Euripide & de Sophocle, où la vérité triomphe, ou le vice est condamné, & dont quelques-unes ne sont pas indignes de la majesté de l'Ecriture qui en a fourni les sujets.[56]

Que si nous n'avons pas esté plus heureux pour le poëme épique, que les Romains pour la Tragédie, nous avons du moins le plaisir de voir Homère devenu François, parler notre Langue, comme s'il avoit esté élevé a l'Académie, & par là se reconcilier avec des personnes de grand mérite, qui n'avoient

54. It is curious that in writing for and in the Académie neither Fénelon nor Valincour makes any direct use of its own tradition of eloquence, so admired within its conventions.

55. That Valincour knew the *Anti-Lucrèce* is known from his time at Sceaux (see above, chap. 5.); that he admired it less in private is suggested in a letter to Gualterio, below, chap. 8, n. 34.

56. Racine but not his followers, it would seem, and surely not Genest, whose *Joseph* is Mme du Maine's success (Letter to Noailles, 1 Jan. 1711, *RHLF* 5 [1912], 466.) There is no reference ever to Crébillon.

d'autres défauts à luy reprocher que d'avoir escrit tant de merveilles dans une Langue qui n'estoit pas la nostre.[57] (276–77)

History's vitality, in its turn, is also infused with a prominently displayed concern for religion. Allusions to Academicians' writing (Claude Fleury's ecclesiastical history and Renaudot's research on oriental religions) supplement a straightforwardly humanistic description of the utility of history which "offre tous les jours des secours nouveaux à ceux qui veulent s'y instruire par rapport à la Guerre, à la Politique, aux Lois & aux coustumes de l'Estat , *& aux véritez mesmes*" (278; my emphasis).

The more surprising development in this tableau, and the innovation of its content, is the inclusion in "bonnes lettres" first of science and mathematics, then of crafts ("ateliers" that open "nouveaux chemins au Commerce"). An enthusiastic amateur scientist, who enjoyed the conversations of Cassini, Valincour the administrator of naval affairs had good reason also to celebrate the achievement of *Le Neptune français* (1693), as he does in his inclusiveness. The expansion of categories in this newly inclusive Academic discourse orients its message and presuppositions in the direction of the *Encyclopédie*'s enterprise.

La Médecine, l'Anatomie, & la Chimie font tous les jours de nouvelles descouvertes qui sont aussitost rendues utiles à tous les hommes dans cette Histoire qu'on appelle l'Histoire de la Nature & qui fait *tout l'honneur à Nostre Nation & à nostre siècle*. L'Algèbre mesme & la Géométrie du haut de leurs speculations les plus abstraites sont descendues dans les boutiques & dans les ateliers; elles y dirigent les Arts utiles à la vie, elles montent sur les Vaisseaux dont elles ont déterminé la construction, elles en calculent la route, elles vont aux extrémités du monde perfectionner l'Astronomie & la géographie, & ouvrir de toutes parts de nouveaux chemins au Commerce. (278–79; my emphasis)

It was for Fleury's ears especially that this vivid tableau was assembled. Organized by three main points, and a tightly constructed logical development of them, Valincour's good "sermon" maintains, as

57. Valincour's friendship and esteem for Mme Dacier (see below, n. 76) directs a veritable campaign for her that goes beyond the "anciens et modernes" cause. If his tendency to respect historical precedent (there is no statute prohibiting women) would seem to preclude a literal campaign for her admission, she is made very much present as exemplum to the male audience and far outshines her "present" husband (a trend distinguished by Fern Farnham, *Mme Dacier,* [Monterey: Angel Press, 1976], 106, 132–33).

did the first, that "if the muses require the protection of kings, the greatest kings do not fail to need the muses" (268). Development then sets recommendations to Fleury to protect the Republic of Letters by making this truth obvious to the king. To show that there is a heritage worthy of the king's protection, the second point supported by the demonstration of the central tableau must be that "letters and sciences have become active and industrious in our century," pointedly situating speaker and audience in a new reality. "And in our century they are esteemed only in so far as they render men either more virtuous or more capable of fulfilling their duties in all estates and conditions" (275). At this stage it becomes apparent that continuing lines of praise of humanistic study and its contemporary relevance are offered by a speaker, experienced himself as a tutor, to another—Fleury—responsible for the essential substance and orientation of the king's education. The final, third point—"For those who know how to make good use of it, the study of letters is the study of virtue itself" (280)—with its commonplace underscores and amplifies his final insistence on the needed content of the royal education.

Having carefully constructed and illustrated his case, Valincour concludes soberly. Something may be heard of the schoolmaster attempting to frighten his pupil in the concluding stark representation of the solitariness and difficulty of the craft of kingship, in which books may be more faithful companions and reliable advisers than those persons who surround the monarch. But again, most forcefully, an urgent message that concerned both the regent and Fleury is conveyed: the need for special care, which both in fact took,[58] that the education offered Louis XV would be in the best sense conservative and thereby open to the present and future of a good master of the realm reigning in a new France.

Faites donc entendre au grand Prince que vous instruisez, que les Lettres ne sont pas un simple ornement de l'esprit, & qu'elles sont encore plus nécessaires à un Roy pour scavoir commander qu'à ses Sujets pour savoir obéir. Dans un Estat bien policé, chaque particulier est suffisamment adverti de ses devoirs; ses amis, ses ennemis, les Loix, les Magistrats ne lui permettent pas de les oublier, ni de rien entreprendre qui y soit contraire. Les Rois seuls sont privés de ces utiles secours. Dès que l'âge prescrit par les Loix les met en possession du pouvoir souverain, les conseils, les remonstrances, la justice, la raison

58. In contrast to older views, J. H. Shennan insists on the regent's good intentions and efforts. *Philippe, Duke of Orleans,* pp. 47, 125, 130.

mesme n'ont plus sur eux d'autre pouvoir que celui qu'ils veulent bien leur donner. Que de bons livres soient donc chers à notre Prince, puisqu'ils doivent un jour lui estre si nécessaires; qu'il s'accoutume de bonne heure à les regarder comme de sages conseillers & comme ses amis les plus fidèles. (285–87)

To enforce the image of the future, the "modelle des bons Roys, le père de ses peuples & l'objet éternel de leur amour," Valincour permits himself a final innovation. Louis le grand appears as expected. He is given, however, an unexpected defect, albeit one allegedly shared by Alexander the Great. Louis himself, according to Saint-Simon,[59] spoke freely of his defective early education. But it was an unusual Academician who took the liberty of that same freedom in the concluding moment of a royal panegyric.

Son auguste Bisayeul si librement pourvu par la nature de tous les talens qu'elle peut donner à un homme né pour commander aux autres, a pourtant senti plus d'une fois qu'il manquoit ce qui ne sçauroit estre acquis que par l'estude.

Alexandre au milieu de sa gloire se plaignit de n'avoir pas appris la Langue Latine, & a fait des efforts louables mais tousjours inutiles, à un certain âge, pour réparer cette perte. (287–88)

Like later historians of the Académie, d'Alembert delighted in the story of circumstances that led to the accidental foundation by Valincour of the portrait collection of its members.[60] Villars having offered his own portrait to the company, Valincour mistrusted his personal motives and feared the symbolic presence of this sole portrait of a member amid those only of sovereigns and protectors previously exhibited. To check the move, Valincour donated portraits of Racine and Boileau. A perhaps overly fastidious reservation of an old courtier, d'Alembert suggests, Valincour's actions seems nonetheless admirable to him as a sign of devotion to essential principles of the Académie. The most precious principle of all, the statutory equality of Academicians, is in fact safeguarded by Valincour.[61] The anecdote also gives relief and points historically to Valincour's choice among other possibilities as the best prospective protector of the Académie as it was defined by its

59. "Sa première éducation fit tellement abandonnée, . . . on lui a souvent ouï parler de ces temps avec amertume." *Mémoires* (Truc ed.), 4:950.

60. *Registres* 4:230–31. See Paul Mesnard, *Histoire,* pp. 59–60: gesture protecting "l'égalité . . . jusque là le moins contesté, le plus respecté des privilèges académiques."

61. "L'Eloge du duc de Villars." *Œuvres complètes* (Paris: Belin, 1821), 3:179: "zelé pour l'honneur des lettres, et sentait toute la dignité de cet état, se montrait, par cette raison, l'ennemi déclaré de la plus légère usurpation académique."

statutes and its history. And with that end in view, a decade of varied support of Fleury begun in 1717 will seem to the Academician at its end to have been well worth the effort.[62]

Last Discourse

The discourse of 28 December 1724, with which Valincour received Antoine Portail, *premier président* of the Parlement of Paris, is in several ways exceptional, although it continues and indeed clarifies the personally innovating line of form and content throughout Valincour's Academic writing. Voltaire's praise of it, as "one of the best discourses ever pronounced in the Académie," elaborates suggestive reasons for his judgment (however casual it may have been) that in turn point to the most exceptional feature of a discourse that brought Valincour a different kind of notoriety. Voltaire the satirist remembered the discourse, whose central section generally denounces false poetic vocations and in particular the doings of society abbés whose versifying amounts to a debasement of both poetic and religious vocations. For Voltaire the attack meant a defense of the dignity of true "hommes de lettres" (in the line of his own contribution to *L'Encyclopédie* under that rubric) and, if memorable still in 1752, was fairly tame stuff. As he recalled it,

M. de Valincour attempts to cure the error of a prodigious number of young persons who, taking their rage to write for talent, rush to present bad verses to princes, inundate the public with their brochures, and blame the ingratitude of the century because they are useless to the world and to themselves. He reminds them that the occupations believed the most base are quite above that which they have embraced.[63]

The moralist's severity, in fact increasing with each Academic piece since 1711, was heard by others simply as satire. Bouhier's correspondence buzzes with rumors spread about Paris concerning the identities of Valincour's targets.[64] And the Academician, now among the four

62. See below, chap. 8, pp. 276–77.
63. *Le Siècle de Louis XIV, Œuvres historiques,* ed. R. Pomeau (Pléiade ed., 1957), 1212 (my translation). Bouhier (1 Feb. 1725) also found it well written and, as Valincour wishes, "rempli de réflections utiles. Chose qu'on ne trouve guère en ces sortes de discours." Henri Duranton, ed. *Correspondance littéraire du président Bouhier No. 8: Lettres de Mathieu Marais à Bouhier 1 (1724–1726)* (St.-Etienne: Université de St.-Etienne, 1980), 73. The *Mercure's* review (Feb. 1725, p. 344) reports an "éloge des lettres" and a useful satire "d'en abuser."
64. "On me mande que le discours de Mr de Valincour a soulevé contre lui bien des gens, qui s'y sont cru désignés, si vous en savez quelque nouvelle, vous me ferez

senior members, was himself doubtlessly harassed by inquiries, which may well have driven him to break his usual silence on his writings and to clarify his intentions by unusual self-commentary.

In unpublished letters to Cardinal Gualterio, Valincour first admits that he had wished to annoy a certain audience, of "libertine poets" and aged gallants, and is gratified to have done so.

Le petit discourse que j'ay eu l'honneur ... d'envoyer a fait encore à Paris plus de bruit qu'il ne mérite. Tous les poètes athées ou libertins dont le nombre est grand et ceux qui sont assez fous pour faire des vers amoureux dans leur vieillesse sont entrés en fureur et je ne me mets pas en peine de les appaiser car je m'estois bien attendu à les fascher.[65]

The ultimate reason for this severity, however, is again a renewal of Academic eloquence, which should have real substance, reason (rather than empty frivolities) that should communicate a needed if unpleasant message to society.

Mais j'ay voulu rompre le mauvais usage qui s'étoit introduit dans l'Académie de n'y prononcer que des discours frivoles et où l'on ne trouve que des paroles vuides de sens. J'ay cru qu'en parlant devant les hommes raisonnables on devoit les accoutumer à entendre la raison et la Morale quoy qu'un peu sévère à leur goust et à leurs inclinations.

J'espère que j'en verray un bon succès et que tant de prestres et d'abbés qui passoient leur vie à faire des vers d'amour auront honte à l'avenir de s'employer à un exercice si contraire à leur profession. Si ce n'estoit point trop désirer j'avoue que je serois au comble de mes voeux.[66]

---

plaisir de m'en faire part," Bouhier wrote to Marais, 2 Feb. 1725 (loc. cit., 73). Marais first reveals that "on n'était pas content de Mr de Valincour parce qu'il semblait avoir voulu instruire un premier Président sur les fonctions académiques" (6 Feb., p. 76), then after reading the discourse in the *Gazette de Hollande* guesses La Monnoye as one of its targets (10 Apr., p. 131). When La Monnoye has disagreed, he changes to the côterie of Mme de Lambert: "Entre nous, je crois qu'il en voulait à quelques courtisans de la marquise de Lambert" (17 Apr., p. 133). Despite Valincour's denial, he sticks to this and fastens on Fontenelle (whose *Œuvres diverses* appeared incriminatingly in 1724): "M. de Valincour a beau dire: la *vieillesse indigente* n'appartient point aux courtisans de la Marquise, mais je crois bien qu'ils ont leur fait sur le recueil des folies de jeunesse, qui se reconnaît dans les œuvres de F. redonnées depuis peu (19 Apr., p. 138).

65. B. M. Add MSS. 20395, pp. 212v–13.

66. Ibid. For Valincour's targets there is an *embarras de choix* even within his immediate audience. His remarks on aged *galants* may as well strike Malézieux (like Fontenelle in the audience); Sceaux and Mme du Maine, then, as well as Mme de Lambert's group. In this vein academic instruction may have been more suitable to

In a final move to bolster his authority (which would have astonished Voltaire and which shows the distance between Valincour and the "espirit philosophique"), Valincour more than hints to Gualterio that the approbation of the pope would be of great service to the cause, one of religion as well as letters he had already begun to champion in his tableau of poetry in 1717.

Si le peu de bonne morale que j'ay tâché de mettre dans ce discours pouvoit aller jusqu'aux oreilles de sa Sté et mériter son approbation cela seroit d'un grand poids pour remettre la vertu dans nostre poésie françoise qui depuis quelque temps est horriblement dépravée. Car les muses qu'on appelloit autrefois les filles du ciel semblent estre devenues en France des servantes de cabaret ou de quelques lieux encore plus infâmes et n'avoir plus d'autre employ que d'exciter les hommes à boire et les femmes à faire l'amour. En quoi certainement beucoup de Payens ont esté plus sages que nous.[67]

The deceased Academician it was Valincour's duty to eulogize, abbé de Choisy, had been in earlier days at least a touchy subject for a eulogist and fit Valincour's characterization of gallant abbés. His adventures en travestie, chronicled in his Histoire de Madame la comtesse des Barres, remain a legendary eccentricity (as d'Alembert too saw it).[68] But Valincour does not sacrifice Choisy as he had Callières. He is, to the contrary, given a prominent place—in fact, final periods of development in the section of the discourse in which celebration of the Académie's august Protector is expected. So placed, Choisy becomes the occasion of Valincour's last innovative modification and modulation of the discursive form and tone of his academic eloquence.

Choisy's old age offers an exemplum, in Valincour's presentation, for those who would persist in frivolities. Retired from society and devoting himself exclusively to reading and writing, the eulogist maintains, the first fruits of Choisy's learned solitude were "quelques morceaux choisis de l'Histoire de France" (surely no pun intended);[69] then, "ayant pris des veües plus convenables à son caractere, il entreprit

Portail's predecessor as premier président, de Mesmes, unfortunate sometime collaborator with the duchesse.

67. Ibid. See below, chap. 7, p. 318 for Valincour's high praise for Benedict XIII, newly elected in 1724.

68. "Eloge," Œuvres complètes (Paris: Belin, 1821), 3:36. On Choisy's adventures and "feminism" see Jean Mélia, L'Etrange existence de l'abbé de Choisy (Paris: Emile-Paul, 1921). The tact of Valincour's eulogy is emphasized, pp. 201–4.

69. A contemporary pun had it that Claude Fleury's history was "choisie"; Choisy's, "fleurie."

l'Histoire ecclésiastique, qu'il a eu la consolation d'achever avant sa mort' (143–44).[70] Service to the king is recalled in Choisy's voyage to Siam. The prose style of Choisy's subsequent account of that voyage (praised by Bouhours and Boileau) displays the same qualities evoked in his academic discourse by Valincour: "officieux, & plein d'une politesse qui n'avait rien d'affecté." There may be some nostalgia as Valincour pays this final tribute to the last Academician of the generation his senior when he entered the Académie. He justifies that tribute with a description of a kind of eloquence that would mirror appreciation of Choisy's, just described, but also recalls his own lessons from Bouhours—"noble et sublime, et en même temps naturelle et sans affectation." In his last appearance before the Académie, Choisy's senility had been responsible for his delivering the shortest discourse on record. Valincour turns that last appearance itself into a gesture of regard ("amitié") for the company and, after evoking his infirmities, recreates the moment of hearing the discourse as one of sublime beauty that no regularity in form could have managed to provide.

Son discours . . . n'avoit certainement rien de tout ce qu'on met ordinairement en usage pour attirer l'attention. Mais comme ses paroles partoient du fond de son cœur, & qu'elles estoient animées par une tendre amitié pour celui de nos confrères dont il faisoit la réception; j'observay avec plaisir, que ce discours, tout négligé qu'il estoit, fit plus d'impression sur l'esprit des auditeurs, qu'il n'en eust fait avec tous les ornements & tout l'appareil que l'art auroit peu s'ajouster. (145–46)

D'Alembert, perhaps aided in part by Valincour's concluding images, found Choisy's discourse moving, "plein de sensibilité." Moving to the generalization that follows Valincour's evocation of this moment, one finds a self-justification for it with an esthetics that had served him almost half a century earlier in his criticism of *La Princesse de Clèves*. Capable of striking a response in a younger generation, which would shortly wish to shed its own ideas—as the speaker had—of the "enflures espagnoles" of institutional rhetoric for the "sensible," the "naturel" Valincour had long before sought finds a newly responsive audience.

70. *Histoire de l'Eglise*, 11 vols. (1703–23). Author of works of devotion from the 1680s on and the Académie's eulogy of Bossuet (1704), Choisy clarifies in the latter that the history was undertaken from a suggestion by Bossuet that became a moral obligation. That Valincour will feel similarly (see below, chap. 7, p. 226) is a bond of sympathy between them.

Tant il est vray, que c'est dans ces mouvements du cœur, supérieurs aux règles & aux préceptes, que consiste la véritable éloquence, dont ni l'adresse, ni le travail des Rhéteurs, ne sçauroient approcher qu'imparfaitement.

Le Peintre, le Sculpteur peuvent bien dans une seule figure humaine rassembler toutes les beautés à toutes les proportions des divers originaux vivans, qui leur auront servi de modelle. Ils feront paroistre à leur gré la joye ou la douleur, la terreur ou la compassion. Mais ils ne parviendront point jusqu'à animer leur ouvrage: & ces passions exprimées avec tant d'art, tant d'estude & tant de recherches, ne nous toucheront jamais autant que celles que nous voyons sur le visage d'un enfant, qui les ressent avant que de les connoistre, & qui les exprime, sans le sçavoir, par les simples mouvements de la nature. (147–48)

The blaze of rhetorical glory expected for this moment is, in the 1724 discourse, contained within the central development that recasts more darkly the tableau of 1717. Heavily censorious, Valincour denounces (141–43) numerous debasers of poetry and its proper place in society—from parasites corrupted by wealthy patrons to drinkers inspired by the cabaret to believe themselves poets and fit to "decider avec hauteur sur des choses qu'ils ne sont pas mesme capables d'entendre"; from youthful delusions of poetic gifts,[71] kindled by false praise, to the pathetic dreams of a similarly deluded old age. Worthless citizens and men without self-sufficiency, useless to the realm as well as dangerous to the Republic they all are, the hard judge concludes. Tribute to Louis XIV, to the past, comes here, as by contrast "esprits du premier ordre" are evoked who alone may "tracer eux-mesmes des routes particulières, & suivre le génie qui les entraisne hors du chemin commun des emplois ordinaires de la vie civile" (141).[72] *Laudator tempora se puero* the speaker insistently allows himself to be.

Unlike the writing of these bad citizens, who are content with frivolously self-indulgent writing, Valincour began his discourse with

71. This advice had been personalized for Jean-Baptiste Racine (see below, chap. 8, for his bitterness).

72. Although both Valincour and Daguesseau had encouraged Louis Racine's sacred poetry (the odes, though not published until later, doubtless figuring in Valincour's generalized praise), both discouraged him from the theater. Valincour also dissuaded him from standing for the Académie, because of Fleury's opposition. On the latter, Racine wrote ironically to J.-B. Rousseau of the "chemin commun des emplois ordinaires de la vie civile": "M. de Valincour me conseilla de m'abandonner à mon protecteur, et, au lieu d'être nommé à l'Académie, je fus nommé Inspecteur des fermes. . . . Ainsi vous voyez que je ne suis qu'un financier subalterne." Cited by A. Rouxel, *Chronique des élections à l'Académie* (Paris: Hachette, 1888), 109.

a celebration of the humanistic and civil ideal of the magistrate. It is embodied in the new Academician, Portail, who has learned lessons in the books of great jurisconsults: that "l'austérité des loix a besoin d'estre tempérée par la douceur des Lettres humaines," and that the good magistrate "doit sçavoir rendre la justice aimable dans ses discours, comme il sçait la faire craindre dans ses Arrests, & respecter dans sa conduite" (130). On the way to his own enactment of this ideal, in the eulogy of Choisy that follows his harsh judgments, Valincour seems to be carried away by his own development (and perhaps by an association known to him that commanded respect for Choisy through forebears including Michel de l'Hôpital). At the center of his discourse he arrives at a seemingly anomalous panegyric of the sixteenth-century authors courageous enough to have written the *Satire Ménipée*. This rhetorical ornament would seem to have even less to do with the placid Antoine Portail than do others that also appear—Scipio and Laelius together in leisure or Terence's power to refresh the mind, commonplaces always fresh to Valincour's imagination. Linking his celebration of magistrates to the *Satire*—"Satire ingénieuse, qui couvrant d'un ridicule amer & judicieux, la folie & l'insolence des Ligueurs, retint tant de bon François dans les sentiments de respect & de fidélité, qu'ils devoient à leur Prince légitime" (136)—Valincour ideally associates men of letters and magistrates (co-authors of the satire, according to his beliefs) in the noblest ideals of citizenship. It was a collaboration Valincour himself sought with friends like Daguesseau and Bouhier. And in the idealized community constituted with those friends, he shared in manuscripts of his own that circulated among them views that displayed the qualities admired in the authors of the *Satire Ménipée*. The declaration of 14 May 1724, with its potential for unleashing fanatical actions, had brought the Ligue to his mind and goaded him to his celebration of those authors who had combatted it.[73]

A key to a changed future for Valincour in advancing age lay with enlightened magistrates, as it would for Montesquieu. The reference to the Ligue also suggests that Valincour was troubled by other troubles and disorder, more grave than the quarrel of the ancients and moderns, those of the *Unigenitus* controversy that threatened the faithful and the Church of France itself. With these fears, Valincour had his own reason for turning toward magistrates and for idealizing them as a class through his eulogy of Portail:

73. On this declaration against reformers see above, chap. 5, n. 138. "On sentait courir le souffle qui anime la Satire Ménipée," Leclercq notes (*Histoire de la Régence* 2:89).

Vous escoutez tant de malheureux, qui sans Vous seroient les victimes de la chicane & de la violence, & qui croyent n'avoir plus besoin d'autres défenseurs lorsqu'ils ont peu parvenir à vous faire entendre leurs plaintes. Qualitéz rares, mais absolument nécessaires à celuy qui doit rendre la justice aux autres, & dont Vous n'estes pas seulement redevable à vostre heureux génie, & à la bonté de vostre cœur, mais encore à l'estude de ces Lettres que nous appellons humaines, parce qu'en effet, en donnant de l'agrément & des lumières à ceux qui les cultivent, elles leur inspirent encore de la douceur & de l'humanité. (131–32)

Poetry's Part

In private Valincour allowed himself to speak of the more trying of his colleagues and the Académie with a *raillerie* that is similar enough to Boileau's in his epigrams as to seem a pastiche. The first of two extant epigrams, probably written shortly after election to the Académie, may well have been a pastiche offered to Boileau in sympathy. At the moment he was piqued by La Chapelle, who, in receiving Valincour, had omitted any allusion to Boileau when Valincour was represented as Racine's aide in royal historiography.

> D'où vient donc tout à coup cette horrible gelée,
> Et ce triste acquilon qui mugit dans les airs!
> C'est que l'Académie au Louvre est assemblée:
> La Chapelle et Danchet y recitent leurs vers.[74]

A quite similar piece changes target to the chilly panegyrics of abbé Boutard.[75] Valincour preferred to deliver his stings more quickly, in passing in letters and conversation, and to combine attacks of this sort in a more richly textured verse.

Even during the busy decade 1703–12, from which no poetry by Valincour appears to have survived, he may have exchanged verse with those who would remain old friends from Auteuil, as well as with Boileau himself. After Boileau's death, Renaudot, Fraguier, Mme Da-

74. Published by Adry (1807), 2:326. Boileau had written similarly against Perrault and included La Chapelle in an epigram in 1699 (Adam, nos. 50, 58, pp. 263, 266). On Boileau's quarrel, letter of J.-B. Racine, *MLN* 54 (1939), 174; Maurice Henriet, "Discourse de M. de la Chapelle sur Racine," *Annales de la Société historique et archéologique de Château-Thierry* 5 (1902), 53–67.

75. Adry, ibid. Raillery of Boutard, emblematic of "frozen" panegyrics, is a leitmotif in Valincour's letters to Noailles; e.g., 14 July 1710, 6 Feb., 1711. *RHLF* 11 (1904), 156; 12 (1905), 480: "Je voudrais seulement qu'on se hastast de tuer l'abbé Boutard de peur qu'il vous fasse une ode." The line continues later simply with "abbé B."

cier until her death in 1720 (reported feelingly to Gualterio),[76] and Valincour continue to exchange verse. A "dixain" was addressed to "Anne, ma sœur," apologizing for the state of a "longue épître" she had requested that had already been sent to Daguesseau. The apology ends with a conspiratorial denunciation of contemporary "overproductive" writers, "modernes" in one way or another.

> Anne ma sœur, vous voulez mon ouvrage.
> Vous en pouvez comme moy disposer.
> Bien est-il vray que si j'estois plus sage
> De la donner je devrois m'excuser.
> Non que je veuille en rien vous refuser,
> Mais connoissant qu'en une œuvre si vulgaire
> Il n'est mot capable de vous plaire
> La mettre au feu m'auroit mieux réussi,
> Et plust à Dieu qu'en pussent autant faire
> Tant d'écrivains qui fourmillent icy.[77]

A similar attack also appears to have figured more extensively in an unfortunately now lost "Idylle sur l'Age d'or et sur la déesse Astrée" sent to Mme Daguesseau after one of Valincour's stays at Fresnes. The title and the chancellor's compliment on style worthy of Bion and Moschus (and Ovid)—"noble, simple, grâcieuse"[78]—suggest a continuation of the earlier appreciative paraphrase of Tasso that had complimented Mme Poncet. The aging poet had flattered Mme Daguesseau, the chancellor quips, to the point of making his homelife an age of iron. As in the earlier verse, pastoral elements lead again to satire with its age of iron; Daguesseau congratulates Valincour for his assault upon the "scourge of bad poets."

By 1712 Valincour's poetry was circulating in a wider and differently constituted circle, identified in part by a manuscript note[79] to a posthumous collection of his verse grouped with writings—"in the manner of each"—by M. et Mme Daguesseau, M. et Mme de Torcy,

76. 17 [Sept. 1720]. B. M. Add MSS. 20395, p. 9v (misplaced): "Nous avons perdu Mad Dacier dont V. E. connoissoit le mérite. On a fait sur sa mort une Elegie que je prends la liberté d'envoyer à V. E. Je suis persuadé que vous la jugerez digne d'estre admiré dans le pays même de Tibulle et de Catulle." The elegy is later identified as Fraguier's. News of abbé Renaudot's death is included in the same letter.

77. Published by E. Charavay, letter to Bouhier, 2 Jan. 1729, L'Amateur d'autographes 5 (1866), 285.

78. Œuvres de Daguesseau (ed. Pardessus), 14:318–19.

79. Adry, loc. cit., p. 326.

Mme de Bouzols,[80] and Mme la marquise de Castries-Vivonne.[81] Four poems, composed it appears between 1712 and 1722, and rescued by Adry from Valincour's posthumous papers, show what poetry, with this special audience, became for him in advancing age and new historical perspectives—"Pour moi, qui vois de près le bout de ma carrière," the poet reflects. Exactly contemporary with the mature Academic pieces, this new poetry provides a supplement to them, extending their concerns and broadening their field of textual reference and echo. Private in the sense of intimate, rather than secret, these writings, like his earlier poems, reveal both talent for verse and commitment to poetry. Paralleling his efforts to renew academic eloquence, but in this domain part of a very active and varied current of renewal of poetic genres, diction, and resources,[82] Valincour's reconstituted later verse, in its fullness, forms, and simplicity of diction, is a consciously new poetry. In "manner" it is decidedly satirical, taking its distance (as might be supposed from the academic discourse in 1724) from the contemporary "vers badin" that was transforming the "galanterie" of Valincour's youth. The four poems, given, seemingly by Adry, not wholly appropriate titles, are an ode ("Sur la paix") and three satires ("Caprice," "Le Sens commun," and "Sur un gros rhume") that might better be designated simply "Satires III, IV, V" [following on the second "Requête à Olimpe" (I) and "De Daphnis à Damon" (II)].

"Sur la paix" is a unique excursion by Valincour into the realm of official verse, or so it may seem. Most probably composed about 1712, and addressed to Torcy, as an ode to peace it celebrates the long-awaited and welcome peace of Utrecht of which Torcy had been the architect. For the task the poet's old muse is summoned up for appropriate meter and figures.

> Vous soyez la bien venue,
> Divine et charmante paix ...
> Du peuple qui vous implore
> Ecoutez les cris touchans,

80. Marie-Françoise Colbert de Croissy (1671–1724), eldest daughter of the minister and Torcy's sister. For a portrait, Saint-Simon, *Mémoires* (Truc ed.), 1:275–76.

81. Marie-Elisabeth de Rochechouart-Vivonne, marquise de Castries (1663–1708), great-niece of Mme de Montespan. Valincour's Montespan and Colbert connections thus both continue here too.

82. Specifically the kind of "commitment" Robert Finch describes for Louis Racine, also in "temperament rather than diction" and "qualities rather than forms." *The Sixth Sense,* pp. 262–63, 43, 73.

> Qu'avec vous Cérès et Flore,
> Bacchus et Pomone encore
> Viennent embellir nos champs.
> Bientôt dans leur sacrifices
> Les labourreurs à genoux,
> Vous offriront les prémices
> Des biens qu'ils tiendront de vous.[83] (vv. 1–2, 7–15)

As the "encore" (v. 10) already suggests, the official turns personal; with a parodic break in the Pindaric surface texture, the poet begins a transformation of the ode's formal features for the satirist's use. Peace in the realm is juxtaposed with war in the Republic of Letters. The traditional blaze of glory of the ode's figures of "noble hardiesse" is replaced, given the continuing scandal of this unworthy battle of books, by a pyre ignited by the high indignation of the poet to consume incendiary books. There is nothing faint-hearted in this attack on two men of the Church, harsh in the case of Valincour's fellow Academician Huet.

> Délivrez encore la terre
> De deux maudits écrivains ...
> Que la flamme dévorante
> Brûle et détruise à souhait,
> De l'abbé Tilladet
> La Préface impertinente,
> Et les discourse assomans
> De ce Docteur qui méprise
> Le sublime de Moïse
> Pour admirer les Romains. (vv. 35–36, 46–53)

And this denunciation is prefaced by an invocation of the muse for favor that will carry the poet beyond his earlier verse (and his contemporary efforts in defense of Boileau in the querelle du sublime).[84] With this new strength polemic would here be put to the highest purpose,

---

83. Adry, loc. cit., 295–97.

84. The dispute between Huet and Boileau begun in 1683 was last revived by Boileau's "Xe Réflexion critique sur quelques passages du rhéteur Longin" (1710). Abbé Tilladet reprinted Huet's letter to Montausier (1683) in 1712 in his edition of Huet's *Dissertations sur divers sujets* (see Boileau, ed. Adam, pp. 541–43). Boileau's "Xe Réflexion" was not published collectively until 1713, with a notice by abbé Renaudot. "Sur la paix" may thus contribute in establishing Valincour's co-editorship of that edition. Boileau himself occasionally did mock Pindarics (Adam ed., p. 264). The same scornful tone for Huet remains: letter to Bouhier, 17 Nov. 1729, *RHLF* 31 (1924), 399–400.

the public function of poetry to which it had been summoned by Malherbe. Once again Boileau had shown the way, in the discourse on the ode probably more than in his illustrations of this high tradition of poetry's public mission/commission.

> Pour moi, qui sur le Permesse,
> Nourri par les doctes sœurs
> N'eut jamais d'autres richesses
> Que leurs stériles faveurs,
> Je veux pourtant que l'on voie
> Briller aujourd'hui ma joie,
> Et me courronnant de fleurs,
> Vous faire, ô paix adorable
> Un holocauste agréable
> De deux méchans auteurs ... (vv. 23–32)

"Caprice" ("Satire III") amplifies the poet's indignation along other lines, although ill-advised poets are not forgotten. Initial grand rhetorical questions (vv. 1–23) reject any frivolity that spring might inspire in the poet. There is no place for "insipides sonnettes," love songs to Lycoris, or even the *Pastor fido* ("par l'abbé de Régnier si sottement chanté," it must be said of the Academician). Nor is there a place for ambition, either the poet's in the city (or Académie) or the courtier's. A third member of a trio that constantly occupies Valincour's new poetry is added: the speculator, a fixture of regency society no less than the "age of iron" evoked in these poems. "Près le bout de ma carrière," the poet confides, there is time only for wisdom of a certain kind. In 109 *alexandrins* Valincour offers a sermonizing lesson on "divertissements" that focuses the poem on a commanding Pascalian image of man "esclave de ses propres chimères." The central development greatly amplifies the earlier meditation on this same vision in the "Lettre de Daphnis à Damon."

Man's uniqueness, the poet reasons, is far from an untroubled "grandeur." It sets him rather doubly out of harmony, in the order of nature that encompasses him and within himself—"L'homme est plein de défauts, dont le plus grand peut-être / C'est de vivre et mourir sans se connaître."[85] He is constantly prey to distractions that in both worlds obscure perceptions of proportion. Tension is consequently central to a life that exerts powerful, contrary attractions to order on the one

---

85. Doubtless of generalized inspiration, it is however difficult not to hear Pascal on "disproportion" through this line and the poem generally. No. 22 (pp. 169–76) in the 1670 ed. of the *Pensées*.

hand and on the other to a delusory "freedom" that flees it. Orotund rhetoric and carefully crafted lines support the poet's amplifications. No image is more forcefully planned than that which concludes the poem with a chilling detachment from the new world seen through the verse. "Je verrois les mortels se déchirer entre eux / Pour l'ombre d'un bonheur qui les rend malheureux" (vv. 98–99).

The younger poet, of the "Lettre à Daphnis," had managed to resolve in poetry the tensions that are the subjects of "Caprice." For the poet of "Caprice" there is no resolution and no recourse to the "bel idéal" of the "Lettre." Both poetry and the wisdom that is its raison d'être in the present of this poetic meditation are lost dreams, unattained in the present and uncertain in the future. The ending "en beauté" in the context of personal confession seems, however, less a chillingly cynical detachment from society than a stark statement of loss tinged with bitterness.

> Pour moi, qui vois de près le bout de ma carrière,
> Si le ciel me rendoit ma jeunesse première,
> Que d'un genre de vie, il me laissât le choix,
> J'irois, n'en doutez pas, dans nos champs, dans nos bois,
> Chercher cette innocence, et cette paix profonde
> Qui firent le bonheur et l'enfance du monde.
> Ni l'or, ni les grandeurs ne pourroient me tenter;
> Content de mon état, sans vouloir l'augmenter,
> Libre des embarras, de la cour, de la ville,
> Sans crainte, sans désirs, et spectateur tranquille,
> Je verrois les mortels se déchirer entre eux
> Pour l'ombre d'un bonheur qui les rend malheureux. (vv. 88–99)

Against this, the "bel idéal" of the "Lettre" rings as hollow as those scored in its verse with a formulaic "Heureux qui . . ."

> Heureux qui peut souffrir une règle fidelle,
> Qui tient tous ses désirs à la raison soumis,
>   Et ne faisant rien que par elle,
> Ne veut rien qui ne soit et possible et permis!
>   Toujours d'accord avec soi-même,
>   Toujours dans un repos extrême. (vv. 133–38)

The message that verse is called upon to amplify in "Le Sens commun" ("Satire IV") is sought in a different way but enforces the vision of "Caprice." Beginning with what may seem an anti-Cartesian thesis—"Le sens commun n'est pas chose commune / Chacun, pourtant, croit en avoir assez"—the poet conducts a demonstration in 100 undecorated decasyllabic lines (as though 10^2 might be a part of that proof) of the contemporary truth of his contention: "Tant il est vrai qu'en ce siècle où nous sommes, / Le sens commun est rare chez les hommes" (vv. 102–3). Fortune in this exemplum offers to each person one wish. A "bon bourgeois" arriving late finds very little left:

> Un vase simple et fait sans aucun art,
> Où on lisoit écrit en vieux gothique:
> "Le sens commun est dans cette urne antique;
> Prenez-en, mais sans perdre un moment,
> Car la fortune en donne rarement." (vv. 25–29)

The latecomer, with the mimed reflex of the "bon bourgeois" ("mieux vaut encore quelque chose que rien") is rewarded; those who indulged less stolid ambitions come to a bad end. For them all, Fortune's favors are undermined by an "amour du gain" that is made to appear universal.

The poet has some malicious fun in passing (once again at the expense of the Académie) with a display of Fortune's wares that resembles the Saint-Germain fair.

> Bonheur au jeu, chez les grands libre accès,
> Folle entreprise, et faite avec succès,
> Gros intérêt prise dans la Compagnie,
> Même, dit-on, place à l'Académie,
> Faveur des rois, honneurs et dignités,
> Emplois brillans, quoique non mérités,
> Argent sans peine, en un mot toute chose
> Dont à son gré la fortune dispose, ... (vv. 16–23)

The mimed dialogue that brings social types into this dance of self-interest that paradoxically refuses the gift of common sense again includes poets.

> "Le sens commun! que veut-on que j'en fasse?"
> Disoit un sot, j'en ai du plus exquis;
> Qu'on porte l'urne à monsieur le marquis;
> Que l'on donne à Madame une telle
> Qui fait l'habile, et n'a point de cervelle;
> Qu'on en fournisse à ce grand magistrat,
> Qui se croit sage, et pourtant n'est qu'un fat;
> A cet abbé, dont la veine féconde,
> De méchans vers fatigue tout le monde. (vv. 35–43)

It is finally, however, the speculator/financier who is made the primary beneficiary of the poet's justice.

> Le financier, plus solide et plus sage,
> Fait moins de bruit, amasse davantage,
> Se cache au monde, et marche sourdement;
> De mille écus, acquis, Dieu sait comment,
> Il fait bientôt cent mille écus de rente,
> De jour en jour son bien croît et s'augmente.
> Bientôt on voit comtés et marquisats,
> D'un vil faquin composer les états.
> Des vieux héros le patrimoine antique,
> Devient celui de marquis comique,
> Qui de ces titres enflant ses qualités
> Flétrit ces noms jadis si respectés.
> Mais rarement la déesse volage
> De ses faveurs accorde un long usage.
> On voit bientôt par un retour fatal
> Le gros joueur réduit à l'hôpital,
> Et maudissant son peu de prévoyance,
> Manquant de tout, mourir dans l'indigence.
> Le financier, justement recherché,
> Dans quelque coin fugitif et caché,
> A tous momens, tremble que la Justice,
> Le découvrant, ne l'envoie au supplice.
> Bientôt, chez lui tout est en désarroi,
> On vend ses biens, et tout retourne au roi.
> Mais son pareil voit en vain son naufrage,
> Le mal d'autrui ne le rend pas plus sage;
> Dans quelque bail il cherche à s'engager,
> L'amour du gain lui cache le danger ... (vv. 75–102)

In earlier days of a lighter touch, this prosopopeia (which recalls "Le Printemps") might well have been freed of its frame of "pseudo"-demonstration. But "Le Sens commun" is unrelentingly rigorous and denunciatory for the same reasons that amplified the bitterness of "Caprice"—the fever of speculation caused by Law's schemes chronicled by Valincour himself in his letters to Gualterio between October 1719 and December of 1720.[86] With its self-disgusted avowal of "sagesse

---

86. See above, chap. 5, n. 117. In his disgust Valincour has played on the "old story" of the four merchants (retold also by Helvétius, De l'esprit, 1818 ed., 1:64) and one of his favorite essays by Montaigne, "De la présomption" (II.2): "... le plus juste partage que la nature nous ait fait de ses grâces, c'est celui du sens; car il n'est aucun qui ne se contente de ce qu'elle lui en a distribué." (Pléiade ed., 1964, p. 644).

manqué," "Le Sens commun" is a corollary of the bleak vision of "Caprice."

There is more than a hint of Molière's Alceste and his cascading indignation over the rituals of courtesy in "Sur un gros rhume" ("Satire V"), written most likely during a two-week confinement in 1718.[87] The poet begins with jocular thanksgiving for being spared some public functions by his indisposition.

> Que d'inutiles complimens,
> De souhaits et de révérences!
> Que de trompeuses assurances,
> De vœux, de bénédictions,
> De fausses protestations,
> Qui toujours ne sont que paroles,
> Et paroles des plus frivoles! (vv. 7–13)

Universal "amour du gain" is again the text: "L'argent, l'argent sur toute chose, / C'est le seul but qu'on se propose / De l'argent dans ce qu'on écrit, / Dans ce qu'on fait; dans ce qu'on dit" (vv. 76–80). The Golden Age once more sets off this society saturated by financial self-interest (to the wonderment also of Montesquieu's Persians and the profit of playwrights, it may be recalled). For his chosen interlocutors, Daguesseau and Torcy, the poet incorporates a scene of a ministerial solicitation by an interested caller. An inner monologue of calculation quickly develops into a spectacle of sychophancy.

> Il est fait ministre aujourd'hui,
> Je m'en vais donc dîner chez lui.
> Nous étions au collège ensemble,
> Je m'en souviens, même il me semble
> Que nous devons être parens,
> C'est une amitié de trente ans,
> Vraiment il faut que je le voie;
> "Hé, bonjour, monsieur, quelle joie
> De vous voir en si grand crédit!
> Oh! je l'avois toujours bien dit,
> Non, le roi ne pouvoit mieux faire,
> Vous lui serez fort nécessaire;
> Mais conservez votre santé
> Pour l'Etat, pour sa Majesté.
> Ma foi, plus je vous envisage,
> Plus je vous trouve bon visage;
> *Mais je vous connois* ... Entre nous,

87. Letter to Gualterio, 22 June 1718. B. M. Add MSS., 20395, p. 21.

> Le travail n'est qu'un jeu pour vous."
> Pendant qu'il attend sa réponse,
> Une comtesse qu'on annonce
> Entre, et dit d'un air effaré:
> "Vous voilà comme un déterré;
> Sans mentir le travail vous tue,
> Et je suis tout exprès venue
> Pour vous détourner un moment,
> Car il faut du relâchement.
> N'auriez-vous point eu la migraine?
> En vérité, j'en suis en peine;
> Un de vos gens m'a confié
> Que vous aviez un cor au pied,
> Et j'en sens la douleur extrême,
> Comme si je l'avois moi-même."
> Et puis tirant à l'ècart:
> "Je voudrois bien vous faire part
> De certaine petite affaire
> Que l'on me propose de faire."
> Car c'est là que tendent toujours
> Tous ces pathétiques discours. (vv. 38–75)

Less amusing than this old story for bureaucrats (and readers of Le Sage) is another new element. This time, rather than new money men, it is a mercenary aristocracy ("genre de courtisans nouveaux") that appears, whose members are already actors as familiar in the news,[88] it would seem, as in comedy.

> Plus que ne faisoit autrefois
> La table d'un prince en un mois.
> De là viennent tant de bassesses;
> De là, marquises et comtesses,
> Genre de courtisans nouveaux,
> Descendent au fond des bureaux,
> En foule en assiégant la porte,
> Attendent que le commis sorte,
> Pour demander d'un air soumis:
> "Puis-je espérer le droit d'avis?" (vv. 96–105)

The poem closes with a surprise. As in his Academic eloquence, the poet concludes not with a mythical past but with France past and present. He offers a simulated prayer for its well-being in this verse,

---

88. See Valincour's remarks on noble customers of Law, above, chap. 5, n. 117.

apparently addressed to Daguesseau; the prayer takes final place and textually plays upon both the figure of Michel de l'Hôpital Valincour heroicized and a portrait done by him of the virtues of the chancellor's father.[89] The satirist is not led in his special heat to indict the present, however ferrous, and does not issue his own *Philippiques*. It is rather the royal historiographer who concludes, with the "bel idéal" of the magistrate, summarizing also in himself through his "new poetry" principles of service to the sovereign that are the proper inspiration of that poetry and of a subject who has had the honors of that service (and even of the Académie).

> O France, ô ma chère patrie,
> Seras-tu long-temps flétrie,
> Sans tes autres adversités,
> Par de telles indignités?
>   Ne reviendrez-vous point encore
> O temps heureux que l'on ignore,
> Quoique séparé de nos jours,
> Par des intervalles si courts?
> Temps où la France triomphante,
> Riche, magnifique, brillante,
> Sous le deuxième des Henris,
> Sut faire respecter Paris
> A l'Angleterre, à l'Allemagne,
> Rélégua Charles en Espagne.
> C'était, c'était dans ces beaux jours,
> (Hé! que n'ont-ils duré toujours!)
> Que la femme d'un duc de Guise,
> (Le croira-t-on, quoiqu'on le lise!)
> Petite fille d'un grand roi,
> Grimpant dessus un palefroi,
> Et d'un page à peine suivie,
> Sans craindre le chaud ni la pluie,
> Faisoit gaiement son chemin
> De Paris jusqu'à Saint-Germain;
> C'était dans ce temps mémorable,
> Que cet homme si respectable
> Le chancelier de l'Hôpital,
> En fourchant un mauvais cheval,
> Portant sa chère femme en trousse,

89. Adry (loc. cit., p. 332) cites the portrait: "Peu de gens ont connu la profondeur de son esprit," says Valincour; as in the verse, he celebrates humility by evoking the modesty of equipage, this time on the road to Versailles.

Et peut-être meme sans harnasse
Alloit à sa maison des champs
Passer les beaux jours du printemps.
Faites rentrer ces mœurs en France,
Vous en chasserez l'indigence. (vv. 94–127)

Chapter 7

The Responsibilities of Belief

Vous avez une portion de l'âme de Platon et de M.
Pascal, tant je trouve de resemblance entre leur style et
le vôtre.

Daguesseau to Valincour[1]

Philosophe malgré lui: Letters to Bossuet

In the thick of preparation at Toulon for naval campaigns in 1703, or rather the thin of their delay, Valincour aboard the *Foudroyant* addressed a series of letters on religion to Bossuet and his secretary, Ledieu. He began on 17 September after reflection on remarks by Bossuet challenging the soundness of inquiry that sought to find in prophetic passages of the Old Testament the work of later interpolators. Bossuet's commentary has in the main satisfied him, Valincour writes, remarking that "opponents of prophecy" have been corrected and the truth strengthened.[2] He nonetheless poses a difficulty in the instance of Isaiah 7:14 and Matthew 1:22–23,[3] centered on clarity of evidence, therefore on the existence of prophecy qua prophecy.

Valincour's difficulty is stated and argued initially and throughout with a tight logic that does not give way, at least in his letters, at the conclusion of the epistolary exchange. The text of Isaiah, he proposes,[4] could not reveal to the Jews the coming of Christ; to the contrary, it

1. *Œuvres* (Pardessus ed.), 16:290.
2. Letter of 1 Oct. 1703, *Correspondance de Bossuet* (Urbain-Levesque ed.), 14:112.
3. "The Lord himself, therefore, will give you a sign. It is this: the maiden is with child and will soon give birth to a son whom she will call Immanuel"; "Now all this took place to fulfill the words spoken by the Lord": "The virgin will conceive and give birth to a son and they will call him Immanuel." (Jerusalem Bible).
4. *Correspondance* 14:109. Note to no. 2236 (Ledieu's précis?).

must have led them to believe that Jesus was not the Messiah. Therefore, St. Matthew could not cite it as prophecy; therefore, it is not
prophecy. Proof of the proposition is that in the prophecy the Messiah
must be born of a virgin; the Jews see Jesus as son of a married woman,
and therefore have no means of judging that she is a virgin. The
Messiah must be named Immanuel; Jesus has another name. Therefore,
the Jews were reasonable in believing, within the terms of the prophecy,
that the son of Mary, wife of Joseph, was not the Messiah.

Bossuet in his reply exalts the mystery and reminds his correspondent that, of course, the special quality of the Messiah marked by the
term "born of a virgin" cannot be ascertained by physical means. He
significantly does not have recourse to linguistic clarification from the
Hebrew text[5] (which might have suggested an association of inquiry
with the exegetical methods he had contested). He applies himself
rather to elucidation of the nature of the prophetic sign and its indicative evidence. Indicative evidence is not necessarily immediate evidence, nor need it be recognized by all in the same moment, he affirms,
departing from the Cartesian terms of Valincour's inquiry. "La sainte
vierge l'a sue d'abord; quelque temps après, saint Joseph, son mari l'a
apprise du ciel et l'a crue, lui qui avait le plus d'intérêt. Saint Mathieu
la rapporte comme une vérité déjà révélée à toute l'Eglise." Christ
alone, he adds, has had this distinguishing quality, neither shared nor
contested by any of his great enemies (like Mohammed, Bossuet adds).
After recalling the definition of Immanuel, and referring Valincour to
his own writings (Part II of the *Discours sur l'histoire universelle* and
Liber Psalmorum), Bossuet concludes, as he began, with faith, reaffirm-
ing in this instance the reprobation of the Jews: "La vocation des
Gentils et la réprobation des Juifs sont choses si publiques et si authentiques qu'il faut être aveugle pour ne les voir pas comme les marques
infaillibles de Messie actuellement venu au monde."[6] Bossuet may have
been surprised to receive the response that came in Valincour's letter
ten days later (11 October). After thanking the bishop for the kindness
of his prompt attention and for his instruction, Valincour, by way of
Ledieu, simply restates his difficulty, clearly indicating that its crux
remains:

Je vous prierais de vouloir bien lui dire que le fond de l'objection consiste à
dire que la prophétie d'Isaïe dont il s'agit, non seulement n'éclaircit point les

5. I.e., "almah" signifying maiden or recently married woman.
6. Letter, 1 Oct., p. 112.

Juifs et ne leur montre point que Jésus-Christ était le Messie, et c'est à quoi notre admirable et respectable prélat a divinement répondu, mais que cette même prophétie les aveugle et leur fournit un argument auquel il leur était impossible de trouver la réponse, et c'est sur quoi je désirerais qu'il eût la bonté de m'instruire. . . . Il est même si vrai que cela leur pouvait passer par l'esprit; qu'ils en font l'objection eux-mêmes en disant: "Lorsque le Messie viendra, on ne saura d'où il est; mais pour celui-là, nous savons d'où il vient."[7]

The episcopal guide responded patiently, in two lengthy and eloquent letters (26 October and early [8?] November). Feeling perhaps that reiteration and the emphasis of elaboration were the needed and proper means of bringing his correspondent to a perception of the truth, Bossuet in fact adds nothing more to the arguments and points already made. Since indicative evidence was distributed to be revealed in its time, he repeats, it is not surprising that it was not immediately recognizable to the Jews. It does not follow that "il leur fût permis de tenir leur esprit en suspens sur la mission de Jésus Christ."[8] And other signs were there; the Savior's coming was foretold by so many miracles that "refusal" to believe could only be "manifest infidelity." Again, he reasserts, belief must precede, in the disposition to believe: "Ils devaient donc commencer par croire, et demeurer persuadés que le particulier des prophéties se découvrirait en son temps."

The exchange ended without clearly expressed satisfaction on either side. "Embarrassment," Busson believed,[9] is indicated in the length of Bossuet's last two letters, whereas Valincour's of 25 November concludes with a rationalist's aversion to proof exclusively from faith:

Voilà ce que la véritable religion me propose à croire, alors il n'y a que croire aveuglément, sans preuve, sans raisonnement: *Captivantes intellectum,* le mérite est dans la soumission. Mais quand je dis "Entre toutes les religions du monde, voilà la seule bonne et la seule véritable," alors il faut des preuves pour me déterminer: je puis me tromper dans le choix et je dois le craindre *Videte ne quis vos seducat.* Or il paraît que rien ne peut m'assurer que l'évidence des prophéties.

Personal doubt, indicated here by the first person, can scarcely be promoted, as Busson suggests, to a "crisis" of doubt of an "unquiet spirit nourished on Pascal." If Pascal's "submission *and* use of reason"

7. Letter, 11 Oct., p. 219.
8. Letter, 26 Oct., p. 114.
9. *La Religion des classiques* (Paris: PUF, 1948), 410–11. Bossuet's dissatisfaction on full communication might be inferred from his return to the subject for book-length treatment: *Explication de la prophétie d'Isaïe sur l'enfantement de la sainte Vierge* (1704).

has not been fully satisfied for Valincour in this exchange, the coolness of his letters (transcribed by a secretary) is perceived by Bossuet himself as other than the cause for alarm of a crisis of faith. "I know that your faith is not in need of this instruction," he wrote from long-standing personal knowledge of his correspondent, then exhorted him to future action that may on the one hand already identify the circumstances of Valincour's present inquiries (suggested in the "quand je dis" of the passage quoted above) and on the other indicate future concerns and directions of his writing. "I cannot keep from deploring, as you do," Bossuet continues, "the spirit of incredulity that in fact is to be found among Christians and exhort you with all my heart to inspire in all, when the opportunity arises, a desire to learn what is in fact for them the eternal life."[10]

Valincour's letter of 25 November is of capital importance. It shows a critical mind, already evident in matters of literary judgment and historical evidence, in the different light of philosophical toughness and rigor that is new in the chronology of his now extant writings. Mind is also his subject and is examined with explicit reference to reflection on Pascal. His concern for clarity of evidence, for a reasoned support of faith in mathematics, rather than a cutting edge to separate faith and reason, is more than just suggested in the textual situation of inquiry. Valincour evokes a background of an unquestioning, accepting religion, without need for proofs, which from all indications may describe that in which he was raised. Inevitably Gallican by family tradition of service to the monarch, disinclined to change in forms, seeking clarification when absolutely necessary from bishops, "as in the time of the apostles" as Valincour was pleased to write to Bossuet, the correspondent was—as Fontenelle suggests—like his family devout without excessive piety.[11] Two important passages in the letter of 25 November suggest that this life of devotion is coming to a new degree of consciousness at the moment of writing to Bossuet and is doing so from intentions and for purposes not previously identified by commentators on the letters.[12]

Il semble qu'il n'y a que deux moyens pour obliger un homme à croire une vérité qu'on lui propose pour l'objet de sa créance: ou *l'évidence, qui ne manque*

10. Letter, 1 Oct., p. 112.
11. "Eloge," *Œuvres* (1825), 2:250, 255.
12. Only Henri Busson and Urbain have considered the exchange in detail.

jamais d'entraîner le consentement par sa propre lumière, ou la certitude que l'on a que cette vérité nous est proposée par un être qui ne peut ni tromper lui-même, ni vouloir tromper des autres, parce qu'alors l'autorité tient lieu d'évidence et nous fait croire fermement les choses les plus obscures et même les plus contraires à notre raison. Et pour donner un exemple de ceci, dans *la géométrie, qui est la seule de toutes les connaissances humaines où l'on puisse s'assurer de trouver la vérité,* si je propose à un homme de croire que ... deux lignes qui sont asymptotes prolongées à l'infini s'approcheront toujours et ne se rencontreront jamais, si j'ajoute que l'espace compris entre ces deux lignes prolongées à l'infini, et qui par conséquent est infini par lui-même, est pourtant égal à un espace fini et déterminé que je lui trace sur le papier, alors il pourra me dire que cela lui paraît impossible et inconcevable; mais que si je lui montre que cela est conforme aux démonstrations de la géométrie, dont il connaît la certitude, il ne laissera pas de croire cette proposition sans pouvoir la comprendre.

Il en est de même de la religion. Jamais homme raisonnable ne sera surpris qu'elle propose à croire des choses obscures et au-dessus notre raison; mais tout homme raisonnable, avant que de les croire, voudra être assuré que cette religion est en effet celle qui conserve la parole de Dieu et qui, par conséquent, ne peut jamais être dans l'erreur ni y jetter ceux qui la suivent. *Il faut donc une évidence qui marque tellement la vérité de la religion à tous ceux qui la cherchent, que personne n'en puisse douter* et ne puisse avoir d'excuse légitime pour refuser de croire les choses qu'elle nous offre pour objet de notre créance.

It seems that there are but two means of obliging a man to believe a truth proposed as the object of his belief: either *evidence, which never fails to produce assent by his own lights,* or certainty that one has that the being proposing this truth can neither be deceived himself nor wish to deceive others, in which case authority takes the place of evidence and causes us to believe firmly things that are the most obscure and even contrary to our reason. To give an example of the latter, *in geometry, which is the only of all human knowledge in which one may be sure of finding truth,* if I propose that someone believe that two asymptotic lines prolonged to infinity will always approach one another but never meet, if I add that the space included between these two lines prolonged to infinity, and which consequently is itself infinite, is nonetheless equal to a finite and determined space I mark on my paper, then he can say to me that that seems to him impossible and inconceivable but that if I were to show him its conformity to geometric demonstration, whose certainty he knows, he would not fail to believe this proposition, without being able to understand it.

It is the same with religion. Never will a man of reason be surprised that it proposes for belief things that are obscure and beyond our reason; but every man of reason, before believing those things, will wish to be assured that this reason is in fact that which preserves the word of God and which consequently can never be in error or lead those who follow it into error. *Any evidence that marks the truth of religion must thus mark it for all those who seek it,* so that no one may doubt or may legitimately excuse himself for refusing to believe the things religion offers us as object of our belief.

If read rapidly, with predisposition to hear a spirit of contestation in them, the passages I have emphasized might seem to identify one type of Pascal's interlocutors. If, on the contrary, phrases and points immediately following those saliently quotable extracts are given equal attention ("certainty that one has," "if I propose that someone believe," "Never will a man of reason be surprised," "So that no one may doubt or legitimately excuse himself for refusing to believe"), then the opposite position in dialogue may be equally probable. That Valincour is in fact trying out arguments that he might use as a defender, even "apologist," in dialogue becomes even clearer in a second development, that in which Pascal explicitly figures. Whether from Pascal alone or not, the outline of an apologetic design begins to take shape, in which prophecy must play an integral part as it does for Pascal (as distinguished from miracles, which will not be given that central place).[13] At this stage it may simply have been a previous conversation that sent Valincour, dissatisfied with his part in it, to write to Bossuet. He did not need to have met the "Militaire philosophe" in person[14] to have found among the naval officers at Toulon some sharply articulated opposition to religious orthodoxy for which in the heat of exchanges he did not have ready responses.

Car supposant un homme dans l'état où M. Pascal supposait celui qu'il voulait instruire, c'est-à-dire qui, dans un âge de raison, cherche de bonne foi la véritable religion, dont il n'a aucune connaissance; si cet homme commence par interroger la nature, le soleil, les cieux, et tous les éléments, ils lui diront qu'ils ne se sont pas faits eux-mêmes, mais qu'ils ont été faite par un être supérieur, à qui ils doivent tout ce qu'ils ont d'admirable et surtout l'ordre dans lequel il les maintient depuis tant d'années. Mais, s'il continue à leur demander quel est donc cet être, quels sentiments on en doit avoir, quel culte

13. See Anthony R. Pugh, *The Composition of Pascal's Apologia* (Toronto: University of Toronto, 1984), 248 and passim pp. 249–65. On the recurrent stumbling block, Henri Peyre, "Religion and Literary History," *Historical and Critical Essays* (Lincoln: University of Nebraska, 1963), 153. The immaculate conception had of course been a recurrent source of *raillerie libertine*.

14. The author of the *Difficultés sur la religion proposées au Père Malebranche par M., officier militaire dans la marine* is ca. 1710, but nothing places him in Toulon in 1703. On his religious attitudes, see C. J. Betts, *Early Deism in France* (The Hague: Nijhoff, 1984), 283–86 and passim.

il exige des hommes, ce qu'ils ont à craindre ou à espérer de lui, alors ils ne lui répondront que par un affreux silence.[15]

... C'est alors qu'au milieu infini de sectes et de religions différentes qui ont partagé les hommes dans tous les temps, il découvre un livre très ancien qu'on lui dit être la parole de Dieu et la loi véritable, hors de laquelle il n'y a point de salut. ... Il y trouve des choses au-dessus de sa raison, quelques-unes même qui lui paraissent y être entièrement contraires. Cependant, comme il y voit aussi des choses admirables, il déclare à ceux qui en sont les dépositaires qu'il est prêt à croire tout ce qu'il enseigne et à exécuter tout ce qu'il ordonne, pourvu que l'on lui montre, à n'en pouvoir douter, que ce livre contient en effet la véritable loi de Dieu.

Jusque-là, on ne saurait douter qu'il ne soit dans la disposition la plus raisonnable où un homme en cet état puisse être, car, comme il y aurait de la folie à refuser sa créance aux choses que Dieu nous ordonne de croire, puisque, dès là qu'il est Dieu, nous savons qu'il ne saurait nous tromper, il n'y en aurait pas moins à recevoir légèrement de la main des hommes, sujets à se tromper et à tromper les autres, un livre qu'ils disent être la loi de Dieu, si nous ne sommes pas assurés d'ailleurs que ce livre est en effet ce que l'on assure qu'il est.

Il faut donc trouver des preuves de la divinité de ce livre, et il paraît qu'on ne saurait les trouver que dans les prophéties. Car un homme qui n'a encore aucune connaissance de notre religion ne saurait encore être touché ni par les martyrs, ni par les miracles, voyant que tant d'autres religions manifestement impies et extravagantes se vantent d'avoir les leurs.

Il faut donc lui dire: cette religion que je vous propose comme la seule véritable a été annoncée par des prophéties qui, pour preuve de leur mission, ont prédit des choses surprenantes et extraordinaires qui sont arrivées précisément dans les temps et dans la manière qu'ils l'avaient prédit. Or cet être, quel qu'il soit, qui donne aux hommes le pouvoir de faire des prédictions de cette nature et qui se vérifient par les événements doit non seulement connaître l'avenir, mais encore en être le maître absolu, pour pouvoir disposer toutes choses selon sa parole, et par conséquent, ce ne peut être que le véritable Dieu.

Suppose a man like the one M. Pascal supposed and wished to instruct, that is, of the age of reason, seeks in good faith true religion, of which he has no knowledge; if this man begins by examining nature, the sun, the heavens, and all the elements, they will tell him that they did not make themselves but were made by a superior being, to whom they owe everything admirable they possess and especially the order in which they have for so many years been maintained. But if he continues to ask them what indeed this being is, what

15. To us, the echo here is "Le silence éternel de ces espaces infinis m'effraie" (Brunschvicq, 206); for Valincour, the "univers muet" of Part 7 of the 1670 ed. of the *Pensées* which he follows into Section 9 (2nd ed., pp. 78–79), where figures and prophecy are introduced.

opinions must be held of it, what cult it demands of men, what they have to fear or to hope from it, then they will answer only with a frightful silence.

It is then that amidst infinite sects and different religions that have in all times divided men, he discovers a very ancient book that he is told contains the word of God and the true law, outside which there is no salvation. . . . He finds in it things beyond reason, some even that seem to him entirely contrary to it. However, since he sees things there also that are admirable, he declares to those who are the trustees of that book that he is prepared to believe all that it teaches and to do all that it demands, provided that he be shown beyond any doubt that this book does contain the true word of God.

Up to this point one could not doubt that he is inclined as reasonably as a man in his state can be; for just as it would be foolish to refuse belief in the things that God demands us to believe, it would be no less foolish to receive lightly from the hands of men, subject to deceive themselves and others, a book they say to be God's law without being reassured that this book is in fact what one assures it to be.

Proofs of the divinity of God must thus be found in this book, and it seems that they may be only in the prophesies. A man who has no knowledge yet of our religion could not be moved by the martyrs, or by the miracles, seeing that so many manifestly blasphemous and extravagant religions boast their own.

It is thus necessary to say to him: this religion that I propose to you as the only true religion has been announced by prophesies that for evidence of their mission have foretold surprising and extraordinary things which have happened precisely at the times and in the way they were foretold. Now this being, whatever it may be, that gives men the power to make that kind of predictions and to verify them by events must not only know the future, but must also be the absolute master of it in order to be able to dispose all things according to his word, and consequently cannot be other than the true God.

Had Bossuet lived longer than the year left to him, Valincour might have renewed his consultations, again seeking guidance as he had earlier in Bossuet's writings before addressing the bishop himself. Harassed on many fronts to maintain orthodoxy in his last years, Bossuet would have had no difficulty agreeing with Valincour in the two decades after the bishop's death that the spirit of division or contention continued to plague the realm. He might not either have had doubts if Valincour had addressed to him, as he did to others, his conviction that the number of deists, freethinkers, even atheists, was increasing and that in the new century deism was beginning to have a newly systematic articulation[16] that could exert more seductive intel-

16. It is exactly in the years 1700–1703 that C. J. Betts sees intellectual consolidation of a newly independent (of earlier traditions) deism (Enlightenment/critical), constituted among other texts in Claude Gilbert, *Histoire de Calejava* (1700); Lahontan,

lectual attraction than a text like the "Quatrains du déiste" had on his own generation. With the guide gone, as I shall later present some evidence to suggest, Valincour may have come to a point of feeling the same kind of loyalty that he felt and showed with his systematization of Boileau's doctrine in 1711; that is, of taking Bossuet's exhortation to speak the truth of eternal verities of the faith wherever he could as a personal responsibility to defend doctrine in apologetic writing of his own. In the meanwhile, Valincour transferred to another arena his humanist's faith, with its predisposition to dialogue and reasoned mediation by it, its distrust of fanaticism and aversion to violence. Actively, indeed militantly, he intervened directly and covertly as a concerned Christian layman in the divisions of the Church of France that followed in the wake of the papal bull *Unigenitus dei fillius* promulgated by Clement XI on 10 September 1713. For the rest of Valincour's life the bull remained for him "cette malheureuse affaire."

The *Unigenitus:*[17] Polemics and Unpublished Letters to Gualterio

The denunciation as a Jansenist that shook Valincour in 1714[18] can scarcely have astonished him. The Augustinian tinge of his published as well as privately circulated writings had from the first (1678) provided grounds for allegation of a sympathy with the "Amis de la Vérité." The allegation is still current in the insinuation of the remark that Valincour "passed for having too little faith in human nature."[19] Other visible religious attitudes, like the humanist's respect for individual conscience or the critic's desire for pure source texts, could enforce the "evidence" of Port-Royalist affinities. Association with Racine and

---

Nouveaux voyages (1703), *Traduction d'une lettre d'Hypocrate à Damagette* (1700), previously existing at the conceptual level in relative isolation.

17. Until the collection of articles by Lucien Ceyssens (listing in the bibliography; references here by short titles), the most comprehensive treatment remains J.-F. Thomas, *La Querelle de l'Unigenitus* (Paris: PUF, 1950). An accute, dense and well-documented overview is B. Robert Kreiser, *Miracles, Convulsions, and Ecclesiastical Politics in Early Eighteenth-Century Paris* (Princeton: Princeton University Press, 1978), chap. I (1713–1729). Thomas gives the French text; for an English trans., Anne Freemantle, *The Papal Encyclicals* (New York: Mentor Books, 1956), 85–104.

18. See letter to Mme de Maintenon, cited above, chap. 5, n. 80.

19. Urbain (loc. cit., p. 144): "Ses sympathies jansénistes étaient connues, et il adhéra aux appels interjetés de la bulle *Unigenitus*"; too baldly designated, however, by the *Oxford Dictionary of French Literature* (1966) as "Jansenist."

Boileau (and in print with Pascal) alone could have sufficed. But in 1714, in answering his then unknown "accusers," Valincour solemnly denies to Cardinal de Rohan a doctrinal Jansenism. And he appears to have been believed both by Rohan and at court. The letter of 6 May 1714 has previously remained unpublished:

Puisque V. E. a eu la bonté de vouloir bien être instruite par moi-même de mes sentiments, j'ose la supplier très instamment de vouloir bien en être caution auprès du Roy. Je n'ay jamais osé prendre la liberté de demander une audience à S.M. pour me justifier, et je n'ay paru devant ses yeux qu'en tremblant et craignant d'abuser de la bonté qu'elle avoit de me souffrir en sa présence dans temps où j'avais le malheur de lui déplaire.

J'ose pourtant vous dire, Mgr., que si S.M. savoit ce que j'ai toujours dit et pensé sur l'affaire dont il s'agit elle me jugeroit peut-estre plus digne de ses grâces que de son indignation. Ce que je dis là est bien hardi et ce n'est que la force de la vérité qui me l'arrache, et je sçais en le disant combien c'est un crime horrible de mentir à Dieu et à son Maistre devant qui je crois parler en écrivant ceci.

Pour ce qui est des gens suspects qu'on dit être de mes amis, vous savez, Mgr., qu'avec une certaine réputation que le hasard donne plus que le mérite, il est presque impossible de ne pas avoir pour amis ou pour connoissance la pluspart des gens qui ont de l'esprit ou qui se picquent d'en avoir. Mais je n'ai aucune liaison particulière avec aucun de ces gens-là, si ce n'est tout au plus par rapport à la querelle d'Homere ou à quelques bagatelles d'Académie. Je ne vais jamais à Paris que pour le conseil de Mgr. le comte de Toulouse, je n'y vois personne que ses gens d'affaires, et pendant les voyages de Marly, je demeure à St. Cloud où il ne vient point assurément de gens suspects ni qui parlent des affaires du tems.

Cependant, Mgr., s'il plaisoit au Roy par un excès de bonté dont je ne suis pas digne et que je ne puis obtenir que par vous, me faire marquer par V.E. les personnes dont le commerce a dû me rendre suspect, je m'engagerois de tout mon cœur à m'en séparer de telle sorte, qu'il n'y auroit jamais sur cela la moindre ombre de soupçon.

Il est digne de vous, Mgr., d'employer la confiance que le Roy a si justement en vous pour tirer un innocent du malheureux état où il se trouve sans que sa conscience lui reproche rien qui le lui puisse avoir attiré et qui est plus terrible pour moi que ne seroit la perte de ma fortune et de ma vie.

Je n'ose par respect chercher qui sont mes accusateurs, mais j'espère que le Roy voudroit bien, plein de justice et de bonté comme il est, considérer que cette accusation ne peut guère avoir de fondement, puisqu'il n'en est rien revenu ni au P. Le Tellier,[20] ni a M. de Meaux,[21] ni à vous, Mgr., et que je me

20. The king's confessor was rabidly anti-Jansenist.
21. I.e., now Henri de Thiard, bishop of Toul (1687), Meaux (1704), cardinal de Bissy (1713). Later one of Valincour's *bêtes noires*.

soumets aux plus sévères châtiments si l'on peut jamais prouver que j'aie eu sur tout cela d'autres sentiments. ...[22]

Since Your Eminence has had the kindness to wish to be instructed directly by me on my opinions, I venture to entreat him to confirm them as quickly as possible to the king. I have not been so bold as to request an audience with His Majesty to justify myself and have in his presence only trembled with the fear of abusing his goodness in suffering me to remain in his favor during a time when I had the misfortune to displease him.

I nonetheless dare to say, Monseigneur, that if His Majesty were to know what I have always said and thought on the affair in question, he would perhaps find me more worthy of his grace than of his indignation. To say this is indeed bold, and only the force of truth pulls it out of me, knowing while I speak how horrible a crime it is to lie before one's God and master, before whom I believe myself to be as I write.

As for the suspect persons said to be among my friends, you know, Monseigneur, that with a certain reputation that chance more than merit bestows, it is almost impossible not to have as friends or acquaintances all those persons who think or pride themselves on doing so. But I have had no special relationship with any of those persons, unless through the quarrel on Homer or some bagatelles of the Académie. I never go to Paris except for Monseigneur le comte de Toulouse's council, I see no one except his agents, and during trips to Marly I remain at St. Cloud, where assuredly no suspect persons come or speak of current affairs.

However, Monseigneur, if it were to please the king by an excess of goodness of which I am not worthy and which I can obtain only through you, to designate through Your Eminence the persons whose commerce must have made me suspect, I pledge with all my heart to distance myself from them in a manner that will evermore leave not a shadow of doubt.

It is worthy of you, Monseigneur, to use the confidence the king so rightly has in you to save an innocent person from the unhappy state in which he finds himself, without reproach by his conscience for its responsibility, and which is more terrible for me than would be the loss of my fortune or my life.

I dare not from respect seek to know who my accusers are, but I hope that the king will indeed desire to consider, filled with justice and goodness as he is, that this accusation can hardly be founded, since nothing has come to the attention of Père Le Tellier, M. de Meaux, or you, Monseigneur, and that I submit myself to the harshest punishments if ever it can be shown that I have had on all this any other opinions. ...

After discovering sometime later that his accuser had been Jérôme de Pontchartrain, Valincour wrote to Gualterio, during a visit to Rome by Rohan, about his part in the affair.

22. B. N. MS. fon. fr. 17748, pp. 137–38.

Je ne saurois plaindre V. E. de n'estre pas dans l'aymable solitude du
Corgnolo puisqu'elle est retenue à Rome par l'amitié qui est entre vous et
Mgr. le cardinal de Rohan. C'est un prince que ses grandes qualités élèvent
bien au-dessus de sa dignité et de sa naissance.

Pour moy, je luy ay des obligations du temps du feu Roy dont je conserveray
toute ma vie le souvenir et la reconnoissance, car il m'empecha d'estre chassé
de la cour sur ce que M. de Pontchartrain avoit dit au Roy que j'estois
janséniste et il eut la bonté d'éclairer tellement cette affaire auprès du Roy
que sa Mté. m'a toujours traitté depuis et jusqu'à sa mort avec une bonté
toute particulière.[23]

I cannot pity your Eminence's not having his beloved solitude at Corgnolo
when he is kept in Rome by the friendship that exists between you and
Cardinal de Rohan. He is a prince whose great qualities raise him well beyond
his dignity and birth. For my part, I have obligations to him from the time
of the late king that I shall recall all my life with gratitude, for he kept me
from being expelled from court as a result of M. de Pontchartrain's saying to
the king that I was a Jansenist and he had the goodness to elucidate this affair
with the king in such a way that his Majesty until his death treated me with
very special goodness.

The Jansenist accusation (from the letter to Rohan clearly guilt by
association) derives from other associations than those with the literary
circles and society perhaps mentioned by Valincour as the least compromising. It involves rather the appearance of being among the appellants
(*anticonstitutionnaires*) of the *Unigenitus* (or constitution, as Valincour
always calls it). There were a number of reasons and occasions for
indiscreet praise or endorsement of opposition to the "pure and simple"
acceptance of the bull that the king had assured Clement XI it would
have, when he pressed it upon the pope in 1711 as a final solution of
the "Jansenist problem." With the engineering and dominance of
Cardinal Fabroni,[24] and over the pope's hesitations and doubts, the
final document had extracted 101 propositions from Pasquier Quesnel's
widely approved and read *Réflexions morales*. It was plain to Valincour,
as to all concerned, that the arrangement of these propositions to
consolidate a summa of earlier Jansenist principles was an extortion.[25]
Defense of Quesnel may have been the compromising indiscretion
overheard or reported, since Valincour numbered among his friends
several eminent Oratorians and was intellectually disposed to their

23. 12 Oct., 1721. B. M. Add. MS. 20395, pp. 254v–55.
24. See L. Ceyssens, "Fabroni," (1982), 66–76.
25. Ceyssens repeatedly uses "extorted" to describe the reading of Quesnel. See, on
the genesis of the bull, his study with J. A. G. Tans, "L'*Unigenitus* à Rome" (1981).

program of study.[26] But it was more to the form of procedures that he seems to have objected, and continues to do, first in the demands on the extraordinary assembly of bishops convened by the king to accept the constitution; and other allegiances linked to them more probably prompted indiscretions. The assembly was neither expeditious in deliberations (which lasted from December 1713 through January 1714) nor purely and simply accepting. Forty bishops headed by Rohan accepted in that manner, with only the proviso that the bull be accompanied by their pastoral instruction. But in the closing session a group of eight appellants was led by Cardinal de Noailles,[27] against whom the bull had been particularly aimed.[28] Thus, Valincour could write in March to Cardin Le Bret that the assembly had been a failure:

La paix de l'Eglise n'avance pas, au contraire. Vous aurez su par votre prélat ce qui s'est passé à l'assemblée et au Parlement. M. larch. de Paris s'est cru obligé de publier un mandement pour défendre à toutes les communautés ecclésiastiques de son diocèse de recevoir la Constitution. Le roi le trouve mauvais et a donné ordre à la Faculté de Théologie de s'assembler pour le recevoir. C'est aujourd'hui le troisième séance. Dieu nous garde au milieu de tout cela des fantaisies souvent mal réglées de la Cour de Rome.[29]

The peace of the Church does not advance; to the contrary. You will have learned from your prelate what happened in the Assembly and in Parlement. The archbishop of Paris has believed himself obliged to publish a mandate that forbids all religious communities in his diocese from acceptance of the constitution. The king has disapproved it and ordered the faculty of theology to assemble to accept the constitution. Today is its third meeting. God preserve us in the midst of all this from the often ill-governed fantasies of the court of Rome.

Then three weeks later, with new developments, he repeats the same fear of ill-advised interventions by Rome:

Voilà la paix de l'Europe faite. Celle de l'Eglise ne l'est pas. Il vint hier un courrier de Rome qui apporte à ce qu'on dit des choses très gracieuses pour

26. To Noailles, 23 June 1723: "l'honneur de vous recevoir icy quelqu'un de ces jours avec le Père général de l'Oratoire." *RHLF* 5 (1912), 495.

27. See L. Ceyssens, " 'Unigenitus': son acceptation par l'Assemblée du clergé" (1985), especially pp. 732–45. The *appelants* were Noailles, d'Hervault (Tours), Béthune (Verdun), Clermont (Laon), G. J. B. Noailles (Châlons, brother of the cardinal), Soanen (Senez), Pierre de Langle (Boulogne), V.-F. Desmarets (St.-Malo), Dreuillet (Bayonne).

28. L. Ceyssens, "Le Cardinal de Noailles" (1984): "Il y a du Copernic dans l'histoire de Noailles: elle ne tourne pas autour de la bulle, c'est celle-ci qui circule autour de lui" (p. 169).

29. 3 Mar. 1714, *RHLF* 31 (1924), 403. MS. Bibliothèque de l'Institut, No. 1660.

les Evesques qui ont fait l'instruction pastorale et fort terribles contre M. le Cardinal de Noailles. Il faut prendre patience et prier Dieu qu'il donne une fin à tout cecy, car les hommes n'en sauroient venir à bout. Les bonnes et saintes intentions du Roy ne suffisent pas contre les fantaisies de la cour de Rome et l'ignorance crasse des gens qu'elle employe.[30]

Peace in Europe accomplished! That of the Church is not. A courier arrived yesterday from Rome bringing, I hear, very gracious things for the bishops who did the pastoral instruction and terrible ones against the Cardinal de Noailles. One must be patient and pray God to put an end to all this, for men will not be able to end it. The good and sainted intentions of the king do not suffice against the fantasies of the court of Rome and the crass ignorance of those it employs.

Linked closely to the Noailles family,[31] and an admirer of the integrity of the cardinal,[32] Valincour was also associated with opposition through his friend Daguesseau, who, as *procureur-général* and the "soul" of the Parlement, had expressed opposition to acceptance from the start.[33] The letters to Le Bret that Valincour wrote, containing principles that remain constant throughout his life, already show the Gallicanism at the heart of Daguesseau's continuing defense of the 1682 articles, often seemingly more Gallican than the monarch. The king promised Clement, after the first opposition, that it would be only a "few days" before the opposition would be brought around;[34] Valincour knew the principals, and principles exacerbated beyond men's ability to transcend them, in a different way, beginning with the king's anger that banished Noailles from court and the other appellants to their sees. It is at this point, and in conjunction with Noailles, that Valincour allowed himself to become actively engaged in a new role, but one with which he was already associated publicly; that is, to become a public mediator in the controversy, at the moment of its first anniversary. The resulting fiasco, which thwarted the good intentions of his friends (Rohan but especially Polignac) to give Valincour a role

30. [Apr., 1714]. Transcription in *Catalogue des autographes provenant au cabinet de M. A. Martin* (Paris: Merlin, 1843), 48.

31. Besides the duc, in more than thirty years of friendship, also the maréchale d'Estrées and the future comtesse de Toulouse.

32. See above, letter to A.-M. de Noailles, chap. 5, n. 60.

33. Georges Frêche, *Un Chancelier gallican: Daguesseau* (Paris: PUF, 1969), 18. I understand Valincour to be Gallican in the sense defined here for Daguesseau: pp. 42–43, 57–59 and also by Kreiser, pp. 17–19.

34. Albert Le Roy, *Le Gallicanisme au 18e siècle: la France et Rome, 1700–1715* (Paris: Perrin, 1892), 384–85.

that would expunge the earlier difficulties, ended 1714 for him bitterly if not so dangerously as it had earlier on threatened to be.

Shortly before the departure of Amelot, the king's emissary to Rome,[35] Valincour was drawn into a series of public debates on a compromise. Ultimately, the plan was Voysin's, one in a series of at least five attempts at compromise initiated throughout 1715.[36] As Jean Louail (1723)[37] tells the story, the king's decision to send Amelot to Rome to negotiate a national council, to settle disputes, and to silence Noailles by threat of excommunication if he persisted in opposition was necessitated by the failure of Cardinal de Polignac to act as mediator between Noailles and the king. It was also Polignac's mismanagement that drew Valincour into the debates, since Polignac, without consulting Noailles, had assured Voysin that Noailles was willing to change his position. The spokesman for Noailles's position of intransigence was Mengui, a canon and *conseiller au Parlement,* praised by Louail for "sagacity, talent in public speaking, vast knowledge of the laws, precision, doctrine";[38] facing him as a layman, Valincour is praised as "not less known for the justness of his mind, noble ideas, consummate prudence, and special ability to conciliate skillfully." Quite apart from the machinations, beyond his control and unknown to him,[39] which thwarted his success, Valincour's tone was not, as Louail reports it, entirely in keeping with the prudence praised; it did not show a clear separation from Noailles's position in opposition. "First M. de Valincour granted that there should not and could not be a national council, but held that the enemies of the cardinal de Noailles, unable to repress him formally, would use other means of authority to destroy him. On their part, he further stated, there was only heat, wrath, and derision. Hence, he concluded that His Eminence would

35. On the preparations, see Thomas, *La Querelle,* pp. 90–91. Valincour's letters to Gualterio begin at this moment.

36. See L. Ceyssens, "Autour de la Bulle *Unigenitus.* Les Essais d'accommodement (1714–1715)" (1985). The "third" (pp. 369–75) in August-October involves Valincour (p. 374n).

37. J.-B. Louail, *Histoire du livre des Réflexions et de la Constitution,* 4 vols. (Amsterdam: Nicolas Potgieter, 1723–38), 1:371–72. On Louail and his collaborator, see Thomas, *La Querelle,* p. 15, n. 1.

38. Guillaume Mengui (d. 1728) was a Sorbonne theologian who became a *conseiller au Grand' Chambre* (1709). He was an intransigent Jansenist and *appelant;* see Thomas, *La Querelle,* pp. 172–73.

39. Ceyssens ("Essais d'accommodement," p. 374n) complicates the imbroglio inextricably beyond Louail's account, involving Massillon, Cardinal de Rohan, and P. Gabriel Daniel, the first two the "dupes" of the last.

be wise to get out of the difficulties with the most complaisance possible." Mengui is no less forthright in granting that a council should not take place but is on the one hand more politic, in professing himself loath to proceed where cardinals preceded him, and on the other more recalcitrant in principles. He bolsters Noailles with the reflection that cowardice must be distinguished from weakness and that the virtue of a bishop is all the more real for the testing of persecution. The conditions proposed for the continuation of debate—that Noailles's "compromise" be substantially new, in writing, and have the prior approval of the king, pope, chancellor, Noailles, and the bishop of Meaux [Bissy]—catch Valincour, who is treated coldly. Even so, he persevered, informing the chancellor of his eagerness to do so. But the chancellor advised him to desist. And Louail ends with explanation, only part of the truth of the causes of frustration of other participants besides Valincour, that bespeaks the kind of cynicism about men's abilities to end conflict that Valincour himself reiterated increasingly after 1714: the cardinal de Rohan declared more than once that he had no part in this negotiation and "had only consented to it to keep his confederate Polignac busy."[40]

Valincour's posture of conciliation, however unfortunate in 1714, will be maintained with concerted efforts to show himself of a "third party,"[41] a moderate, first of all concerned pragmatically to "sortir de l'embarras avec toute la condescendance possible." In doing so, he demonstrates that he is neither a Jansenist nor a Jesuit, but rather a good Frenchman (with all the Gallican risks that implies) and a Christian dedicated to the higher good of the Church and the community of faith. Some thirteen years after the letters to Le Bret, Valincour wrote to Cardinal Gualterio on 23 March 1726 what may serve as a summary and balance sheet of an already long correspondence. In short it constitutes a constantly held profession of faith.

Je ne suis ni janséniste ni moliniste mais je vois des fous et des enragés dans les 2 partis qui feront un mauvais usage ... suivant son humeur et ses préventions. Pour moy je voudrois que tout le monde acceptast la constitution

40. Louail's account emphasizes Valincour's victimization by the high prelates, cynically noting in conclusion that Rohan had agreed to Polignac's initiatives "pour occuper l'activité de son confrère."
41. The designation "tiers parti" analyzed by Emile Appolis and especially as applied to Fleury seems justified on the basis of the correspondence with Gualterio that will be presented here. See *Entre Jansénistes et zelanti: Le 'Tiers parti' catholique au XVIIIe siècle* (Paris: Picard, 1960), 60–81.

et c'est le conseil que j'ay toujours donné à quelques Evesques de mes amis, à des prestres, et à des Religieuses[42] qui m'ont consulté, parce que *je crois en effet et je crois très fermement qu'on la peut accepter pour le bien de la paix et sans interesser sa conscience. Mais je ne puis approuver et je n'approuveray jamais qu'on refuse des Explications à ceux qui en demandent de bonne foy* et non dans un esprit d'orgueil ou de contagion. St. Paul qui se faisoit tout à tous pour gagner à Jésus-Christ n'eût jamais refusé des Explications à ceux qui lui en auroient demandé sur les endroits de ses Epîtres que St. Pierre trouvoit obscures et difficiles à entendre.

Mais je m'apperçois que je parle trop pour un Laïque et qu'on me mettroit peut-estre au St. Office si je tenois un pareil discours à Rome.[43]

I am neither Jansenist nor Molinist, but I do see fools and madmen in the two parties who will make ill use of . . . following their humors and preventions. For my part, I wish that everyone would accept the constitution, and that is the counsel I have always given to the bishops among my friends, the priests and religious persons who have consulted me, because *I believe in fact and I believe very firmly that one can accept it for the sake of peace without affecting one's conscience. But I cannot and I shall never approve that explications be refused those who seek them in good faith* and not in the spirit of pride or contagion. St. Paul, who made himself whatever for whomever to bring them to Jesus Christ, would not have refused explications asked on passages of his epistles that St. Peter found obscure and difficult.

But I see that I am saying too much for a layman and that I might in Rome be put to the Holy Office (emphasis mine).

To seek peace and to serve "le culte du vray Dieu et l'honneur de la Religion" after 1714 Valincour relocates his combative activity as he had in the Académie in 1711 at a level beyond local disorders. The 159 letters written to Gualterio between 1714 and 1728,[44] which have remained unpublished and have not been considered in any account of Valincour's career, show the heart of the activity of the "honnête homme" at the height of that career. For a voice of moderation to be heard at Rome becomes to him a matter of increasing urgency, just as from his earliest letter to Gualterio he wishes that for the good of the "affair" the cardinal's special disposition and gifts were still in Paris. "Plust à Dieu, Monseigneur, que V. E. fust encore icy comme elle estoit

42. Valincour's expression seems simply to mean religious women.

43. 23 Mar. 1726. B. M. Add MS. 20395, p. 103 (my emphasis). Valincour jokes here but sometimes (infrequently) uses a code. The "chiffre avec M. de Valincour" is in B. M. Add MS. 20582, pp. 71–73.

44. Gualtieri (or Gualterio), Filippo Antonio (1660–1728), polymath and diplomat. Legate at Avignon before being nuncio. Cardinal in 1706 (Clement XI). Resident in Rome from 1706. See *Hierarchia* 5 (1667–1730); Boze, *Histoire de l'Académie d'Inscriptions* 7:386–93.

l'an passé. Sa présence, sa sagesse, et ses lumières y seroit bien utiles pour finir à la satisfaction du Pape et du Roy une affaire plus importante qu'aucune autre qu'il y ayt eu depuis plusieurs siècles. Mais il ne convient pas à un simple laïque comme moy de parler que de ce qui me regarde." (1v)[45] ["Might it have pleased God that Your Eminence be here as he was last year! His presence, his wisdom, and his lights would be useful indeed for concluding to the satisfaction of the pope and the king an affair that is more important than any other for a number of centuries has been. But it is proper for a simple layman like me to speak only of what concerns him."] On familiar terms with the cardinal, who during his stay in France as nuncio (1701–1706) had enjoyed the hospitality of Boileau at Auteuil as well as other learned circles and had visited again in 1711–12, Valincour becomes his most faithful Parisian correspondent.[46] Although there is much more in the letters than news of the constitution, that news is absent from almost none of them and grows significantly over the years. With the blessings, one would suppose, of successive governments that renewed honors bestowed first by Louis XIV on the francophile Gualterio,[47] Valincour

45. 30 July 1714. Dates and references to B. M. Add. MSS. 20395 are henceforth given parenthetically.

46. Valincour's letters are the most numerous and chronologically extended of those extant among Gualterio's papers. Besides a file of correspondence with the royal family and Mme de Maintenon (20316) and Orléans (20315), Torcy and Chavigny, there are also exchanges with Dubois (20321, Nov. 1718–Mar. 1723), Cardinal Fleury (20322, 1717–27), Ch.-J. Colbert de Croissy (20397, 1707–10), Ch.-M. Le Tellier (ibid., 1707), Mailly (ibid., 1701–10), Bissy (20367, 1706–27, the most extensive after Valincour's), Callières (20368, 1706–14). Saint-Simon's extensive letters (weekly from 1706 [Mémoires 6:57] through 1728) are no longer extant except for a very small group and some minutes: see Armand Baschet, *Le Duc de Saint-Simon et le cardinal Gualterio* (Paris: Epernay, 1878) and especially François Formel, "Etat chronologique de la correspondance actuellement connue du duc de Saint-Simon avec le Cardinal Gualterio," *Cahiers Saint-Simon* 6 (1978), 35–53; also Saint-Simon, *Mémoires* (Truc ed.), 7:471–76; Ceyssens, "Le duc de Saint-Simon" (1985), 517–19; Georges Poisson, *M. de Saint Simon,* 2nd ed. (Paris: Mazarine, 1987), 171 and passim. Letters from French Benedictines were published by D. U. Berlière, "Lettres inédites au Cardinal Gualterio," *Revue bénédictine* 24 (1904), 415–19.

47. He was given the abbey of St. Rémi (dioc. Reims) by Louis XIV and asked to return to France (which he promised to do every five years, but after 1713 he sent his nephews). In 1716, the regent awarded him St. Victor (Orléans to Gualterio, 21 Feb. and 6 Mar. 1716, B. M. Ad MSS. 20315, pp. 37–38); after the accession of Louis XV, he was made *commandeur de l'ordre du Saint-Esprit* (Letters from the duc de Bourbon, 8 Feb. and 12 June 1724, B. M. Add. MSS. 20316, pp. 174, 179). If pressure as well as information was wished by correspondents, Gualterio's position noted by Ceyssens is ironically ill-suited for it: "... à Rome où dominait le cardinal Fabroni, il se trouvait

assiduously keeps the news and a certain point of view from Paris available to him. Polignac, who may have misguided him in 1714, is nonetheless acclaimed to Gualterio as the author of the *Anti-Lucrèce,* which "has all the magnificence and graces of Lucretius's poetry but put to a more noble end . . . to the cult of the true God and the honor of religion."[48] In a more modest way, Valincour dedicated his letter writing to the same end.

Early in 1716, Valincour provides a summary of the affair; despite the best intentions, it is stalled. Only God, it seems to him, can break the impasse created by the fury of both parties.

L'affaire de le constitution n'avance point par la faute ou plutost la fureur des deux parties. M. le duc d'Orléans, M. le Chancelier [Voysin] sous ses ordres, Mgrs les cardinaux de Noailles et de Rohán ont fait tout ce qu'on pouvoit attendre d'eux. C'est à Dieu à faire le reste et à rendre le sens et la raison aux testes qui en sont dépourvues et qui en sont en grand [sic]. Mais si le Pape pouvoit voir le sort irréparable que cela fait à la Religion, il en seroit touché et prendroit des mesures tout opposées à celles qu'on a prises jusqu'à présent pour finir cette malheureuse affaire. (s.d. [1716?], 9v–10)

The affair of the constitution does not advance by the fault or rather the fury of both parties. The duc d'Orléans, the chancellor [Voysin] on his orders, and the cardinals de Noailles and de Rohan have done all one could expect from them. God must accomplish the rest and restore sense and reason to heads devoid of it and much in evidence. But if the pope was to see the irreparable consequences of this for religion, he would be touched and take measures to end this unfortunate affair just the opposite of those taken until now.

In July, he has little hope that the high expectations for change aroused by the latest mission to Rome[49] will be any more fulfilled than they had been by Amelot's journey. He expands with a familiar Tassonian evocation of the lost Golden Age:

Il est temps de finir et le mal n'a que trop duré. *O bella età de l'oro non già perchè di latte s'en corse il fiume.* Mais parce qu'on n'y parloit ni d'acceptation relative, ni absolue, ni de P. Quesnel, ni de constitution, ni de cent autres choses pareilles qui troublent la paix de l'Eglise et le repos des fidèles. Cependent le Turc menace l'Italie et fera peut estre des progrès dont on se repentira très inutilement lors qu'il ne sera plus temps de s'y opposer. Il y a

---

en disgrâce." But Gualterio was still "bien placé, d'autant plus loquace qu'il était aigri et fort à même de le renseigner sur les affaires de Rome et de la bulle." ("Le duc de Saint-Simon," pp. 518–19).

48. For the context of the letter, 31 Aug. 1724, see below, chap. 8, n. 34.

49. By Chevalier, see Thomas, *La Querelle,* p. 108; Leclercq, *Histoire de la Régence* 1:168ff.

bien longtemps que je vois avec regret que toutes ces malheureuses disputes ne durent que faute de s'entendre de part et d'autre. On ne peut douter que M. le Cardinal de Noailles, et les Evesques attachés à lui n'ayent pour le Pape tout le respect qu'ils doivent. On ne peut douter non plus de la droiture des intentions de sa Sainteté, mais les relations qui viennent icy de M. Chevalier font voir qu'on n'estoit point instruit à Rome de la manière dont les choses s'estoient passées icy au sujet de la première acceptation. (8–8v)

It is time to conclude it and harm by it that has lasted only too long. "O bella età de l'oro non già perchè di latte s'en corse il fiume." But only because one spoke neither of absolute nor of relative acceptance, nor P. Quesnel, nor the constitution, nor a hundred like things that trouble the peace of the Church and the repose of the faithful. Meanwhile the Turks threaten Italy and will perhaps make inroads that will be repented uselessly when there will no longer be time to oppose them. For a long time I have seen with regret that all these unfortunate disputes persist only because of a lack of understanding on both sides. One cannot doubt Cardinal de Noailles and the bishops attached to him have all the respect they should for the pope. One cannot doubt also the uprightness of His Holiness's intentions. But the accounts that arrive here by M. Chevalier show that one was not instructed in Rome on the ways in which things came to pass here in the first acceptance.

At the end of the year Valincour reports the imminent resumption of deliberations and sarcastically compares the constitution to Helen of Troy, with a final turn to include censorship in that sarcasm.

On va recommencer à tenir des séances ou des sessions, quoy qu'il n'y ayt point de concile sur l'affaire de la constitution qui [ne] pourroit bien dire comme Hélène dans Homère: "Malheureuse que je suis que ne m'a-t-on étouffée dans le moment qui m'a vu naistre plustost que me laisser vivre pour causer tant de troubles et divisions." Je supplie au moins V.E. de se souvenir que c'est Homère qui parle et non pas moy et qu'Homère peut dire tout ce qu'il lui plaist sans craindre d'estre mis à l'inquisition ni mesme à l'index. (29 Nov.; 12)

Meetings or sessions are to recommence, although there is no council on the affair of the constitution that could not well say like Helen in Homer: "Unhappy am I not to have been smothered at birth rather than live to cause so many troubles and divisions." I beg Your Eminence to remember that it is Homer speaking and not I and that Homer may say all he pleases without fear of being put to the Inquisition or even on the Index.

Just before the appointment of Daguesseau as chancellor in February of 1717, the two new year's letters have lost any play of sarcasm. Straightforward severity and pleas seem more fitting for the moment:

Je ne parleray point à V.E. de l'affaire de la constitution, ni des maux qu'elle cause dans l'Eglise pendant que Mgrs les cardinaux de Noailles et de

Rohan font de bonne foy tout ce qui dépend d'eux pour la finir. Il y a des deux costés des subalternes brouillons et entestés qui employent toute leur adresse à leur fureur pour empêcher qu'elle ne finisse. Ces gens là sont très punissables. Mais les maux qu'ils causent n'en sont pas moins grands et le Père commun des fidèles devroit bien employer sa bonté pour les finir, car sa puissance ne suffit pas. (19 Jan.; 13v–14)

I will not speak to Your Eminence of the affair of the constitution or the ills it causes the Church while Cardinals de Noailles and de Rohan do in good faith all they can to conclude it. There are on both sides quarrelsome and stubborn subalterns who use all their skills in their fury to prevent its conclusion. These men are most deserving of punishment. But the ills they cause are no less great and the Father of all the faithful should use his goodness to finish them, for his force will not suffice.

Je souhaitterois fort pour la paix de l'Eglise et le repos de l'estat que le Pape voulût bien consulter V.E. sur ce qui se passe icy au suject de la constitution. Il n'y a point de bon chrétien ni de bon François que ne tremble à la vue des choses qui sont sur le point d'arriver par l'acharnement des deux partis. La cour de Rome se repentira un jour de n'en avoir pas prévenu les suites et peut estre qu'alors le mal sera irréparable. Si V.E. estoit icy je suis bien assuré que sa sagesse, ses lumières, et ses bonnes intentions auroient empêché les choses d'en venir au point où elles sont. (30 Jan.; 15–15v)

I would strongly wish for the peace of the Church and the repose of the state that the pope might be willing to consult Your Eminence on what is happening here on the constitution. There is not one good Christian or good Frenchman who does not tremble at the sight of the things about to take place through the relentlessness of the two parties. The court of Rome will one day repent not having forestalled the results and then the damage will perhaps be irreparable. If Your Eminence were here I am sure that his wisdom, lights, and good intentions would have prevented things from coming to their present point.

Sure that things are in good hands with Daguesseau, Valincour does not press his exhortations with Gualterio for a while. But he does not leave opportunities to pursue his line. With the gift of his Academic discourse of 1717, he wrote as he had spoken about the scandal of disorder caused by the "War of Homer" when the nation was at peace:

J'espère . . . que V.E. conviendra qu'il vaudrait mieux qu'on imprimast douze harangues à Paris par semaine et que jamais on n'y eust imprimé tous les écrits qui ont esté faits pour et contre la constitution. Je dis pour et contre, car il seroit nécessaire de les brusler tous pour avoir la paix qui est le plus grand des biens. (31 July; 17v)

I hope that Your Eminence will agree that it would be better to print a dozen harangues a week in Paris than ever to have all the writings for and against the constitution. I say for and against, since it would be necessary to burn them all in order to have that peace which is the greatest of goods.

Then again the following year, with the gift of the second edition of the Académie's *Dictionnaire,* more eloquently he expands:

Mais de quel prix et de quel mérite ne seroit-il point si parmy tant de mots dont il donne la véritable explication il en avoit pu donner une assez claire et précise de tous les mots de la constitution pour faire cesser les funestes disputes qu'elle cause depuis si long-temps. Et combien sont encore plus funestes les suites de ces disputes! La nouvelle que l'on a apprise avec étonnement de ce qui a esté fait à Rome a obligé et même contraint ceux qui estoient menacés de prendre les précautions que l'on peut prendre en cas pareil,[50] mais ce n'est pas aux laiques ni aux profanes à parler sur cette matière. Je crois cependant qu'il leur est permis de faire comme quand il tonne: prendre de l'eau bénite, faire le signe de la croix, et n'avoir point de peur quand leur conscience ne leur reproche rien. (25 Sept.; 25–26)

What value and what merit would this book not have if among so many words of which it gives true explanations it had been able to give a clear and precise one to all the words of the constitution and cause to cease the fateful disputes it has so long caused. And how much more fateful are the continuations of those disputes! The news learned with astonishment here about what has happened in Rome has obliged and even constrained those who were threatened to take the precautions one may in such cases. But it is not for the layman and the secular to speak on this matter. I believe however that it is permissible to do as when it thunders: to take holy water, to make the sign of the cross, and to have no fear when their conscience reproaches them with nothing.

This calm letter, with its rapprochement to the simple of heart and would-be restraint, is the first letter to be written after the disgrace of Daguesseau and his exile to Fresnes.[51] New tones and form follow as frustration dictates an apocalyptic lament.

Il semble que les 4 anges qui ont toute puissance de nuire à la terre et à la mer soient déchaînés et qu'il n'y ayt plus de voix qui les retienne ni de serviteurs de Dieu qui méritent d'estre marqués au front et d'estre préservés des malheurs qui menacent tout l'univers. L'Eglise aussi troublée que les Estats temporels n'est plus en estat de leur procurer la paix dont elle se prive

---

50. The *Pastoralis officii* (8 Sept. 1718). See Thomas, *La Querelle,* pp. 135–36. Cf. Valincour's comments to A.-M. de Noailles, above, chap. 5, n. 120.

51. The regent had abruptly taken the seals from him (and passed them to d'Argenson) on 28 Jan. 1718. He remained at Fresnes until 7 June 1720. See above, chap. 5, n. 118.

elle même. Il ne m'appartient pas d'entrer dans le détail de ces affaires, mais j'en say assez pour croire que si St. Cyprien et St. Athanase pouvoient descendre du ciel en France ils seroient bien étonnés d'y trouver ce qu'on nous envoye de dehors et plus étonnés encore d'entendre les discours et de lire les écrits de quelques uns de nos Evesques dont je voudrois pouvoir louer le zèle mais dont je suis bien éloigné d'admirer la science. (7 Nov.; 29v–30)

It seems that the four angels that have the power to destroy the earth and the seas have broken loose and that there is no voice to restrain them nor any servant of God whose brow is marked to preserve him from the ills that menace all the world. The Church, as troubled as temporal states, is no longer in the position to procure for them the peace of which it deprives itself. It is not my place to enter into the detail of these affairs, but I know enough about them to believe that if St. Cyprian and St. Athanasius were to descend from heaven to France they would be astonished indeed to find here what is sent to us from outside and still more to hear the discourse and read the writings of some of our bishops whose zeal I should like to praise but whose science I am far from admiring.

The outburst of November 1718, following the more humble moment of constraint and mortification, reflected a climactic event that seemed the frustration of the entire course of the regent's attempts since 13 September 1715 to urge Clement to a speedy resolution of the "affair" that would forestall imminent schism, and a moderation of tone in clear, restrictive explication that would permit relative acceptance (thereby safeguarding the Church of France in its independence and his own doctrinal integrity). The regent's phrasing and its representation of urgency are very similar to Valincour's in his subsequent letters intended to keep Gualterio—and Rome—informed.

Je voudrais que le pape fût en état d'en juger par lui-même; et quand Sa Saintété aurait vu de près les esprits aussi échauffés qu'ils le sont, les évêques animés contre les universités, et les universités contre les évêques, l'episcopat divisé, le second ordre entraîné dans la même division . . ., en un mot le schisme prêt à éclater de toutes parts, je prendrais la liberté de demander à Sa Sainté s'il m'est, je ne dis pas permis, mais même possible d'attendre tranquillement un événement aussi triste.[52]

I would wish the pope were in a position to judge by himself; if he could see minds inflamed as they are, bishops animated against universities, universities against bishops, the episcopate divided, the second order drawn into the same division . . ., in a word schism at the point of erupting from all sides, I would

52. Quoted by Jean-Christian Petitfils, *Le Régent* (Fayard: 1986), 335.

take the liberty to ask His Holiness not whether it is permissible but whether it is even possible for me to await calmly such a sad event.

The Parlement refused to register this intractable "law," convinced that papal infallibility would thereby gain full force with it, and the government sent the nuncio's pouch back unopened.[53] Thus in the letters of early 1719, Valincour returns to the pope's intractability and its responsibility with resonant Scriptural authority.

Voilà l'Europe dans d'étranges convulsions, la guerre d'Espagne, la mort du Roy de Suède, et surtout la constitution. Est-ce que sa Sainteté ne voudra jamais comprendre qu'il n'est pas juste de donner des anathemes et des malédictions à des chrétiens qui lui demandent à genoux des explications et que l'Evangile dit qu'un père même méchant ne donne point un scorpion à son fils qui lui demande du pain. (19 Jan.; 36v)[54]

Europe is in strange convulsions with the Spanish war, the death of the king of Sweden, and above all the constitution. Will his Holiness never understand that it is not just to give anathemas and maledictions to Christians who seek explications on their knees and that the Gospel says even a cruel father does not give a scorpion to his son who asks him for bread.

And at Easter he leaves for the retreat at St. Cloud with the determination to find peace for himself and to offer his prayers for its advent in a troubled world.

Je vais passer les festes dans mon hermitage de Saint Cloud ou j'espère n'entendre parler ni d'Espagne, ni d'Angleterre, ni du Roy Jacques ni du Roy Georges, ni même de la constitution et où je ne songeray aux affaires publiques que pour prier Dieu qu'il accorde à toute la chrétienté la paix et le repos dont elle a tant besoin. (26 Mar.; 37v)

I am going to spend the feast days in my hermitage at St. Cloud, where I hope not to hear either of Spain or England or King James or King George or even the constitution and where I shall think of public affairs only in praying God to accord all Christianity the sense and peace of mind it so much needs.

Having succeeded in neither goal, he returns after some philosophical musing to a blunt indictment of papal responsibility:

Il est en effet extraordinaire qu'il n'y ayt dans tous les pays que nous connoissons pas un seul endroit où un homme sage et qui voudroit passer la

---

53. Ibid.
54. The precedence of the "Affaire" over concern for war should be noted. In his scriptural quotation Valincour has fused Matthew, 7:9: "Or what man of you, if his son asks for bread, will give him a stone?" with the Old Testament punishment (e.g.,

vie en philosophe pust se promettre de n'estre point exposé ou aux foudres de la guerre ou à ceux du Vatican. Dieu nous délivre des uns et des autres. (13 May 1719; 39)

It is in fact extraordinary that there is not anywhere in all the countries that we know a single place where a wise man who would like to live his life philosophically can assure himself not to be exposed to the thunderbolts of war or those of the Vatican. God save us from both.

From the summer of 1719 through January 1720, Valincour's letters take a new turn. For the first time he names names in opposition and relays documents directly, strictly speaking, despite his usual denunciation of both sides. He gives up his professed third-party status along with the layman's fitting humility on the substance of matters beyond him. The writing that prompted the change, already condemned by Parlement and burnt, was the letter published by Mailly, archbishop of Rheims.[55] Even though Valincour cannot at first credit the authorship, he quotes from Isaiah to capture the moment.

On ne peut s'imaginer que ce soit un prélat comme M. l'archevesque de Rheims. Du moins si c'est lui il n'a pas pris les Epistres de St. Paul pour modèle. Depuis le temps que dure cette malheureuse affaire on a fait de part et d'autre assez d'écrits pour remplir l'Eglise de St. Pierre toute grande qu'elle est, et il y en auroit eu assez pour convertir ou pour confondre tous les hérétiques du monde si les écrivains avoient voulu attaquer l'hérésie au lieu de s'attaquer les uns les autres. "Cumque superba foret Babylon spolianda trophiis bella geri placuit nullos habitura triumphos."[56] La postérité sera étonnée et même indignée de voir tout ce qui a esté dit, fait, et écrit de part et d'autre, car puisque l'on est assez malheureux pour voir deux partis dans l'Eglise il faut avouer de bonne foy qu'il y a des fanatiques dans les deux partis et les plus emportés sont presques toujours ceux qui savent le moins de quoy il s'agit. Dieu nous délivrera des uns et des autres quand il lui plaira. (25 June; 42–43)

One cannot imagine that a prelate like the archbishop of Rheims is the author. If he is, he has not taken the epistles of St. Paul as his model. Since the beginning of this unhappy affair there have been enough writings on each side to fill the church of St. Peter, as vast as it is, and enough to confound and to convert all the heretics in the world if writers had wished to attack heresy rather than each other. "Cumque superba foret Babylon spolianda

---

1 Kings, 12:11: "My father chastised you with whips but I will chastise you with scorpions.").

55. François de Mailly (1658–1721), archbishop of Reims (1710), cardinal (1719). His letter, attacking the royal declarations of 7 Oct. 1717, was condemned by the Parlement on 19 March. See Thomas, La Querelle, 117, 131–33.

56. Valincour returns to Isaiah (21:9) and couples it with Revelation (28:2).

trophiis bella geri placuit nullos habitura triumphos." Posterity will be astonished and even indignant to see all that has been said, done, and written on
each side; for since one is so unfortunate as to see two parties in the Church
it must be confessed in good faith that there are fanatics in the two parties
and that those most carried away are always the ones who know the least
about what the question really is. God will deliver us from both sides when
it pleases him.

When the authorship is confirmed and the bishop of Soissons is
reported to also have published an inflammatory letter, the prophet
denounces both, then returns to the pope.[57] If he has spoken before of
the models of St. Cyprian and St. Anthanasius, he is now more
outspoken on the spiritual health of the pope (who was physically
unwell).

Puisque Vostre Eminence n'a pas vu la lettre de M. l'archevesque de
Rheims, je crois, monseigneur, ne pas faire une chose qui vous soit désagréable
en vous l'envoyant. Je ne say quel jugement on en fait à Rome où vous me
mandez que l'on en a des copies, mais elle a esté également désapprouvée icy
par les gens les plus échauffés des deux partis et détestée par tous les bons
François qui savent les loix et les maximes de leur patrie. On dit que l'Evesque
de Soissons vient d'en publier une autre encore plus outrée et dont j'envoyeray
copie à V. E. s'il m'en tombe une entre les mains.
    Si quelque chose peut donner mauvaise opinon d'un parti c'est lui voir de
tels défenseurs, car je ne crois pas que dans toute l'Eglise de Dieu il y ayt
deux Evesques qui ayent moins d'esprit et moins de lumières. Ils signent et
adoptent ce qui leur est présenté et même imposé par des gens qui ont pris
tout pouvoir sur eux et l'on peut dire de ces 2 evesques qui ne laissent pas
d'avoir de bonnes qualités, "magis ex alieno jecore sapiunt quam ex duo." Le
mal est que ceux qui les gouvernent "habent jecur ulterosum."
    On est fort informé icy du mauvais estat de la santé du Pape et des efforts
que font des gens qui sont en France pour engager sa Sainteté à pousser les
choses à la derniere extremité. Cela n'est pas honorable pour eux surtout dans
un temps où nous savons que le St. Office est partagé sur cette malheureuse
affaire et qu'il s'y trouve des personnes bien intentionnées qui trouvent qu'on
n'en a déjà que trop fait et qui condamnent par avance tout ce qu'on pourroit
faire de plus. Plust à Dieu que le Pape voulût se rappeler dans la mémoire la
conduite de ses saints prédécesseurs surtout durant les 6 premiers siècles de

57. Jean-Joseph Languet de Gergy (1677–1753), bishop of Soissons since 1702.
Elected to the Académie, 1721. Condemnation of three of his writings by Parlement
(5 June 1719) was followed by an open letter of protestation to the regent. See Thomas,
La Querelle, p. 140; Leclercq, *Histoire* 3:109. Valincour the Gallican here, as often,
puts the emerging notion of papal infallibility into question and of course will also
not accept the constitutional theory that a regent has limited rather than plenary
exercise of the king's authority.

l'Eglise. C'est avec ces saints là qu'il doit passer l'Eternité et il seroit fâcheux qu'ils eussent à lui reprocher de n'avoir pas suivi leurs exemples. (9 Aug.; 45–46)

Since your Eminence has not yet seen the letter of the archbishop of Rheims, I believe I shall not be amiss in sending it. I do not know what judgment has been made on it in Rome, where you tell me there are copies. But it has been equally disapproved here by the most heated in both parties and detested by all good Frenchmen who know the laws and maxims of their nation. It is said that the bishop of Soissons has just published another that is even more outrageous and that I shall send Your Eminence if a copy falls into my hands.

If anything can discredit a party it is the appearance of this kind of defenders, for I don't believe that in all God's Church there are two bishops who have less mind and fewer lights. They sign and adopt whatever is presented to them and even imposed upon them by those who have exerted full power over them; and even though it can be said that these two bishops are not lacking good qualities, "magis ex alieno jecore sapiunt quam ex duo." The evil is that those who govern them "habent jecur ulterosum."

We are well informed of the poor state of the pope's health and of the efforts made by persons here in France to engage His Holiness to push things to the final extremity. That is not honorable, especially at a time when the Holy Office is divided on this unhappy affair and includes persons with good intentions who find that all too much has already been done and condemn in advance anything more that could be done. May it please God that the pope call to mind the conduct of his sainted predecessors, during the first six centuries of the Church especially. It is with those saints that he will have to spend eternity; and it would be vexing if they were to rebuke him for not having followed their examples.

In November, then in January, as a revealing codicil to what will be clearly a political testament, Valincour professes himself less than vexed that Mailly has not received the promotion he avidly sought. "Il fait depuis longtemps pour obtenir le chapeau beaucoup de choses qui, selon mon avis, le rendent très indigne de l'obtenir jamais" (19 Nov.; 51v–52). [He has long done things to obtain the cardinal's hat that in my view make him forever very unworthy of receiving it.] But he adds, peace for the Church is worth a cardinal's hat (1 Jan. 1720; 56v).[58]

The information that there is indecision at this moment in Rome might suffice to explain Valincour's heightened tone and changed

58. Mailly's. See Leclercq, *Histoire* 3:110–12; Jean Carreyre, *Le Jansénisme durant la Régence* (Louvain, 1929–33), 2:257–61, 284–87. Carreyre points out that Gualterio at this moment supported Dubois for the cardinalate; Valincour did also, it would seem, ironically in view of later events of 1722–23 (see above, chap. 5, n. 129 and text).

tactics. The writings of both bishops contravened the regent's "pacific declaration" of 7 October that had forbidden all further appeals, legal proceedings, or contestations. That declaration had fulfilled Valincour's own fondest desires for silence. But it is revealing that Valincour had not addressed this kind of denunciatory, circumstantial letter to Rome in 1717 when the appellant Bishops Soanen (Senez), Colbert de Croissy (Montpellier), Langle (Boulogne), and La Broue (Mirepoix) had convinced Cardinal de Noailles, the Sorbonne, and others to remain incalcitrant and themselves had registered at the Châtelet their open appeal for a national council.[59] Nor again that the cardinal de Noailles was not specifically incriminated by the letter writer when he pursued his own appeal to the pope in response to *Pastoralis offici* and at the same time resigns from the *conseil de conscience*. Although continuing reference to fanatics in *both* parties may retrospectively refer to both the appellants and Noailles, they do not lessen what may then have been a strong sympathy for the appellant cause, which always lingers in Valincour's letters to Gualterio. Two important changes had occurred by the closing days of 1719. The regent had in June renewed his ban on contestation, oral or written; and Noailles had publicly assumed a moderate position.[60] The way lay open for a good Frenchman to hope again for a conclusive compromise. Privately, the regent had hardened his line against opposition, as Valincour may have known through his friend Saint-Simon;[61] publicly, Valincour may have assumed it to be as it always has been and supported it wholeheartedly for what it represented: political Gallicanism that allowed him to view the bishop of Rheims, and others like him to follow, first of all as the enemies of good Frenchmen.

In 1720–21, Valincour wrote as many letters to Gualterio as he had in the first five years of his correspondence; and the frequency of letter writing accelerates to an at least monthly rhythm. News of the affair had previously always had an important place in his letters. But now it dominates them. The primary cause of this increased activity was the *corps de doctrine,* the compromise document on the bull negotiated

<hr/>

59. See Petitfils, *Le Régent,* pp. 339–40.

60. *Première Instruction pastorale de son Eminence Monseigneur le Cardinal de Noailles . . . au Clergé Seculier & Regulier de son Diocese, sur la Constitution 'Unigenitus,'* (Paris: Delespine, 1719). The letter to the Pope of 2 June 1717 is, however, republished with it (pp. 377–94).

61. With the economic chaos ("désolation dans le gouvernement des affaires"— Barbier), and Parlement's opposition, his impatience is more than understandable; on Orléans's anger, Barbier, *Journal* 1:77 and Petitfils, *Le Régent,* pp. 568–69.

by the regent with a commission of the clergy including Noailles, which Valincour happily reports to Gualterio as the compromise and peace of our bishops.[62] Returning to praise of its authors throughout the year 1720, and proclaiming that "cela seul suffiroit pour honorer sa régence à jamais" (14 Apr.; 61v: "That alone would suffice to honor his regency evermore."), Valincour sees the negotiation as the solution and the victory of reason. In his enthusiastic first communication of the news to Gualterio, on the eve of its signing at the Palais-Royal (13 March) by Cardinals de Noailles, de Bissy, de Rohan, de Gesvres, and de Mailly, almost all *constitutionnaires* and moderate opposition, Valincour minimizes the opposition he nonetheless foresees. (In fact the recalcitrants were reduced to the bishops of Boulogne, Marseilles, Mirepoix, Montpellier, Palmiers, some curés and Sorbonne doctors.)

Je ne puis m'empêcher de ... faire part à V.E. de l'heureuse nouvelle de l'accommodement et de la paix de nos Evesques au sujet de la constitution. C'est Mgr le duc l'Orléans qui seul a fini cette grande affaire par sa patience et sa fermeté, et il a rendu à l'Eglise et à l'Etat le plus grand service qu'il leur pouvoit rendre. Et jamais ni l'un ni l'autre n'en doivent perdre la mémoire.

M. le cardinal de Rohan s'est conduit dans la fin de cette affaire comme il avoit fait dès le commencement avec une candeur, une droiture, et un amour pour la paix qu'on ne sauroit assez louer. Et c'est à lui après Mgr le duc d'Orléans qu'on a la plus grande obligation de l'accommodement. M. le Cardinal de Bissy à son ordinaire n'a fait que jetter difficultés sur difficultés et cela à tel point que Mgr le duc d'Orléans qui est la douceur et la patience même fust obligé de lui dire qu'on finiroit bien l'affaire sans lui.

Demain tous les cardinaux et les evesques doivent signer un corps de doctrine pour montrer leur unanimité dans la foy et suivant lequel M. le cardinal de Noailles acceptera la constitution. Ce qu'on peut faire sans tirer à conséquence, car je ne crois pas que la cour de Rome songe à nouveau en envoyer d'autres de longtemps d'icy.

Quoy que par la grâce de Dieu tous nos prélats soient d'accord, ce n'est pas à dire que la paix soit entièrement rétablie, car les jansénistes et les jésuites vont estre également mécontents de ce qui aura esté fait. Peut-estre même que les universités en auront quelque peine d'abord, mais ceux qui voudront bien penser quel mal c'est qu'on schisme dans l'Eglise et quelles suites horribles il peut avoir jugeront bien qu'il faut soumettre leurs préventions et leurs resentiments particuliers au bien de la paix qui est le partage annoncé par les anges aux hommes qui ont le cœur droit et les intentions pures. (12 Mar.; 59v–60)

62. Saint-Simon sees the hand of Dubois (*Mémoires* 6:628, 370); Valincour evidently wishes to place primary responsibility elsewhere (i.e., the regent and Daguesseau but also the sometime collaborators Massillon and Père de La Tour, Superior General of the Oratoire, responsible for aiding Noailles in the redaction of the *corps de doctrine*).

I cannot keep from informing Your Eminence of the happy news of the compromise and peace of our bishops on the constitution. It is the duc d'Orléans by himself who concluded this great affair by his patience and firmness, and he has rendered the greatest service to the Church and the state. Neither should ever forget it.

The cardinal de Rohan acted in the conclusion as he had from the start with a candor, uprightness, and love for peace that is beyond praise. It is to him after the duc that we are most indebted for the compromise. Cardinal de Bissy as usual only piled difficulties on difficulties to the point that the duc, who is gentleness and patience itself, was obliged to inform him that the affair could be concluded without him.

Tomorrow all the cardinals and bishops must sign a *corps de doctrine* to show their unanimity in the faith, after which the cardinal de Noailles will accept the constitution. That can be done without consequences, for I do not believe that the court of Rome will think of sending us others for a long time.

Although by the grace of God all our prelates are in agreement, that is not to say that peace is entirely re-established, for both Jansenists and Jesuits are going to be equally discontent with what has been done. Even the universities will perhaps at first have some trouble. But those who will be willing to think what an evil a schism is in the Church and what horrible consequences it can have will indeed judge that they must submit their biases and private resentments to the good of peace which is the gift shared by the angels with men of upright heart and pure intentions.

From April, on his return to the city, through the summer, Valincour finds in Paris what he had expected: "troubles and divisions" from the inflexible opposition that insists on "full and pure" rejection of a document read as an inversion of the principles of Christian religion that could not be corrected by any turning of the terms for a "good sense" (14 Apr. 1720; 61v). There are men of piety and merit in both parties, Valincour grants; but in them both there are "madmen and fanatics like the riff-raff of an army that fights with rocks and foul speech" (7 July; 66v).[63] Neither reason nor authority has any effect on this kind of passionate prejudice, he repeats with regret, especially as he is obliged to report that the university has sent a deputation to the Parlement at Pontoise (where it was exiled in July) to exhort it to take no part in the regent's compromise. The university had thereby

63. The description is very close to that of hangers-on in Guise's army, who discredited his honor. See above, chap. 4. The term *goujats* does not seem to be leveled specifically at the lower clergy, which remained increasingly involved through grievances over hierarchical inequities. Valincour nowhere explicitly recognizes this side of the "affair."

incurred his strong "disapproval" (17 Aug.; 68v). The chancellor's name, however, is added to the repeated list of the regent, Cardinals de Rohan and de Noailles, those who had done all that was possible for the progress of the plan—in the instance, Parlement's registration on 4 August of the *corps de doctrine* as the "Déclaration du Roy touchant la conciliation des Evêques du Royaume à l'occasion de la Constitution *Unigenitus*."[64] Declaring to Gualterio on 16 August that the only means to restore reason was a year's time spent in silence on the constitution, and deploring loose accusations, Valincour must have been delighted with the declaration's fifth and final article. It specified the regent's general promise in the preamble to quell "false zeal and partisan spirit": it prohibited any accusations of His Majesty's subjects as "Jansenist, schismatic, or heretic."

Daguesseau's reappearance on the scene, which reenforces Valincour's assent, came about through agreement with other articles, specifically the second, which insured the integrity and inviolability of the French Church (and its right to appeal to a future council). But the chancellor's participation was not gained or enjoined without difficulties. Not counting on the Parlement, the regent took on 23 September the extraordinary measure of pushing the registration through the *Grand Conseil*. With the blessing of Saint-Simon, who had treated the matter at length in several letters to Valincour,[65] the comte de Toulouse accompanied the regent and the Princes of the Blood in that session. Reporting on the aftermath to Gualterio (7 Oct.; 70–70v), Valincour hopes for two positive results from that registration: that the Parlement will be reestablished in Paris; and that Noailles's pastoral decree will be published. He professes himself unable to understand the difficulties raised on the *Grand Conseil* by the new nuncio (i.e., Massei: 3 Nov.; 73) from whom he had hoped for more enlightenment than had come from the invariable difficulties created by his predecessor (Bentivoglio: 7 July; 66v). As for Valincour's hopes, Noailles signed the pastoral letter accepting the bull as explicated on 16 November. Daguesseau, drawn also by hopes of reestablishing Parlement in Paris, fully supported and was reconciled with the regent. Full registration in Parlement followed on 4 December. For Daguesseau,

64. On the "accommodement," see Thomas, *La Querelle,* 143–45; Leclercq, *Histoire* 3:117–19; Carreyre, *Le Jansénisme* 2:275–81, 3:42–43; Kreiser, *Miracles,* 36–39.
65. *Mémoires* 7:437–39 (letters); 6:630–31 and Barbier, *Journal* 1:73–74 (Toulouse's presence in the procession).

there was passionate denunciation from fanatical appellants; but for the lawyer Barbier—and Valincour—among others, this registration and the chancellor's actions symbolized ultramontane defeat.[66]

Sadly, Valincour closes the year (30 Nov.; 79) with news that the publication of Noailles's pastoral decree[67] has not yet given peace to the Church and concludes with new praise for the regent's "excellent esprit, sa patience, et ses bonnes intentions." But resigned, he looks now to heaven rather than to time as the only solution; heaven must give, in its time, "illam quam mundus fare non potest pacem," the phrase recurring like a psalmist's litany in his later letters. He had succeeded in quieting his own anger, which had flashed quickly at the pope earlier in the year. Unreasonable opposition was to be expected from some quarters; but that it should come from the pope is a scandal to Valincour's mind. The kind of logic and explanation expected from and respected by Bossuet seems with Clement to have no hold.

Ce qui m'étonne, c'est d'apprendre que le Pape témoigne n'estre pas content de l'accommodement dont il devroit, suivant l'avis de tous les gens bien intentionnés, remercier Mgr. le duc d'Orléans. Sa Sainteté ne peut pas douter, si elle prend la peine de relire la constitution, qu'elle ne soit remplie de termes durs, difficiles à bien expliquer, et capables d'exciter du trouble parmy les fidèles. Ce qui n'est que trop certain, puisqu'elles y ont excité. . . . Mais le mal est fait. Il le faut réparer et en empêcher les suites. Or quel moyen plus convenable pour cela que celui qu'a trouvé Mgr le duc d'Orléans que d'engager comme il a fait les Evesques appellants et acceptants à accepter cette constitution en lui donnant un sens très catholique et en rendant ce sens public pour l'instruction et l'édification des fidèles? Sa Sainteté ne prétend pas qu'on accepte sa Bulle sans lui donner aucun sens, et pour parler comme l'Ecole, *ab omni sensu.* Cela ne se peut proposer à des gens raisonnables. Elle trouveroit mauvais aussi qu'on rejettast en lui donnant un sens hérétique que surement elle n'a pas et qu'elle ne peut avoir. Il faut donc qu'elle consente qu'on lui en donne un catholique. (14 Apr., 61v–62)

What astonished me is to learn that the pope has shown himself not satisfied with the compromise for which he should, following the opinion of all well-intentioned persons, thank the duc d'Orléans. His Holiness cannot doubt, if he takes the trouble to reread the constitution, that it is filled with terms that are hard, difficult to explain, and capable of troubling the faithful. That is

---

66. On Daguesseau's Gallican "volte-face" and its controversial significance, see Frêche, *Un Chancelier gallican,* pp. 37, 42–44, 59; Barbier is very close to Valincour's terms of praise: *Journal* 1:83.

67. Soanen, Langle, and Colbert send "respectueuses remontrances" to the king, published as a *Lettre* in mid-January and presented to the regent in February. Rohan is sent to Rome at this moment. See Thomas, *Le Querelle,* 146.

only too certain, since they have done so. But the harm is done. It must be put right and consequences forestalled. And what more fitting way to do that than the duc d'Orléans's engagement of appellant and accepting bishops to accept this constitution by giving it a very catholic sense and making that sense public for the instruction and edification of the faithful? His Holiness does not suppose that his bull may be accepted without giving it any sense, *ab omni sensu,* to speak as the Schools do. That cannot be proposed to thinking persons. He would find it wrong too for it to be rejected for an heretical sense that it surely does not and cannot have. It is therefore necessary that he consent for it to be given a catholic sense.

With the satirist's old tones, and more pique than anger, he cannot resist remarking (7 Oct.; 70v): "Pour moy, je suis persuadé que les affaires de l'Eglise n'en iroient pas plus mal quand il y auroit un jésuite de moins dans le sacré collège." ["For my part, I am convinced that the Church's affairs would not worsen if there were one fewer Jesuit in the sacred college."] Heavily sarcastic, Valincour imagines a skillful philosopher in Rome, examining its maxims and dogma for their conformity with those of the apostles: he would have the same experience as Boccaccio's Jew with Roman morals and draw the same conclusions (24 Jan. 1721; 86v). In Augustus's time it was said, "fumum et opes strepitumque Roma," he began the letter; today, it is in Paris as well as Rome only "fumum et strepitum," and lucky one is if that is all one must contend with.

The letters continue their angry outbursts and denunciatory sarcasm until the death of Clement. Even Loyola, if he returned to earth, would say "enough" to him (19 February 1721), just as it should be repeated that the regent has done more than enough. For the first, Valincour grants that there are in Paris a "grand nombre d'hommes considérables par leur vertu et par leur habileté" (88v: "great number of men worthy of consideration for their virtue as well as their skill") who fear that the regent has in fact done too much and who may have a case. Even in response to Gualterio's news of the pope's death, angry resentment tinges charity in an ambivalent benediction. "I hope that he may find tranquillity in the other world to equal the perturbation he caused during his lifetime in a Church perhaps not yet ready to see its end." (28 March 1721; 91v: "Je souhaitte qu'il trouve autant de repos en l'autre monde qu'il a causé de trouble à l'Eglise durant sa vie et dont nous ne sommes peut-estre pas prests de voir la fin.")[68] The letter writer

68. Valincour in "private" thus goes further than the *Histoire des Réflexions* that is judged "peut-être trop loin" (Thomas, *Le Querelle,* 147): alluding first to a "politique

hurries on to fuss over the emperor's influence on the conclave, as he had from the first news of the pope's final illness the preceding December. With bitter sarcasm, he proceeds to subtract from the French delegation those cardinals who, with Rohan, might have contributed enlightenment ("qui a le plus d'esprit et de capacité") in the choice of Clement's successor—Gesvres for reasons of health, Polignac especially who cannot afford the voyage, and Noailles for reasons needing no elaboration. This leaves Mailly, whose zeal is "undiminished either by the biretta or by Parlement's condemnation of his writings," (24 Jan.) and Bissy: "Je ne say si leur présence sera aussi agréable à la cour de Rome et au pape futur qu'elle l'auroit dû estre au feu Pape pour le service duquel ils ont fait tant de choses extraordinaires et publié tant d'ecrits qui ont perdu tout le merite dans le moment de sa mort." (28 March; 92v: "I do not know whether their presence will be as agreeable to the court of Rome and the future pope as it must have been to the late pope, in whose service they did so many extraordinary things and published so many writings that have lost all their merit at the moment of the pope's death.") This last description of the changed fortune of these writings is a revealing indicator also of basic changes in the shape of Valincour's subsequent letters to Gualterio.

With the death of Clement and the election of his successor, Innocent XIII (Conti, 1721–24), Valincour's letters to Gualterio relax considerably and become progressively quieter through the reign of Innocent and his successor, the Dominican, Benedict XIII (Orsini, elected 1724), "a sainted man venerated in France."[69] The first letters referring to Innocent simply offer prayers for his guidance (8 September 1721; 101v; 18 October; 106). It is as though the letter writer remembered his Tacitus, sometimes quoted to Gualterio as to others, that violent desire for quiet grows into a great tumult (*Annals* 1, 80), or after recommending so often the model of St. Paul, he felt the spirit of quiet he preached (I Thessalonians, 4:11 or Philippians, 4:7) following on that phrase of Isaiah he knew well—"In peace shall be your strength" (30:15). And

---

humaine, parce qu'on sait que ces vues entrent beaucoup à Rome dans les affaires les plus importantes de la religion," then concluding that Clement XI "a jeté dans l'Eglise une pomme de désordre et une source de division et de trouble, qui a souvent fait dire à la plupart de ceux mêmes qui ont accepté, qu'il eût été à souhaiter que la Bulle ne fût jamais paru."

69. Thomas (*Le Querelle,* 149) refers to the "espèce de trêve bizarre que fut le pontificat d'Innocent XIII," which Valincour among others evidently read as a favorable sign at least until summer 1722. Benedict XIII was on the other hand known in France to be more open to Augustinian doctrine (and was seventy-five when elected).

as if to obey his own preaching on a year's silence, none of the seventeen letters to Gualterio written in 1723 refer to *Unigenitus.*

The strength of faith is there in the letters, even in the unquiet letter of 24 January 1721. After regretting that passionate division still persists despite the publication of Noailles's pastoral decree, with its exemplary wisdom and moderation (he maintains), Valincour first remarks again like the prophet:

Dans cent ans d'icy nostre postérité rougira et rira en même temps de voir les excès et les comportements ridicules où nous sommes portez de part et d'autre dans une querelle qui estant regardée alors sans passion et sans interrest ne parroitra qu'une pure question de mots et de Grammaire.

In two hundred years our posterity will blush and laugh at the same time to see the ridiculous excesses and behavior into which we are drawn by a quarrel that will then be regarded without passion and self-interest as a pure matter of words and grammar.

In short, "une peste a infecté les esprits dans la chrétienté comme elle infecte les corps en Provence" (86).[70] But nonetheless, he concludes, "Toutes les folies ne feront point de tort à la Religion, parce qu'elle est éternelle et inaltérable." [A plague infects minds in Christendom as it infects bodies in Provence. . . . All the follies will do no harm to religion, because it is eternal and unalterable."] Another certainty also underlay and fostered his growing detachment of philosophy supported by faith. Clement's death first, then his successor's agreement not to break silence on the affair—as well as his known position on grace—removed what Valincour apparently felt to be the last real threats to the compromise of 1720 that duly registered as law of Church and realm remained for him, through the regency and thereafter, reason's rightful and triumphant restoration of order. The reality in its direct literal sense of schism seems to recede (but is in no way replaced by higher tolerance for diversity).

If the letter writer relaxes and now enjoys letters that continue through 1725 the pace and volume of those established in 1720–21, in no way "devalued like the currency," he quips to the correspondent celebrated as a "man who does so much honor to humanity," he remains vigilant in his observations of the divisions that plague man's minds and distort their behavior. His ritually repeated identification of "fous

70. The epidemic in the south gives the simile forcefulness. It was felt as disastrous on a national scale. The comte de Toulouse gave 200,000 liv. for plague relief (Leclercq, *Histoire* 3:90).

et enragés" on both sides of issues begins to have the ring of Ecclesiastes: "madness and folly" (1:17; 2:12), vanity as afflicting as the "gathering and heaping" he denounced as the "contagion" of Law's schemes; he continually deplored unnecessary and dangerous books, that of the inevitably human folly of "the making of books there is no end." Thus he regrets the appearance in November 1721 of the "Lettre des Sept Evêques."[71] After reporting that following their particular biases and interests judges have on the one hand proclaimed it a masterpiece worthy of the first centuries of the Church and on the other a work filled with heresies, he moderates in a now typical position:

Pour moy, qui grâces à Dieu ne suis d'aucun parti et à qui il n'est permis d'examiner ces sortes d'écrits qu'en qualité de médiocre académicien, je trouve que les écrivains ont manqué à la premiére régle de la rhétorique qui est de chercher à concilier la bienveillance de celui qu'on veut persuader. Ce n'est pas qu'ils n'ayent marqué avec des termes très expressifs le profond respect qui est dû au Pape et qui est encore mieux gravé au fonds de leur cœur qu'il n'est exprimé dans leur lettre. Mais je crains que ce qui est dit du pape défunt et de la révocation de la constitution ne déplaise à S. Sté sur tout dans un temps où l'on peut prendre des voyes plus douces par l'accommodement approuvé par tant d'autres Evesques et fait par les soins et sous l'autorité de Mgr le duc d'Orléans. On a fort loué l'application du passage de st Basile qui est en effet très beau et qui convient fort aux conjonctures présentes. Mais une application ne sert jamais ou ne doit jamais servir de principe à une décision, car on pourroit donner à Pierre le justaucorps de Gautier qui lui conviendroit fort parce qu'ils seroient tous les deux de même taille. Mais cela n'empêchera pas que ces deux hommes ne fussent infiniment différents l'un de l'autre et qu'ils méritassent des traittements différents. (29 Nov.; 108–108v)

For my part, who thanks to God am of no party and am permitted to examine these kinds of writings only as an average Academician, I find that the writers missed the first rule of rhetoric, which is the "captatio benevolentiae." It isn't that they have not marked with the most expressive terms the deep respect that is due the pope and which is still better engraved in their hearts than in their letter. But I fear what they say of the late pope and the revocation of the constitution may displease His Holiness, especially at a time when more gentle approaches are possible through the compromise approved by so many other bishops and made by the application and under the authority of the duc d'Orléans. The application of the passage of St. Basil has been much praised and in fact is very fine and pertinent in present circumstances. But

71. Dated 9 June 1721, the letter (86 pp. in French and Latin) appeared in November over the signatures of the bishops of Tournai, Palmiers, Senez, Montpellier, Boulogne, Auxerre, Mâcon. It was sent to Rome by way of Germany. Summary in Thomas, pp. 152–54.

an application never serves as a principle for decision and must not, for one could give to Peter the *justaucorps* of Gauter that would be his size. But the two men would not thereby fail to be infinitely different and to merit different treatments.

The following year, Valincour returns to the "Lettre," when he has read the pope's reply and letter to the regent. The hearts he had born witness to may be unchanged; he does not speak of them. Only the ill-advised heads of friends, who had not consulted him, are his concern. Had he been consulted, he would surely have advised against a publication that could only embitter minds and keep this "mauvaise affaire" eternally alive. He turns away with an invocative of faith: "Il faut que Dieu s'en mesle et qu'il nous donne 'illam quam mundus dare non potest pacem' " ["God will have to enter in and give us 'that peace which the world cannot give' "] (18 July 1722; 122).[72] The same procedure takes place when it is a matter of the "other side," the publication by Bissy and Languet de Gergy of two "heavy tomes."[73] "It would have been more useful to be quiet," Valincour comments, then quotes Ecclesiastes—"faciendi plures libros non est finis." "The more one writes on grace," he continues, "the clearer it will be that it is impossible to explain. St. Paul said that long ago, and one can take his word for it" (3 September; 129v).[74] Earlier in the year, it had been a question of the appearance of an "impertinent" *Histoire de l'Eglise depuis l'an 1700 jusqu' au présent.*[75] As Valincour describes it, the history is an apology of the constitution that treats the most "respectable" persons insolently ("one will not suspect the Fathers of the Oratoire of being the authors"). Reflecting, God's gift of silence seems, more than his gift of language, what is needed in this strangest of quarrels, in which all err, the strangest "since men have been men, that is, subject to act against reason" (11 January; 110v–111).

Hopeful as he is with the election of Benedict XIII, and especially

72. Present disorder in the church evoked through St. Basil's epistles (61 and 69) is thus reinvoked in the same terms by Valincour. The "Letter of the Seven Bishops" was condemned by the Holy Office on 8 January 1722 and a papal letter by Innocent XIII in July deploring the bishops' disobedience.

73. Bissy, *Instruction pastorale,* 376 pp. Dated 7 June 1722. See Thomas's summary, pp. 168–73; Languet de Gergy, *5e Instruction pastorale* (lre Partie, 25 Mar. 1722; 2e Partie, 25 Sept. 1722). See Carreyre, *Le Jansénisme* 3:268ff.

74. At this point and through 1725, in this insistence on human error and on the mystery of grace, both Valincour's Augustinianism and his "tiers parti" status are perhaps clearest.

75. Unidentified.

with the renewed use of councils, Valincour repeats on several occasions that his work is troubled. He is particularly aggrieved when a long remonstrance by the bishop of Montpellier (Colbert de Croissy) and a lengthy account of the death of the bishop of Boulogne (Langle)[76] appear. Is the clock turning back to 1717? he must have wondered; this time, as in 1722, the appellants on whom he had then remained silent, perhaps in sympathy, he calls to order. The two parties yet at each others' throats are nonetheless in agreement on one thing, he reports—that God has given us a saint for pope. It is frivolous to trouble his prospects and "consolation" in ending the long-standing disputes.

Je désapprouve fort, quoy qu'ils puissent contenir de bonnes choses. . . . La prudence chrétienne voudroit qu'on supprimast ces sortes d'Ecrits lors qu'on voit qu'ils ne peuvent causer aucun bien et faire un effet tout contraire. Je ne les envoye point. (30 July 1724; 197–97v/9 September; 202–202v)

I strongly disapprove, although they may contain some good things. . . . Christian prudence would require the suppression of these kinds of writings when they can cause no good and can do its opposite. I am not sending them.

And it is at this point that special praise is sent to Gualterio of Polignac, then visiting Rome, praise of the right use of writing for the glory of religion (that is a part of the climate of the last Academic eloquence condemning that ethical frivolity of writing). Along with a Latin inscription for a portrait bust of Polignac he includes a "sixain" of his own composed at Fontainebleau on the author of the *Anti-Lucrèce*.

> Tel fut le vainqueur d'Epicure:
> Et des faux Esprits sort l'Ennemi redouté;
> Qui de leurs vains détours perçant la nuit obscure
> A leurs yeux éblouis montra la vérité
> Et dans les jeux de la nature
> Du Dieu qui la soutient fit voir la majesté. (31 August; 199v)

After praising God for the successful conclusion of the pope's council and affirming that his example will carry more authority than the laws and constitutions of his predecessors, Valincour announces the appearance of a new, inordinately long pastoral letter by Cardinal de

---

76. *Remonstrances au Roi* by Colbert de Croissy was condemned by the *Conseil d'Etat* in September and the bishop was removed; Bayeux's condemnation of two *constitutionnaire* works brought the conseil's condemnation of all three. See Thomas, pp. 182–85. Valincour's finding some "bonnes choses" in Boulogne's work despite his own dismissal of these writings may have come from his long friendship with Langle.

Bissy. His response is a summary, in its terseness, of his advice to others and his own counsel since 1722. The very long letter "will be less useful than the shortest of those of St. Paul to Titus or to Philemon" (8 July 1725; 228v). "Fous et fanatiques," he reasons earlier in the year, who trouble peace, could not seriously in their folly suppose they understood grace better than St. Augustine or St. Paul (26 January; 211v); why do they not listen silently to them? Much will depend on the pope's response now to Noailles (6 August; 233), who remains for Valincour among the "hommes très éclairés, gens de bien" that are to be found in both parties. "God will put his hand to it when it will please Him to do so," he affirms with faith that remains steadfast at the end of 1725. "The angel of Noël has not yet brought peace for all men of good will. God will give it, when it shall please him, to the Church and to the court of France" (29 December; 242). Ironically perhaps this hope is accompanied by a recommendation of a Jesuit (Père Charlevoix) who is said to Gualterio to be a "très bon sujet et capable de faire honneur à sa compagnie."

Metaphysics and Daguesseau

The "serious study" of metaphysics, Valincour wrote to Bouhier in 1725, had long occupied him and was not yet finished. And the "vanity" of metaphysics, he concludes, has become progressively more apparent to him.[77] That study may go back as far as the letters to Bossuet. It certainly does at least to 1722, when Daguesseau wrote his conversations with Valincour into his *Méditations métaphysiques,* ten dense and tortuous essays undertaken and left finally unfinished during his second exile.[78] The chanellor's letters are of some assistance, though they have confused the issues,[79] in clarifying a position and a project that are identifiable enough from the paraphrases Daguesseau gives of

77. Letter of 29 Dec, *L'Amateur d'autographes* 5 (1866), 382.
78. *Œuvres* (ed. Pardessus), vol. 14, 636pp. Dating by Dom Marcel Pierrot, "D'Aguesseau et l'humanisme." *Le Chancelier Henri-François D'Aguesseau* (Limoges: Desvilles, 1953), 55.
79. Since neither the Pardessus nor 1743 edition of Daguesseau's letters fully identifies correspondents, and manuscripts are seemingly not extant, possibilities for confusion are many. The long letters on creation, substance, and infinity are most probably not addressed to Valincour (Pardessus, 16:1–78, 138–47, 155–95, 326–28). These include the discussion of Cudworth's *The True Intellectual System* attributed to the exchange by Francis Monnier, who appears to have had little knowledge of Valincour (*Le Chancelier D'Aguesseau,* [Paris: Didier, 1860], pp. 268–73).

his interlocutor's arguments and an accompanying characterization of Valincour beyond the exchange qualifying his intentions.

Valincour has been strongly influenced by a reading of Locke, most probably in Coste's translation (1700).[80] He begins with his conviction that there is no innate idea of justice, therefore no justice prior to positive law. Like Locke, he departs from Malebranche and the Cartesian tradition and abandons a preliminary definition of substance.[81] He first asks the kind of question that he had posed for Bossuet about prophecy. How could we recognize proof that natural ideas of the just and unjust exist? Arguments are piled up. If they were natural, nature would have given them to all men. But diversity of laws demonstrates the falsity of that assertion. If there were a universal natural law, men would at least recognize it when shown its principles, as they do the axioms of geometry. But men do not. If they did, why would they exult in injustice as they do? Can an indivisible substance, as we would understand the soul to be, reconcile these two contrary dispositions any more than a geometer could say that a line is straight and curved at the same time? And if these natural principles exist, why should men be any more hard put to express them as clear ideas than a mathematician to set forth his axioms? No moral principle has the same necessary effect upon the will that those mathematical axioms do upon intelligence, even the first principle—"ne faites pas à un autre ce que vous ne voudriez pas qu'un autre vous fît." Questions having been pushed to this point, Valincour oversteps Locke[82] and seeks elsewhere both his metaphysics and its social inferences.

Moving closer to Hobbes, Valincour insists that love of fellow man may be a first principle only if we discover a different world from that in which we live. Tertullian may have said of the first Christians— "Voyez comme ils s'aiment"; "Voyez comme ils se haïssent" is a truer

80. Valincour does not seem to have known English. Locke's plain style, discernible in Coste, was almost certainly an attraction, as was the view of the "Epistle" that Valincour himself echoes on the "vague and insignificant forms of speech, and abuse of language, ... passed for mysteries of science."

81. Here and in the following I use the paraphrase by Daguesseau of Valincour's position in the "Première Méditation," 14:6–16 and the "Deuxième," passim. It is Book I of Locke that is in question. On Locke and Malebranche, see John Yolton, *Locke* (Oxford: Clarendon, 1985), 3, 150; Paul Hazard, *La Crise de la conscience européenne* (1961 ed.), 225–28.

82. On the "objective rule and measure emanating from God and ascertainable by human nature," see John Locke, *The Second Treatise on Government* (New York: Liberal Arts, 1952), section 14 and Introduction by T. P. Peardon, p. xiii.

picture of the present. Brotherly love ("charité fraternelle") is an automatism now, like the gregariousness of animals. Together in a theater, with the "représentation d'une belle tragédie," tears are shed; "au sortir du spectacle," a man who has just wept over an imaginary plight "verra d'un oeil sec des malheurs réels, et refusera inhumainement le moindre secours à une famille qui meurt de faim."[83] In that real world, it is asserted with direct paraphrase from Hobbes, men are rival brothers caught in the pursuit of "une guerre fatale de tous les hommes contre tous les hommes."[84] Rather than a love of justice, which importunately constrains men's desires, what rules them in this world is uniquely "le désir de leur conservation dans l'être et dans le bien-être."

It is in this natural and universal desire that one must seek the "origine de la société, le fondement des lois, la source de tout ce qu'on appelle justice." If illusions on a natural justice engraved in the heart are dispelled, our minds may be freed for appropriate actions. More profoundly than in his verse, the satire of "Le Sens commun," Valincour takes an anti-Cartesian line, with a proposition that echoes Pascal's on true happiness (in God): "Ce qu'on appelle justice n'existe ni hors de nous ni dans nous," he begins.[85] The conclusion on authority, combining principle and counsel, is in fact reflected in Valincour's increasing stringent assertions of the necessity for obedience to authority—to the monarchical principle (as in Hobbes's *De cive*)[86] and to law even when it may become repressive. It is Descartes's provisional ethics (Part III of the *Discours de la méthode*) that underwrites this kind of "social contract."

Ce qu'on appelle justice n'existe ni hors de nous ni dans nous. Ce n'est pas un point fixe et certain, que notre intelligence puisse saisir. . . . La justice n'est qu'un rapport ou une conformité à ce qui est juste; mais le juste est aussi difficile à définir que la justice. Ainsi . . . puisqu'elle consiste dans la conformité avec un objet, il faut nécessairement ou que cet objet soit la volonté

83. *Méditations*, p. 10. Since Valincour will include "Spectacles" among the subjects of his later dialogues, this example seems an important thematic link. See below, chap. 8, pp. 284–85.

84. *Méditations*, pp. 11–12. Cf. Hobbes, *Leviathan*, ed. M. Oakeshott (Oxford: Clarendon, 1960), part I, pp. 83–85.

85. As a resolution of the stoic/epicurean (Lafuma 407): "Le Bonheur n'est ni hors de nous ni dans nous: il est en Dieu et hors et dans nous."

86. Valincour had surely read the *De cive* in Sorbière's translation (1652). For what I take to illuminate Valincour's later justification of authority, see Christiane Frémont, "L'Enfer des relations," *Recherches sur le XVIIeme siècle* 7 (1984), 83.

connue et certaine d'un être supérieur, ou qu'il ne soit autre chose que ce qui est utile pour notre conservation.[87]

What is called justice exists neither outside us nor within us. It is not a fixed and sure point that our intelligence can grasp. ... Justice is nothing other than a relationship or a conformity with what is just; but the just is as difficult to define as justice. Thus ..., since it consists in conformity with an object, it must by necessity be either the known and certain will of a superior being or something else that is useful for our conservation.

In the dialogues, Daguesseau refuses to accept Valincour's Lockean premise and shows no inclination whatsoever to enter into musings on Hobbes's vision of the world. Galvanized by this aggressive irony and the bleakness of a vision of man's wretchedness without God (the sense of the compliment previously cited that Valincour shares in the spirit of both Plato and Pascal), the chancellor's own shared doubts are willfully repressed for a re-enunciation of Cartesian metaphysical certainties. As Jean Carbonnier has acutely observed, the "wager against his friend Valincour" pushes Daguesseau to defend a natural law demonstrable by the light of reason alone, religion becoming for him the perfection of reason; Voltaire would have applauded the tactic, Carbonnier concludes, identifying the position as an answer to Pascal as much as to Valincour.[88] The question then becomes the extent to which Valincour has played devil's disciple and led his interlocutor into this paradoxical position. Daguesseau had invited him to take a strong stand; an invitation to which he had answered: "Metaphysics in nothing,"[89] a proposition that is clearly not either the equivalent of that made to Bouhier in 1725 about its vanity or consistent with a series of others made to him in the last quarter of that year indicating a use of metaphysics as a means to an end. That end, in retrospect already perceptible in the correspondence with Bossuet, is more clearly divulged in Daguesseau's quite similar characterization of Valincour's intentions in taking the position he had argued. The chancellor, self-proclaimed disciple of Descartes, does not share the enthusiasm for Locke of course; and Hobbes, for him, is simply the bogeyman atheistic-politician symbolizing, as he did, any and all extremities of materialism, determinism, individualism, and ethical relativism. Locke is thus

---

87. *Méditations*, pp. 14–15.
88. Jean Carbonnier, "L'Importance de D'Aguesseau pour son temps et pour le nôtre." *Le Chancelier Henri-François D'Aguesseau*, p. 39.
89. "La métaphysique n'est rien." Cited by Francis Monnier, loc. cit., p. 269.

the first term in a regression, just as the philosophy of Ralph Cudworth may represent to him a similar move toward containing that regression. Daguesseau is then quite careful to dissociate the "real" Valincour from his possible misrepresentation.

If Valincour cannot "entertain the notion of perceiving justice by the mind," the chancellor discriminates, he possesses it nonetheless "always present in his heart." Unlike the common run of men, he is "always just in practice and unjust only in theory." Having rejected the possibility that his interlocutor may be a Pyrrhonist, Daguesseau can only conclude that Valincour is following in the line of Pascal, with all the implications that association may summon up.

Le philosophe qui m'engage à méditer sur cette mattière ... s'il paroît dégrader en un sens notre raison, ce n'est que pour mieux établir la nécessité de la révélation: c'est par un excès de zèle et comme par une sainte jalousie pour la loi divine, qu'il se plaît à rabaisser et à décrier.[90]

The philosopher who engages me in meditation on this matter ... for all of appearing in one sense to degrade our reason only does so to establish all the better the necessity of revelation: it is only by an excess of zeal and a godly jealousy for divine law that he takes pleasure in humbling and disparaging the mind.

Pascal's strategy "soumission *et* usage de la raison," is thus Valincour's strategy.

Strictly speaking, a specific project of writing an apologetic work is not yet fully disclosed by Daguesseau's characterization. Although it may seem closer, and Valincour more disposed to it than in the Bossuet correspondence, that project may well have come only near or after the end of the exile that closed for Daguesseau in 1727. Other events intervene to move the writer on the one hand to lighten pessimism about the limits of even the best minds caught up in controversy and consequently the recurrently expressed doubts about "doing the good in this world one would like to do" and on the other hand to translate into a practically oriented, didactic text what Daguesseau perhaps too easily neutralized as abstraction. At the moment of Daguesseau's characterization, however, Valincour may indeed have been satisfied simply to move to the exchange of translations

90. *Méditations,* p. 13. Daguesseau's note identifies Valincour. "Méditation II" then includes in the "Sommaire": "Mais il n'auroit pas dû décrier la loi naturelle, sous prétexte de mieux établir la nécessité de la révélation."

of Plato's *Crito*[91] that by mutual agreement was an appropriate choice of the use of the two friends' leisure time of exile.

The exchanges with Bouhier, extended to him with a sense of renewal on Valincour's part, repeat points already made to the chancellor but with a clearer suggestiveness of purpose than it is possible to recover at second hand from Daguesseau. "Quis leget haec?," he comments revealingly with Persius, of a lengthy poem in Greek proving the immortality of the soul,[92] the inference being that the happy few may, but that those in need of its message either cannot or will not. A similar question is at the source of critiques of Malebranche and Leibniz: "Who can read that?" Both thinkers are, Valincour gladly acknowledges, among the greatest of the century. But the "visions connues" of his friend Malebranche and the "système harmonique" of Leibniz, though quite different, are, as Valincour's scornful characterizations already imply, "ridiculous and absurd."[93] Mathematics, in their case as in others', may be wrongly used; but Valincour does not for that reason give them up. They must once again find, he implies, the place given to them by Pascal. Lucian is this time enlisted to mock the vogue that would not work.

La géométrie transcendante qui est devenue si fort à la mode marque également l'étendue et la petitesse de l'esprit humain. La lune se plaint à Jupiter dans quelque endroit des dialogues de Lucien de ce que les astronomes l'importunent et passent les nuits à prendre sa mesure comme s'ils voulaient lui faire un habit. Il n'y a point de parabole ou d' hyperbole qui ne pust faire la même plainte contre les géomètres, *mais du moins ont-ils la satisfaction de trouver toujours la vérité et les métaphysiciens ne l'ont jamais.*[94]

Transcendental geometry that has become so fashionable shows equally the extensiveness and the smallness of the human mind. The moon complains to Jupiter somewhere in Lucian's dialogues of importuning astronomers who

91. B. N. MS. Supp. fr. 3771. 7 pp. Daguesseau's more polished translation: *Œuvres* (ed. Pardessus), 16:458–70.

92. 9 Sept. 1725, *RHLF* 31 (1924), 375. Allusion is to a poem by Gilbert Gaulmin.

93. Letters of 17 and 29 Dec. 1725, ibid., 379, 382. Valincour refers to Malebranche as "de mes amis," but I have been unable to find any trace of the friendship in direct or indirect correspondence. On their friendship, the link with Daguesseau, and differences ("Malebranche n'aimait pas les vers; Valincour détestait la métaphysique"), see André Robinet, *Malebranche vivant. Œuvres de Malebranche* (Paris: Vrin, 1967), 20:367–69. He is eager to read the *Critique de la Recherche de la Vérité* by Simon Foucher (rev. ed., 1693) on 17 Dec. The sole reference to Leibniz here, to the *Système nouveau,* would seem to echo Bayle's "general impression of obscurity." See W. H. Barber, *Leibniz in France* (Oxford: Clarendon, 1955), 62–63.

94. Letter of 29 Dec. 1725, *L'Amateur d'autographes* 5 (1866), 282 (my emphasis).

spend their nights measuring her as though they wished to make her a garment. There is no parabola nor hyperbola that could not make the same complaint about geometers. *But at least they have the satisfaction of always finding the truth, which metaphysicians never have.* (my emphasis)

Finally, the concerns voiced to Gualterio about the impiety of the Republic of Letters to which the Academic discourse of 1724 was directed have a year later been generalized. Whatever the extent and combination of deist texts and practice were that had caused Valincour to take stock of his arguments in 1703, the currency of deism seems to him rampant both in Paris and at court two decades later. Briefly to Bouhier, he notes the position he has already been taking in conversations that will need to be developed in a "long discourse."

Pour les déistes et même les athées dont le nombre augmente tous les jours à Paris et à la Cour, je n'ai trouvé qu'un seul moyen de leur fermer la bouche et le voici: pour demeurer tranquilles dans le parti que vous avez pris, il vous faut une démonstration plus que géométrique, que certainement vous n'avez pas. Mais pour déterminer à suivre, même suivant les règles de la raison humaine, ce que la religion chrétienne me prescrit, il suffit que j'aie des motifs de crédibilité, et certainement j'en ai d'aussi considérables que ceux qui me font croire que César et Cicéron ont existé, donc, etc. Mais cela renferme la matière d'un long discours.[95]

As for deists and even atheists, whose numbers grow every day in Paris and at court, I have found only one means of closing their mouths, which is this: to remain unassailable in the position you have taken, you must have a demonstration beyond the geometrical one, which certainly you do not have. But to determine me to follow what the Christian religion prescribes, even following the rules of human reason, it suffices that I have dispositions to belief; and certainly I do have them, ones that are as worthy of consideration as those that make me believe that Caesar and Cicero existed, thus, etc. But all this contains the matter for a long discourse.

It will be at Saint-Cloud that the "long discourse" will be elaborated in the form of dialogues, continuing in correspondence with Bouhier and with other interlocutors who will be visitors there. That elaboration will be added to the scenes of activity that continue to be depicted in letters to Gualterio in which metaphysics is never explicitly an issue. Through 1725 those letters reveal an active life, even in the

95. 9 Sept. 1725, *RHLF* 31 (1924), 375. Should additional confirmation of Valincour's opinions for 1722 be needed, it is offered most recently by Pierre Clair's "photographie de l'opinion." *Recherches sur le XVIIeme siècle* 6 (1983), 24–38 and 179–84 on "De la conduite qu'un honnête homme doit garder pendant sa vie."

philosophical retreat of the library of Valincour's "hermitage," broken occasionally by memorably represented scenes of melancholy, as migratory birds pass overhead, young fruit trees are contemplated, or Rome is desired "on the wings of a dove."[96] Coming to terms there in difficult accommodation with the realities of human nature expressed to Daguesseau, Valincour had the sustaining myth of the consolation of study, which outlasts intact the destruction of the bust of Socrates and the volumes of Cicero and Horace.[97] To sustain his projects, as the continuity of his life, there was also centrally the guide of a clarified faith found in meditation upon St. Paul, as Locke had found it in other circumstances of controversy and as Bossuet had preached it.[98]

96. B. M. Add MSS. 20395: 10 Mar. 1723 (p. 138), 26 Apr. 1723 (p. 140), 13 Mar. 1725 (p. 217v), especially 24 Jan. 1721 (p. 85).

97. "Du repos, de la vertu et de l'innocence . . . loin des préventions du vulgaire" (10 Oct., 1723, ibid., p. 131v). The letter of 30 Nov. 1720 (ibid., 78v–79) describes a bust of Socrates as a central feature of the library.

98. The method of Locke's reading of St. Paul is from his initial identification of a "clear, plain, disinterested preaching of the Gospel, a preaching without any hidden design, or the least mixture of any concealed, secular interest" similar to Valincour's. For the remarkable summary/gloss of Locke's *Paraphrase, Commentary,* and *Essay* on St. Paul, *Works* (London, 1823), vols. 8–9 by Peter A. Schouls, which could stand as a guide to Valincour's reading: *The Imposition of Method* (Oxford: Clarendon, 1980), "Appendix," p. 244ff. Bossuet's panegyric (Pléiade ed., pp. 349–69).

Part IV

The Shape of a Life:
The Limits of *honnêteté*

Chapter 8

Last Years (1726–1730)

Je regrette sensiblement ce pauvre homme. Il avait cent
bonnes qualités et pas un defaut nuisible à ses amis.

D'Olivet to Bouhier, 18 January 1730[1]

The fire of the night of 13 January 1726 that left "not a book, a page,
or a painting" from Valincour's 7,000–volume library, collection of
portraits, and "forty years' accumulation of personal papers" sent a
chill through bookish circles. Four hours of the fire, an accident caused
by the negligence of a sleepy servant, destroyed Valincour's life at
Saint-Cloud as he had constructed it and much of his past. Close
friends worried about the man, shaken by this loss in his seventy-third
year. Daguesseau wrote to Valincour, solicitous of his health after the
trauma and wishing Fresnes were close enough to serve as a shelter.
But repeating the earlier tribute to his friend's faith, Daguesseau
reassured him that he had no need of resources other his own to
overcome this adversity. "J'en conçois que la métaphysique sans la
religion est bien inutile," he now agreed, "mais la dernière est si forte
et si bien affermie chez vous, que je suis persuadé qu'elle vous aura
mis audessus d'un si triste événement" ["I understand that metaphysics
without religion is indeed useless, but your religion is so strong and
so sure that I am convinced that it will lift you above this sad event"].[2]
To Gualterio, Daguesseau, and especially to Bouhier, Valincour was
frank in expressing regrets for his losses. All the riches of Samuel

---

1. *Correspondence littéraire du Président Bouhier. No. 3: Lettres de Pierre-Joseph
Thoulier, abbé d'Olivet (1719–1745)*, ed. H. Duranton (St.-Etienne: Université de St.-
Etienne, 1976), 140.

2. *Œuvres* (ed. Pardessus), 16:331–32. A second similar compliment in a second
letter, p. 333.

Bernard could not recover them, he wrote; and he refused to play the Stoic: "Aussi ne feray-je pas le philosophe mal à propos avec vous. Je vous avoue que l'affliction n'est pas médiocre ... Dieu veuille me donner la force de la supporter."³ ["I will not play the philosopher unsuitably with you ... I confess that my affliction is not an ordinary one ... May God give me the strength to support it."]³ Passing through Saint-Cloud afterward, he admitted to Bouhier, he had needed two months to find the heart to look in the direction of his old hermitage.⁴ But by 9 February strength of mind had been found. After informing Bouhier that the offending servant had been kept on, he concluded with fine resolution: "Je n'aurais guère profité de mes livres si je ne savais pas les perdre." ["I would scarcely have profited from my books if I did not know how to lose them."]⁵ Although his health remained fragile—two months' pulmonary disorders followed the fire, numerous bouts with gout and colds in 1727 and 1728, an unidentified illness in 1729 that d'Olivet feared would be fatal—by 10 February 1726 it might seem to an outsider that business had resumed as usual. In a short letter to Gualterio that day, he reported having forwarded papers to the minister Chavigny and commented much in his usual tone on the twin concerns of peace in Europe (not so much in danger as the purveyors of the news would have believed) and in the Church (where it continued to be elusive).⁶

In part perhaps to occupy his mind, d'Olivet recruited Valincour to translate the fourth "Tusculan Disputation" with a team including himself, Bouhier, Fraguier, and Nicolas Gédoyn. Each translator was to do one disputation, his own commentary, and read all the others' work. Bouhier would provide the critical apparatus and Rémond a preface situating the friends' enterprise in their walks at Auteuil and Saint-Cloud. All the participants were "zealous to immortalize our association," d'Olivet assured Bouhier.⁷ Although a somewhat miscellaneous conversation, the fourth disputation's Stoic exposition of philosophical remedies for various "disorders of the soul" might have offered some good therapy. But Valincour had little interest in Stoicism in itself, and as a passing sarcastic dismissal of "that idiot Poseidonius"

3. Letter of 27 Jan. 1726 published by Cazes, ed., *Lettres à la marquise****, "Introduction," 65.
4. 24 July 1726. *RHLF* 31 (1924), 384.
5. Cazes, 66.
6. B.M. Add. MSS. 20395, p. 249.
7. 9 July 1726. *Correspondance littéraire du Président Bouhier. No. 3* (1976), 108–9.

indicates,[8] he had neither need nor inclination to seek that specific remedy for his ills. The pleasures of the learned association with friends might have seen him through, if he had chosen retirement at this moment; but as d'Olivet informed Bouhier, their friend Valincour was simply too busy elsewhere.[9] A year earlier Valincour had written to Gualterio about the demands on him and had given an accounting of his life that centered in his career. This accounting would be clarified rather than modified by the aftermath of the 1726 fire, which forced Valincour to reconstruct his life and to reflect on the limits that health and age imposed upon him.

Il y a 40 ans que je suis chargé d'affaires honorables pour moi à la vérité, mais qui deviennent pénibles et fatiguantes dans un aage où on ne doit plus songer qu'à celles de l'autre monde et à passer en repos le peu de temps qui reste à vivre en celuy-cy. Je trouverois tout cela auprès de V. E. et je ne voudrois point d'autre employ que celui de concièrge ou *villicus* du Corgnolo. Mais il y a des chaînes et des engagements qu'on est obligé de soutenir toute sa vie quand on les a portés un certain nombre d'années.[10]

For forty years I have been charged with affairs that have been honorable, truth to tell, but which become arduous and tiring at an age when one should think only of those of the other world and live the little time remaining in this world with peace of mind. I should find all that with your eminence and would wish no other employ than gatekeeper (or *villicus*) at Corgnolo. But there are chains and undertakings one is obliged to sustain all one's life when they have been born a certain number of years.

These duties and pledges, resumed in February 1726, maintained the high ideals of service—to the realm, the Church of France, and the Republic of Letters—the same ideals that in the earlier part of his career had informed both the honorable effort to fulfill charges and the honorable leisure of the writer, both of which had contributed to establishing the "merit" of the "honnête homme."

Service to Toulouse took first place, already in 1725 in alliance with Fleury. James Pritchard's recent statement about "officers of the pen," that they "defined for themselves what it meant to be the king's confidential agent,"[11] may always have been true of Valincour. He himself had defined, for the good of the state, the charge of *secrétaire*

8. 8 Sept. 1725 to Gualterio. B.M. Add. MSS. 20395, p. 236v.

9. 25 Dec. 1726, 20 Feb. 1727. Loc. cit., pp. 112, 114.

10. 19 April 1725. B.M. Add. MSS. 20395, p. 220v.

11. *Louis XV's Navy, 1748–1762* (Kingston and Montreal: McGill-Queen's, 1988), 37.

général de la marine and had made a good part of that definition his dedication to the admiral's statutory and administrative place as well as his material privileges. Alliance with Fleury (after association for a decade in the Académie and friendship of shared moments of leisure) relocated the occupations of the "confidential agent" in ways that made for some perhaps difficult compromises when the bishop became first minister in summer of 1726 (though without assuming the title). In February Fleury still remained, as he had been since gaining control of the newly constituted *conseil de conscience* in 1723, an inflexible and indeed violent *constitutionnaire*. After as before Benedict XIII's new efforts to make peace with Cardinal de Noailles (through the "twelve propositions" dissociated from the 1720 "corps de doctrine" Valincour heartily praised[12]), the bishop had opposed compromise by explications of *Unigenitus*. He continued to wish Noailles expelled and to collaborate with both Jesuits and the curia to that end. As both Dorsanne's running commentary on the bishop's exploits and Georges Hardy's careful archival investigation show, by February 1726 it had become clear to all—including the pope—that the peace of the Church depended on the bishop of Fréjus. It appeared by July that he was ready politically to give a new conciliatoriness a try.[13] Valincour for his part could hope that Fleury's past inquisitional rigor (not too strong a word, since he at one point had wished to invoke a decree of the Inquisition) would no longer be brought to bear against individual members of the clergy. Magistrates among Valincour's friends had been harshly singled out, as had been Père La Tour, whose integrity he admired. Valincour could be under no illusion about mildness that professed to detest "tout ce qui peut être soupçonné de violence,"[14] but could perhaps believe in seconding and aiding the "third party" position politically orchestrated from July 1726 by Fleury and his key advisers (Rohan, Bissy, and Polignac). Master of the king's councils as well as the Church's "conscience" (at least its *conseil* and the "feuille des bénéfices"), for the "bien de l'état" (and of course Toulouse's) Fleury could not be ignored. As Valincour had advised generally in 1723 on first ministers, pragmatically there was "no other decision than to be the declared friend" and

12. 23 Feb. 1727 to Bouhier, *RHLF* 31 (1924), 389: referring back: "le mandement du Cardinal de Noailles qui a fait en ceci tout ce qu'un bon et saint et sage prélat pouvait faire pour le bien de la paix. Mais le Bissy s'est encore avisé de chicaner."
13. See Georges Hardy, *Le Cardinal de Fleury et le mouvement janséniste* (Paris: Champion, 1925), 38–39.
14. Ibid., p. 127, quoting A. A. E. 1262, p. 31.

morally there is "never a good party except that which has the person of the king and royal authority."

If Fleury led Valincour to new prominence in the Académie, his influence did not stop there. It determined certain directions in Valincour's letters to Gualterio. Both directly and in more indirect ways, it also contributed to the reordering of priorities in his personal writing of history, poetry, and dialogues. The responsibilities of a lifetime, like its pleasures, are in fact redirected rather than abandoned in the new apartment offered Valincour by the duc d'Orléans (who also gave hospitality to some *appellants*). Society at the château of Saint-Cloud, with the duc's increasing reclusiveness, was largely what Valincour wished—occasional. If the change were not otherwise known, letters to Bouhier might seem still written from the old library. The ideal library in fact changed little. Nor did Valincour's pleasures of poetry and of criticism, of writing, and of reading new texts against older ones; these remained in his last years the source they had earlier been of both serenity and energy.

Valincour's first obligation, to Toulouse, was to reconstitute as best he could the personal papers destroyed by the fire. He duly supervised the transcription and notarizing of the provisions of the charges and other documents from the Parlement's registers (the copies remaining in the comte's papers). He continued also to take part through 1729 in the household council. On 19 July 1726, he was again delegated for a mission that long experience had trained him to deal with: a "Sommaire de ce que m'a dit M. le duc du Mayne" that day records an interview on possible petitions for lost "honors." As in the past, and with Fleury's opinion now in mind it would seem, the memo begins with a decisive "Que votre Altesse n'y consent point."[15] Nothing was presented in fact by Toulouse or Maine. In the meanwhile, since 1725, Valincour had seemingly continued his own campaign for the admiral's "assured status," again depending on Fleury. He must have felt a particular pleasure—perhaps he felt he had gone as far as might— when an announcement came that Barbier was also pleased to record in his *Journal* in 1727: "On a rendu à M. le comte de Toulouse le détail de la marine qu'il avoit autrefois comme grand amiral, et que l'on avoit donné au secrétaire d'Etat de la marine, en sorte que M. de Maurepas, qui l'est, ira travailler à présent avec le portfeuille chez M.

15. A.N. 300 API; 91. The single-folded folio-size page is in part indecipherable; the issues are an "estat fixe" for the prince de Dombes and duc de Penthièvre.

le comte de Toulouse." ["The internal economy of naval affairs, which had been given to the secretary of state for naval affairs, has been returned to the comte de Toulouse. Henceforth M. de Maurepas, who is secretary, will take the portfolio to the comte's residence to work on it."][16] A good new start, for both Toulouse and the duc de Penthièvre, remained then for Valincour as a sense of achievement; that nothing came of it was left for others' disillusion after his death.[17] And so was the rumor that Toulouse might be first minister, which, for all its improbability, the ever-cautious adviser would doubtless have found dangerous gossip and an alarming possibility.[18] Barbier, reacting in 1737 to this rumor with the conviction that finances were in the best shape ever, thought it a pity that the cardinal should retire. For similar reasons so would Valincour, though he knew from 1723 and 1726 that, like his own professed desires to retire, the cardinal's wishes could mean something very different.

There may be a direct link between the new situation of the admiral in 1727 and a private memoir written by Valincour for Fleury shortly after his assumption of the government: "On the State of Europe in 1726" (Monmerqué's title).[19] That memoir may be only one (others were to follow) that Valincour was encouraged to and did write in 1726—with his old directness of speech, independent opinion not necessarily in agreement with Fleury's, and challenging questions salted with characteristic *raillerie* (in this instance again on papal infallibility). The fidelity and discretion once promised Mme de Maintenon, and with Toulouse a lifetime affair, are sworn first on the record of friendship: "La bonté dont il plaît à Votre Eminence de m'honorer depuis tant d'années, et le fidèle dévouement que j'auray pour elle toute ma vie, semblent m'autoriser à luy rendre compte de tout ce que je crois utile à son service." ["The goodness with which your eminence

16. *Chronique de la régence et du règne de Louis XV (1718–1763) ou Journal de Barbier* (Paris: Charpentier, 1858), 2:18. Barbier notes that the arrangement had been made during a visit by the king to La Rivière, then settled at Rambouillet. Obviously, by 1727 the comtesse de Toulouse has taken over the greater part of Toulouse's relations with the king.

17. Despite the comtesse's prodding (and life-size toy frigates on the canal at Rambouillet with retired sailors to sail them, Mme Guenard reveals), the duc de Penthièvre showed no interest in the navy or naval administration. Cf. J. Pritchard, loc. cit., p. 47.

18. *Journal de Barbier* 3:76. Toulouse's death in 1737 of course put an end to any speculation.

19. *Mémoires du marquis de Villette* (Paris: Renouard, 1854), xlvii-xlix.

has been pleased to honor me for so many years and the faithful dedication I will have for your eminence all my life seem to authorize me to report all that I believe useful to your eminence's service."] The first two points made, concerning peace and the economy, forcefully put in terms that exactly recall statements made in 1710, are seemingly the ends that for Valincour—as for many others, like Barbier,— justified some of Fleury's means: "Une année de guerre peut ruiner le royaume." ["A year of war can ruin the kingdom."] Ten years' peace is needed to repair its finances and for "the absolute necessity of liquidating the king's debts, which can be done only by very violent but absolutely necessary measures." The preacher here was of course addressing the already converted. Fleury's measures of budget trimming, administrative reorganization, and currency stabilization that were underway would continue (and long after remained that part of his administration most approved by later historians, with his peace diplomacy close behind.)[20] Before developing his specific points about alliance with England, Valincour throws in a red herring, though he is once again preaching to a believer—this time on the policy of keeping the princes of the blood from positions of power. The old courtier is playing a dangerous game, it would appear, to ensure the credibility of the faithful servant of Toulouse, to say nothing of himself, then the guest of the duc d'Orléans: "Les Princes inquiets, mal contents et voulant un changement, leur donnera-t-on des armées à commander? les retiendra-t-on dans le royaume?" ["Will the princes, restless, discontent, and wishing a change as they do, be given armies to command? Will they be confinable within the kingdom?"]

The larger part of the memoir, given to considerations of alliance with the English, is informed by Valincour's old mistrust of them focused in sharply insistent questions about their reasons for seeking alliance and their commercial advantage, which, as Valincour foresaw, would be considerable. The balancing of profits and losses must be done carefully, he insists, since it is a matter of the law of survival of societies. In this last official memoir, eloquence is put fully to service of the state. In closing, the Academician redirects the last development of his 1719 compliment to the king, bidding the minister who had heard that compliment to include him among the needed, plain-speaking advisers upon whom he can depend. In posing his pointed

20. See H. Carré, *Louis XV*, pp. 100–101; Arthur M. Wilson, *French Foreign Policy during the Administration of Cardinal Fleury* (1936; Rpt. Westport: Greenwood, 1972), 47–56, 101 and passim.

questions, he also serves Toulouse, giving ample place to a strong plea for the navy, for which Valincour to the end made himself a spokesman.

Or, que peut gagner la France dans la guerre où les Anglois veulent l'engager? Rien. Que peut-elle perdre? Tout, et se perdre elle-même. Que peuvent perdre les Anglois? Rien; on n'ira pas les attaquer dans leur isle, ni prendre Londres. Que peuvent-ils gagner? Tout ce qu'ils souhaitent: détruire et faire périr les forces maritimes et le commerce de la France, de la Hollande et de l'Espagne; s'assurer l'empire de la mer, dont ils se mettent visiblement en possession. Ils chassent à force ouverte nos pêcheurs de morue de dessus le grand banc; ils font trembler l'Europe et l'Amérique à la vue de trois escadres qu'ils ont armées et qu'ils ont fait agir, sans en donner aucune participation à la France, à qui ils proposent de tout sacrifier pour eux. ... Mais ces Anglois qui sont si fort de nos amis, ne seront-ils jamais nos ennemis? ne l'ont-ils jamais esté? ... Cette amitié qu'ils nous vendent si cher durera-t-elle plus longtemps que l'utilité qu'ils en retirent? et s'ils viennent à se tourner contre nous dans le fort d'une guerre où ils nous auront engagés, où serons-nous? Notre Marine détruite; pas un vaisseau à mettre à la mer; la plupart des officiers hors d'estat de servir; les costes exposées, les ports ruinés faute de réparations; nos colonies d'Amérique n'ayant pas de quoi faire la moindre résistance, et pouvant estre enlevées d'un coup de main. (xlviii)

Now what can France gain in the war in which the English wish to engage it? Nothing. What can it lose? Everything, including itself. What can the English lose? Nothing; one will not go and attack them on their island nor take London. What can they gain? Everything they wish: destroy and eliminate forever the maritime forces and the commerce of France, Holland, and Spain; ensure for themselves dominion over the seas that they visibly number among their possessions. They pursue our cod fishers with open arms from the grand bank; they make Europe and America tremble with the sight of three armed squadrons that they have put into action, without offering any part in them to France, which is asked to sacrifice everything for them. ... But will these English who are such good friends to us never be our enemies? Have they never been? Will this friendship that they sell us so dearly last longer than the usefulness they extract from it? And if they turn against us in the thick of a war in which we shall be engaged, where shall we be? Our navy destroyed; not a seaworthy vessel; the majority of naval officers not in a state to serve; the coasts exposed, ports in ruin for want of repairs; our American colonies without the means to make the slightest resistance and able to be taken by a raid.

Having saved nothing from the history of the realm, Valincour moved quickly (as he did in reconstituting Toulouse's papers) to save what he could by retrieving from abbé Vatry a copy lent to him of the manuscript *Eloge historique du roi sur ses conquêtes depuis l'année 1672*

jusqu'en 1678 by Racine.[21] That he did not give serious consideration
to the possibility of recreating the lost narrative himself, and completing
it, is indicated by a confession to Bouhier retold to Leclerc shortly after
Valincour's death. The picture it gives of the royal historiographer
differs greatly from the commitment Valincour made in the 1711
placet to the king. "You have doubtless seen Valincour's eulogy in the
discourse of his successor [in the Académie]," Bouhier wrote: "It is
supposed there that he had much advanced the history of the late king
and that his continuation had perished in the fire at St. Cloud. Nothing
could be more false. He *often* said himself to me that he had never
written a line of that history, any more than had Despréaux. They had
let it lie with Racine, who from time to time read extracts to the king
and in the end had also given up the task ("besogne") from which
perhaps nothing now remains."[22] Bouhier's ignorance of the *Eloge
historique* and its authorship suggests that he did not know everything.
What of Valincour's own perished in the fire remains his secret. But
there is no reason to suppose that between 1711 and 1714 he did not
make a start at writing. That writing and its project would have been
interrupted by the king's displeasure in 1714, then again by the series
of events that made the project seem increasingly inadvisable for
Valincour in his position as secretary to Toulouse. The decision to
sell his charge of *secrétaire du cabinet* in 1718–19, after that series of
discouraging events, may also signal his final decision to abandon his
own plans for continuation of the official history of the reign. The
decision not to take up the project of official history, or indeed any
project of historical writing, in the last years, may have been an
intellectual decision determined only in part by a busy schedule and
much more by both the nature of that history and the place an historian
had in a changed society.

For the kind of history Valincour had once written, the panegryic
had always been an element in tension with critical evaluation of
evidence. That critical focus, to his mind the responsibility of the
"honnête" historian, had also presented a double risk of misreading—
for both the historian and for his readers—which, with Fleury's con-

---

21. The detail is given in the preface to Féron's publication of the *Eloge* (Paris:
Bleuet, 1784). See E. Magne, *Bibliographie générale des œuvres de Nicolas Boileau-
Despréaux* (Paris: Giraud-Badin, 1929), 1:198. For the text, Racine, *Œuvres*, ed. R.
Picard (Pléiade ed., 1966), 207–64.

22. Letter of 10 April 1730. B.N. MS. fon. fr. 24413, p. 770.

trols in 1726–30, meant for more than one historian either discrediting censorship or actual imprisonment. The form demanded by the genre of official history may have seemed in 1726 also doubly questionable to Valincour. Intellectual limitations inherent to the genre are Valincour's first reason for not continuing, as he alleged in the letter written to d'Olivet on Racine. Doubtless admiring Racine's *Eloge historique*, for its qualities of clarity in chronological narrative focus and accuracy of technical information,[23] Valincour did his friend's reflections on historical method little discredit to include in them doubts about the beauties of eulogistic elements inevitably there. He repeats in his 1729 letter almost textually the allegation he had made in 1711 that the historical enterprise was contrary to both Racine's and Boileau's "génies" and tellingly once more dissociates himself. History may indeed have been his own way, as early on he had felt it to be. But that way did not lie with the new historiographers who replaced his old friends and colleagues. Not fully explicit, as his historiographical successor Duclos shortly would be facing a similar dilemma,[24] Valincour was clear enough for his first readers to see that he did not care to be associated with Père Gabriel Daniel nor to write the kind of history he had published.[25]

Touchant l'histoire du feu Roi, dont vous me demandez particulièrement des nouvelles, je n'ai, Monsieur, qu'un mot à vous répondre; Despréaux et Racine, après avoir quelque temps essayé ce travail, sentirent qu'il étoit tout à fait opposé à leur génie; et d'ailleurs *ils jugèrent avec raison que l'histoire d'un prince tel que le feu Roi*, et remplie d'événements si grands, si extraordinaires en tout genre, *ne pouvoit, ni ne devoit être écrite que cent ans après sa mort, à moins que de vouloir ne donner que de fades extraits de gazettes, comme ont fait les misérables écrivains qui ont voulu se mêler de faire cette histoire* (my emphasis).[26]

23. On the *Eloge's* qualities, R. Picard, *Œuvres de Racine* 2: 193–94; the interference of eulogistic rhetoric and the ideal of historical style, N. Ferrier-Caverivière, *L'Image de Louis XIV dans la littérature française de 1660 à 1715* (Paris: PUF, 1981), 208–12.

24. *Mémoires secrets sur le règne de Louis XIV, la Régence et Louis XV, Œuvres complètes* (Paris: Fain, 1806), 1:102: "Le Père Daniel jésuite, fut chargé et eut soin d'appuyer dans son Histoire de France sur les grands établissemens des bâtards de nos rois. Sitôt que l'ouvrage parut, le roi en parla avec éloge, en recommanda la lecture; il falloit le lire ou l'avoir lu. Daniel en eut le brevet d'historiographe de France avec une pension. J'espère que ces mémoires ne me feront pas regarder comme historien à gages."

25. Daniel's *Histoire de France* began to appear in 1696; he was named historiographer in 1713. See F. Fossier, "A Propos du titre d'historiographe sous l'ancien régime." *Revue d'histoire moderne et contemporaine* 32 (1985), 389. No pension for Daniel, however, is documented (nor for Valincour).

26. *Histoire de l'Académie française*, ed. C.-L. Livet (Paris: Didier, 1858), 2:334.

Concerning the history of the late king, on which you especially ask for news, I have, sir, a short answer. After having attempted this work for a while, Despréaux and Racine felt that it was entirely contrary to their talents; and moreover *they judged reasonably that the history of a prince like the late king,* filled with such great events, in every way extraordinary, *could not and should not be written until a hundred years after his death, unless colorless gazette entries are all that is wanted, as has been the case with the wretched writers who have wished to enter into the writing of this history.*.

Valincour's decision to reserve what time he had left for the potentially more directly effective uses of history he made of it in memoirs like those of 1725 and 1726, and to avoid the polemical interference that published history would almost inevitably incur, may in its scruples have extended as far as suppression during his lifetime of Racine's *Eloge historique.*[27] Desiring peace as ardently as he did in his last years, it may have seemed to Valincour as inadvisable to publish that glorification of war as it was inappropriate for him—or another— either to rewrite the history of Louis XIV's last wars (whose costs he had too keenly felt to wish to mask with ornaments or style) or to turn his account into a criticism, even implicit, of monarchy during the early years of a new reign. Either way, the old ideal of an historical style "où la vérité toute pure sera" would be impossible. Valincour the humanist reached his limit (again separating him from the *philosophes* to come)—silence—which was also the final solution he shared with Fleury on *Unigenitus*.

The position taken in letters to Gualterio, until the cardinal's muchregretted death in 1728,[28] in itself varies little from that developed through the earlier letters of impassioned, then increasingly detached chronicling, which in the end could see no solution as "final" except the hearts of men touched by God's grace. The "third party" statement of that position, with which I began as a résumé, in fact is the starting point of the last period of Valincour's letter writing and its attempts to continue to present Gualterio with a true picture, for his use, of events and the climate of opinion in France. It antedates (on 23 March 1726),[29] if only slightly, Fleury's new orientation, and astutely evaluates

27. In his detailed consideration of the attribution of the *Eloge*, Raymond Picard does not discuss the means by which the manuscript arrived at first publication in 1730 (after a privilege of 29 June 1729 to the printer Mesnier) among the works of Pellisson. See R. Picard, "Le 'Précis historique' est-il de Racine?" *Revue d'Histoire littéraire de la France* 58 (1958), 157–58.

28. A public memorial service was held for him in Paris. See G. Poisson, *Monsieur de Saint-Simon*, 420.

29. See above, chap. 7, n. 43 and text.

the circumstances that led to the cardinal's own changed tactics. It was also preceded by a veritable campaign of letter writing lobbying for Fleury's elevation, which continued until the pope named the new cardinal in October. At least two letters a month during the last years continue to oppose fanaticism in the "two parties" and to call for explications of the original articles in the proper spirit of charitable instruction.

Pessimism grows in these last letters as the detached writer observes continuing obstructions of reason's triumph and compromising violence. The "nothingness of the world and the vanity of its seemingly most important occupations" is central to Valincour's reflections in 1727.[30] He is revolted by the abundant evidence that "men like to harm one another" and "heartily consent to trouble others' peace," the more so as nowhere but in that peace can the sure guide be found that is needed to restore the Church (29 July; 230v). It is no longer a matter of blame or sympathy for *appellants* or *constitutionnaires*. Judgment of violence, blame, and punishment must be God's, the letter writer feels; but he nonetheless supplements his often-invoked prayers with the continued letter writing. Earlier doubts about councils are set aside when the "bref magnifique" addressed by Benedict to the bishop of Embrun heightens hopes for the Council of Embrun (9 and 23 August; 311, 313). The exile that was its punishment of Bishop Soanen leaves Valincour with sadness and neither a triumphant sense of the victory of truth nor Voltaire's blazing indignation. If there is no denunciation of the ambitions of Tencin, condemning his use of the council,[31] there is a sense that too high a price has been paid for reason's way. Here, as repeatedly, and in some of Valincour's last words to Gualterio, silence must prevail with prayers that God should provide His guidance—even by a miracle. "On ne peut trop louer les bonnes et saintes intentions du Pape, mais dans la disposition où sont les espirits il faut pour rendre ces bonnes intentions efficaces que Dieu y verse une bénédiction particulière." ["The saintly intentions of the pope cannot be overpraised; but given minds disposed as they now are, in order to

30. 28 May 1727; the following from 29 July 1725. B.N. Add. MSS. 20395, pp. 305–305v, 230v. It is seemingly on the basis of letters like these that Jean Sareil refers to Valincour as "l'austère ami de Racine." *Les Tencin* (Geneva: Droz, 1969), 63.

31. For a review of the Council of Embrun and Tencin's place, see B. Robert Kreiser, *Miracles, Convulsions, and Ecclesiastical Politics in Early Eighteenth-Century Paris* (Princeton, 1978), 47–48 and n. 98. On Valincour's later reservations, see below n. 61.

render those good intentions efficacious God needs to infuse them with a special blessing."][32] At the time of his death, Valincour may have believed that the peace of the Church had been achieved; [33] he knew too well the policies that had won it, however, to believe that a special blessing had truly changed even "bons François."

"I try to keep myself as far as possible away from the great events that agitate our court," Valincour wrote at the moment of occupying his new apartment, just in time to observe the fall of the duc de Bourbon's government and the advent of Fleury. Reflections are ready on the fall from high place and the wise man's preference for the "average and even unremarkable" life. Something of Toulouse's "retirement" may echo in the bitterness of Valincour's observations on these losses of high employ: "On ne sent plus le plaisir de les avoir eues, qui était en effet bien frivole, et l'on est rongé, le reste de sa vie, du regret, encore plus frivole, d'en être privé." Even trying to keep a distance from events, as Valincour observes, he was "near the storm, shaken and drawn into it," necessarily, as secretary of the "prince he served." Nonetheless, at St. Cloud he re-established in the first summer after the fire his old habits of diverse readings. Verses from Montemay-or's *Diana*, worthy of Tibullus, delighted him, as did the Italian pastoral poets Sannazaro and Fracastoro, whom he had lavishly praised earlier to Gualterio with a list of his Italian readings[34] but now found inferior to Virgil in wisdom and in seemliness (Valincour unusually uses the Greek "to prepon"). In addition to the poets he reads Bouhier's own *Traité de la succession des mères* (Briasson, 1726). At first as fearful as he would be for an unprepared trip to China, he declares finally that the clarity of the treatise would convert him to exclusive reading of law books if they were as well written. He enjoys the correspondence of Blazac and Chapelain, recommended by Bouhier, and is pleased to

32. 23 Aug. 1727. B.M. Add. MSS. 20395, pp. 313–13v.

33. On the "entreprise de pacification" at the beginning of 1730, see G. Hardy, *Le Cardinal de Fleury*, p. 187. Valincour would have approved Daguesseau's measures in 1728–29.

34. On the Portugese poems, 24 Apr. 1726. *RHLF* 31 (1924), 379; the Italians, 23 Nov. 1725, ibid. On 3 Oct. 1723 (B.M. Add. MSS. 20395, 156v) he wrote to Gualterio that "Je connois Dante, Petrarque, le Tasse, l'Arioste, le Marin dont je ne fais pas grand cas, Guarini, Fulvio Testi, Redi et Filicaia. Et de tous ceux là celui que je crois le plus Poete c'est l'Arioste." The catalogue was in response to Gualterio's request to supply a list of the eight "meilleurs poetes français" for a parnassus at his villa of Corgnolo. Boivin composed accompanying inscriptions for the statues of his choices: Racine, La Fontaine, Boileau, Marot, Malherbe, Racan, and Corneille. Later with some embarrassment he added Polignac (31 Oct. 1724, ibid., 198v).

284 · Limits of *honnêteté*

alter judgment based on his earlier distaste for Balzac's rhetorical epistolarity. Polemics occupy him also. He especially admires J.-B. Cadry's *Apologie des Chartreux que la persécution excitée contre eux au sujet de la bulle 'Unigenitus' a obligé de sortir de leurs monastères* (Amsterdam: Potgieter, 1725). Revealing some earlier reading that set a high standard, he judged it "très sage et très bien faite" ["Very sagacious and very well done"] and "much superior to that for Port-Royal done by Sacy." The bishop of Soissons's latest production falls far below this praise.[35] He is tempted by the new, expensive folio edition of Quintilian with glosses by Claude Caperonnier. But, like Montaigne in his last years, Valincour by 1726 had little use for glosses and wished the texts themselves to be his companions and from them pleasures that would include their power to explain more than shield the mind from the world. While waiting for Simon Foucher's critique of Malebranche, for which he had hinted to Bouhier, he turned in his writings in different but related ways to problems occupying his mind. It will at least not be distracted by the "deluge of epic poems" he promised not to read and left with the comment that "it is curious that they were by our most mediocre versifiers" (11 July 1725).

The spectacle and experience of violence, to which Valincour often alludes in 1726, directed in part the specific critical project that took shape in the first set of his dialogues, "Contre les spectacles," begun in May and planned to extend to four dialogues. The interlocutors, with himself, were to be his former "amis particuliers," M. de Pomponne and the comte de Fiesque, "who thought very differently on this matter."[36] In both the first and second dialogues Valincour was centrally concerned with the Aristotelian notion of catharsis, an "imagination ridicule" that is typically mocked as less sensible than a dose of rhubarb and senna. The stumbling block is the empirical nature of a "purging of the passions by exciting them," through tragedy as problematic to

35. A polemic against the Benedictines of Saint-Corneille de Compiègne. Valincour points out another doubtful use of the Pascalian model (*Les Provinciales*) this time on falsification of papal bulls, whose dating by Gergy he also criticizes. 31 Oct. 1725, *RHLF* 31 (1924), 378. The praise of the *Apologie* is 23 Nov., ibid.

36. Letter of 19 May, ibid., 381. A close friendship with Jean-Louis-Mario, comte de Fiesque (d. 1708), aide de camp during the campaigns of 1692 and 1693, is something of a surprise. "Il avait de l'espirit et de la lecture," according to Saint-Simon, and was much a *mondain* (see *Mémoires*, Truc ed., 1:1052, 719). Although the Pomponne given the "anti-theatre" side of the dialogue might be the marquis (who was among the signers of Héricourt's marriage contract), it is more likely to be Henri-Charles, abbé de Pomponne, *conseiller d'église* in 1711, brother-in-law of Torcy.

Valincour's mind as it is elsewhere and as troubling as the discrepancy, noted to Daguesseau, between tears in the threatre and the indifference to human suffering in the streets when the play has ended. Having found that Dacier's glosses failed even to see the real question, and no satisfaction in conversation with Rémon "le grec,"[37] Valincour asks for Bouhier's opinion on the status of the text. They agree that it is corrupt. Although elsewhere Valincour may deplore the fact that a woman as intelligent as Mme Riccoboni must make her living in the theatre,[38] his dialogues against theatrical representation were not then to be simply declamatory moralism (in the vein of the prince de Conti's). Linked to his metaphysical meditations, as with his experience, they were an inquiry into the dramatic poem as "mild narcosis,"[39] thus an examination of the nature of esthetic experience and its limits. In his technical concern, his former preoccupation with plot-structure is also still there. Usually deferring to Bouhier's superior erudition, he significantly does not when Bouhier's "too reasonable" rectification of Aristotle's text writes out the "di'apaggelias" (*Poetics*, 6:2). Congratulating Bouhier on admiration that he himself shared for the controversial narration by Théramène (*Phèdre,* Act 5), he also reminds him to keep in mind the specificity of narrative distinguishing tragedy from epic (as perversely he had reminded others long before on *La Princesse de Clèves*).

Bouhier's notes on the "enormous copybook" of the first two dialogues are ready by early July and with Daguesseau's[40] stimulate the

37. The eldest son of the *fermier-général* Rémon "le diable," who is the source of several anecdotes for Bouhier's amusement. On his writings, see the extended note by A. Monglond, *RHLF* 32 (1925), 260–61.

38. Letter to Gualterio, 17 May 1725. B.M. Add. MSS. 20395, p. 223v.: "Nous avons icy une guerre de littérature qui ne fera tort ni à l'Estat ni a l'Eglise. Un homme qui ne sut guere l'italien s'est avisé de traduire en françois la Jerusalem du Tasse et il y a fait beaucoup de fautes. Une comedienne de la troupe italienne nommée la Delle Riccoboni a fait imprimer une lettre où le pauvre traducteur est fort mal traitté, et où cette femme fait voir qu'elle n'a pas moins d'esprit que de connaissance des belles lettres. En lisant ce qu'elle a écrit on ne peut s'empescher d'estre fasché de voir qu'une personne qui a tant de merite soit reduite à faire un mestier si abject que celui de monter sur le theatre pour faire rire le public."

39. Cf. Freud, *Civilization and its Discontents* (New York: Norton, 1962), 28.

40. Daguesseau's "Sur les Dialogues de M. de Valincour, contre les Spectacles" (Pardessus ed., 16:290–91) is only a cover letter seemingly to the longer reflections, "Remarques sur le discours qui a pour titre 'De l'imitation par rapport à la tragédie,'" (ibid., 243–82). The author, according to Daguesseau, "paroît avoir voulu se réduire à traiter ces deux dernières questions ... pourquoi toute imitation nous plaît en tant qu'imitation, et pourquoi celle qui est l'âme de la tragédie, fait de plus fortes impres-

author, who feels rejuvenated. "I feel a daimon like Socrates's, which says to me 'Tu ne cede bonis sed contra audentior ito' " (24 July; 384). His answers to both critics will be incorporated in revision of the second dialogue, finished by 6 August but not yet ready to be seen. In the meanwhile, preoccupations with the Académie intervene, as they often had and continued to do in the last years of assiduous attendance, when abundant justifications could have been found for absences.

Some of the "liberté académique" Valincour had always jealously safeguarded was impinged upon by his being the guest of the duc d'Orléans. Always opposed to outside pressures on elections, whether from Sceaux or the "cabale lambertine" (as he called Mme de Lambert's influence), he was distressed to feel the need to back Orléans's candidate, Mirabaud, judged a "double fat" for his style in translating Tasso and especially the "even more impertinent manner in which he has judged Boileau" (6, 8 August: 384–5). The latter reference is revealing, as is the bit of Amyot quoted to express his discontent with obligation to Orléans: "Qui en maison de Prince entre, devient serf de libre qu'il était quand il vint." ("Who enters a prince's house, serf becomes, the freeman gone who came there.") More than a reflection on his past, this proverb and the reminiscence of Boileau in 1726 are interesting for the reflection they cast on the "client" of Fleury that Valincour had become and was recognized to be in the Académie. By a chance similar to that which made him eulogist of both Racine and Boileau, he had first in 1717 received the bishop, then complimented him with the king in 1719, finally in 1726 offered the Académie's compliment on his ministry of state. In that new compliment, he sustained the metaphor of that paid to the king in 1719, and enthusiastically commended the garden of French culture to this new gardener/protector of Academic traditions. The "fruits of our labors" are now in the charge of this "sagacious economist" whose "vigilant beneficence" will serve to render its "fields fertile and its harvests abundant and will neglect neither the cultivation nor the ornaments of the gardens, knowing full well that

---

sions que toutes les autres" (273). The independent nature of the development of four points then developed "pour rendre sa dissertation plus pleine et plus parfaite," like the first half of the letter's exposition of Aristotle on imitation, reveals nothing of Valincour's dialogue. A following "Conjectures sur le véritable sens de la définition qu'Aristote a donné de la Tragédie" (ibid., 282–87) was perhaps solicited from Daguesseau at the same time as Bouhier's opinion on catharsis. Here too the letter is an independent treatise.

the flowers that come to beauty through his tending themselves beautify the places where they are cultivated."[41]

The gardener, as inclined to intervene in Academic affairs as the "late king," threatened to enact the fable of the Scythian philosopher. Valincour, up to a point, may have shared Fleury's opinions on the impossibility of Voltaire's candidature or even on "abominable passages" in Montesquieu's *Les Lettres persanes*, which were temporarily suppressed in accordance with the cardinal's desires. But Valincour could not have been fully in agreement with the spirit of Fleury's censorship. The keeper of the flame of Boileau's values, assiduously conducting his own brand of "beneficent vigilance," might well have preferred Voltaire's presence to Gergy's, which symbolized in the once splendid sanctuary of the muses an iron age of mediocrity (stagnation in the Académie is also denounced frankly by d'Olivet, among others). Assiduity may then have been as much in the interest of the garden—and the spirit of friendship in letters whose collegiality among its workers was the more humble corollary of the ideal of transcendence of contentiousness—as the gardener with whom Valincour more than occasionally discussed Academic affairs. La Motte's eulogy, in a central development linking Valincour's continued reputation for academic ideals and his gift for friendship, suggests that the "confidential agent" of Fleury may have had a more "official" charge of monitoring Academic affairs. The absence of any extant correspondence between the two men makes the suggestion improbable, as does Valincour's long record once more of conciliatoriness (apparent even in attempts to avoid voting for the exclusion of Saint-Pierre, by absenting himself during the proceedings). That a tempering opinion, some adversarial questions, even a bit of ironic perspective might be of service to Fleury here as elsewhere, with some insistence on the value of investments added, perhaps appropriate for a time of budget trimming, may have been La Motte's reasons for praise of his friend Valincour's last years of active participating in the Académie. "The long friendship with which he was honored by the illustrious cardinal, born for the glory of the king and the peace of nations," he began, "became so to speak a public good. M. de Valincour used it only to protect merit and believed he could serve the minister, as well as those seeking his favor, by his recommendations. Strengthened by his own disinterest, he went

41. *Recueil ... de l'Académie* (Paris: Coignard, 1726), 37,

as far as importunity in the interest of others. The minister merited the friend he was."[42]

Relations with Fleury freed Valincour in his last years from one kind of writing. In ironic compensation for the decision to abandon historical writing, he was excused from producing "official verse," which had never been to his taste. When Bouhier asked him for a copy of an exchange of "official" verse between Fleury and Valincour, he took some pains to recover a copy and to explain the circumstances of its composition. When the young king rallied from scarlet fever in November 1728, Valincour explained, he had discreetly inquired of Fleury whether a *Te Deum* from the Académie would be appropriate. His Eminence replied that a "madrigal" would suffice. Despite those he had heard during the quarter, again as director, Valincour composed his own and was "marvelously pleased" with its versification and "tour singulier." But Daguesseau was not so enthusiastic and the poet "threw it into the fire."[43] The verse finally sent to Fleury in place of the first curled with a long familiar irony (which had the misfortune of "vexing" Bouhier when he did receive the retrieved copy).

> Un Madrigal sur la santé du Roy
> N'est pas, Seigneur, une petite affaire:
> Vous même vous savez la douleur et l'effroy
>   Que pour une tete si chère
> Inspira du danger l'ombre la plus légère.
> Mais si tost que du ciel le visible secours
> Sans l'art des médecins eut assuré ses jours
> Quelle joye à l'instant succède à la tristesse:
> Que de feux allumés, que de chants d'allégresse!
> Pour voir ce prince aimé quels doux empressements!
> Combien dans tous les cœurs de tendres sentiments!
> Pour les exprimer il faudroit un Homère.
> C'estoit son grand talent, il vous manque aujourd'huy,
> Et, si vous en doutez essayez-le pour lui.
> Aussi bien tout le jour n'avez vous rien à faire.[44]

Fleury returned the irony in a compliment that let it be understood that duty had been done and no more was required. Not content to let the game lapse, Valincour returned yet another compliment thanking the minister for his favor. Its amplification of what was in fact a

---

42. *Recueil . . . de l'Académie* (Paris: Coignard, 1730), 17.
43. Letter to Bouhier, 28 Dec. 1728, *RHLF* 31 (1924), 392.
44. Letter to Bouhier, 19 Dec. 1728, *L'Amateur d'autographes* 5 (1866), 283.

minor incident (a token bombardment of Tunis by one French squadron to avenge a diplomatic insult) into a new Punic War ends the game and Valincour's excursions into "official verse" with a trump of mock-heroic satire that explodes the genre.

> Celui qui détruisit et Carthage et Numance
>   Ne crut pas indigne de lui
> De faire en s'amusant, sous le nom de Térence,
>   Ces vers qu'on admire aujourd'hui.
> Le prélat qui de nostre France
> Devient le plus fidèle et le plus ferme appui
> Sous le nom d'abbé B. cachant son Eminence
> Fait des vers qu'avoueroit et Voiture et Térence.
>   D'où je tire une conséquence
>   Et c'est qu'avant qu'il soit six mois
>   Sous ses auspices les François
>   Iront abattre l'insolence
>   Du reste des Carthaginois.[45]

Valincour never kept copies of his occasional verse, he wrote typically to Bouhier, then was embarrassed when he inadvertently sent to him some lines on a cold a second time and received them back corrected.[46] He had always mocked at his poetic muse, periodically picturing himself with the lyre trying to make repairs or other work disappear with his song. He had nonetheless in his youth the desire to be more than an occasional versifier, and pretensions to being a poet in his middle years. Both seem to have gone in the exchange with Fleury. But just as he could see the sublime elsewhere, the elderly poet could glimpse the direction he might have taken to find it in poetry if he were a younger man in 1729. After writing his own elaborate tribute to the new dauphin, he admitted to Bouhier that he had heard two lines on the Pont-Neuf whose simplicity had captured the event

45. Ibid., 284. Charavay gives Fleury's compliment in response and a letter of 2 Jan. 1729 to Bouhier in which Valincour recounts a visit to the minister when the *fermiers-généraux* were in audience. "Les Académiciens viennent toujours les mains vuides," the cardinal greeted him; "Je lui répondis: C'est ce qui vois trompe, car en voilà une où j'ay mon mouchoir. Cela se tourna en plaisanterie qui dura un quart d'heure sans qu'aucun des gens qui estoient là osast ouvrir la bouche. Je sortis avec eux: ils se serroient pour me faire place et me regardoient avec vénération, mais au diable l'un qui m'offrit de me prester seulement 100 pistoles." Disdain of moneymen thus continues in this ironic courtier's performance.

46. Letter of 27 Feb. 1729, *L'Amateur d'autographes* 5 (1866), 285. Valincour's last words on his poetry are then: "C'est beaucoup qu'elle paroisse supportable la première fois, mais elle ne méritoit pas d'être lue la deuxième."

more satisfyingly.[47] Other kinds of writing made prior claims; first of friends that put him in touch with a sublimity he had long meditated upon, then his own dialogues.

Meditating in 1727 on tragedy, as he would in the letter to d'Olivet "On Racine" and the "Observations on Sophocles's *Œdipus*" that were in 1729 his last completed writings, Valincour revealed a preference withheld in the idealized historical harmonization of his earlier academic eloquence. Dissatisfied with Fontenelle's "Vie de Corneille" ("too long on wit and short on good sense, especially in the comparison of Corneille with his rival"), Valincour countered that "there is more true sublimity in *Britannicus*, *Mithridate*, and *Athalie* than in all the declamations of Corneille" (February 1727; 388). Critics displeased with the letter Valincour wrote on Racine, which he described as an "unshaped mass of anecdotes," have inferred that there may be more critical acumen in this one remark than in the entire letter.[48] As a favor to d'Olivet, who had asked him for information on several Academicians for his continuation of the *Histoire de l'Académie*, Valincour had written his letter at Fontainebleau *stans pede in uno*, literally, since he was suffering from gout. Pressing publication as usual, and annoyed by Coignard's delays in getting the *Histoire* through the press, d'Olivet sent Valincour's letter on unrevised, and much embarrassed his collaborator.[49] Even more than for remarks on the history of the reign, Valincour was taken to task for revealing a passing temptation to suicide during Racine's last illness, when he was often at his friend's side.[50] That Racine was human was very much Valincour's line in the letter, devoted as he always was to the illuminating truth of the Plutarchian detail: "en parlant d'un homme aussi grand que Racine, les plus petits faits intéressent." ["When speaking of a man as great as Racine was, the smallest details are of interest."] Although he might

47. 4 September 1729, *RHLF* 31 (1924), 397: "Et quoiqu'il soit bien petit / On ne voit que Monsieur son père / Qui soit plus grand que lui" are the lines of which Valincour says: "Je voudrois l'avoir fait et n'en avoir jamais fait d'autres."

48. After Racine's sons, the editors C.-L. Livet (loc. cit., p. 237, n. 1) and P. Mesnard (*Œuvres de Racine*, 1:204–5), R. Picard was irritated to the point of wishing the letter away with most other eighteenth-century pieces of similar nature. *La Carrière de Jean Racine*, 11; "Etat présent des études raciniennes." *L'Information littéraire* 8 (1956), 85–88.

49. 1 Dec. 1729 to Bouhier, *RHLF* 31 (1924), 401.

50. See Racine, letters of 27 Feb. and 16 May 1698, and especially 24 Oct. to J.-B. Racine: "M. de Valincour et M. l'abbé Renaudot m'ont tenu la meilleure compagnie du monde: . . . ils n'ont presque pas bougé de ma chambre" (*Œuvres*, ed. Picard), 2:593, 610, 638–39.

in deference to Racine's family have deleted this passage in revision, he obviously felt that its disclosure neither incriminated "true religion" nor needed the cosmetic rhetoric of a "fine death" topos. Anecdotes are recounted that became an integral part of Racinian tradition— Racine's reading Greek in the woods at Port-Royal and learning a romance by Heliodorus by heart, his recitation by heart at Auteuil of *Œdipus* (which opened new access to the text for Valincour), winning Colbert's favor or enjoying the protection of Henri-Jules de Condé, being "saved" by workers at Versailles who mistook his recitation from *Mithridate* as the cries of a man in danger. Valincour saw no need, he remarked to d'Olivet, for sustained analysis of the plays that his correspondent could do as well or better than he. But he offers some critical remarks nonetheless on the modern play he most admired— *Phèdre*—and some historical rectifications.

During the *cabale* over *Phèdre*, Valincour testifies to having seen Racine "in despair." And why should he not have been, the critic asks, when this kind of reception and Pradon's worthless play troubled the fortune "of the most nearly perfect work ever given to our theater" (332). Arnauld had admired it too and declared it highly moral. Approving Arnauld's judgment in all things, Valincour differs significantly with him over the question posed about the morality of creating a "Hippolyte in love." That love "dilutes" the play ("l'affadit"), even diminishes its tragedy, he will concede, but finally, as in the instance of Mme de Lafayette's Nemours, the cost of this "blemish" is not great. Hippolyte's love is set in "admirable verse" and the character of Aricie is "the perfection of beauty."

A defense is also made of the comedy of *Les Plaideurs*. Having enjoyed the comedy and what he calls Racine's "bitter mockery" ("raillerie amère"), Valincour deplores again an inadequate measurement of it by its first "failure." That it brought guffaws from the "very serious late king" is to his mind a better test. But the final seal of approbation is Molière's; even no longer a friend of the author, he had left the theater declaring that "those who mocked the play deserved to be mocked," a lesson Valincour had taken for his own earlier criticism. Savoring comic espisodes, and delighted to recount this one for his old friend, Valincour tells of the return of the comedians from Versailles elated by their triumph, their awakening Racine late, and his neighbors' conviction that the law the playwright had mocked was exacting its justice (333). Some justice is also accorded Corneille, "incapable of base jealousy," Valincour judges (333). When advising that Racine should abandon dramatic poetry (after hearing an act of *Alexandre*), he had merely shown his failure as a critic. Indicating that he had not sought to explore problems of catharsis in Corneille's critical writings, Valincour concludes that "the talent for making excellent verse and excellent judgment of poets and poetry may sometimes not be found in the same head" (337). That Corneille preferred Lucan to Virgil was enough to clinch his point. The backhanded compliment of being an excellent technician is also paid, elsewhere, to Malherbe in a revision of earlier admiration. "A fine organmaker," and not much more, the critic who wanted more concludes.[51]

Before his death in 1726, Jean Boivin had asked Valincour and d'Olivet to see certain of his writings through press. For Boivin's translation of *Œdipus* Valincour provided a "dedicatory epistle,"[52] which was finished in December of 1728 but put back to rest for a last six weeks before final rereading and submission to d'Olivet on 23 January 1729. D'Olivet had wanted a full-scale critical preface and was only partially satisfied with the relaxed, even casual liminary piece Valincour provided, with compliments to Boivin's erudition and once again an excuse of modesty for not displaying his own learning. He is more willing to recall the discussions with Boivin in which he had raised certain critical questions, amazingly consistent in their terms of enunciation with the esthetics brought to bear a half century earlier in discussion of *La Princesse de Clèves*. Valincour is in fact centrally concerned with only one question on the subject of *Œdipus*, a fault that Boivin had dealt with as he did his friends, who were habitually justified as long as possible and then excused. In criticism, Valincour rejoins, this is excessive charity, needless since "ces fautes ne détruisent ni la réputation du Poète ni le mérite de ses Tragédies."[53]

The crux of Valincour's difficulty with this tragedy, qualified as "perhaps the greatest ever," is the degree of ignorance of Laius's murder that Œdipus displays; some lines of exposition to deal with poetic

51. "Par rapport à la poésie, comme je regarde un excellent facteur d'orgues par rapport à la musique: grande justesse dans l'oreille, adresse infinie à accorder ses tuyaux pour en tirer une harmonie merveilleuse, et rien au delà." Letter to Bouhier, 2 Nov. 1729, *L'Amateur d'autographes* 5 (1866), 286. Similarly, 11 Oct. 1729, *RHLF* 31 (1924), 398.

52. This seems to be Valincour's reference on 23 Dec. 1728 to Bouhier. *RHLF* 31 (1924), 392. On d'Olivet's part in the project, *Correspondance littéraire du Président Bouhier. No. 3* (1976), 128, 133. The volume including also a translation of Aristophanes's *The Clouds* appeared by 26 Oct. 1729.

53. The text used is that reprinted by Goujet. *Bibliothèque française* (1731), 20–26.

probability are proposed. Surely, he reasons as before (and once again dissatisfied with Dacier's commentary to *Poetics* 16), the ignorance is *in* the play (Act II, v. 4 is cited) and not beyond it, as commentators have alleged. Criticism then typically is extended to these critics, including two "quite frivolous rules in the *Poetics*." Developing his esthetic presupposition, the critic reassembles as examples of *vitia* forms of expression admired as much as the tragic. The first scene of Terence's *Woman of Andros* (taking him back to his first literary love) contains technically faulty exposition; but it does not keep this play from being as great in its genre as is *Œdipus* among tragedies. The claims of comedy, of thoughtful laughter in Lucian, Rabelais, Molière as well as Terence that was Valincour's personal preference in discourse, put it finally on a par with tragedy, whose claims for edification are on trial in his dialogues on imitation. A paragraph of examples drawn from paintings, and containing the argument taken earlier from Quintilian's passage on Timanthes, is added, with the most significant instance being Le Brun's "beau Tableau" of "The Family of Darius." Valincour recalls having pointed out, in discussion with Le Brun, that the mother's gaze is turned from the son and directed rather toward the wife and daughters. No discussion with Le Brun is reported; only a pause occurs in the text. It evokes an earlier silence in discussion when, in a reflective moment, painter and critic seemingly paused before this focal point of the sublime, constituting the painting one that "could never have been done except by a very great painter." Without explicit comment, this development follows a reference to Racine's *Iphigénie*. What could be more "ridicule" than the image literally evoked by the lines "Tout reconnut mon père; & ses heureux vaisseaux / N'eurent plus d'ennemis que les vents & les eaux"? But what does it matter? Having said his last words on Racine, Valincour concludes with a merciless autopsy of Corneille's *Œdipe*.

There was no need to worry about the "madness" that might be inspired by Voltaire's *Œdipe*, Valincour quips sarcastically, with a lingering trace of the subjects of his dialogues, which disappear from correspondence after the elation of revision on 6 August 1726. A less acerbic, ambiguous reference is made to the *Henriade*, "a novel on Henri IV that will be praised and not read."[54] Valincour perhaps surprisingly prefers *Paradise Lost* (although Milton's "more than poetic

54. On *Œdipe*, 22 Dec. 1729 to Bouhier. *RHLF* 31 (1924), 402; *Henriade*, 20 Sept. 1729, ibid., 396.

enthusiasm for the Bible overwhelms the simplicity of Scripture").[55] Admirer of Swift, from an odd angle, Valincour is not one of Pope, even when a translation of the preface to Pope's *Homer* is dedicated to him. His "lead" is from Bouhier; and it is negative, as Valincour's experience of English readings tends to be: "I judged as you did Pope's poem. His discourse on Homer printed in the little volume addressed to me shows more reading than wit and taste. We have more advantage over the English in poetry and belles-lettres than they do over us in geometry."[56] Fascinated by Voltaire, Bouhier elicits from his correspondents commentaries on the turbulent author's every doing and much speculation on his motivations and character. Valincour does not let himself be drawn beyond his personal judgments or taste for Voltaire's writings. In other ways the letters to Bouhier, the most often admired of Valincour's writings, in their chatty informality show that the pleasures of writing to Bouhier had their reticences and some resistances on both sides.

At the center of a network of correspondents spanning a good part of European learning, Bouhier was a master at leading the most diverse persons—scientists, philosophers, historians, jurists, philologists, for a start—into being and delivering themselves. A generation younger than Valincour, and an avid literary historian, he wished from Valincour anecdotes and a newsletter from the Académie (as an "absentee" member since his election in 1727). Valincour was delighted to provide it in epistolary conversations that pleased them both and sometimes rose to sharpness that was not just wit or *médisance* (maliciousness). Had Valincour lived another decade, Voltaire's "novel of the soul," metaphysics as he treated it, rather than the "novel on Henri IV," coupled with the new directions of his scientific writing might have challenged Valincour's mind and led him to pursue his own second series of dialogues on metaphysics (and religion). Bouhier, it has been shown, already was the guide to others whose intellectual developments resembled Voltaire's.[57] Valincour could ask him some disconcerting

55. 20 Sept. 1729, ibid.

56. 26 Oct. 1728, *L'Amateur d'autographes* 5 (1866), 283. In a description of the volume to Bouhier, d'Olivet identifies the translator who dedicated his work to Valincour as "M. Perelle, conseiller au Grand Conseil, petit bossu tout plein d'espirit." *Correspondance littéraire du Président Bouhier, No. 3* (1976), 126.

57. See Ira O. Wade, "Notes on the Making of a *Philosophe*: Cuenz and Bouhier." *Literature and History in the Age of Ideas* (Columbus: Ohio State University Press, 1975), 97–123.

questions, in addition to judgments that were not always predictable; after reading the treatise on "succession des mères," he inquired whether Judge Bouhier, now in possession of the consolidated knowledge, felt that he could preside over a trial on the question in court. "Esprit voltairien"?—Valincour had several other affinities with it. If Bouhier's pedantry in correcting Valincour's last verse were in "correcting" the first series of dialogues even a bit less suffocating than Daguesseau's earnest thoroughness, it would not perhaps seem surprising that the first never reached print and that even the existence of the second series was not divulged to Bouhier. Valincour continued to entertain him and to use his learning mainly as a thesaurus for quotations from Cicero or others and for discrete inquiries on Greek vocabulary.

The anecdotes, on himself as much as his more famous friends, are a benefit for later readers, as in the instance of the famous reflection on La Bruyère for Bouhier in 1725 that, for all of its frequent quotation, has scarcely ever been of interest as a reflection on Valincour himself at the threshold of his last years and at the point of a new project of writing.

Pour La Bruyère, qui a été fort de mes amis, il ne devait guère qu'à lui-même ce qu'il a écrit, et M. le Prince Henri Jules, dont j'ai eu l'honneur d'être le favori, était bien plus capable de marquer aux écrivains le ridicule de leurs écrits que de leur fournir des idées ou de bon mots. La Bruyère pensait profondément et plaisamment; deux choses qui se trouvent rarement ensemble. Il avait non seulement l'air de Vulteius, mais celui de Vespasien ('faciem nitentis'), et toutes les fois qu'on le voyait, on était tenté de lui dire: 'utere lactuis et mollibus,' etc. C'était un bonhomme dans le fond mais que la crainte de paraître pédant avait jeté dans un ridicule opposé, mais qu'on ne saurait définir, en sorte que, pendant tout le temps qu'il a passé dans la maison de M. le duc, où il est mort, on s'y est beaucoup moqué de lui.[58]

For La Bruyère, who was a close friend, he owed what he wrote only to himself, as Prince Henri Jules, whom I've had the honor of knowing, was more apt to point out writers' ridicule than to furnish them with ideas or bons mots. La Bruyère thought profoundly and amusingly, two things that rarely go together. He not only had the air of Vulteius, but also Vespasian's ("faciem nitentis"), and every time that one saw him it was tempting to say: "utere lactuis et mollibus," etc. He was a good man basically but was so afraid of appearing pedantic that he was driven to a ridiculous opposite extreme

58. 31 Oct. 1725, *RHLF* 31 (1924), 377.

that it would be difficult to define but which had the result of making him always in the household of the duc—where he died—much mocked.

A flashy bon mot with a facile put-down in its prescription of laxatives? Valincour's reflection may rather seem to readers of the *Caractères* to enact critically the "profond/plaisant" he admires there and to spark thought as he generally liked to do through it (here too perhaps there is some hesitancy over a personal analogue to the opposite of pedantry that is itself a nameless extreme,—"overwriting," it has been suggested for La Bruyère).[59] The nature and human significance of La Bruyère's gritty "ridicule" is also in question as Valincour, who had used his verbal talents differently, does show his particular superiority—an easier wit and more comfortable accommodation to social *honnêteté* and the style by means of which some part of his success had been won. Valincour may not have had La Bruyère's desire for vengeance by writing; there is in the Bouhier letters nonetheless enough anger to extinguish rather than to fire the desire to complete the second series of dialogues and the project of giving his meditations on religion to the world around him.

Unlike the Gualterio letters, those to Bouhier are unquiet, denunciatory with the *saeva indignatio* of the young satirist Valincour, the imitator of Juvenal (and Boileau's first manner), had been and still was in some of the letters to Noailles and Le Bret twenty years earlier. Scornful and dubious about the canonization of the "monk Hildebrand, who made such fuss and follies under the name Gregory VII," he will view him gladly as a Don Quixote figure ("who would be committed to an asylum today," however); but he ends with the bon mot of Henri IV, now applied to the sacred college—that it did not collectively have enough brains to fill a silver teaspoon—then and yet adds, for himself: "Eheu! quam perfatuae sunt tibi Roma togae! N'allez pas croire que ce vers soit de Buchanan ou de Bèze, il est de Martial." ["Don't go believing that this verse is by Buchanan or Bèze; it is by Martial."][60] He is revulsed by the posthumous fate at Rome of Cardinal de Noailles's good intentions.[61] And he does not stop at Rome. Without

---

59. Cf. Floyd Gray on Cliton, the obsessive eater as a figure of La Bruyère obsessed with writing and caught up in grotesque exaggeration. The writer is deformed as well as transformed by writing. *La Bruyère: Amateur de caractères* (Paris: Nizet, 1986), 133 and passim.

60. 8 July 1729, *RHLF* 31 (1924), 394. The canonization dated from 1606; only the fixing of the feast day, in 1728. On the pope's "manifeste" on the "vengeur de la liberté romaine," see G. Hardy, *Le Cardinal Fleury*, pp. 162–67.

61. 16 Aug. 1729, *RHLF* 31 (1924), 395.

feeling the need for the cover of a code, and perhaps with his other almost exact contemporary Soanen in mind, he deplores the prospect of the creation of a Cardinal de Tencin and bluntly adds that the bishop of Embrun had been of no credit to the cardinal who used him.[62] At the end of the same month, Valincour was obviously relieved and refreshed to be able to praise a panegyric of Saint Louis by a humble preacher who had "ni pain ni chemise" and to ask Bouhier archly where in Cicero he can find the citation "in jocis seriisque amicum omnium horarum" that Bouhier himself of course personifies.[63]

Daguesseau's commentary[64] on what may be Valincour's second series of dialogues is uncertain because of undisclosed dating and unavailing because of the chancellor's tendency to elaborate treatises rather than to write letters. It does not confirm, as one might like to find in it, the intentions or the specific directions of an apologetic work affirmed increasingly between 1725 and the end of 1727. Daguesseau does suggest that it is not a good idea to have the theologian of the dialogue admit to not having read Hobbes. The form of the second series of dialogues in manuscript cannot be even tentatively reconstructed in outline until the *Ouvrages posthumes* are recovered. Valincour's own high demand remains in mind with a nagging doubt that with discouragement he had not taken them far. "La meilleure marque qu'un auteur puisse avoir de la bonté de son ouvrage est la confiance qu'il sent en lui-même de l'exposer aux objections. . . . C'est ainsi qu'en usa Descartes quand il composa ses *Meditations*," ["The best indicator an author can have that his work is good is the self-confidence he feels in exposing it to objections. . . . So it was that Descartes proceeded when he wrote his *Méditations*,"] he affirmed to Bouhier.[65] It was a difficult model. And in 1729 his health generally failed, leaving the author occasionally wandering, d'Olivet confided. One would like to find, however, in a reflection on Maraldi to Bouhier, the outline of a new project of apologetic writing that would once again concentrate Valincour's powers of mind, as they earlier had been concentrated in reflection on Pascal. Regretting the death of Maraldi, who had often shared with him the developments of his research, Valincour payed

62. Ibid.
63. 30 Aug. 1729, ibid. The priest was abbé Signy.
64. *Œuvres* (ed. Pardessus, 16:147–53). Fiesque is given the explication of Hobbes. A new character, the comte de Saint-Pol, figures also, as does a Docteur "que se charge de détruire ce système."
65. 23 Dec. 1728, *RHLF* 31 (1924), 392.

tribute to the shape of a life he had at moments wished his own to take. "Le pauvre M. Maraldi," he wrote to Bouhier on 1 December 1729 and, adding Cassini to his tribute, continued: "Il n'y a peut-être de philosophes ni de mathématiciens, après M. Pascal, si pleinement persuadés des vérités de la religion avec une si grande soumission et une si parfaite simplicité de cœur." [There were no philosophers or mathematicians, after M. Pascal, so fully persuaded of the truths of religion, with such great submission and so perfect simplicity of heart.][66]

The letter that Saint-Simon wrote to his old friend from La Ferté in 1728 doubtless pleased Valincour as much as had Bouhier's honorific association of the old "hermitage" at St. Cloud and its master with Horace.[67] "Que vous êtes sage et heureux, Monsieur, et quelle vie la vôtre! Tout le suc, tout l'utile, tout le vray s'y trouve sans le voile de la vie commune, sans l'étalage de la dévotion, ny les ragousts et les inconvénients de la retraitte" ["How wise and happy you are, Monsieur, and what a life you have! Everything essential, everything useful, everything true is there unobscured by everyday life, by display of devotion, or by the confusions and annoyances of retirement"], the duc expanded and then contrasted his own perturbations.[68] For all his pleasure in the idealization, Valincour would know that this truth was partial, that his own life was often unquiet, that the servant of Toulouse, of the "bien de l'état" and its way through Fleury, the impatient Academician, and the intolerant commentator on the "Affaire" did not perfectly fit this rhetorical celebration of friendship. Friendship, in letters as in faith, however, may also have been felt as having transcended the networks and conferences of the bureaucratic structures that had materially shaped his life. After following that life, the "conventional" terms of Valincour's last testament may similarly seem more than those of just any "honnête homme."[69] Any of his unfinished writings found after his death should be burnt, he stipulated, with something more than ritual diffidence. With the same sense of humility he knew that in his last writings he had not made the vital step from feeling the intolerable—the violence that is born at the heart of

66. *RHLF* 31 (1924), 401.
67. Horace, *Odes* 1:37, v.25 is quoted by Valincour from Bouhier's letter. The citation is identified by A. Monglond. Letter of 24 July 1726 *RHLF* 31 (1924), 282.
68. 27 Dec. 1728, *Mémoires* (Truc ed.), 7:455–56.
69. I have had only the extracts of Valincour's will given by Charavay, Catalogue 703 (May 1960).

conviction—any more than the contemporaries he criticized had done. Both would need to await their time. But he had begun and repeatedly sought, through his critiques of reason's fanaticisms, the way of witness to difference that seems to Paul Ricoeur, for one, the route toward a true tolerance.[70] With this humility and the confidence of a lifetime he finally entrusted his family and his writings to his friends and "literary executors," Torcy, Daguesseau, and Fleury. Always shrewd, Valincour knew that both were likely to be cared for, and that the writings would not by these friends be rushed vainly into perishable print.

70. On distinction and its problems, Paul Ricoeur, "Tolérance, intolérance, intoléra-ble." *Bulletin de la Société de l'Histoire du Protestantisme Français* 134 (1988), 135–50.

Bibliography I

Jean Baptiste Henry du Trousset de Valincour

*(*designates items known indirectly from bibliographies)*

A. Verse

Published Verse

1. *Rondeau*: "Avant qu'il soit peu, la Belle." 7vv.
2. *Air*: "Je craignois vostre inconstance." 8vv.
3. *Air*: "Vous croyez que vos soins & vostre Complaisance." 12vv. Luynes (1680)[1]
4. *Ode*: Horace XI du 1er Livre: "De la fin de nos jours." 16vv. *Mercure* (1681)[2]; Bouhours (1693, 1701)[3]; Ménage (1715, 1729)[4]; La Martinière (1727)[5]; Goujet (1745)[6]; Des Guerrois (1855)[7]
5. *Le Printemps*: "Olimpe, de qui les appas." 87vv. Bouhours (1693); *Moetjens (1694);[8] Lafeuille-Uitwerf (1694);[9] Goujet (1745)

1. *Nouveau recueil des plus beaux vers mis en chant, augmenté de tous les airs les plus nouveaux et de plusieurs grands récits et autres couplets de Madame la Comtesse de La Suze* (Paris: Guillaume de Luynes), pp. 530–31, 534. Bibliothèque de l'Arsenal, 8B.11365.
2. Vol. 13 (février 1681), p. 73.
3. *Recueil de vers choisis par le R. P. Bouhours* (Paris: Gosse, 1693), pp. 39–40; 89–92 (No. 5); 58–60 (No. 6); 53–57 (No. 7). For 2nd ed. (1701) see also Lachèvre, *Bibliographie des recueils collectifs* 2, p. 120; 3, p. 327.
4. *Ménagiana ou les bons mots et remarques critiques, historiques, morales, et d'érudition de Monsieur Ménage*, ed. La Monnoye (Paris: Delaulne), 2, pp. 216–17.
5. *Essai d'une nouvelle traduction d'Horace, en vers françois, par divers auteurs, avec un discours sur les satires & les épitres* [ed. Bruzen de la Martinière] (Amsterdam: Uitwerf), p. 27. Koninklijk Bibliotheek (The Hague) 765j30.
6. *Bibliothèque poétique ou nouveau choix des plus belles pièces de vers en tout genre, depuis Marot jusqu'aux poëtes de nos jours* (Paris: Briasson), 4, pp. 126; 114–16 (No. 5); 112–14 (No. 6); 123–25 (No. 7); 117–19 (No. 8). Co-editor is Lefort de La Morinière.
7. Charles Des Guerrois, *Le Président Bouhier* (Paris, 1855), p. 136.
8. *Recueil de pièces et nouvelles, tant en prose qu'en vers* (La Haye: Adrian Moetjens). Quoted from F. Lachèvre, *Bibliographie* 1, p. 230; 3, p. 327.
9. *Nouvelles fables choisies et mises en vers par les plus célèbres auteurs français de ce temps*

6. *Le Rossignol en cage*: "Un rossignol dont le ramage." 49vv. Bouhours (1693, 1701); Moetjens (1694); Lafeuille-Uitwerf (1694); Goujet (1745)

7. *Lettre de Daphnis à Damon*: "Il est une heure après minuit." 145vv. *MS. Vitry-le-François 79.[10] Bouhours (1693, 1701); Goujet (1745)

8. *Consolation à Damon sur la mort de sa sœur*: "Quand ne sçus, cher Damon." 52vv. Bouhours (1701); Goujet (1745)

9. *Le Rossignol*: "Pour garder certaine toison." 272vv. MS. B.N. fon. fr. 19144. Schouten (1699)[11]; La Fontaine (1710, 1718, 1721, . . .);[12] Vergier (1743)[13]

10. *Le Tonnerre* (?): "Il est assez d'amans contents." 189vv. Vergier (1743)[14]

11. *Le Sens commun*: "Le Sens commun n'est pas chose commune." 100vv.

12. *Sur la paix*: "Vous soyez la bienvenue." 53vv.

13. *Caprice*: "Le Printemps vient enfin ranimer la nature." 99vv.

14. *Sur un gros rhume*: "Rhume qui me tient dans ma chambre." 137vv.

15. *Sur de mauvais vers*: "De tes vers la douceur extrême." 8vv.

16. *Epigramme*: "D'où vient donc tout à coup cette horrible gelée." 4vv. Adry (1807)[15]

17. *Epigramme*: "Un rhume vient m'ôter la parole." 10vv. Charavay (1866);[16] Monglond (1924)[17]

18. *Madrigal*: "Un madrigal sur la santé du Roy." 15vv.

19. *Réplique par rapport au dessein que l'on avoit de détruire Tripoli*: "Celui qui détruisit et Carthage et Numance." 13vv.

(Amsterdam-La Haye: La Feuille-Uitwerf). Collection not mentioned by Lachèvre containing poems listed by him in Moetjens anthology. L.C. Coll. Toinet 658.

10. *Cat. gén. des MSS.*, Vol. 13 (Paris, 1891), p. 46. The MS. is no longer in the library's collections (communication from the librarian).

11. *Recueil de quelques pièces nouvelles et galantes, tant en prose qu'en vers* (Utrecht: Antoine Schouten), pp. 12–27. L.C. Coll. Toinet 760. Vv. 1–83 are unique to this printing, figuring neither in the MS. nor later in reprintings.

12. See L. Moland (*Œuvres complètes de La Fontaine*, Paris, n.d. [1872–76], 3, pp. 365–67). 1762 reprinting first has attribution to Valincour: "Le Rossignol, Par M. Lamblin [?], Conseiller au Parlement, de Dijon, ou par M. Du Trousset de Valincour, d l'Académie française" subsequently reprinted (See Rochambeau, *Bibliographie des œuvres de La Fontaine*, Paris, 1911, p. 285). Lachèvre (*Bibliographie* 3, p. 327) attributes the *conte* to Valincour.

13. *Contes, nouvelles et poésies diverses du Sieur Vergier et de quelques auteurs anonymes* (Rouen: Besongne), 1, pp. 364–74. Attributions to Vergier by Beuchot (*Biographie universelle*, s.v. "Vergier"); A.C. Lee (*The Decameron: Its Sources and Analogues*, London, 1909, p. 162).

14. *Contes*, Vol. 1, pp. 21–29. Attribution to Valincour only by Titon du Tillet (*Le Parnasse françoise* [Paris, 1732], p. 647).

15. *La Princesse de Clèves* (Paris: Sourds et Muets), 2, pp. 291–95 (No. 11); 295–97 (No. 12); 298–303 (No. 13); 303–307 (No. 14); 308 (Nos. 15–16). B.N. R² 46455. Published from now lost *Ouvrages posthumes*.

16. *L'Amateur d'Autographes*, 5, pp. 285; 283 (No. 18); 284 (No. 19): 285 (No. 20).

17. *RHLF* 31, p. 400.

20. *Dixain à Madame Dacier*: "Anne ma sœur, vous voulez mon ouvrage." Charavay (1866)

Unpublished Verse

21. *Requeste de Lisette à Olimpe*: "C'en est fait, je m'en vais mourir." 54vv. MS. B.N. fon. fr. 19144, p. 90.
22. "Vingt fois de vous louer ayant fait le dessein." 121vv. MS. B.N. fon. fr. 19144, pp. 91–92.
23. "La femme est toujours femme." 20vv. MS. B.N. fon. fr. 19144, p. 98.[18]
24. *Chanson à Mme de Maintenon*: "Estre dans un cachot bien noir." 80vv. M.S. B.N. fon. fr. 12625, pp. 49–52.
25. *Le Devoit Nuptial: Sur le mariage de l'Empereur*: "Un grand benest qu'on appelloit Jannot." 116vv. M.S. B.N. fon. fr. 12625, pp. 181–83.

B. Prose Works and Eloquence

Published Works

1. *LETTRES/A/MADAME LA MARQUISE ***/SUR LE SUJET/DE LA/ PRINCESSE DE CLEVES./* A Paris/Chez Sebastien Mabre-Cramoisy/ . . . /M.DC.LXXVIII. Avec privilège de sa Majesté. [17 juin 1678]. 1 vol. 12°. 370 pp.

    (b) idem. Chateau-Gaillard, 1678. 12°. 275pp.[19]

    (c) idem. Paris: Gabriel Huart, 1691. 12°. 370pp.[20]

    (d) idem. ed. Adry. Paris: Sourds et Muets, 1807.[21]

    (e) idem. ed. Cazes. Paris: Bossard, 1926.

    (f) idem. Farnborough: Gregg International, 1971. Facsimile of 1a.

    (g) idem. ed. Groupe d'étude du XVIIe siècle de l'Université François Rabelais. Tours, 1972. Facsimile of 1a.

2. *LA VIE/DE/FRANÇOIS/DE LORRAINE/DUC DE GUISE/* Suivant la Copie imprimée/A Paris/Chez Sebastien Mabre-Cramoisy . . . / M.DC.LX-XXI. Avec privilège de sa Majesté. [16 avril 1681]. 1 vol. 12°. 174pp.[22]

    (b) idem. Mabre-Cramoisy, 1681. 12°. 139pp. (Newberry Library 53–3341)

    (c) idem. n.p., n.d. 120. 113pp.[23]

    (d) *THE LIFE/OF/FRANCIS/OF LORRAIN/DUKE OF GUISE/*

18. Transcription (?) attributed to Valincour by title note of La Fontaine's "La Matron d'Eprèse" (*Contes* 5, 6), vv. 177–96.

19. Pirated printing according to Toinet (note, L.C. copy. 32–6048) perhaps prior to Mabre-Cramoisy printing.

20. B.M. Besançon, 244, 356. No variants; same title page as 1st printing.

21. *La Princesse de Clèves* 2, 1–290.

22. "Suivant la Copie imprimée" suggests a fine reprinting of 2b. There are no variants.

23. Pirated printing (?). B.N. Ln[29] 9403a. No variants.

London/Printed for R. Bentley and M. Magnes/from the French of J. B. H. du Trousset de Valincour/by F[errand] S[pence]. 1 vol. 12°. 136pp.[24]

3. DISCOURSE/PRONONCE/DANS L'ACADEMIE FRANÇOIS/ Le Samedy vingt-septième Juin M. DC. LXXXXIX/Par MONSIEUR DE VALINCOUR . . ./A Paris/Chez Jean Baptiste Coignard. M.DC.LXXXXIX. 1 vol. 19pp. B.M. 731.e.6(6).

   (b) Recueil de Plusieurs Pièces d'Eloquence et de Poesie présentées à l'Académie françoise. Paris: Coignard, 1699, pp. 135–62.

   (c)Recueil des Harangues, Amsterdam: aux dépenses de la Compagnie, 1709. vol. 2, pp. 465–78.

4. DISCOURS/PRONONCE/DANS L'ACADEMIE FRANÇOIS/Le vingt-cinquième de Juin M.DCCC.XI/A la Réception de/ M. L'ABBE D'ES-TREES/Par MONSIEUR DE VALINCOUR . . . */A Paris/ Chez Jean Baptiste Coignard, M.DCC.XI. 1 vol. 40.[25]

   (b) Recueil . . . Académie françoise, 1711, pp. 295–315.

   (c) Œuvres de Nicholas Boileau Despréaux, Paris: Espirit Billiot, 1713.[26]

5. Edition with Eusèbe Renaudot (?). ŒUVRES/de/NICHOLAS BOILEAU/DESPREAUX/Nouvelle Edition, reveue et augmentée./A Paris,/Chez Esprit Billiot . . . /M.DCCXIII. 1 vol. 4°. Avec privilège de sa Majesté [26 avril 1711] au sieur ***.[27]

6. Avis sur les occupations de l'Académie, imprimé par ordre de la Compagnie: Pour obeir à ce qui est porté dans la déliberation du 23 novembre 1713. Paris: Coignard, 1714. *MS. Mazarine. A 16260 Rés.[28]

   (b) Œuvres de Fénelon, ed. P. de Querbeuf, 1787, Vol. 3, pp. 449–601.

   (c) idem., ed. J.-A. Lebel, 1824, Vol. 21, pp. 145–55.[29]

24. Translator identified in B.M. copy 10662aa.

25. Cited by J. R. Miller (Boileau en France au dix-huitième siècle, Baltimore, 1942, p. 124, n. 7).

26. Subsequent reprintings cited by E. Magne Bibliographie générale des oeuvres de N. Boileau-Despréaux, Paris, 1929): 1713. Amsterdam (Magne No. 562); 1714. Amsterdam (563, 564); 1715. Liège (567); 1716. Genève (568, 569); Liège (570); 1717. Amsterdam (571, 572, 574); 1718. Amsterdam (575, 576); 1720. Amsterdam (579); 1721. Amsterdam (581); 1722. La Haye (582); 1724. Genève (583); 1726. Paris (584); 1729. La Haye (588, 590, 592), Amsterdam (589, 591); 1735. Paris (593), La Haye (594); 1740. Paris (597), 1746. Dresden (603); 1747. Paris (605); 1757. Paris (609); 1759. Glasgow (313); 1767. Dresden (613); 1768. Paris (614); Utrecht (320); 1769. Paris (615); 1772. Paris (616); Venezia (744); 1793. Saint-Brieuc (353); 1810. Paris (377).

27. See Magne, Bibliographie, No. 559. Valincour's and Renaudot's editorship have been questioned without direct evidence disproving it by R. Jasinski ("Les Papiers de Jean-Baptiste Racine III," Cahiers raciniens 1 (1957), p. 174). A school text published by Flammarion, n.d. [1892 and frequent reprintings] attributes notes reproduced from 1713 ed. to Valincour.

28. Variants from this now lost MS. are given by Charles Urbain (RHLF 6, 1899, p. 367, n. 1) with a demonstration of Valincour's authorship (ibid., pp. 367–74).

29. Attributed yet to Fénelon in Traités divers (Paris: Didot, 1853), 463–70.

7. *Réponse de M. de Valincour alors Directeur de l'Académie au Discours prononcé par M. de Fleury, ancien Evesque de Fréjus, Précepteur du Roy.* [1 avril 1717]. *Recueil ... Académie françoise*, 1717, pp. 265–88.

8. *Preface. Dictionnaire de l'Académie Françoise ...* 2e éd. Paris: Coignard, 1718.

    (b) *Dictionnaire ...* 7e éd., 1884, pp. xii–xxv.

9. *Compliment fait à Sa Majesté ... le Samedy 22 de Juillet 1719. Recueil ... Académie Françoise.* 1719, pp. 223–25.

10. *Réponse de M. de Valincour au Premier Président* [Portail, 28 décembre 1724]. *Recueil ... Académie françoise*, 1724–25, pp. 127–48.

11. *Compliment fait A S. E. Monseigneur le Cardinal de Fleury, à Fontainebleau, le Lundi 23 septembre 1726, par M. de Valincour.* *Paris: Coignard, 1726. 1 vol. 4°.[30]

    (b) *Recueil ... Académie Françoise*, 1726, pp. 33–37.

12. *Lettre de M. de Valincour sur Jean Racine.* In Abbé d'Olivet, *Histoire de l'Académie françoise depuis 1652 jusqu'à 1700.* *Paris: Coignard, 1729.

    *(b) idem. Coignard, 1730.

    *(c) idem. Amsterdam: J. F. Bernard, 1730.

    *(d) idem. Coignard, 1743.

    (e) idem., ed. Ch. Livet. Paris: Didier, 1858, Vol. 2, pp. 327–39.

13. *Observations critiques de M. de Valincour sur l'Oedipe de Sophocle. A M. l'abbé d'Olivet* [23 janvier 1729]. In Goujet, *Bibliothèque française*, 1731, pp. 20–26.

14. *Dialogue entre MM. Daguesseau, l'abbé Renaudot, Racine, Despréaux, et de Valincour.* [1691?].[31] In *La Princesse de Clèves*, ed. Adry, 1807, Vol. 2, pp. 309–23.

    (b) idem. *Œuvres de Boileau.* Ed. Daunou, 1810, Vol. 2, pp. lvii–lix.

15. *Caractère et traits remarquables de M. et Mme Daguesseau.* [1716?].[32] Adry, 1807. Vol. 2, pp. 332–35.

16. *Traité sur les Prises, pour l'usage de M. le Comte de Toulouse, Amiral de France, Par M. de Valincour.* In Eugène Sue, *Histoire de la Marine française*, 1836. Vol. 4, pp. 40–52.[33]

17. *De l'Origine de l'établissement des congés dans la Méditerranée et dans l'Océan.* Sue, 1836. Vol. 4, pp. 53–58.

18. *Mémoire sur la Marine de France* (1725). In Monmerqué *Mémoires du marquis de Villette.* 1854, pp. li–lxviii.[34]

30. Copy, Harvard University Library.

31. Date suggested by Adry (p. 329). Adry, Daunou, and Sainte-Beuve (*Portraits littéraires*, 1843, Vol. 1, p. 15, n. 2) imply that Valincour recorded an actual conversation. Published from the *Ouvrages posthumes*.

32. Henri Daguesseau (1635–1716), "Conseiller d'Etat" and father of the chancellor. Eulogistic tone suggests a date of composition perhaps shortly after his death. Published from the *Ouvrages posthumes*.

33. Location of MS. not mentioned by Sue or its most recent commentator, A. de Wismes (*Jean Bart et la Guerre de Course* (Paris, 1965), 201).

34. Published from the *Ouvrages posthumes*.

19. *Mémoire sur l'Etat de l'Europe en 1726, remis par M. de Valincour au Cardinal de Fleury.*[35] Monmerqué, 1854, pp. xlvii–xlix.

Prose Works in MSS

20. Translation. *Le Criton, par Mr de Valincour.* MS. B.N. Supp. fr. 3771. 7pp.
21. *Mémoire* (avril 1716). MS. B.N. Collection Clairambault 720.[36] 3pp.
22. *Mémoire sur la Course* (16 juillet 1711). MS. Archives de la Marine G 144 No. 9.[37] 63pp.
23. *Mémoire. de M. de Valincour sur la conduite qu'il estimoit que S.A.S. Mgr le comte devoit tenir avec M. le Duc, lors de son avenement.* 10 9bre 1723. A.N. 300 AP 1:91, no. 15. 17pp.

35. Extract only. Published from the *Ouvrages posthumes.*
36. *Cat. gén. des MSS.*, ed. Lauer (Paris, 1923), p. 338. In "Recueil des pièces concernant les différences des pairs de France avec les présidents à mortier du Parlement de Paris."
37. Second, draft copy. No. 8. 33 pp. Cf. B.N. MS. fon. fr., 16731, pp. 47ff.

Bibliography II

A. Works Especially on Valincour

Adry, J. L., ed. *La Princesse de Clèves; Lettres à Madame la marquise****. 2 vols. Paris: Sourds et Muets, 1807. Vol. 2.

Beaurepaire, Charles. "Pierre Legendre, marchand de Rouen." *Normandie* 10 (1895), 193–205.

Broglie, prince Emmanuel de. *Le Portfeuilles du Président Bouhier et fragments de sa correspondance littéraire*. 2 vols. Paris: Hachette, 1896.

Cazes, Albert, ed. Valincour, *Lettres à Madame la marquise*** sur le sujet de la Princesse de Clèves*. Paris: Bossard, 1926. "Introduction," 11–86.

Charavay, Etienne. "Valincour et la Président Bouhier." *L'Amateur d'autographes* 5 (1866), 280–86.

Charnes, Jean-Antoine de. *Conversations sur la critique de La Princesse de Clèves*. Ed. François Weil et al. Tours: Université François Rabelais, 1973. Facsimile of Paris: Barbin, 1679.

Chupeau, Jacques, et al., eds. *Lettres à Madame la Marquise****. Tours: Université François Rabelais, 1972. "Introduction," i–xiii.

Dédéyan, Charles. *Madame de Lafayette*. 2nd ed. Paris: SEDES, 1965, 93–103.

De Jean, Joan. "Lafayette's Ellipses: The Privileges of Anonymity." *Publications of the Modern Language Association of America* 99 (1984), 884–902.

———. "*La Princesse de Clèves*: The Poetics of Suppression." *Papers on French Seventeenth Century Literature* 18 (1983), 79–97.

Demailly, Paul. *Notice sur la vie et les œuvres de J. B. H. de Valincour*. Ham, 1884.

Dens, Jean-Pierre. *L'Honnête homme et la critique du goût au XVIIe siècle*. Lexington, Ky: French Forum, 1981, 127–38.

Depping, Georges B. "Lettres de Phélypeaux, comte de Pontchartrain." *Bulletin du Comité des monuments écrits de l'Histoire de France* 2 (1850), 52–92.

Dulong, Gustave, Rev. of *Valincour, Lettres à Madame la marquise****, ed. A. Cazes. *Revue d'Histoire littéraire de la France* 33 (1926), 633–34.

Faguet, Emile. "Un critique homme du monde au XVIIe siècle: Valincour." *Revue des Deux-Mondes* 51 (1909), 372–98.

Foisset l'aîné. "Valincour." *Biographie universelle*. Vol. 42. Paris: Didot, 1827.

Fontenelle, Bernard Le Bovier de. "Eloge de M. de Valincour" (1730). Rpt. *Œuvres de Fontenelle*. Paris: Salmon, 1825, vol 2, 250–57.

Fossier, François. "A Propos du titre d'historiographe sous l'ancien régime." *Revue d'histoire moderne et contemporaine* 32 (1985), 361–417.

Fournel, Victor. "Valincour." *Nouvelle Biographie générale*. Vol. 45. Paris: Didot, 1878.

Genette, Gérard. "Vraisemblance et motivation." *Communications* 11 (1968), 5–21. Rpt: *Figures II*. Paris: Seuil, 1969, 71–99.

Goujet, Claude and Lefort de La Morinière. *Bibliothèque poétique ou nouveau choix des plus belles pièces de vers en tout genre depuis Marot jusqu'aux poëtes de nos jours*. 4 vols. Paris: Briasson, 1745. vol. 4.

Henriot, Emile. "Valincour, l'ami de Racine." *Courrier littéraire du Temps* 64 (9 December 1924), 87–92.

Hepp, Noémi. "Esquisse du vocabulaire de la critique littéraire de la querelle du Cid à la querelle d'Homère." *Romanische Forschungen* 69 (1957), 332–408.

Jal, Auguste. *Dictionnaire critique de biographie et d'histoire, errata et supplément pour tous les dictionnaires historiques d'après des documents authentiques inédits*. 2nd ed. Paris: Plon, 1872.

Jasinski, René. "Les Papiers de Jean-Baptiste Racine." *Cahiers raciniens* 1 (1957), 154–74.

Lachèvre, Frédéric. *Bibliographie des recueils collectifs de poésies publiés de 1597 à 1700*. 4 vols. Paris: Leclerc, 1901–1905. Vols. 2, 3.

La Faye, Jean Leriget de. "Discours." *Recueil de plusieurs pièces d'éloquence et de poësie présentées à l'Académie françoise*. Paris: Coignard, 1730, 1–10.

La Motte, Houdar de. "Réponse de M. de La Motte." *Recueil de plusieurs pièces d'éloquence et de poësie présentées à l'Académie Françoise*. Paris: Coignard, 1730, 11–24.

Laugaa, Maurice. *Lectures de Madame de Lafayette*. Paris: Colin, 1971.

Lyons, John. "Narrative, Interpretation and Paradox: *La Princesse de Clèves*." *Romanic Review* 72 (1981), 383–400.

Magne, Emile. *Le Cœur et l'esprit de Madame de Lafayette*. Paris: Emile-Paul, 1927.

———. Rev. of *Valincour, Lettres à Madame la marquise****, ed. A. Cazes. *Mercure* 192 (15 September 1926), 147–48.

———, ed. Mme de Lafayette. *Romans et nouvelles*. Paris: Garnier, 1958.

Miller, Nancy. "Emphasis Added: Plots and Plausibilities in Women's Fiction." *Publications of the Modern Language Association of America* 96 (1981), 36–48.

Monglond, André, ed. "Les Dernières années d'un ami de Racine: Valincour et ses lettres au Président Bouhier, 1725–1730." *Revue de l'Histoire littéraire de la France* 31 (1924), 364–408; 32 (1925), 260–61.

Monmerqué, J. L. N., ed. *Mémoires du marquis de Villette, publiés pour la Société de l'Histoire de France*. Paris: Renouard, 1854.

Moréri, Louis. *Le Grand dictionnaire . . . augmenté par l'abbé Goujet*. Paris: Libraires associés, 1759. Vol. 10.

Nicéron, Jean-Pierre. *Mémoires pour servir à l'histoire des hommes illustres dans la république des lettres avec un catalogue raisonné de leurs ouvrages*. 43 vols. Paris: Briasson, 1728–45. Vol. 24.

Niderst, Alain. "Valincour." *Dictionnaire des littératures de langue française*. Ed. J.-P. de Beaumarchais et al. Paris: Bordas, 1984. Vol. 3.

―――, ed. Lafayette. *Romans et Nouvelles*. Paris: Garnier, 1970. "Introduction," vii–xliv.

Pélissier, Léon-G. "Les Correspondants du duc de Noailles: lettres inédites de Valincour." *Revue d'Histoire littéraire de la France* 10 (1903), 671–89; 11 (1904), 140–55; 12 (1905), 469–95.

Pingaud, Bernard. "Un critique de salon: Valincour." *Les Lettres Nouvelles* 7 (25 March 1959), 49–50.

Pizzorusso, Arnaldo. *La Poetica del Romanzo in Francia, 1660–1685*. Rome: Sciascia, 1962.

Ramsay, Jerome. "Valincour and the Critical Tradition." *Modern Philology* 66 (1968), 325–33.

Rouben, César. "Valincour, Charnes et la querelle de La Princesse de Clèves." *French Literature Series* 4 (1977), 56–74.

Russo, Paolo. "La Polemica sulla Princesse de Clèves." *Belfagor* 16 (1961), 555–602; 17 (1962), 271–98, 385–404.

Sainte-Beuve, Charles–Augustin. "Histoire du Chancelier Daguesseau par M. Boullée" (1851). *Causeries du lundi*. 3rd ed. Paris: Garnier, 1862, vol. 3, 407–27.

―――. "Madame de Lafayette" (1836). *Portraits de femmes*. Nouvelle ed. Paris: Garnier, 1845, 249–87.

Scott, John W. "The Digressions of the Princesse de Clèves." *French Studies* 2 (1957), 315–22.

Sue, Eugène. *Histoire de la marine française*. 5 vols. Paris: Bonnaire, 1836. Vol. 4.

Tastet, Tyrtée. *Histoire des quarante fauteuils*. Paris: Lacroix-Comon, 1866. Vol. 3.

Titon du Tillet, Evrard. *Le Parnasse françois*. Paris: Coignard, 1732.

Urbain, Charles. "Les Premières rédactions de la lettre à l'Académie." *Revue d'Histoire littéraire de la France* 6 (1899), 367–407.

Vallée, Oscar de. "Valincour et Louis Racine à Fresnes." *Moniteur universel* (29 August 1859), 995–96.

Voltaire, François Marie Arouet. *Le Siècle de Louis XIV. Publié par M. de Francheville*. 2 vols. London: Dodsley, 1752. Vol. 2.

Waller, R. E. A. *The Relations between Men of Letters and the Representatives of Authority in France, 1715–1723*. D.Phil. Diss.: Oxford, 1971, 421–34.

Williams, C. G. S. "The Diamond of *courtoisie* and the Dragonnades of 1681: Valincour's *Vie de François de Lorraine*." *Literature and History in the Ages of Ideas. Essays on the French Enlightenment Presented to George R. Havens*. Columbus: Ohio State University Press, 1975, 31–56.

―――. *Jean Baptiste Henri du Trousset de Valincour (1653–1730)*. Ph.D. Diss.: Yale University, 1970.

B. Other Works

(* Indicates references to Valincour)

Académie française. **Registres de l'Académie française*. Ed. Camille Doucet. 4 vols. Paris: Firmin-Didot, 1895–1906.

*Acerra, Martine, José Merino, Jean Meyer, eds. *Les Marines de guerre européennes, XVIIe-XVIIIe siècles*. Paris: Presses de l'Université de Paris-Sorbonne, 1985.

Actes et mémoires des négociations de la paix de Ryswick. 4 vols. The Hague: A. Moetjens, 1699.

*Adam, Antoine. *Histoire de la littérature française au XVIIe siècle*. 5 vols. Paris: Domat, 1956.

———. *Du mysticisme au révolte. Les Jansénistes du XVIIe siècle*. Paris: Fayard, 1968.

*Alembert, Jean Le Rond d'. *Mélanges de littérature, d'histoire, et de philosophie*. 5 vols. Amsterdam: Chatelain, 1759.

———. *Œuvres*. 5 vols. Paris: Belin, 1821–22. *Vol. 3.

Allentuch, Harriet. "Pauline and the Princesse de Clèves." *Modern Language Quarterly* 30 (1969), 171–82.

*Almanach royal, 1699–1730.

Antoine, Michel. *Le Conseil du Roy sous le règne de Louis XV*. Geneva: Droz, 1970.

Apostolidès, Jean-Marie. *Le Roi-machine. Spectacle et politique au temps de Louis XIV*. Paris: Minuit, 1981.

Appolis, Emile. *Entre Jansénistes et Zelanti. Le Tiers parti catholique au XVIIIe siècle*. Paris: Picard, 1960.

*Argenson, René-Louis de Paulmy, marquis d'. *Mémoires et journal inédit*. 5 vols. Paris: Janet, 1857–58.

Aubigné, Agrippa d'. *Histoire universelle*. Ed. Baron de Ruble. 2 vols. Paris: Renouard, 1886.

Aucoc, Jean-Léon. *Lois, statuts et règlements concernant les anciennes académies*. Paris: Hachette, 1889.

Auerbach, Erich. *Mimesis*. Trans. W. Trask. Princeton: Princeton University Press, 1953.

Barber, William H. *Leibniz in France from Arnauld to Voltaire. A Study in French Reactions to Leibnizianism, 1670–1760*. Oxford: Clarendon Press, 1955.

*Barbier, Edmond-Jean-François. *Chronique de la Régence et du règne de Louis XV (1718–1763)*. 8 vols. Paris: Charpentier, 1857.

Barnwell, Harry T. *The Tragic Drama of Corneille and Racine. An Old Parallel Revisited*. Oxford: Clarendon Press, 1982.

Barthes, Roland. *Sur Racine*. Paris: Seuil, 1963.

*Baschet, Armand. *Le Duc de Saint-Simon et le cardinal de Gualterio. Mémoire sur la recherche de leur correspondance (1706–1728)*. Paris: Epernay, 1878.

Bausset, Cardinal de. *Histoire de Bossuet*. Paris: Outhenin-Chalandre, 1841.

Bayard, Françoise. *Le Monde des financiers au XVIIe siècle*. Paris: Flammarion, 1988.

Bayle, Pierre. *Dictionnaire historique et critique*. 4 vols. Rotterdam [Geneva: Fabri & Barillot], 1715. 3rd ed. *Vol. 2 ("Guise").

———. *Lettre à M. L.A.D.C. touchant les comètes*. Cologne [Rotterdam]: Marteau, 1682.

———. *Lettres choisies*. 3 vols. Rotterdam: Fritsch and Böhm, 1714. *Vol. 1.

Becq, Annie. *Genèse de l'esthétique française moderne. De la Raison classique à l'Imagination créatrice, 1680–1814*. 2 vols. Pisa: Pacini, 1984.

Benoist, Elie. *Histoire de l'Edit de Nantes*. 4 vols. Delft: Beman, 1683–95.

Betts, Christopher J. *Early Deism in France. From the so-called "déistes" of Lyon (1564) to Voltaire's "Lettres philosophiques" (1734)*. The Hague: Nijhoff, 1984.

Bibliothèque françoise. Ed. C. Goujet. *Vols. 1 (1730), 5 (1736).

Bibliothèque françoise, ou Histoire littéraire de la France. Ed. J.-F. Bernard. (Amsterdam). *Vol. 2 (1723).

Bissy, Henry de Thyard, Cardinal de. *Mémoire contre l'appel de la bulle Unigenitus au futur concile fait en 1717*. N.p., 1719.

———. *Remarques de M. le cardinal de Bissy sur le projet de mandement de M. le cardinal, présenté de sa part à MM. les cardinaux. . . .* N.p., n.d.

Bluche, François. *Louis XIV*. Paris: Fayard, 1986.

———. *Les Magistrats de la cour des monnaies au XVIIIe siècle*. Paris: Les Belles Lettres, 1966.

———. *Les Magistrats du Grant Conseil au XVIIIe siècle*. Paris: Les Belles Lettres, 1966.

———. *Les Magistrats du Parlement de Paris au XVIIIe siècle (1715–1771)*. Paris: Les Belles Lettres, 1960.

———. *L'Origine des Magistrats du Parlement de Paris au XVIIIe sièle*. Paris: Mémoires de la Féderation des Sociétés historiques et archéologiques de Paris et de l'Ile-de-France, vols. 5/6 (1956).

———. *La Véritable hiérarchie sociale de l'ancienne France. Le Tarif de la première Capitation* (1695). Geneva: Droz, 1983.

———. *La Vie quotidienne au temps de Louis XIV*. Paris: Hachette, 1984.

Bolingbroke, Henry St. John, Viscount. *Letters and Correspondence*. 3 vols. London: Robinson, 1798. *Vol. 3.

Boileau, Nicolas. *Œuvres complètes*. Ed. A. Adam and Françoise Eschal. Paris: Gallimard-Pléiade, 1966.

Boislisle, Arthur de. *Correspondance des contrôleurs généraux des finances avec les intendants des provinces*. 3 vols. Paris: Imprimerie Nationale, 1874–97.

Borgerhoff, E. B. O. *The Freedom of French Classicism*. Princeton: Princeton University Press, 1950.

*Bossuet, Jacques Bénigne. *Correspondance*. Ed. Ch. Urbain and E. Levesque. 15 vols. Paris: Hachette, 1909–25.

———. *Œuvres complètes*. Ed. F. Lachat. 31 vols. Paris: Vivès, 1862–66.

*Bouchard, Marcel. *De l'Humanisme à l'Encyclopédie. L'Esprit public en Bourgogne sous l'ancien régime*. Paris: Hachette, 1930.

312 • Bibliography

Bouhours, Dominique. *Entretiens d'Ariste et d'Eugène*. 2nd ed. Paris: Mabre-Cramoisy, 1671.
———. *La Manière de bien penser dans les ouvrages de l'esprit*. 3rd ed. Paris: Brunet, 1745.
———. *Remarques nouvelles sur la langue françoise*. Paris: Mabre-Cramoisy, 1675.
*Bouillé, René, marquis de. *Histoire des ducs de Guise*. 2 vols. Paris: Amyot, 1849.
*Bourgeois, Emile. *La Diplomatie secrète au XVIIIe siècle. Ses débuts. Le Secret du Régent et la politique de l'abbé Dubois (Triple et Quadruple Alliances, 1716–1718)*. Paris: Colin, 1909.
Brantôme, Pierre de Bourdeilles, sr de. *Œuvres*. Ed. Prosper Mérimée. 13 vols. Paris: Jannet, 1858.
Bray, René. *La Formation de la doctrine classique*. Paris: Nizet, 1927.
Brink, C. O. *Horace on Poetry: The "Ars poetica."* 2 vols. Cambridge: Cambridge University Press, 1971.
*Broglie, prince Emmanuel de. *La Société de l'Abbaye Saint-Germain-des-Prés au XVIIIe siècle: Bernard de Monfaucon et les Bernardins*. 2 vols. Paris: Hachette, 1891.
*Bromley, John S. "The Loan of French Naval Vessels to Privateering Enterprise (1688–1713)." *Les Marines de guerre européennes. XVIIe–XVIIIe siècles*. Ed. Martine Acerra, et al. Paris: Presses de l'Université de Paris-Sorbonne, 1985, 65–90.
*Brosses, Charles, baron de Montfalcon. *Lettres de Charles de Brosses à Ch. C. Loppin de Gemeaux*. Paris: Firmin-Didot, 1929.
*Brossette. *Correspondance entre Boileau et Brossette; Mémoires sur Boileau Despréaux*. Ed. E. Laverdet. Paris: Techener, 1858.
Brumfitt, J. H. *Voltaire Historian*. Oxford: Oxford University Press, 1958.
Brun, Victor. *Guerres maritimes de la France: Port de Toulon, ses armements, son administration, depuis son origine jusqu'à nos jours*. 2 vols. Paris: Plon, 1861. Vol. 1.
Brunel, Lucien. *Les Philosophes et l'Académie au dix-huitième siècle*. Paris: Hachette, 1884.
*Busson, Henri. *La Religion des classiques*. Paris: PUF, 1948.
*Bussy, Roger de Rabutin, comte de. *Correspondance*. Ed. L. Lalanne. 6 vols. Paris: Charpentier, 1859.
*Buvat, Jean. *Journal de la Régence (1715–1723)*. Ed. E. Campardon. 2 vols. Paris: Plon, 1865.
Carré, Henri. *Le Règne de Louis XV (1715–1774)*. Paris: Hachette, 1911.
Carreyre, Jean. *Le Jansénisme durant la Régence*. 3 vols. Louvain: Bureau de la Revue d'Histoire Ecclésiastique, 1929.
Castelvetro, Ludovico. *On the Art of Poetry*. Trans. and E. Andrew Bongiorno. Binghamton: Medieval & Renaissance Texts and Studies, 1984.
———. *Poetica d'Aristotele vulgarizzata e sposta*. Ed. Werther Romani. Rome-Bari: Laterza, 1978.

*Castries, duc de. *Le vieille dame du quai Conti. Une histoire de l'Académie française.* Paris: Perrin, 1978.

*Castro, Eve de. *Les Bâtards du soleil.* Paris: Olivier Orban, 1987.

Ceyssens, Lucien, O.F.M. "Autour de la bulle 'Unigenitus': son Acceptation par l'Assemblée du clergé." *Revue d'histoire ecclésiastique* 80 (1985), 364–414; 732–59.

———. "Autour de la bulle Unigenitus: le duc de Saint-Simon." *Revue belge de philosophie et d'histoire* 63 (1985), 513–53.

———. *"Autour de le bulle Unigenitus: les Essais d'accommodement (1714–1715)." *Antonianum* 60 (1985), 343–95.

———. "Autour de la bulle Unigenitus: Madame de Maintenon (1635–1719). *Augustiniana* 36 (1986), 101–54.

———. "Autour de la bulle Unigenitus: le Pape Clément XI." *Bulletin de l'Institut historique belge de Rome* 43–44 (1984), 253–304.

———. "Autour de la bulle 'Unigenitus': le P. Guillaume Daubenton, S. J. (1648–1735)." *Augustiniana* 33 (1983), 330–81.

———. "Autour de la bulle Unigenitus, V: le P. Louis Doucin, S. J. (1652–1726)," *Antonianum* 58 (1983), 448–73.

———. "Autour de la bulle 'Unigenitus': le P. Timothée Pescherard de la Flèche, capucin." *Collectanea Franciscana* 53 (1983), 281–300.

———. "Autour de l'Unigenitus: le Cardinal de Noailles." *Lias* 11 (1984), 169–252.

Ceyssens, Lucien and J. A. G. Tans. "L'Unigenitus à Rome (1712–1713): Les Jugements théologiques portés sur les 155 propositions de Quesnel denoncées au Saint-Office." *Lias* 8 (1981), 3–77.

Le Chancelier Henri-François d'Auguesseau. Limoges 1668–Fresnes 1751. Limoges: Desvilles, 1953.

*Charavay. Catalogue, No. 703 (May, 1960). Valincour's will.

Chartier, Roger, M. Compère, and D. Julia. *L'Education en France du XVIe au XVIIIe siècles.* Paris: SEDES, 1976.

Cicero. *Tusculan Disputations.* Ed. J. E. King. London: Heinemann, 1921.

Clair, Pierre. *Libertinage et incrédules (1665–1715?). Recherches sur le XVIIeme siècle* 6 (1983), 13–289.

Clémént, Pierre. "Mme de Montespan, Bossuet et Louis XIV." *Revue des Questions historiques* 4 (1868), 437–88.

———. ed. *Lettres, instructions, et mémoires de Colbert.* 7 vols. Paris: Imprimerie Nationale, 1861–1873.

Colbert, Charles-Joachim. *Lettre de MM. les évêques de Senez, de Montpellier et de Boulogne au roi, au sujet de l'arrest du Conseil d'Etat de Sa Majeste, du 31 décembre 1720, portant suppression de leurs mandemens du mois de septembre de la même année et de l'acte d'appel qui y est joint.* N.p., 1721 (January).

———. *Lettre circulaire de M. l'évêque de Montpellier aux évêques de France.* N.p., 1724 (2 May).

Colton, Judith. *The Parnasse françois: Titon du Tillet and the Origins of the Monument to Genius.* New Haven: Yale University Press, 1979.

Cottrell, Robert D. *Brantôme: The Writer as Portraitist*. Geneva: Droz, 1970.

Dacier, André. *Poétique d'Aristote, traduite en français*. Paris: Barbin, 1692.

*Daguesseau, Henri-François d'. *Œuvres complètes*. 13 vols. Paris: Libraires associés, 1769–79.

———. *Œuvres complètes*. Ed. Jean-Marie Pardessus. 16 vols. Paris: Fantin, 1819.

———. *Lettres inédites*. Ed. D. B. Rives. 2 vols. Paris: Imprimerie Royale, 1832.

*Dangeau, Philippe de Courcillon, marquis de. *Journal avec les additions inédites du duc de Saint-Simon*. Ed. Feuillet de Conches. 19 vols. Paris: Didot, 1854–60.

Demorest, Jean-Jacques. "L'Honnête homme et le croyant selon Pascal." *Modern Philology* 53 (1956), 217–20.

Des Guerrois, Charles. *Le Président Bouhier*. Paris: Ledoyen 1855.

Dessert, Daniel. *Argent, pouvoir et société au Grand Siècle*. Paris: Fayard, 1984.

Dompnier, Bernard. *Le Venin de l'hérésie*. Paris: Editions du Centurion, 1985.

*Doncieux, Georges. *Un Jésuite homme de Lettres au XVIIe siècle. Le Père Bouhours*. Paris: Hachette, 1886.

*Dorsanne. *Journal de M. l'abbé Dorsanne, contenant tout ce qui s'est passé à Rome & en France, dans l'Affaire de la Constitution Unigenitus*. 2 vols. Rome: Aux dépens de la Société, 1753.

Drouet, Joseph. *L'Abbé de Saint-Pierre: l'homme et l'œuvre*. Paris: Champion, 1912.

*Duchêne, Roger. *Madame de Lafayette: la romancière aux cent bras*. Paris: Fayard, 1988.

*Duclos, Charles. *Mémoires secrets sur le règne de Louis XIV, la Régence et le règne de Louis XV. Œuvres complètes*. Paris: Fain, 1806. Vols. 5–6.

Dulong, Gustave. *L'Abbé de Saint-Réal: étude sur les rapports de l'histoire et du roman au XVIIe siècle*. 2 vols. Paris: Champion, 1921.

*Dumas, Auguste. "Le Conseil des prises sous l'ancien régime, XVIIe et XVIIIe siècles." *Nouvelle Revue de droit français et étranger*. 3e Série, vol. 29 (1905), 317–77; 477–522; 613–78.

Du Plaisir. *Sentiments sur les lettres et sur l'histoire avec des scrupules sur le style*. *Ed. Philippe Hourcade. Geneva: Droz, 1976.

Eves, Charles K. *Matthew Prior: Poet and Diplomatist*. New York: Columbia University Press, 1939. Rpt. Octagon, 1973.

Ewert, Alfred. "Of the Precellence of the French Tongue." Oxford: Clarendon Press, 1957.

*Farnham, Fern. *Madame Dacier*. Monterey, CA: Angel Press, 1976.

Faure, Edgar. *La Banqueroute de Law. 17 Juillet 1720*. Paris: Gallimard, 1977.

Fénelon, François de Salignac de la Mothe. *Lettre à l'Académie*. Ed. Ernesta Caldarini. Geneva: Droz, 1970.

Ferrier-Caverivière, Nicole. *L'Image de Louis XIV dans la littérature française de 1660 à 1715*. Paris: PUF, 1981.

———. *Le Grand Roi à l'aube des Lumières, 1715–51*. Paris: PUF, 1985.

*Fevret de Fontette, Charles M., ed. *Bibliothèque historique de la France, contenant la catalogue, imprimés & manuscrits, qui traitent de l'histoire de ce royaume, ou qui y ont rapport; avec des notes critiques et historiques, par feu Jacques Lelong.* 5 vols. Nouvelle éd. Paris: J. T. Herissant, 1768–78.

Filion, Maurice. *Maurepas: ministre de Louis XV (1715–1749).* Montreal: Leméac, 1967.

*Finch, Robert. *The Sixth Sense: Individualism in French Poetry, 1686–1760.* Toronto: University of Toronto Press, 1966.

Formel, François. "Etat chronologique de la correspondance actuellement connue du duc de Saint-Simon avec le Cardinal Gualterio." *Cahiers Saint-Simon* 6 (1978), 35–53.

*Forneron, Henri. *Les Ducs de Guise et leur époque.* 2 vols. Paris: Plon, 1877.

*Fossier, François. "La Charge d'historiographe du seizième au dix-neuvième siècle." *Revue historique* 258 (1977), 73–92.

Frêche, Georges. *Un Chancelier gallican: Daguesseau.* Paris: PUF, 1969.

Freemantle, Anne. *The Papal Encyclicals in their Historical Context.* New York: Mentor, 1956.

Frémont, Christiane. "L'Enfer des relations." *Recherches sur le XVIIeme siècle* 7 (1984), 69–87.

Fumaroli, Marc. *L'Age de l'Eloquence: Rhétorique et "res literaria" de la Renaissance au seuil de l'époque classique.* Geneva: Droz, 1980.

———. *"From 'Lives' to Biography: The Twilight of Parnassus." *Diogenes* 137 (Spring 1987), 1–27.

———. "Rhétorique d'école et rhétorique adulte: remarques sur la réception européenne du traité 'du sublime' au XVIIe et au XVIIIe siècle." *Revue d'Histoire littéraire de la France* 86 (1986), 33–51.

*Geoffroy, Auguste. *Madame de Maintenon d'après sa correspondance authentique.* 2 vols. Paris: Hachette, 1887.

Gohin, Ferdinand. *La Fontaine: études et recherches.* Paris: Garnier, 1937.

Gossman, Lionel. *Medievalism and the Ideologies of the Enlightenment: La Curne de Sainte-Palaye.* Baltimore: The Johns Hopkins University Press, 1968.

*Goyet, Thérèse. *L'Humanisme de Bossuet.* 2 vols. Paris: Klincksieck, 1965.

Gray, Floyd. *La Bruyère: Amateur de caractères.* Paris: Nizet, 1986.

Groethuysen, Bernard. *Origines de l'esprit bourgeois en France. I. L'Eglise et la Bourgeoisie.* Paris: Gallimard, 1927.

Grubbs, Henry A. *Jean-Baptiste Rousseau: His Life and His Works.* Princeton: Princeton University Press, 1941.

Guenard, Madame. *Vie du duc de Penthièvre.* 2 vols. in 1. Paris: A. Egron, 1803.

Haight, Jeanne. *The Concept of Reason in French Classical Literature, 1635–1690.* Toronto: University of Toronto Press, 1982.

Halliwell, Stephen. *Aristotle's Poetics.* Chapel Hill: University of North Carolina Press, 1986.

Hardy, Georges. *Le Cardinal de Fleury et le Mouvement janséniste.* Paris: Champion. 1925.

*Haussonville, comte G. P. O. d' and G. Hanotaux. *Souvenirs sur Mme de Maintenon*. 3 vols. Paris: Calmann-Levy, n.d. [1904].

*Hazard, Paul. *La Crise de la conscience européenne*. Paris: Fayard, 1961.

Henriet, Maurice. "Discours de M. de la Chapelle sur Racine." *Annales de la Société historique et archéologique de Château-Thierry* 5 (1902), 53–67.

Histoire de l'Académie royale des Inscriptions et Belles Lettres Paris: Imprimerie Nationale, vols. *1 (1717), *5 (1719), 7(1721).

Hobbes, Thomas. *Leviathan*. Ed. Michael Oakeshott. Oxford: Clarendon Press, 1960.

Horace. *The Odes and Epodes*. Ed. C. E. Bennett. London: Heinemann, 1964.

———. *Satires, Epistles, Ars poetica*. Ed. H. R. Fairclough. London: Heinemann, 1966.

*Hozier, comte Charles d'. *Armorial général de la France*. Paris: Collombat, 1738–41. Registre Premier, Pte. 2.

Huart, Suzanne d'. *Archives de la Maison de France (Branche d'Orléans). Tome I: Fonds de Dreux*. Paris: Archives Nationales, 1976.

Huppert, George. *The Idea of Perfect History*. Urbana: University of Illinois Press, 1970.

Jaeger, Gérard. *Qu'est-ce que l'Académie française? à quoi sert-elle? A propos du rapport de Chamfort sur les Académies (1634–1803)*. Paris: La Pensée universelle, 1978.

*Jal, Auguste. *Glossaire nautique*. Paris: Firmin-Didot, 1848.

Jenkins, E. H. *A History of the French Navy from its Beginnings to the Present Day*. London: Macdonald and Jane's, 1973.

Jouan, René. *Histoire de la marine française*. Paris: Payot, 1970.

Klaits, Joseph. *Printed Propaganda under Louis XIV*. Princeton: Princeton University Press, 1976.

Kreiser, B. Robert. *Miracles, Convulsions, and Ecclesiastical Politics in Early Eighteenth-Century Paris*. Princeton: Princeton University Press, 1978.

Labatut, Jean-Pierre. *Les Ducs et pairs de France au XVIIe siècle*. Paris: PUF, 1972.

Labrousse, Elisabeth. *Une foi, une loi, un roi? La Révocation de l'édit de Nantes*. Paris: Payot, 1985.

La Bruyère, Jean de. *Œuvres*. Ed. Gustave Servois. 3 vols. Paris: Hachette, 1865–82. *vol. 1.

*La Chesnaye-Desbois, F. A. A. de and M. Badier. *Dictionnaire de la noblesse*. 3rd ed. Paris: Schlesinger, 1876. vol. 19.

*Lacour-Gayet, Georges. *La Marine militaire de la France sous le règne de Louis XV*. Paris: Hachette, 1910.

Lafayette, Marie-Madeleine Pioche de La Vergne, comtesse de. *Correspondance*. Ed. André Beaunier. 2 vols. Paris: Gallimard, 1942.

———. *La Princesse de Clèves. Romans du XVIIe siècle*. *Ed. Antoine Adam. Paris: Gallimard, 1958.

La Fontaine, Jean de. *Contes et nouvelles*. *Ed. Paul Lacroix. Paris: Bibliophile Jacob, 1863.

———. *Œuvres diverses*. Ed. Pierre Clarac. Paris: Gallimard-Pléiade, 1958.

Languet de Gergy, J. Joseph. *5e Lettre pastorale contenant une réfutation du Mémoire donné en 1719 sous les noms de Mgrs les évesques de Senez, de Montpellier, et de Boulogne . . . de la lettre au pape sous le nom de 7 évesques de France dattée du 9 juin. . . .* Paris: R. Mazières, 1722–23.

La Roncière, Charles de. *Histoire de la marine française.* 2nd ed. 6 vols. Paris: Plon, 1909–32.

Lebeau, Sylvain, ed. *Nouveau code des prises, ou recueil des édits, déclarations, lettres patentes sur la course et l'administration des prises depuis 1400 jusqu'à présent.* Paris: Imprimerie de la République, An VII–IX.

Le Clerc, Josse. *Bibliothèque.* In *Richelet, Dictionnaire de la langue françoise ancienne et moderne.* 3 vols. Lyon: Duplain, 1728. *vol. 1.

*Leclercq, Dom Henri. *Histoire de la Régence pendant la minorité de Louis XV.* 3 vols. Paris: Champion, 1921.

*Ledieu, François. *Les Dernières années de Bossuet: Journal de l'abbé Ledieu.* Ed. Ch. Urbain and E. Levesque. 2 vols. Paris: Hachette, 1928–29.

Leffler, Phyllis. "The *histoire raisonnée,* 1660–1720: A Pre-Enlightenment Genre." *Journal of the History of Ideas* 37 (1976), 219–40.

Le Roy, Albert. *Le Gallicanisme au XVIIIe siècle. La France et Rome de 1700 à 1715. Histoire diplomatique de la bulle Unigenitus jusqu'à la mort de Louis XIV.* Paris: Perrin, 1892.

Le Roy Ladurie, Emmanuel. "Rangs et hiérarchie dans la vie de cour." *Travaux de Linguistique et de Littérature* 22 (1985), 60–77.

*Lever, Maurice. *Le Roman français au XVIIe siècle.* Paris: PUF, 1981.

Lewis, Warren H. *The Sunset of the Splendid Century.* New York: Doubleday Anchor, 1963.

Livet, Georges. *L'Intendance d'Alsace sous Louis XIV, 1648–1715.* Paris: Les Belles Lettres, 1956.

Locke, John. *Essai philosophique concernant l'entendement humain.* Trans. Coste. Ed. Emilienne Naert. Paris: Vrin, 1983.

———. *A Paraphrase and Commentary on the Epistles of St. Paul and an Essay for the Understanding of St. Paul's Epistles by Consulting St. Paul Himself. The Works of John Locke.* London: Tegg et al., 1823. vols. 8–9.

———. *The Second Treatise of Government.* Ed. T. P. Peardon. New York: Liberal Arts Press. 1952.

*Losme de Montchesney, Jacques de. *Bolaeana, ou bons mots de M. Boileau.* 2 vols. Amsterdam: Lhonoré, 1742.

*Louail, J.-B., and J.-B. Cadry. *Histoire du livre des Réflexions morales sur le Nouveau Testament et de la Constitution Unigenitus.* 4 vols. Amsterdam: Potgieter, 1723–1738.

*Magne, Bernard. *Crise de la littérature française sous Louis XIV: Humanisme et nationalisme.* 2 vols. Paris-Lille: Champion/Atelier Reproduction des Thèses, 1976.

Magne, Emile. *La Château de Saint-Cloud.* Paris: Calmann-Lévy, 1932.

Mailly, Francois de. *Lettre de Mgr l'archevesque duc de Reims à Messigneurs les cardinaux, archevesques et évesques du royaume, qui sont soumis à la bulle Unigenitus*. Reims: Multeau, 1719.

———. *Lettre de Mgr l'archevesque de Reims à Mgr l'évesque de Boulogne, du 29 avril 1723. Réponse de Mgr l'évesque de Boulogne du 12 mai 1723*. N.p., n.d.

Maimbourg, Louis. *Histoire du luthérianisme*. 2nd ed. 2 vols. Paris: Mabre-Cramoisy, 1681.

Maintenon, Françoise d'Aubigné, marquise de. *Mémoires et lettres*. 16 vols. Maestrich: Dufour et Roux, 1789.

———. *Lettres*. Ed. Marcel Langlois. 5 vols. Paris: Letouzey, 1935–39.

*Malebranche, Nicolas. *Œuvres complètes*. Ed. André Robinet. 20 vols. Paris: Vrin, 1958–70.

*Marais, Mathieu. *Journal et Mémoires sur la Régence et le Règne de Louis XV*. Ed. Lescure. 4 vols. Paris: Firmin-Didot, 1863–68.

———. **Letters de Mathieu Marais à Bouhier*. 2 vols. In *Correspondance littéraire du Président Bouhier, No. 8*. Ed. Henri Duranton. St.-Etienne: Université de Saint-Etienne, 1980.

Marmier, Jean. *Horace en France au XVIIe siècle*. Paris: PUF, 1962.

Martimort, Aimé-Georges. *Le Gallicanisme de Bossuet*. Paris: Editions du Cerf, 1953.

Martin, Henri-Jean. *Le Livre français sous l'Ancien Régime*. Paris: Promodis, 1987.

———. *Livre, pouvoirs et société à Paris au XVIIe siècle (1598–1701)*. 2 vols. Geneva: Droz, 1969.

Matoré, Georges. *Histoire des dictionnaires français*. Paris: Larousse, 1968.

Mélèse, Pierre. *Donneau de Visé*. Geneva: Droz, 1936.

*Mélia, Jean. *L'Etrange existence de l'abbé de Choisy*. Paris: Emile-Paul, 1921.

Ménagiana. Nouvelle édition. 2 vols. Paris: Delaulne, 1729. *Vol. 2.

Menant, Sylvain. *La Chute d'Icare: la crise de la poésie française, 1700–1750*. Geneva: Droz, 1981.

Mesnard, Paul. *Histoire de l'Académie française depuis sa fondation jusqu'en 1830*. Paris: Charpentier, 1857.

Miller, John R. *Boileau en France au dix-huitième siècle*. Baltimore: The Johns Hopkins University Press, 1942.

Molière, Jean-Baptiste Poquelin. *Théâtre*. Ed. Robert Jouanny. 2 vols. Paris: Garnier, 1962.

Mongrédien, Georges. "Un épigrammatiste du XVIIe siècle. J. de Cailly." *Revue de France* 1 (1931), 300–33.

*Monnier, Francis. *Le Chancelier d'Aguesseau: sa conduite et ses idées politiques*. Paris: Didier, 1863.

Montgolfier, Bernard de. *Ile Saint-Louis*. Paris: Ville de Paris-Musée Carnavalet, 1980.

Moore, Will G. "Boileau and Longinus." *French Studies* 14 (1960), 56–61.

———. *French Classical Literature: An Essay*. Oxford: Clarendon, 1961.

Mouligneau, Geneviève. *Mme de Lafayette romancière?* Brussels: Editions de l'Université de Bruxelles, 1980.

Mousnier, Roland. *Les Institutions de France sous la monarchie absolue, 1598–1789.* Vol. 1: *Société et Etat*; vol. 2: *Les Organes de l'Etat et la société.* Paris: PUF, 1974, 1980. Trans. Brian Pearce. Chicago: University of Chicago Press, 1979, 1984.

―――. *La Plume, la faucille et le marteau.* Paris: PUF, 1970.

Murray, Timothy. *Theatrical Legitimation: Allegories of Genius in Seventeenth-Century England and France.* New York: Oxford University Press, 1987.

Nelson, Robert J. *Corneille and Racine; Parallels and Contrasts.* Englewood Cliffs: Prentice Hall, 1962.

Noailles, Adrien-Maurice, duc de. *Mémoires.* Ed. Petitot and Monmerqué. Paris: Foucault, 1829. Vols. 72–74.

Noailles, Louis-Antoine, Cardinal de. *Première Instruction pastorale de son Eminence le Cardinal de Noailles, Archevesque de Paris au Clergé seculier & regulier de son diocese sur la Constitution 'Unigenitus.'* Paris: J.-B. Delespine, 1719.

*Olivet, Pierre-Joseph Thoulier, abbé d'. *Lettres (1719–1745).* 2 vols. Ed. Henri Duranton. In *Correspondance littéraire du Président Bouhier, No. 3.* St.-Etienne: Université de St.-Etienne, 1976.

Orcibal, Jean. *Louis XIV et les protestants.* Paris: PUF, 1951.

Orléans, duchesse d'. *Lettres de la Princesse Palatine (1672–1722).* Ed. Olivier Amiel. Paris: Mercure de France, 1982.

Ormesson, comte Wladimir d'. *Le Clergé à l'Académie.* Paris: Wesmaël-Charlier, 1965.

Pascal, Blaise. *Pensées de M. Pascal sur la religion et sur quelques autres sujets qui ont esté trouvés après sa mort parmy ses papiers.* 2e ed. Paris: Desprez, 1670.

―――. *Pensées.* Texte établi par Louis Lafuma. Paris: Seuil, 1962.

*Paul, C. B. *Science and Immortality: The Eloges of the Paris Academy of Science (1699–1791).* Berkeley: University of California Press, 1980.

Paul, Pierre. *Le Cardinal Melchior de Polignac.* Paris: Plon, 1922.

*Pélissier, Léon-G. "Les Correspondants du duc de Noailles: lettres inédites de Le Verrier, Eusèbe Renaudot." *Revue d'Histoire littéraire de la France* 6 (1899), 621–39; 7 (1900), 624–44.

Pellisson-Fontanier, Paul and Pierre-Joseph Thoulier d'Olivet. *Histoire de l'Académie française.* Ed. C.-L. Livet. 2 vols. Paris: Didier, 1858, *vol. 2.

Péronnet, Michel. "Les Assemblées du Clergé de France et la révocation des édits de religion (1560–1685)." *Bulletin de la Société de l'Histoire du Protestantisme Français* 131 (1985), 453–79.

Petitfils, Jean-Christian. *Mme de Montespan.* Paris: Fayard, 1988.

―――. *Le Régent.* Paris: Fayard, 1986.

*Peyre, Henri. *The Failures of Criticism.* Ithaca: Cornell University Press, 1967.

―――. *Historical and Critical Essays.* Lincoln, NE: University of Nebraska, 1963.

Phillips, Henry. *The Theatre and Its Critics in Seventeenth-Century France.* Oxford: Oxford University Press, 1980.

*Picard, Raymond. *La Carriére de Jean Racine*. Paris: Gallimard, 1961.
————. *"Etat présent des études raciniennes." *L'Information littéraire* 8 (1956), 85–88.
————. *"Le 'Précis historique' est-il de Racine?" *Revue d'Histoire littéraire de la France* 58 (1958), 157–64.
Pierrot, Dom Marcel. "D'Aguesseau et l'humanisme." *Le Chancelier Henri-François d'Aguesseau. Limoges 1668–Fresnes 1751*. Limoges: Desvilles, 1953, 52–58.
Plutarch. *Lives*. Trans. J. and W. Langhorne. London: Tegg, 1825.
Poisson, Georges. *Monsieur de Saint-Simon*. 2nd ed. Paris: Fayard-Mazarine, 1987.
Polignac, Melchior, cardinal de. *L'Anti-Lucrece, Poeme sur la religion naturelle*. Trans. M. de Bougainville. Lyon: Perisse. 1780.
Pritchard, James. *Louis XV's Navy, 1748–1762. A Study of Organization and Administration*. Kingston and Montreal: McGill-Queen's University Press, 1988.
Pugh, Anthony R. *The Composition of Pascal's Apologia*. Toronto: University of Toronto Press, 1984.
Quéniart, Jean. *La Révocation de l'Edit de Nantes: Protestants et catholiques en France de 1598 à 1685*. Paris: Desclée de Brouwer, 1985.
Quesnel, Pasquier. *Instructions chrétiennes et prières à Dieu pour tous les jours de l'année, tirées des "Réflexions morales du Nouveau Testament."* Paris, 1701.
Quintilian. *Institutio oratoria*. Ed. H. E. Butler, 4 vols. London: Heinemann, 1930.
Racevskis, Karlis. *Voltaire and the French Academy*. Chapel Hill: North Carolina Studies in the Romance Languages and Literatures, 1975.
Racine, Jean. *Œuvres complètes*. Ed. Pierre Clarac. Paris: Seuil, 1962.
————. *Œuvres complètes*. Ed. Paul Mesnard. 8 vols. Paris: Hachette, 1885–1888. *Vols. 1, 7.
————. *Œuvres complètes*. Ed. Raymond Picard. 2 vols. Paris: Gallimard-Pléiade, 1966. *Vol. 2.
————. *Principes de la tragédie en marge de la poétique d'Aristote*. Ed. Eugène Vinaver. Paris: Nizet, 1951.
Racine, Louis, *Œuvres*. Ed. Geoffroy. 5 vols. Paris: Le Normant, 1808. *Vol. 2 (includes "Epistre à M. de Valincour"); Vol. 5 (*Mémoires sur la vie et les ouvrages de Jean Racine*).
Ranum, Oreste. *Artisans of Glory: Writers and Historical Thought in Seventeenth-Century France*. Chapel Hill: University of North Carolina Press, 1980.
Rapin, René. *Les Réflexions sur la poétique de ce temps et sur les ouvrages des poètes anciens et modernes*. Ed. E. T. Dubois. Geneva: Droz, 1970.
Rébelliau, Alfred. *Bossuet historien du protestantisme. Etude sur l'Histoire des variations et sur la controverse entre les protestants et les catholiques au XVIIe siècle*. Paris: Hachette, 1892.
Rech, M. Gilbert. "D'Aguesseau et le jansénisme." *Le Chancelier Henri-

François d'Aguesseau. Limoges 1668–Fresnes 1751. Limoges: Desvilles, 1953, 119–32.

Recueil des édits, déclarations, et arrests du conseil, concernant les Gens de la Religion Prétenduë Réformée, les quels ont été Registrez en la Cour de Parlement depuis l'année 1664. Dernière Edition. Rouen: Besongne, 1721.

Religion, érudition et critique à la fin du XVIIe siècle et au début du XVIIIe. Ed. Jacques Solé. Paris: PUF, 1968.

Ricoeur, Paul. "Tolérance, intolérance, intolérable." *Bulletin de la Société de l'Histoire du Protestantisme Français* 134 (1988), 435–50.

Rigaud, Louis. "D'Aguesseau, philosophe du droit." *Le Chancelier d'Aguesseau. Limoges 1668–Fresnes 1751.* Limoges: Desvilles, 1953, 59–65.

Rollin, Charles. *De la manière d'enseigner et d'étudier les Belles-Lettres.* 4 vols. Paris/Leyden: Vve Etienne, 1748/1749.

Romier, Lucien. *Les origines politiques des guerres de religion.* 2 vols. Paris: Perrin, 1913–14.

Rosso, Corrado. *Les Tambours de Santerre. Essais sur quelques éclipses des Lumières au XVIIIe siècle.* Pisa: Goliardica, 1986.

*Rousseau, J.-B. *Correspondance de J.-B. Rousseau et de Brossette.* Ed. Paul Bonnefon. 2 vols. Paris: Cornély, 1910. *Vol. 2.

*Rouxel, Albert. *Chronique des élections à l'Académie française.* Paris: Firmin-Didot, 1888.

Rubin, David L. "Image, Argument, and Esthetics in *La Critique de l'Ecole des femmes.*" *Romance Notes* 15, Supplement No. 1 (1973), 98–107.

*Rudler, Gustave. "L'Histoire et la fiction dans la *Princesse de Clèves.*" *Revue du Seizième Siècle* 5 (1917–18), 231–43.

Schouls, Peter A. *The Imposition of Method. A Study of Descartes and Locke.* Oxford: Clarendon Press, 1980.

Saint-Evremond, Charles de Marguetel de Saint-Denis, sr. de. "De la vraie et de la fausse beauté des ouvrages d'esprit." *Œuvres.* London: Tonson, 1735. Vol. 6, 144–82.

Saint-Germain, Jacques. *Samuel Bernard. Le Banquier des rois.* Paris: Hachette, 1960.

*Saint-Simon, Louis de Rouvroy, duc de. *Mémoires.* Ed. Gonzague Truc. 7 vols. Paris: Gallimard-Pléiade, 1953.

———. *Mémoires.* Ed. Yves Coirault. 7 vols. (published to date). Paris: Gallimard-Pléiade, 1983.

Sainte-Beuve, Charles–Augustin. *Causeries du lundi.* 3rd ed. 15 vols. Paris: Garnier, 1857–72. *Vols. 3, 4, 9, 12, 13.

*Sareil, Jean. *Les Tencin.* Geneva: Droz, 1969.

Sauvy, Anne. *Livres saisis à Paris entre 1678 et 1701.* The Hague: Nijhoff, 1972.

Schaeper, Thomas J. *The French Council of Commerce, 1700–1715. A Study of Mercantilism after Colbert.* Columbus: Ohio State University Press, 1983.

Segraisiana. Paris: Libraires associés, 1721.

Sévigné, Marie de Rabutin-Chantal, Marquise de. *Correspondance.* Ed. Roger Duchêne. 3 vols. Paris: Gallimard-Pléiade, 1972–1978. *Vols. 2, 3.

Shennan, J. H. *The Parlement of Paris*. Ithaca: Cornell University Press, 1968.
————. *Philippe, Duke of Orléans, Regent of France*. London: Thames and Hudson, 1979.
Soanen, Jean. *Lettres de Messire Jean Soanen, évêque de Senez*. 2 vols. Cologne: Aux dépens de la Compagnie, 1750.
Solé, Jacques. *Bayle polémiste*. Paris: Robert Laffont, 1972.
*Sourches, Louis-François du Bouchet, marquis de. *Mémoires*. Ed. Cosnac and Bertrand. 13 vols. Paris: Hachette, 1882–1893.
*Staal de Launay, Marguerite, baronne de. *Mémoires*. Coll. Petitot-Monmerqué. Paris: Foucault, 1829. Vol. 87.
Stanton, Domna. *The Aristocrat as Art: A Study of Honnête Homme and the Dandy in Seventeenth- and Nineteenth-Century French Literature*. New York: Columbia University Press, 1980.
Stegmann, André. *Les Caractères de La Bruyère*. Paris: Larousse, 1972.
Strosetzki, Christoph. *Rhétorique de la conversation. Sa dimension littéraire et linguistique dans la société française du XVIIe siècle*. Trans. Sabine Seubert. Tübingen: Biblio 17, 1984.
*Symcox, Geoffrey. *The Crisis of French Sea Power 1688–1697. From the "guerre d'escadre" to the "guerre de course."* The Hague: Nijhoff, 1974.
Taillemite, Etienne. "Colbert et la marine." *Un Nouveau Colbert*. Ed. Roland Mousnier. Paris: SEDES, 1985, 217–27.
————. *Colbert, Secrétaire d'Etat de la marine et les réformes de 1669*. Paris: Académie de Marine, 1970.
————. "Le Haut-Commandement de la marine française de Colbert à la Révolution." *Les Marines de guerre européennes*. Ed. Martine Acerra, et al. Paris: Université de Paris-Sorbonne, 1985, 249–69.
————. **L'Histoire ignorée de la marine française*. Paris: Perrin, 1988.
————. "Les Problèmes de la Marine de guerre au XVIIe siècle." *XVIIe Siècle* 86–87 (1970), 21–37.
————. "Une Utilisation originale des forces navales: L'expédition de Duguay-Trouin à Rio-de-Janeiro." *Annales de la société d'histoire et d'archéologie de l'arondissement de Saint-Malo*, 1973, 207–22.
Tallemant des Réaux, Gédéon. *Historiettes*. Ed. Antoine Adam. 2 vols. Paris: Gallimard-Pléiade, 1961.
Tavenaux, René. *Le Catholicisme dans la France classique, 1610–1715*. 2 vols. Paris: SEDES, 1980.
————. *Jansénisme et politique*. Paris: Colin, 1965.
Thomas, Jacques-François. *La Querelle de l'Unigenitus*. Paris: PUF, 1950.
Thou, Jean–Augustin de. *Histoire des choses arrivées de son temps*. Trans. Pierre Du Ruyer. Paris: Courbé, 1659.
Torcy, Jean-Baptiste Colbert, marquis de. *Journal inédit, pendant les années 1709, 1710, 1711*. Ed. Frédéric Masson. Paris: Plon, 1884.
Truchet, Jacques. "La Division en points dans les sermons de Bossuet." *Revue d'Histoire littéraire de la France* 52 (1952), 316–29.
————. *Politique de Bossuet*. Paris: Colin, 1966.

*Turgeon, F. K. "Unpublished Letters of Jean-Baptiste Racine to the abbé Renaudot." *Modern Language Notes* 54 (1939), 172–84.

Van der Crysse, Dirk. "L'Honnête homme selon le duc de Saint-Simon." *Revue belge de philologie et d'histoire* 48 (1970), 775–83.

Villedieu, Marie Desjardins, dame de. *Les Désordres de l'amour.* Ed. Micheline Cuénin. *Introduction, xiii–lxiv. Geneva: Droz, 1970.

*Vinaver, Eugène. *Racine and Poetic Tragedy.* Manchester: Manchester University Press, 1955.

Voiture, Vincent. *Lettres et autres ouvrages.* 2 vols. Amsterdam: Mortier, 1709.

Voltaire, François Marie Arouet. *Voltaire's Correspondence.* Ed. Theodore Besteman. 107 vols. Geneva: Institut et Musée Voltaire, 1953–1965.

———. *Lettres philosophiques.* Ed. Raymond Naves. Paris: Garnier, 1962.

———. *Œuvres complètes.* Ed. Louis Moland. 52 vols. Paris: Garnier, 1877–85.

———. *Œuvres historiques.* Ed. René Pomeau. Paris: Gallimard-Pléiade, 1957.

*Vuillart, Germain. *Lettres à Louis de Préfontaine, 1694–1700.* Ed. Ruth Clark. Geneva: Droz, 1951.

Wade, Ira O. "Notes on the Making of a *Philosophe*: Cuenz and Bouhier." *Literature and History in the Age of Ideas. Essays on the French Enlightenment Presented to George R. Havens.* Columbus: Ohio State University Press, 1975, 97–123.

Watson, Richard A. *The Breakdown of Cartesian Metaphysics.* Atlantic Highlands, NJ: Humanities Press, 1987.

Weinberg, Bernard. *The Art of Jean Racine.* Chicago: University of Chicago Press, 1963.

Weingartner, Rudolph H. *The Unity of Platonic Dialogue.* New York: Library of Liberal Arts, 1962.

*Whiteman, Anne, and J. S. Bromley, eds. *Statesmen, Scholars and Merchants: Essays in Eighteenth-Century History Presented to Dame Lucy Sutherland.* Oxford: Clarendon Press, 1973.

*Williams, C. G. S. *Madame de Sévigné.* Boston: G. K. Hall, 1981.

Wilson, Arthur M. *French Foreign Policy during the Administration of Cardinal Fleury, 1726–1743. A Study in Diplomacy and Commercial Development.* New York: Columbia University Press, 1936. Rpt.: Octagon Books, 1972.

*Wismes, baron Armel de. *Jean Bart et la guerre de course.* Paris: Julliard, 1965.

Wolf, John. *Louis XIV.* New York: Norton, 1968.

Wood, Allen G. *Literary Satire and Theory: A Study of Horace, Boileau, and Pope.* New York: Garland, 1985.

Yolton, John. *John Locke: An Introduction.* Oxford: Blackwell, 1985.

*Zimmerman, N.-P. "La Morale laïque au commencement du XVIIIe siècle. Madame de Lambert." *Revue d'Histoire littéraire de la France* 24 (1917), 42–64, 440–55.

Zuber, Roger. *Les "Belles infidèles" et la formation du goût classique.* Paris: Colin, 1969.

Index

Martial, 296
Martine (Toulouse's estates manager), 141
Massei, Bartholomeo (nuncio), 253
Massillon, Jean-Baptiste (bishop of Clermont), 153, 237n.39, 251n.62
Maulévrier, Charles Andrault de Langeron, abbé de, 154
Maupointet, Ambroise, 18
Maurepas, Jean-Frédéric Phélypeaux, comte de, 180n.147, 181 and n.149, 275, 276
Mazarin, 176
Medici, Catherine de', 113, 116–17
Medici, Marie de', 176
Ménage, Gilles, 56
Mengui, Guillaume, 237 and n.38, 238
Mercure Galant, Le, 57, 71 and n.3, 152, 205n.63
Mesmes, Jean-Antoine III de, 166
Mesnard, Paul, 8, 123n.60, 198n.46, 204n.60, 290n.48
metaphysics, 6, 10, 61, 147, 216, 261–68, 271, 294
Mézeray, François Eudes de, 110
Le Militaire philosophe (Difficultés sur la religion proposées au Père Malebranche), 228 and n.14
Miller, Nancy, 2n.2
Milton, John, 19 and n.21, 293–94
Mirabaud, Jean-Baptiste de, 285n.38, 286
Missions étrangères, 138n.22
Molière, Jean-Baptiste Poquelin, 69, 70, 80, 90, 91, 93, 162, 291
monarchical ideology (Valincour), 18, 105, 113, 151, 176, 200n.52, 210, 263, 275, 281
Monmerqué, J. L. N., 8, 10, 276
Monnier, Francis, 261n.79, 264n.89
Mons, siege of, 29, 127, 128n.69
Montaigne, Michel de, 77, 106n.13, 218n.86, 284
Montespan, Françoise-Athénaïs de Rochechouart, marquise de, 22n.38, 23, 40, 58–59, 136, 140n.27, 213
Montesquieu, Charles Secondat, baron de, 210; *Lettres persanes,* 99, 219, 287
Montmayor, Jorge, 283

Montmorency, Anne, connétable de France, 112, 116
Montmorency, Isabelle de Harville de, 70n.1
Montreuil, Mathieu de, 149
Moore, Will G., 83n.24, 124n.62
Mortemart, Louis II de Rochechouart, duc de, 149
Morville, Charles-Jean Fleuriau, comte de, 174n.131
Moschus, 212
Moyens sûrs et honnêtes pour la conversion de tous les hérétigues (anon.), 117n.40
Murray, Timothy, 89n.31

Namur, battle of, 30, 35
naval administration (*La Marine*): admiral, status and provisions, 25–26, 36–37, 137, 142–43, 166, 181, 182, 274–76, prize tenth, 28, 38–39, 146–47; admiralties, 26, 31, 33, 45, 167n.104, 170; code, 23, 28, 37, 145; conseil de la marine (Regency), 161, 169 and n.113, 171, 174 and n.131, 180; conseil des prises, 26, 28, 30, 31 and n.63, 32–33, 37, 38, 45, 137, 141, 143–48; and minister, 25, 31, 36, 137, 138, 182; *course,* memoirs on, 9, 142–45, 158n.75, 180; passports, 26, 27–28, 31 and n.64, 129n.74, 150; ports, 39, 145, 147, 169, 179–80, 278; secrétaire général, 26, 27, 31, 39, 137, 141; Valincour's place in, 2 and n.3, 22, 37, 39 and n.91, 45, 156, 179, 182, 273–74, 277–78
naval history (by Valincour), 27–28, 179–82, 277, 281
Neptune français, Le, 202
Nine Years War, 4 and n.8, 27, 29–31, 126–30, 146–48; See also: Ryswyck, Treaty of
Noailles, Adrien-Maurice, duc de, 42, 47, 133, 138, 141, 149, 155–56, 161, 170, 171, 175; Valincour's letters to, 23, 42, 134, 148–49, 163, 164, 169, 175, 178, 179, 182, 296
Noailles, Louis-Antoine, cardinal de, 47, 154, 161n.87, 171, 177n.135, 235–36, 237, 241, 242, 250–253, 257, 261, 274 and n.12, 296